实用英语作文精选

A Selection of Practical English Compositions

主　编：张震久　袁宪军
副主编：王　磊　田娅丽　安素卿
编　委：安素卿　高　山　关海霞　何顺红
　　　　李辉娟　李艳芝　吕月璞　史　琳
　　　　田娅丽　王　磊　王文圣　吴志花
　　　　袁宪军　张　苒　张震久
英语顾问：[美] Ruth Bell

北京大学出版社
PEKING UNIVERSITY PRESS

图书在版编目(CIP)数据

实用英语作文精选/张震久,袁宪军主编. —北京:北京大学出版社,2010.9
ISBN 978-7-301-17804-1

Ⅰ.①实… Ⅱ.①张…②袁… Ⅲ.①英语－写作－自学参考资料 Ⅳ.①H315

中国版本图书馆CIP数据核字(2010)第183221号

书　　　名：实用英语作文精选
著作责任者：张震久　袁宪军　主编
责　任　编　辑：孙　莹
标　准　书　号：ISBN 978-7-301-17804-1/H·2641
出　版　发　行：北京大学出版社
地　　　　址：北京市海淀区成府路205号　100871
网　　　　址：http://www.pup.cn
电　　　　话：邮购部 62752015　发行部 62750672　编辑部 62754382
　　　　　　　出版部 62754962
电　子　信　箱：zbing@pup.pku.edu.cn
印　刷　者：北京宏伟双华印刷有限公司
经　销　者：新华书店
　　　　　　　890毫米×1240毫米　32开本　19.375印张　693千字
　　　　　　　2010年9月第1版　2010年9月第1次印刷
　　　　　　　2011年6月第2次印刷
定　　　价：39.00元

未经许可,不得以任何方式复制或抄袭本书之部分或全部内容。
版权所有,侵权必究
举报电话:(010)62752024　电子信箱:fd@pup.pku.edu.cn

本书特点

- 本书"写作入门谈"简明浅易,既突出最基本的英文短文写作方法,又适应考试需求,对学习者具有直接的借鉴意义;
- 模拟范例文字准确,行文流畅,中心突出,易于仿写;
- 难易兼顾,繁简适宜,可供不同层次的学习者使用;
- 题材广泛,内容充实,有利学习者扩大知识面,增加信息储备。

前　言

　　《英文模范作文新字典》自1996年问世以来,受到众多学习者的欢迎,对广大学习者英文短文写作能力的提高及在各种英语写作考试中发挥英语写作水平起到了积极作用,因而得到专家的认可和推荐(见全国学位与研究生发展中心组织编写的《英语试卷评析与应用指导》P46)。其中一些精彩篇章被多种同类书籍所引用。

　　为进一步帮助读者开启进入自由作文空间的大门,给读者以新的阅读的惊喜,写作的榜样,我们经过不懈努力,在保持原书题材广泛、体裁多样、短小精悍、文字浅显、易于模仿、便于吸收等特色的基础上,再次精心选材,精心撰写,精心分类,剔除了部分较为枯燥乏味的旧篇章,增添了二百余篇新短文和一些新栏目,更名为《实用英语作文精选》,选篇题材广泛,或富有哲理,或幽默风趣,或简洁明快,或鼓舞人心,或时尚新颖,或令人深思,使之更具实用性、文化性和可学性,会给读者以新的感受。

　　从读者反馈的意见和我们从事教学实践的经验看,本书除利于通过仿写提高短文写作能力外,尚有以下作用。

　　有助于提高口头作文水平,即口语能力。讲话题(Talk on the topic)要求围绕话题组织语言,实际上就像写短文一样,要求对某一要点或某一方面进行连贯清晰的叙述、说明、分析、评述和判断。其基本模式和具体方法完全可参照提供的短文写作模式和具体方法,因而熟读本书有助于就某一话题连续说上两三分钟(十几句话),提高口头表达能力。

　　有助于提高语篇听力能力。学习本书中的短文,要读一读,背一背。反复的朗读和背诵是综合性的语言操练活动。语言学家、翻译家吕叔湘先生在《中国人学英语》中强调,中国人学英语必须"耳到、眼到、口到、手到"。读出声来,自然会增加听觉印象,有助

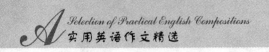

于在听力中识别相关话语中的逻辑性,从而提高听力理解能力。

有助于提高理解和欣赏能力。朗读和背诵本书中优秀短文,不仅有助于在语境中记单词和语法结构,而且可以记住文中一些精彩、精辟的语句。如短文"If I Were a Boy Again"中的"Life is very much like a mirror; if you smile upon it, it smiles back upon you; if you frown and look doubtfully on it, you will have a similar look in return."就值得细细品味。有些佳句,反复咏读后会体味到一种只能用英语意会,难以用汉语言传的情感和意境,如一些有关 Love 的短文。

有助于提高学习者的思辨能力。作文,哪怕是短文,首先具备一定的思辨能力。若脑中空空如也,笔下自然无话可写。本书中新篇章的内容丰富,贴近生活实际,洞察时代脉搏,突出人文主题,体现人文关怀,关注学习者情感体验和身心发展。一些议论文章虽短小,但思路清晰,思维缜密,含义深刻,富有启迪意义,能给学习者一种智力上的满足,并使智慧本身成为学习使用语言的促进力量,在吸收语言营养的同时吸收思维的营养,提高布局运思、谋篇论事的思辨能力。

本书精选短文约五百篇,分为 74 个栏目,每栏目之下,列同类文章四五篇到二十余篇。许多栏目可互为参考,互为借鉴。如第 1 栏"我们的学校"可与第 2 栏"学校生活"互参,因为其中短文均以青年学子的视角探索校园生活的不同侧面;第 54 栏"生活面面观"可与第 55 栏"人生感悟"互参,因为其中短文所涉及的均是人生百态,世事沧桑。互参有助于开拓思路,丰富表达方式。

本书的读者主要是那些有目标,有动力,有毅力的青年学子。对他们来说,学习是一种乐趣,是获取知识的必经之途。在学习本书时,只要坚持"读一读,背一背,写一写",定可全面增强语言应用能力和应试能力。西方有格言说"The power of knowledge consists not so much in its wide spectrum as in its wide application."(知识的力量与其说在于广博,不如说在于广泛应用。)谨望此书读者能在学习中应用,将知识化为力量。

编者
2010.5.6

Contents
目 录

英语短文写作入门谈 ·· (1)
  一、两点建议 ·· (1)
  二、提高组词造句的能力 ·· (7)
  三、段落的写作方法 ·· (15)
  四、各种文体的基本写作技巧 ·································· (19)
  五、培养挖掘写作内容的能力 ·································· (35)
  六、作文考试的命题形式 ······································ (42)
  七、口头作文提示 ·· (59)

No. 1 Our School（我们的学校） ······························· (76)
  (1) Our College ·· (76)
  (2) Our College Campus ······································ (77)
  (3) Our Library ·· (77)
  (4) Our Classroom ·· (78)
  (5) My Bedroom ·· (79)
  (6) A Teacher's Lounge ······································ (80)
  (7) A Major Problem in My College ························ (80)

No. 2 Life at School（学校生活） ······························ (82)
  (1) My View on Elective Courses ·························· (82)
  (2) How to Eliminate Cheating on Campus ·············· (83)
  (3) Living a Colorful Life on Campus ···················· (83)
  (4) Does College Life Simply Mean Getting a Degree? ······ (84)
  (5) How to Improve Students' Mental Health ·········· (85)
  (6) Reduce the Negative Effect of Online
       Games on Campus ·· (86)
  (7) How to Relieve Pressures ······························ (87)

(8) Should Class Attendance Be Rigidly Required? .... (88)
(9) On Your Own .... (89)
(10) University Life .... (89)
(11) My First Day on Campus .... (90)
(12) My First Year at College .... (91)
(13) My Opinion of Students Taking a Part-time Job .... (92)
(14) Should College Students Do Part-time Job? .... (93)
(15) The Students' Associations .... (94)
(16) A Sports Meet .... (94)
(17) What Do You Think about Grades? .... (95)

No. 3 **Teachers and Students**（老师·学生）............... (97)
(1) Our English Teacher .... (97)
(2) Teacher's Social Status .... (98)
(3) The Most Desirable Personal Qualities in a Teacher ...... (99)
(4) My View on Teacher-student Relationship .... (99)
(5) An Angel on the Platform .... (100)
(6) Changing Criteria for Good Students .... (101)
(7) My Favorite Teacher .... (102)
(8) Confucius as a Teacher .... (103)
(9) An Ideal Teacher .... (104)
(10) A True, Good Student .... (104)

No. 4 **Schoolmates and Friends**（同窗好友）............. (106)
(1) My Best Friend .... (106)
(2) How to Get on Well with Our Classmates .... (106)
(3) A Friend in My Memory .... (107)
(4) My Friend .... (108)
(5) Mary and Jane .... (109)

No. 5 **Extracurricular Activities**（课外活动）............ (110)
(1) After-class Activities on Campus .... (110)
(2) A Basketball Match .... (111)
(3) A Basketball Game .... (111)
(4) Visiting a Museum .... (112)

No. 6　Vacation（假期生活）⋯⋯⋯⋯⋯⋯⋯⋯⋯⋯（114）
　　（1）How I Spent My Summer ⋯⋯⋯⋯⋯⋯⋯⋯⋯（114）
　　（2）Summer Memories ⋯⋯⋯⋯⋯⋯⋯⋯⋯⋯⋯⋯（115）
　　（3）How I Passed My Summer Vacation ⋯⋯⋯⋯（116）
　　（4）My Summer Vacation ⋯⋯⋯⋯⋯⋯⋯⋯⋯⋯⋯（117）
　　（5）The Happy Vacation Life ⋯⋯⋯⋯⋯⋯⋯⋯⋯（117）
　　（6）How to Spend Sundays ⋯⋯⋯⋯⋯⋯⋯⋯⋯⋯（118）
　　（7）During the Summer Holidays ⋯⋯⋯⋯⋯⋯⋯（119）
No. 7　Way of Study（学习之道）⋯⋯⋯⋯⋯⋯⋯⋯⋯（121）
　　（1）Why Do We Attend College? ⋯⋯⋯⋯⋯⋯⋯（121）
　　（2）Reading Selectively or Extensively? ⋯⋯⋯⋯（122）
　　（3）Book Knowledge or Practical Experience? ⋯（123）
　　（4）Should Students Be Skeptical about
　　　　 What's Taught? ⋯⋯⋯⋯⋯⋯⋯⋯⋯⋯⋯⋯⋯（124）
　　（5）Good Study Habits ⋯⋯⋯⋯⋯⋯⋯⋯⋯⋯⋯⋯（124）
　　（6）Self-study ⋯⋯⋯⋯⋯⋯⋯⋯⋯⋯⋯⋯⋯⋯⋯⋯（125）
No. 8　Language Learning（语言学习）⋯⋯⋯⋯⋯⋯（127）
　　（1）Writing an Essay ⋯⋯⋯⋯⋯⋯⋯⋯⋯⋯⋯⋯⋯（127）
　　（2）Foreign Language Learning ⋯⋯⋯⋯⋯⋯⋯⋯（128）
　　（3）Gateway to the World ⋯⋯⋯⋯⋯⋯⋯⋯⋯⋯（129）
　　（4）Successful Language Learners ⋯⋯⋯⋯⋯⋯（130）
　　（5）Learning English at College ⋯⋯⋯⋯⋯⋯⋯（131）
　　（6）Advantages and Disadvantages of
　　　　 Electronic Dictionary ⋯⋯⋯⋯⋯⋯⋯⋯⋯⋯⋯（132）
　　（7）How I Overcome Difficulties in Learning English ⋯⋯（133）
　　（8）Worldwide Fervor in Learning Chinese ⋯⋯⋯（134）
　　（9）The Use of Dictionary in Language Learning ⋯⋯（135）
　　（10）On Developing Speaking Ability ⋯⋯⋯⋯⋯（136）
No. 9　Language and Communication（语言与交流）⋯⋯（137）
　　（1）Means of Communication ⋯⋯⋯⋯⋯⋯⋯⋯⋯（137）
　　（2）The Gift of Conversation ⋯⋯⋯⋯⋯⋯⋯⋯⋯（138）
　　（3）The Charm of the Chinese Language ⋯⋯⋯⋯（139）

(4) Advantages of Written Communication ……… (140)
(5) Advantages of Oral Communication ……… (140)
(6) Key Differences in the Communication Patterns of
　　Men and Women ……………………………… (141)
(7) Face-to-face Communication ……………… (142)

No. 10　Examination（考试） …………………… (144)
(1) On Examinations ……………………………… (144)
(2) Examination ………………………………… (145)
(3) Some Disadvantages of Examination ……… (146)
(4) The Negative Sides of Closed-book Exams …… (146)
(5) Is the Test of Spoken English Necessary? …… (147)
(6) About Examinations ………………………… (148)
(7) The Night Before Examination ……………… (149)

No. 11　Way to Success（成功之路） …………… (150)
(1) Pride Goes Before a Fall …………………… (150)
(2) No Pains, No Gains ………………………… (150)
(3) Is Failure a Bad Thing? …………………… (151)
(4) Competition ………………………………… (152)
(5) How to Achieve Success …………………… (153)
(6) Opportunity or Determination ……………… (154)
(7) Opportunity and Success …………………… (155)
(8) My View on Opportunity …………………… (155)
(9) On Work Efficiency ………………………… (156)
(10) The Importance of Confidence ……………… (157)

No. 12　Make Full Use of Time（爱惜光阴） …… (159)
(1) Time …………………………………………… (159)
(2) Make Full Use of Time ……………………… (160)
(3) Youth ………………………………………… (161)
(4) Spending Our Leisure to the Best Advantage …… (162)
(5) The Value of Time …………………………… (163)

No. 13　On Books（书籍与读书） ………………… (164)
(1) Companionship of Books …………………… (164)

(2) Reading Makes a Full Man …………………… (165)
　　(3) The Choice of Books …………………………… (166)
　　(4) Books for Recreation …………………………… (167)
　　(5) Novel Reading …………………………………… (168)
　　(6) Advantages of Marking Books ………………… (169)
　　(7) Reading the Classics …………………………… (169)
　　(8) The Pleasure of Reading ……………………… (170)
　　(9) Will E-books Replace Traditional Books? …… (171)

No. 14　Happiness (幸福观) ………………………… (173)
　　(1) How to Obtain Happiness …………………… (173)
　　(2) How to Be Happy …………………………… (174)
　　(3) Work and Happiness ………………………… (175)
　　(4) Wealth and Happiness ……………………… (176)
　　(5) Life Can Be Happy and Meaningful ……… (177)
　　(6) We Need Humor in Our Life ……………… (178)

No. 15　Ideals and Wishes (理想与愿望) ………… (179)
　　(1) Wishes ………………………………………… (179)
　　(2) Ideals ………………………………………… (180)
　　(3) Young People Should Have Ideals ………… (181)
　　(4) The Aim of a Young Man …………………… (182)
　　(5) If I Were a Boy Again ……………………… (183)
　　(6) Where to Go after My Graduation ………… (184)
　　(7) On Faith ……………………………………… (185)
　　(8) Beliefs ………………………………………… (186)

No. 16　On Will (立志) ……………………………… (187)
　　(1) Where There Is a Will, There Is a Way …… (187)
　　(2) Perseverance ………………………………… (188)
　　(3) Rome Was Not Built in a Day ……………… (188)
　　(4) Don't Stop Halfway ………………………… (189)
　　(5) Discontent …………………………………… (190)
　　(6) Man's Strong Will …………………………… (191)
　　(7) Self-reliance ………………………………… (192)

　　　　(8) Making Decision ·· (193)
　　　　(9) Enjoy Challenges ·· (193)
No. 17　Self-cultivation（道德修养）······························· (195)
　　　　(1) On Selfishness ·· (195)
　　　　(2) On the Misbehaviors of Chinese Tourists Abroad ······ (196)
　　　　(3) How to Prevent Cheating in Exams ························ (197)
　　　　(4) Sense of Independence ··· (197)
　　　　(5) On Virtues ·· (198)
　　　　(6) Patriotism ··· (199)
　　　　(7) Honesty ·· (200)
　　　　(8) Bravery ··· (200)
　　　　(9) Thrift Is Always a Good Virture ···························· (201)
　　　　(10) To Be Patient ·· (202)
　　　　(11) Our Responsibility ··· (203)
No. 18　Good Manners（文明礼貌）······························· (205)
　　　　(1) Good Manners（Ⅰ）·· (205)
　　　　(2) Good Manners（Ⅱ）··· (206)
　　　　(3) Voluntary Blood Donation ···································· (207)
　　　　(4) Politeness ·· (208)
　　　　(5) Punctuality ·· (209)
No. 19　Friendship（友谊）·· (211)
　　　　(1) Friendship ··· (211)
　　　　(2) Making Friends ·· (212)
　　　　(3) How to Make Friends ··· (213)
　　　　(4) My Ideal Friend ··· (214)
　　　　(5) On Making Friends ··· (214)
　　　　(6) On Friendship ·· (215)
No. 20　Habit and Hobby（习惯和爱好）······················ (217)
　　　　(1) Habit ·· (217)
　　　　(2) Good Habits Affect People ···································· (218)
　　　　(3) To Rise Early ··· (218)
　　　　(4) My View on Burning Night Oil ······························ (219)

(5) Bad Habits ⋯⋯⋯⋯⋯⋯⋯⋯⋯⋯⋯⋯⋯⋯⋯⋯ (220)

(6) Hobbies ⋯⋯⋯⋯⋯⋯⋯⋯⋯⋯⋯⋯⋯⋯⋯⋯⋯ (221)

(7) Philately ⋯⋯⋯⋯⋯⋯⋯⋯⋯⋯⋯⋯⋯⋯⋯⋯ (222)

No. 21 Education（教育） ⋯⋯⋯⋯⋯⋯⋯⋯⋯⋯⋯⋯⋯ (224)

(1) Online Education ⋯⋯⋯⋯⋯⋯⋯⋯⋯⋯⋯⋯ (224)

(2) Attend a College Abroad ⋯⋯⋯⋯⋯⋯⋯⋯ (225)

(3) Are Children Overburdened? ⋯⋯⋯⋯⋯⋯⋯ (226)

(4) On Students Choosing Lecturers ⋯⋯⋯⋯⋯ (226)

(5) Quality Education ⋯⋯⋯⋯⋯⋯⋯⋯⋯⋯⋯⋯ (227)

(6) Is Study Pressure Good for University Students? ⋯⋯ (228)

(7) Does Higher Education Cease to Be Useful? ⋯⋯⋯ (228)

(8) Graduate School Rush ⋯⋯⋯⋯⋯⋯⋯⋯⋯⋯ (229)

(9) Active Classes or Passive Classes? ⋯⋯⋯⋯⋯ (230)

(10) The "Hope Project" ⋯⋯⋯⋯⋯⋯⋯⋯⋯⋯ (231)

(11) The Reform of the College Curricula ⋯⋯⋯ (232)

(12) Hard Life Is Good for Children ⋯⋯⋯⋯⋯ (233)

(13) The Advantages and Disadvantages of
    Private Tutoring ⋯⋯⋯⋯⋯⋯⋯⋯⋯⋯⋯⋯ (235)

No. 22 Children and Childhood（儿童与童年） ⋯⋯⋯⋯ (237)

(1) When I Was a Child ⋯⋯⋯⋯⋯⋯⋯⋯⋯⋯ (237)

(2) My Childhood ⋯⋯⋯⋯⋯⋯⋯⋯⋯⋯⋯⋯⋯ (238)

(3) My Boyhood Days ⋯⋯⋯⋯⋯⋯⋯⋯⋯⋯⋯ (239)

(4) A Better Understanding Between Parents
    and Children ⋯⋯⋯⋯⋯⋯⋯⋯⋯⋯⋯⋯⋯⋯ (240)

No. 23 Recollections of the Past（往事的回忆） ⋯⋯⋯ (241)

(1) My Days in the Middle School ⋯⋯⋯⋯⋯⋯ (241)

(2) Farewell to My Middle School Life ⋯⋯⋯⋯ (242)

(3) A Terrifying Experience ⋯⋯⋯⋯⋯⋯⋯⋯⋯ (242)

(4) A Meaningful Day to Remember ⋯⋯⋯⋯⋯ (243)

(5) My Surprise Birthday Party ⋯⋯⋯⋯⋯⋯⋯ (244)

(6) Farewell to Home-village ⋯⋯⋯⋯⋯⋯⋯⋯ (245)

No. 24 Profession（职业与择业） ·· (246)
    (1) College Students' Job Hunting ·························· (246)
    (2) How to Succeed in a Job Interview ···················· (247)
    (3) Why Do Graduates Find Jobs Irrelevant to
        Their Majors? ·· (247)
    (4) Suitability Is the Key to a Good Job ·················· (248)
    (5) Choosing the Right Careers ······························· (249)
    (6) On College Students Supporting Rural
        Construction ·· (249)
    (7) My View on Job-hopping ·································· (250)
    (8) Teaching — My Profession ································ (251)

No. 25 Health（健康） ··· (252)
    (1) How to Keep Healthy ······································· (252)
    (2) Staying Healthy ·· (253)
    (3) Health Improvements in Developing Countries ······ (253)
    (4) How to Lose Weight ·· (254)
    (5) Health and Life ·· (255)
    (6) People's Knowledge of AIDS in China ··············· (256)

No. 26 My Parents（我的父母） ··· (258)
    (1) Motherly Love ·· (258)
    (2) My Beloved Mother ··· (259)
    (3) My Mother ··· (260)
    (4) The Busiest Person in My Family ······················· (261)
    (5) Parents Are the Best Teachers ··························· (262)

No. 27 My Hometown（我的家乡） ····································· (263)
    (1) My Hometown（Ⅰ） ··· (263)
    (2) My Hometown（Ⅱ） ·· (264)
    (3) My Birthplace ··· (264)
    (4) Home Sickness ··· (265)

No. 28 Love and Marriage（爱情与婚姻） ···························· (266)
    (1) Love ··· (266)
    (2) International Marriages ······································ (267)

(3) Being Single ……………………………………… (267)
　　　(4) Marriage and Partner Relationship ………………… (268)
No. 29　Family（家庭）……………………………………… (270)
　　　(1) The Chinese Family Structure ……………………… (270)
　　　(2) Family and Personal Development ………………… (271)
　　　(3) My Family ………………………………………… (272)
　　　(4) Is Family Influence Critical? ……………………… (272)
　　　(5) Honour Our Parents ………………………………… (273)
　　　(6) Resist the DINK Fad ……………………………… (274)
　　　(7) A House Is Not a Home …………………………… (276)
No. 30　Festivals and Holidays（新年佳节）……………… (277)
　　　(1) Chinese New Year: Tradition in Change …………… (277)
　　　(2) The Chinese New Year ……………………………… (278)
　　　(3) The Lunar New Year's Celebration ………………… (279)
　　　(4) The Mid-autumn Festival …………………………… (280)
　　　(5) The Miao Dragon-Boat Festival …………………… (280)
　　　(6) Confucian Festival ………………………………… (281)
No. 31　City Life and Country Life（城市与农村生活）…… (283)
　　　(1) Living in a Big City ……………………………… (283)
　　　(2) How to Solve the Housing Problem in Big Cities …… (284)
　　　(3) Supermarkets ……………………………………… (285)
　　　(4) Country Life ……………………………………… (286)
　　　(5) Pleasure of the Country …………………………… (286)
　　　(6) A Rainy Day in the Countryside …………………… (288)
　　　(7) Enjoyment of Country People ……………………… (288)
　　　(8) Where to Live — In the City or the Country? ……… (289)
　　　(9) The Night Life in Dalian …………………………… (290)
No. 32　Sports（体育）……………………………………… (291)
　　　(1) Sports in Our Country ……………………………… (291)
　　　(2) Women in Sports ………………………………… (292)
　　　(3) Physical Exercise and Mental Advantages ………… (293)
　　　(4) Physical Exercise and Social Advantages ………… (294)

(5) Prize and Competition ……………………………… (294)
(6) The Importance of Physical Exercise ……………… (295)
(7) Beijing Olympics Volunteer in My Eyes ………… (296)
(8) Chinese Basketball ……………………………… (297)
(9) Swimming ……………………………………… (298)
(10) Mountain-climbing …………………………… (299)
(11) Skiing ………………………………………… (299)
(12) Wake Up Your Life by Walking ……………… (300)

No. 33 Recreations（消遣与娱乐）……………………… (302)
(1) Recreations ……………………………………… (302)
(2) Ways of Relaxing ……………………………… (303)
(3) Music …………………………………………… (303)
(4) A Kite …………………………………………… (305)
(5) A Walk in the Rain …………………………… (305)
(6) A Walk on the Seashore ……………………… (306)
(7) An Art Exhibition ……………………………… (307)
(8) The Game I Like Best ………………………… (307)
(9) Mountain Climbing …………………………… (308)
(10) Swimming in Winter ………………………… (309)
(11) Pet Dogs ……………………………………… (310)
(12) Pop Star as Icon of Reform ………………… (311)
(13) Why the Youngsters Like Popular Music ………… (311)

No. 34 Excursion（郊游）………………………………… (313)
(1) Our Spring Day Walk ………………………… (313)
(2) An Excursion …………………………………… (314)
(3) A Happy Outing ……………………………… (315)
(4) A Moonlight Picnic …………………………… (315)
(5) A Visit to Mount Lion ………………………… (317)

No. 35 Tourism（旅行与旅游）…………………………… (318)
(1) Tourism ………………………………………… (318)
(2) Travelling ……………………………………… (319)
(3) Travelling by Air ……………………………… (320)

  (4) Which Mode of Travel Do You Like? ……………… (320)

No. 36　Transportation（交通工具）………………………(322)
  (1) Automobiles ………………………………………… (322)
  (2) Private Cars in Large Cities ……………………… (323)
  (3) Bicycles ……………………………………………… (323)
  (4) Cars for Tomorrow ………………………………… (324)
  (5) Taxi …………………………………………………… (325)

No. 37　Dwellings（民居）………………………………… (326)
  (1) My Home …………………………………………… (326)
  (2) My Flat ……………………………………………… (326)
  (3) My New Home ……………………………………… (327)

No. 38　Money（金钱问题）……………………………… (329)
  (1) Money ………………………………………………… (329)
  (2) Money and Greed ………………………………… (330)
  (3) My View on Bank Loan …………………………… (331)
  (4) Can Success Be Measured in Terms of Money? …… (332)

No. 39　Generation Gap（代沟）………………………… (333)
  (1) What Kind of Life to Live — Realistic
    or Romantic? ……………………………………… (333)
  (2) Mutual Understanding Is Important ……………… (334)
  (3) Generation Gap Between Parents and Children …… (335)
  (4) The Generation Gap ……………………………… (335)

No. 40　Women（妇女问题）……………………………… (337)
  (1) On Women's Problems …………………………… (337)
  (2) Women in Our Society …………………………… (338)
  (3) Women Are as Perfect as Men …………………… (339)
  (4) Women — Still as Second-class Citizen ………… (339)
  (5) Women's Liberation: a Long Way to Go ………… (340)
  (6) Send Women Home and Double Men's Salary …… (341)

No. 41　Population（人口问题）………………………… (342)
  (1) Population Explosion ……………………………… (342)
  (2) Population Control ………………………………… (343)

　　　　(3) China's Population Problem in Rural Areas ·········· (343)
　　　　(4) How to Solve the Problem of Employment
　　　　　　and Population ·· (344)
No. 42　Traffic Problem（交通问题）·························· (346)
　　　　(1) Modern Transportation ······························ (346)
　　　　(2) Only Stricter Traffic Laws Can Prevent Accidents ······ (347)
　　　　(3) Problems Brought About by Automobiles ··········· (348)
　　　　(4) Pile-up Traffic Accidents ···························· (348)
　　　　(5) A Road Accident ····································· (349)
No. 43　Environmental Protection（环境保护）············· (351)
　　　　(1) Pollution ··· (351)
　　　　(2) Cars and Air Pollution ······························ (352)
　　　　(3) Water Pollution ······································ (353)
　　　　(4) Deserts ··· (354)
　　　　(5) Let's Plant More Trees ····························· (354)
　　　　(6) Man and the Environment ·························· (355)
　　　　(7) Protecting Natural Environment ···················· (356)
　　　　(8) How to Save Wild Animals ························· (357)
　　　　(9) Earth Day ·· (358)
　　　　(10) Limiting the Use of Disposable Plastic Bags ········ (358)
　　　　(11) Noise Pollution ······································· (359)
　　　　(12) Man Is to Survive ··································· (360)
　　　　(13) Relationship Between Man and Nature ············ (360)
No. 44　Resources（资源）······································· (362)
　　　　(1) Water ··· (362)
　　　　(2) Shortage of Fresh Water ···························· (363)
　　　　(3) Rivers ·· (363)
　　　　(4) Food ·· (364)
　　　　(5) Land Resources ······································· (365)
　　　　(6) Land Use Today ······································ (366)
No. 45　Energy Supply（能源）································ (368)
　　　　(1) Energy Resources ···································· (368)

  (2) Solar Energy ……………………………………… (368)
  (3) Electricity …………………………………………… (369)
  (4) Save Every Drop of Water …………………………… (370)
  (5) Different Forms of Energy ………………………… (371)

No. 46 Economic Development (经济发展) ………………… (372)
  (1) Management ………………………………………… (372)
  (2) Advantages and Problems of Private Enterprises …… (373)
  (3) What Is Commerce ………………………………… (374)
  (4) Tasks of Production Managers …………………… (375)
  (5) Preserve Every Inch of Farmland ………………… (375)
  (6) Made in China or Created in China ……………… (376)
  (7) The World Exposition ……………………………… (377)
  (8) Peace and Development: The Themes of
    the Times ………………………………………… (378)

No. 47 Science and Technology (科学技术) ………………… (379)
  (1) Effect of Advanced Technology on Human Beings …… (379)
  (2) Space Travel ………………………………………… (380)
  (3) Do We Need Space Exploration? …………………… (380)
  (4) Material Science in the 21st Country ……………… (381)
  (5) Advantages and Disadvantages of Cell Phones …… (382)
  (6) The Digital Age …………………………………… (382)
  (7) Modern Technology and Human Intimacy ………… (383)

No. 48 Computer and Internet (计算机与网络) …………… (385)
  (1) Computers …………………………………………… (385)
  (2) Computer and Man ………………………………… (386)
  (3) Internet—a Two-edged Sword …………………… (387)
  (4) Positive and Negative Effects of Computers ……… (388)
  (5) Away from Net-bar Campaign …………………… (389)
  (6) Shopping on the Internet ………………………… (389)

No. 49 Television (电视) ……………………………………… (391)
  (1) Television …………………………………………… (391)
  (2) My Favourite TV Programme …………………… (392)

   (3) The Harmful Effect of TV on Children ……… (392)

   (4) Television Is Doing Irreparable Harm ……… (393)

No. 50 Mass Media（传播媒介） ……………………… (395)

   (1) The Mass Media ……………………………… (395)

   (2) Newspapers and Television ………………… (396)

   (3) Newspapers …………………………………… (396)

   (4) The News Media ……………………………… (397)

No. 51 Advertisements（广告） ……………………… (399)

   (1) Advertisements ………………………………… (399)

   (2) The Arguments on Advertising: For and Against …… (400)

   (3) Advertisement Paper ………………………… (401)

No. 52 Daily Happenings（生活琐记） ……………… (402)

   (1) Haste Comes Not Alone ……………………… (402)

   (2) A Miserable Moment ………………………… (403)

   (3) Catching Cold ………………………………… (403)

   (4) Seeing a Doctor ……………………………… (404)

   (5) Fortune-telling ………………………………… (405)

   (6) Sending Gifts ………………………………… (406)

   (7) Daydreaming ………………………………… (407)

   (8) A Glimpse of the Market …………………… (407)

No. 53 Social Issues（时事话题） …………………… (409)

   (1) Law and Order ………………………………… (409)

   (2) Fight Against Crime ………………………… (410)

   (3) Cooperation and Competition ……………… (411)

   (4) Challenges …………………………………… (411)

   (5) Problems in Our Grain Production ………… (412)

   (6) The Gap Between the Rich and the Poor …… (413)

   (7) Certificates or a Sound Education ………… (414)

   (8) What Should We Learn from Americans? …… (415)

   (9) Care for Our Community …………………… (416)

   (10) Patriotism …………………………………… (417)

   (11) Copyright Infringements …………………… (418)

(12) The Effect of the Global Financial Crisis .... (418)
(13) The Growth in the Number of Foreign Visitors
    to China .... (419)
(14) Unemployment .... (420)
(15) On Food Safety Issues .... (421)
(16) The Aging Problem .... (422)

No. 54 **Aspects of Life（生活面面观）**................... (423)
(1) Finding Meaning in Life .... (423)
(2) What Is the Best Preparation for Life .... (424)
(3) Is Social Skill Important? .... (425)
(4) Are Pets Good for People? .... (426)
(5) Some Fire Hazards Around Us .... (426)
(6) Euthanasia .... (427)
(7) Dining Out in a Fast Food Restaurant .... (428)
(8) Fate .... (429)
(9) Do "Lucky Numbers" Really Bring Good Luck? .... (430)
(10) My View on Fake Commodities .... (430)
(11) The Problem of Workplace Safety .... (431)
(12) Youth More Liberal .... (432)
(13) Say No to Pirated Products .... (433)
(14) My View on the Income Disparity .... (434)
(15) My View on Lottery .... (434)
(16) Making Decisions .... (435)
(17) Changing Fashions .... (436)
(18) On Clothes .... (437)
(19) On Personal Privacy .... (437)
(20) Starbucks Should Leave the Forbidden City .... (438)
(21) Wenchuan Earthquake .... (439)
(22) Should Free Music Downloads Be Banned? .... (440)

No. 55 **Perception in life（人生感悟）**..................... (441)
(1) The Best Age to Be .... (441)
(2) Satisfied or Dissatisfied .... (442)

（3）A Fall into the Pit, a Gain in Your Wit .... （443）
　　（4）Don't Be Complaining All the Time .... （443）
　　（5）On Learning about Life .... （444）
　　（6）Don't Hesitate to Say "No" .... （445）
　　（7）Reactions to Disappointment .... （446）
　　（8）Enthusiasm .... （447）
　　（9）You Are What You Think .... （447）
　　（10）The Gap Between the Rich and the Poor .... （448）
　　（11）Change Is Opportunity .... （449）
　　（12）Being Thankful .... （450）
　　（13）A Day without Hope Is a Day without Sunshine ...... （450）
　　（14）Smile .... （451）
　　（15）Packaging .... （452）
No. 56　Suicide（自杀问题） .... （453）
　　（1）Suicide .... （453）
　　（2）Young People's Suicide .... （453）
　　（3）Suicide Among Students .... （454）
　　（4）On Opening Psychological Courses .... （455）
　　（5）How to Improve Students' Mental Health? .... （456）
No. 57　Natural Phenomena（自然现象） .... （458）
　　（1）Earthquakes .... （458）
　　（2）Gravity .... （459）
　　（3）Typhoons and Earthquakes .... （459）
　　（4）UFO .... （460）
No. 58　Climate（气候） .... （462）
　　（1）Climate .... （462）
　　（2）Weather .... （463）
　　（3）Weather Forecasts .... （463）
No. 59　Tree-planting（植树造林） .... （465）
　　（1）Preservation of Forests .... （465）
　　（2）Trees and Man .... （466）
　　（3）Forest .... （466）

　　　　(4) Make Our Cities Greener ················ (467)

No. 60　Animals（动物）························ (469)
　　　　(1) Pets ·································· (469)
　　　　(2) The Sheep ··························· (470)
　　　　(3) The Dog ····························· (470)
　　　　(4) The Tiger ···························· (471)
　　　　(5) The King of Beasts ··················· (472)
　　　　(6) Camels in the Desert ················· (473)
　　　　(7) Birds ································ (473)
　　　　(8) Animal Protection ···················· (474)

No. 61　Flowers（花卉）······················· (475)
　　　　(1) Flowers(Ⅰ) ··························· (475)
　　　　(2) Flowers(Ⅱ) ··························· (476)
　　　　(3) Flowers(Ⅲ) ··························· (477)

No. 62　Natural Produce（物产）··············· (478)
　　　　(1) Coal ································· (478)
　　　　(2) Paper and Its Uses ··················· (479)
　　　　(3) Cotton ······························· (479)
　　　　(4) Sugar ································ (480)
　　　　(5) Tea ·································· (481)
　　　　(6) Silk ·································· (482)

No. 63　Beautiful Sights（日月星辰）··········· (484)
　　　　(1) Sunrise on the Western Hills ·········· (484)
　　　　(2) The Sun ······························ (484)
　　　　(3) Sunset ······························· (485)
　　　　(4) The Rising of the Moon ··············· (486)
　　　　(5) The Moon ···························· (486)
　　　　(6) Stars ································· (487)
　　　　(7) Sunrise ······························ (488)
　　　　(8) A Moonlit Night ····················· (489)

No. 64　Changes of the Weather（风云雨雪）··· (490)
　　　　(1) Listening to the Wind ················ (490)

　　　　(2) Clouds ·· (490)
　　　　(3) Summer Clouds ······································ (491)
　　　　(4) A Thunder Storm ···································· (492)
　　　　(5) A Shower ··· (493)
　　　　(6) Snow ··· (494)
　　　　(7) A Snowfall ·· (495)
No. 65　Scenery of the Four Seasons（绚烂四季）············ (496)
　　　　(1) The Four Seasons ··································· (496)
　　　　(2) Spring ·· (497)
　　　　(3) Spring Falls on Us ·································· (498)
　　　　(4) Summer ··· (498)
　　　　(5) A Pleasant Summer ································· (499)
　　　　(6) Autumn ·· (500)
　　　　(7) Winter ··· (500)
　　　　(8) My Favourite Month ································ (501)
No. 66　Sketches of Natural Scenes（山水的描写）············ (503)
　　　　(1) A Bay in the Moonlight ···························· (503)
　　　　(2) A Bay ·· (503)
　　　　(3) A Calm Sea ·· (503)
　　　　(4) A Pond ·· (504)
　　　　(5) A Brook ··· (504)
　　　　(6) Lakes ·· (505)
　　　　(7) A Moonlit Valley ···································· (505)
　　　　(8) A Beautiful Precipice ······························ (505)
　　　　(9) A Village in the Evening ·························· (506)
　　　　(10) The Great Wall ····································· (506)
　　　　(11) Mount Tai ··· (507)
No. 67　Sketches of Animals and Birds
　　　　（飞禽走兽的描写）····································· (509)
　　　　(1) Swallows ·· (509)
　　　　(2) Ducks ·· (509)
　　　　(3) The Hens of a Farmyard ·························· (509)

    (4) Horses ·· (510)

    (5) A Lean Ox ······································ (510)

    (6) Dogs ··· (510)

    (7) Sheep ·· (511)

    (8) Cat ·· (511)

    (9) Stork ·· (511)

    (10) Sea-gull ······································ (512)

    (11) Crows ·· (512)

    (12) Eagle ··· (512)

No. 68 **Sketches of Fish and Insects（鱼虫的描写）** ········ (513)

    (1) Fish（Ⅰ） ······································ (513)

    (2) Fish（Ⅱ） ····································· (513)

    (3) A Butterfly ···································· (513)

    (4) Butterflies ····································· (514)

    (5) The Croak of Frogs ····························· (514)

No. 69 **Sketches of Human Figures（各色人物的描写）** ····· (515)

    (1) Myself ··· (515)

    (2) Grandma and Mother ··························· (516)

    (3) My Father ····································· (517)

    (4) My Grandmother ······························· (517)

    (5) A Young Man ·································· (518)

    (6) The Lady ······································ (519)

    (7) An Old Lady ··································· (519)

    (8) A Kind Person ································· (520)

    (9) An Outstanding Worker ························· (520)

    (10) My Friend ···································· (521)

No. 70 **Comparing and Contrasting（对照比较）** ·········· (522)

    (1) Different Ways of Living ······················· (522)

    (2) Two Friends ··································· (522)

    (3) Two Girl Classmates ··························· (523)

    (4) My Parents ···································· (524)

    (5) Two Sisters ···································· (524)

(6) College and High School ·················· (525)
　　(7) Spoken English and Written English ············· (526)
　　(8) The Sun and the Moon ·················· (526)
　　(9) Differences Between the Two Models ············ (527)
　　(10) Similarities and Differences Between My High School
　　　　 and College Lives ·················· (528)
　　(11) Different Social Customs Between Americans
　　　　 and Chinese ···················· (529)
　　(12) A Comparison Between Two Kinds of Clothes ······· (530)
No. 71　Procedure（操作程序）················ (531)
　　(1) Making Bread ···················· (531)
　　(2) How to Make Hamburgers ··············· (532)
　　(3) How to Take Photographs ··············· (532)
　　(4) Change a Wheel ··················· (533)
No. 72　Writing Based on Pictures（图表及图画说明）······ (534)
　　(1) Area and Population of the Continents ·········· (534)
　　(2) Cooperation ····················· (535)
　　(3) Touch Online or Contact Directly ············ (536)
　　(4) College Students' Booklist ··············· (537)
　　(5) Average Monthly Rainfall in Country A and
　　　　 Country B ····················· (538)
　　(6) How to Use Water Properly ··············· (539)
　　(7) An Incident ····················· (540)
　　(8) Sex Discrimination ·················· (541)
　　(9) The Swallow ···················· (542)
No. 73　Letters（书信）···················· (544)
　　A. Private Letter（私人书信）··············· (544)
　　　(1) A Letter from a College Volunteer Teaching in the
　　　　　Rural Area of Gansu Province ············ (544)
　　　(2) A Letter to My Teacher on Teachers Day ······· (545)
　　B. Social Letter（社交书信）··············· (545)
　　　(1) A Letter of Congratulation ············· (545)
　　　(2) A Letter of Thanks ················ (546)

  (3) A Letter of Acceptance ······················· (547)
  (4) A Letter of Regret ····························· (547)
 C. Other Letters (其他书信) ······················· (548)
  (1) A Letter of Application for Financial Aid ········ (548)
  (2) A Letter of Application for a Place at the Graduate
    School of Physics ····························· (548)
  (3) A Letter of Introduction ······················· (549)
  (4) A Letter of Recommendation ··················· (550)
  (5) An Application for a Scholarship ··············· (551)
  (6) A Letter for Applying a Post ··················· (551)
  (7) A Letter to a Reader ·························· (552)
  (8) A Letter to a House Agency ··················· (553)
  (9) Application Letter ···························· (553)
  (10) A Leter of Apology ·························· (554)
  (11) A Letter of Application ······················· (555)
No. 74 Practical Writings (应用文) ··············· (557)
 A. Note (便条) ·································· (557)
  (1) Asking for Sick Leave(Ⅰ) ···················· (557)
  (2) Asking for Sick Leave(Ⅱ) ···················· (557)
  (3) Asking for Business Leave (Ⅰ) ················ (558)
  (4) Asking for Business Leave (Ⅱ) ················ (558)
 B. Message (留言) ······························· (559)
  (1) Asking a Friend to Give a Ring ················ (559)
  (2) Transmitting a Telephone Message ············· (559)
  (3) Saying Good-bye ····························· (559)
  (4) Requesting to Borrow Something ················ (560)
  (5) To Inform a Friend of Putting off a Meeting ······ (560)
 C. Notice (启事) ································· (560)
  (1) Lost ·· (560)
  (2) A Wrist Watch Lost ··························· (561)
  (3) Found ······································· (561)
  (4) A Briefcase Found ···························· (561)

(5) For Sale ·· (561)
  (6) Needed ·· (562)
  (7) Book Wanted ·· (562)
 D. Poster（海报）·· (562)
  (1) Lecture ·· (562)
  (2) Talk ··· (562)
  (3) Basketball Match ··· (563)
  (4) Women's Volleyball Match ·································· (563)
  (5) This Week's Film ··· (564)
 E. Notice（通知）·· (564)
  (1) Notice of the President's Office ···························· (564)
  (2) Notice of the General Affairs Service ······················· (564)
  (3) Notice of the Library Office ································ (564)
  (4) Notice of the English Department ··························· (565)
  (5) Notice of the Students Union ······························· (565)

Appendix(附录) ··· (566)
 1. 英语章段写作常用词语 ··· (566)
 2. 英语写作常用过渡性词语及其实例 ······························ (574)
 3. 英语作文常用格言和引语 ······································ (576)

英语短文写作入门谈

一、两点建议

英文写作是英语学习的主干课程,是大学英语四、六级、托福、雅思、硕士入学、硕士学位(一级)、英语专业四级和八级的必考项目,也是令许多学生头疼的项目。在我们辅导过的学生当中,不少人曾提出过这样的问题,不管你把写作的理论法则讲得如何清楚,把作文技巧讲得如何透彻,但题目到手,仍不得其门而入。实际上,学生们的确有这种困难,因而我们试图在此定出几种极为明确的入门方法,使学生牢记并付诸实践。此后,每逢遇到一个题目,便能够如法炮制。虽不能凭这些方法写出超级妙文,但至少可以使学生接到题目后,总会有话可说,有文可作,可以达到一般考试对短文写作的基本要求。在谈具体方法之前,先提两点建议。

1. 模仿范例

过去小学生受启蒙教育,多以描红模子练习毛笔字。稍有长进以后又以字帖习之。尽管在一些人看来,这或许并不是什么高明的练字法,但许多人之所以能写出一手逸雅劲爽、神采飞扬的好字,甚至成为独具风格的书法家,不能不说是得益于这种练字的苦功夫。如果说初练毛笔字需要用描红模子、字帖作为范例来练习用笔、学习结构的话,那么,对初学用英文作文的中国学生来说,也需要模仿范例,而后方可得心应手、落笔成章。"熟读唐诗三百首,不会作诗也会吟。"已道出了在初学写作时模仿的重要性。需要说明的是,初学英文写作,我们要模仿的不是相当于"唐诗"那样的经典作品,不是类似于《葛底斯堡演说》(The Gettysburg Address)那

1

样不朽的名家名作，而是本书所收录的一些与考试作文相似的、浅近实用的文章。这些对于初学者堪称作文的范文，本书涉及的内容极为广泛，所有的范文均与中国的国情或当前世界各国共同存在和关注的社会问题有关，因此在考试中碰到类似内容、题目的可能性极大。即使在考试中碰不到你所背诵的范文，在举例或论述时，其相关内容及所使用的句式也足资可鉴，甚至可以灵活运用，将其吸收到自己的作文中去。例如，下面一些考试的基本句式可供借鉴。为便于掌握，将这些句式分为三类：

1）指出一种倾向，引述事实或现状，提出一个问题或看法。此类句子可称之为观点句或主题句。

（1）Although old people in the United States and in my country, China, are treated the same in some ways, in other ways they are treated differently.

（2）With the accelerated pace of modern life, more and more city-dwellers are eager to take a vacation outside the city for a change.

（3）We cannot ignore the fact that there are many students who have difficulties in English learning.

（4）In the past decade, there have been great changes in people's diet.

（5）It is well known to us that the computer plays a very important role in the age of knowledge economy.

（6）From the graph given above, it can be seen that people's living standard has been greatly improved in the past decade.

2）分析原因，进行比较，阐述不同观点或进行反面论述。此类句子可称之为说明句或支持句。

（1）There are three possible reasons for this.

（2）The advantages of B outweigh any benefit we gain from A.

（3）Unfortunately, however, tourism also gives rise to a number of problems.

（4）As a matter of fact, science has also brought new and complicated problems to the world.

（5）However, other people argue that big cities are confronted with many problems.

3）对全文阐述的内容进行概括和总结，就文章讨论的问题说明个人的看法、提出解决办法或建设性的建议。这类句子可称之为结论句。

（1）From what has been discussed above, we may come to the conclusion that examination is necessary. However, its method should be improved.

（2）Personally, I think the plane, the modern means of transportation, has more advantages than disadvantages, and it is more convenient for us to travel by plane.

（3）In my opinion, the computer will never replace man because it has no intelligence of its own.

（4）The influence of TV is so serious that parents will have to be on their guard at all times in order to make sure that their children are not being harmed by exposure to it.

（5）In order to narrow the generation gap, both groups should respect each other, listen to the words of each other and discuss their problems patiently.

灵活地模仿使用简单明确的英文句型和语法结构，是提高英文口头、笔头表达能力的有效途径。例如，在谈论读书类的作文中，会发现这样一个阐述观点的句子：Reading is to the mind what food is to the body.（读书对于精神如同食物对于身体一样。）这是英语中比较两种相似关系的句型，即 A 之于 B 犹如 C 之于 D，其英语句型可归纳为 A is to B what C is to D。从语法上来看，该句型中 what 是一个关系代词，由 what 引起的从句是"A is"的表语，即：A is what C is to D to B。我们"照葫芦画瓢"，可以写出许多表示相似关系的句子：

The army is to the people what fish is to water. (军民关系犹如鱼水关系。)

Science is to the human mind what air or water is to the body. (科学之于人类思想正如水或空气之于身体。)

Shakespeare is to literature what Beethoven is to music. (莎士比亚对于文学的贡献如同贝多芬对于音乐的贡献。)

What sculpture is to a block of marble, education is to the soul. (＝Education is to the soul what sculpture is to a block of marble.) (教育之于心灵,犹如雕刻之于大理石。)

Thoughtfulness is to friendship what sunshine is to a garden. (体贴对于友谊,犹如阳光对于花园。)

在谈论美德的作文中,有这样一句话:As fire tries gold, so adversity tries virtue. (正如烈火试炼真金,逆境试炼人的美德。)

这是英语中比较两种相似情况的句型,即正如C之于D,A之于B也同样。其英语句型可归纳为 As C is to D, so is A to B。在这个句型中,as 引导的是从句,so 之后为主句。照这一句型,可以写出许多表示相似情况的句子:

As the earth moves round the sun, so the moon moves about the earth. (像地球绕太阳运行一样,月亮绕地球运行。)

As bread nourishes the body, so books enrich the mind. (面包滋养身体,书籍培养智慧。)

As I would not be a slave, so I would not be a master. (正如我不愿当奴隶,我也不愿意当主子。)(林肯语)

在谈论立志的作文中,有这样一篇:Where there is a will, there is a way. 许多学习者早已学会并记住了这句话,但只把它看成中文成语"有志者事竟成"的英文对应说法,而不会灵活运用。实际上,Where there is... there is... 这样一个简明的语法结构可以用来表达许多思想。例如:

Where there is life, there is hope. (有生命就有希望。或:留得青山在,不怕没柴烧。)

Where there is money, there is power.（有钱就有权。）

Where there is examination, there is examination-oriented education.（有考试就有应试教育。）

实际上，英文中所有的短语和句式，都可以根据不同内容而灵活运用。例如，依照前面提到的用于文章开头的观点句或主题句第二个例句的句式，可以表达下列不同的意思：

（1）With the (rapidly) growing popularity of computers / private cars / golf / tennis / pianos / fast food / coca cola / mobile phones / house interior decoration / going abroad to study / traveling / beauty salons / credit cards / supermarkets / pets in China, the quality of our lives has been considerably changed.

（2）With the (rapid) growth of our economy / population / private enterprises / housing industry, many problems such as water shortages, traffic jams industrial pollution and chaotic management are beginning to surface.

（3）With the development of science and technology / market economy / electronics industry, more and more people come to realize that…

学习者平时要多积累这样的表达方式，并逐步学会用于自己的短文写作中，以迅速提高写作能力。

学语言，汉语也好，英语也好，在很大程度上都是一种模仿。如果有"通幽"的"捷径"的话，那就是背诵，要埋头背，下苦功夫背，背到滚瓜烂熟，虽不能说"书中自有黄金屋，书中自有颜如玉"，但书中自有单词，自有句型，自有语法规则是不言而喻的。背诵不仅提高笔头作文能力，也会毫无疑问地提高口头作文能力，培养弥足珍贵的"语感"，有了语感就会受用不尽，更何况一般考试中的笔头作文与 TSE（Test of Spoken English）涉及的话题都是一样的。可以说，背诵、模仿是提高英语写作能力的"笨办法"，也是最佳办法。大学者钱钟书曾说：最聪明的人是以最笨的方法做学问的人。这话是颇有见地的。这个笨办法就是博闻强记。

2. 勤于实践,养成正确的语言习惯

自贯彻《大学英语教学大纲》,举行全国大学英语四、六级统测(CET)以来,大学英语教育有了长足进步。但从几年来 CET 单项统计的结果看,作文一项的分数提高幅度较小。作文一项占 CET 的 15%,而一般院校作文平均分数一直在 5 分上下徘徊。CET (以及上文提到的其他考试)写作部分是对考生运用语言进行交际的能力的综合检测;写作所反映的是学生实际语言水平的一种综合能力。造成写作成绩处于低谷的主客观原因很多。学生缺乏必要的写作实践,特别是缺乏基本的写作技能,是问题的关键所在。因而,提高写作水平的关键在于加强运用英语的实践。

正是由于缺乏运用英语的实践,学生的作文中往往出现一些似是而非、违反英语基本语法规则的句子,有时整篇作文几乎找不到一个完整的正确句子。这样的作文按阅卷标准只能得 2 分。实际上,语篇与写作技能(即下文将读到的篇章结构:introduction, body, conclusion;怎样承上启下等)虽然重要,但本书的读者毕竟有中文写作基础,掌握起来不会太难。因此,突破写作关首先要从练基本功做起。

据我们对考生作文中所犯错误的调查分析,常犯的错误大致有以下几类:

(1)编造词语,如 door ticket(门票,应为 entrance ticket 或 admission ticket);high-speed road(高速公路,应为 expressway);comfortable death(安乐死,应为 mercy killing 或 painless death 或 euthanasia);sky wire(天线,应为 aerial 或 antenna)等;

(2)大小写、标点符号以及拼写错误;

(3)可数名词和不可数名词、集体名词、名词复数特殊变化的误用;

(4)动词不规则变化的误用;

(5)主谓语不一致、数的不一致及代词指代关系不一致;

(6)动词用法错误,包括时态、语态、不及物动词用作及物动词,以及动词的单复数等;

(7) 比较级错误,包括特殊变化不熟悉及用法错误;

(8) 句子不完整,包括:① 缺少主语、谓语或谓语的一部分,如在 will/can 后直接接表语,写出 I can happy 之类的句子;② 在 there be 后直接接句子,如 There are many people live there;③ 将 because 和 when 等引导的从句独立成句子;

(9) 词性误用,如形容词用作主语,名词用作谓语等;

(10) 同根词、同形词、同音词混用;

(11) 连词误用,导致复合句结构不当;

(12) 介词误用,如 in the playground(应该用 on);

(13) 常用短语用错,如用 on the other hand 表示递进关系;

(14) 句型用错,影响表达;

(15) 一段文字中主语变换过多,造成不连贯或重点不突出;

(16) 通篇只使用主语+谓语+宾语或用最简单、最基本的句型,虽无大的语法错误,却被视为 baby English(婴儿英语)。

从上述所列问题可以看出,多数考生写作的主要问题还是集中在不能写出正确的、有一定句型变化的句子方面,即基本写作技能问题。

必须着重指明的是,考生在写作时所犯的大部分错误与其说是知识不足,毋宁说是技能不够。如果把这些错误编成改错题,让考生改正,可以肯定地说,绝大多数人是能判断出正确答案的。所以说,写出正确的、有一定句型变化的句子的关键,在于勤于实践和模仿,以养成正确的语言习惯。学习者不妨按照考试要求,多写几篇作文,先置于一旁,过几天后再拿出来,自己认真改正语言方面的错误。这样才能在写作中,特别是在时间紧迫的考试作文中,不犯或少犯那些本来可以避免的典型错误,以提高考试成绩。

二、提高组词造句的能力

1. 句子结合

为了使上文中提到的"婴儿英语"得以改进,在作文中避免句式的趋同单一,我们可以依照英语"形合"(hypotaxis)的特点,利用英语中各类起连接作用的词,把那些每句话只含有一个信息的简单句结合为有一定句型变化、内容上有一定深度的较长的句子,即句子结合(sentence combining)。句子结合也称为句子的延伸转换。

句子结合有限制性练习(closed exercises)和开放性练习(open exercises)两种。迄今教科书中所涉及的有关练习多属第一种。例如:

The place seemed to be enveloped in a glow.
Jill stood in the place. (insert *where*)
A glow gleamed on her red hair. (insert *which/that*)

三个简单句可结合成为一个含有两个定语从句的较长的复合句:

The place where Jill stood seemed to be enveloped in a glow which (or that) gleamed on her hair.

开放性的句子结合练习则比较灵活。例如下列8个只含一个单一信息的单句可按照不同的语法手段,结合成较长的、含信息量较大的简单句、并列句或复合句。①

(1) My friends waited in line.
(2) I waited in line.
(3) The line was long.
(4) We waited to buy tickets.
(5) We finally got the tickets.
(6) The tickets were for a concert.
(7) The rock group gave the concert.
(8) The rock group was popular.

前四个句子可以用两种不同的语法手段结合为一句话:

My friends and I waited in a long line for tickets.

---

① 本例选自 Allan A. Glathorn 等编著的《作文技巧》,Science Research Associates, Inc., Chicago, 1980.

My friends and I waited in a long line to buy tickets.

后四句话也可用两种不同的语法手段结合为一句话：

We finally got tickets that were for a concert which was given by a rock group that was popular.

We finally got the tickets for a concert by a popular rock group.

还可以用不同的语法手段把这 8 个简单句结合成为一句话。例如：

My friends and I waited in a long line, but we finally got the tickets for a concert by a popular rock group.

My friends and I, having waited in a long line for the tickets to a popular rock group's concert, finally got them.

After we waited in a long line, my friends and I finally got the tickets for a rock concert given by a popular rock group.

这种句子结合练习可帮助学习者利用学过的语法知识写出在句法上比较成熟的富有表现力的句子，提高写作技巧。

下面的几组例子显示出如何使用英语中各类起连接作用的词和语法手段，使句子有机结合，使之更富连贯性，并使原来呆板单一的句式变得长短交替有序，且意思表达得清晰明确，主从有别。

（1）She studies at Beijing Normal University. She attends classes every morning and listens to the teacher attentively. She reviews her lessons after class and does her homework. She is hardworking and usually studies late into the night. She is a good student.

试比较：Being a student at Beijing Normal University, she attends classes every morning, during which time she listens to the lecture attentively. Her homework and her preparation for the lessons take much of her spare time and sometimes keep her up until late into the night. She is hardworking and in everybody's opinion a good student.

(2) Many teachers can give students information. Very few can inspire students to learn. Information is of little use to the student. Soon he will leave college. Then he will forget what he has memorized. He must be inspired to learn on his own.

试比较：Many teachers can give students information, but few can inspire them to learn. When a student leaves college, the information he has memorized will be of little use and will soon be forgotten. What he needs most is the ability to learn on his own.

(3) I spent half of my childhood in a small village. The village is very beautiful. There are green hills surrounding the village.

试比较：I spent half of my childhood in a beautiful small village surrounded by green hills.

(4) The old man began to tell us the story of his life. He was fifteen. He ran away to sea. He traveled to South America, China, and Australia. Then he was too old to work. He came to this country to live with his relatives. Now he thinks all the time about the "good old days". He was young then.

试比较：The old man began to tell us the story of his life. When he was fifteen, he ran away to sea. He traveled to South America, China, and Australia. When he was too old to work, he came to this country to live with his relatives. Now he thinks all the time about the "good old days" when he was young.

段落(4)全部使用简单句，显得生硬、单调、平铺直叙。修改的段落中交叉使用了简单句和复合句，其效果就明显不同了，不仅结构更紧凑，而且更简洁，读来抑扬顿挫。

2. 句式多样化

例1

Every year, millions of college students will sit for the post-graduate entrance examination.

这是一篇英语作文的第一句。这句话说明现象：每年有大量大学生参加研究生入学考试。这一意念还可以用下列句式表达：

(1) Every year, there are millions of college students sitting for the post-graduate entrance examination.

这句话用 there be 句型引出客观存在的现象。现在分词短语 sitting for... 是修饰 students 的定语。短语动词 sit for 在此处意为"应考"，"参加考试"。又如：More students than ever before have sat for their post-graduate entrance examination this year.（今年参加研究生入学考试的学生比往年都多。）sit for 另一个重要的意思是"为（当模特儿或照相等）摆姿势"。

(2) The annual post-graduate entrance examination appeals to millions of college students.

这是一句由主谓宾（SVO）构成的简单句。短语动词 appeal to 意为"有吸引力"，相当于一个及物动词。短语动词的使用往往成为语言亮点。

(3) The post-graduate entrance examination is an annual event which draws millions of college students.

这是一句带有限定性定语从句的复合句。这里使用限定性定语从句是为了突出说明中心词（an annual event）所具有的特性：它吸引了许许多多的大学生。

例 2

[1]In recent years, there has been a steady increase in college enrollment. [2]To many high-school students, it's definitely good news, for they would have better chance of receiving higher education.

这是一篇有关高考英语作文的第一段。文中第一句话用 there be 句型引出现象，表达客观情况：近年来高校扩招人数稳步增长。这一意念可以用下列不同句式表达：

(1) In recent years, college enrollment has increased steadily.

这句话以 college enrollment 作为信息要素或"物称主语"（亦

称为"非人称主语"),用主谓(SV)结构。

(2) In recent years, most universities have steadily increased their enrollment.

这句话以 universities 作为物称主语,用主谓宾(SVO)结构。

(3) Recent years has witnessed a steady increase in college enrollment.

这句话以 recent years 作为物称主语,用主谓宾(SVO)结构。值得一提的是,相对而言,英语在选择主语时,往往用不能主动发出动作或无生命的事物词语。这种句式往往带有拟人化色彩,结构严密,言简意赅。如:1949 saw the founding of the People's Republic of China. (1949年,中华人民共和国成立。)

文中的第二句话说明扩招对高中生们说来是好消息,是好事,因为这增多了他们受高等教育的机会。这一意念也可以用下列三种句式表达:

(1) It's definitely good news to many high-school students, for they would have better chance of studying in higher education institutes.

这是一个并列句,第一个分句以 it 指代上文的 increase in college enrollment,用主谓补(SVC)结构,由表示原因的并列连词 for 连接,第二个分句用主谓宾(SVO)结构解释性地说明为何这对许多高中生说来是好消息。副词 definitely 很好地起到了强调语气的作用。

(2) It means better chance of receiving higher education, so high-school students take it as favorable news.

这句话同样用 it 指代"扩招",两个分句均用主谓宾(SVO)结构。以并列连词 so 连接的分句表示结果:所以高中生们把它当作好消息。

(3) High-school students welcome the practice, for they would have better chance of receiving higher education.

这句话也是由表示原因的并列连词 for 连接的并列句,两个分句均用主谓宾(SVO)结构。这句话的主语是 students, they, 以人的角度叙述客观事物,与汉语人称化的说法相同。

上述示例表明,句式多样化的目的在于准确地表达思想,增强作文的可读性。不管句式如何转换,其句子结构必须严谨,表意必须清晰,决不可为多样化而多样化,造成句子冗长,啰嗦,破坏了以"形合"为特点的英语句子的严谨性。

3. 发挥汉译英练习在学习英文组词造句中的作用

汉译英练习是英语教学实践中常用的笔语练习之一。对英语作为外语学习的中国学生说来,它是英文写作训练不可或缺的手段,也是锻炼"准确"的笔语的有效途径。无论是组词造句还是组段连篇,汉译英练习不但有利于复习和巩固所学过的语言知识,也有助于培养运用英语表达思想的能力和使用语言的准确性。

大学生是知识分子成人群体。他们多年来已经形成的固定的汉语习惯,诸如语言体系的、语序的、句型的、句子结构方面的以及思维方式时时在干扰着他们对英语语言习惯的学习和掌握,因此语感差以及写出 Chinese English 之类的错误在所难免。许多学生在初做汉译英练习时往往按照汉语句子的表达习惯逐字翻译,而置英语表达习惯于不顾。译出的句子结构汉语化,含义似是而非。因此,认真进行汉译英笔头练习,使学生从中自觉地,能动的比较汉语和英语这两种语言各自的特点和规律,变母语对习得英语的消极作用为积极作用,进而培养英语语感,逐渐克服和避免笔语中的 Chinese English。

许多指导学习英文写作的著述认为,从写作角度看,将母语译成英语是不可取的,应该直接用英语思维。实际上这种看法只是理想中的写作境界,与实际并不相符。

在英语短文写作中,"三段式"即 introduction-body-conclusion 的写作方法已被广泛接受和采用。一篇由十几句话组成的一百多个字词的文章,除几个常用的扩写方法外,谈不上更多的写作技巧。对大多数学生说来,在语感尚未形成之前,这种写作实际上无法排除心里进行的汉语—英语的翻译和对比。因此,学习者不防结合作文题目与要求有针对性的做一些组词造句类型的汉译英笔头练习。然后再使用适当的扩展方法组段连篇。

例如我们可以针对议论民办大学的短文 Private Colleges 拟出以下几个句子，通过汉译英的方式进行写作前的组词造句练习：

(1) 随着我国高等教育事业的稳步发展，每年都有成千上万的中学毕业生被许多民办大学录取。

With the steady development of higher education in China, thousands of middle-school graduates are admitted by hundreds of privately-funded colleges each year.

(2) 民办大学的快速发展是有其社会根源的。

The rapid growth of these schools has its own social roots.

(3) 经济的快速发展需要大量的受过良好教育的人才。

The rapid economic growth creates a huge demand for well-educated people.

(4) 为满足这种社会需要，政府鼓励建立新型的民办大学。

To meet the social needs, our government encourages the establishment of new colleges with individual or collective funds.

(5) 许多中国人的家庭有能力负担上民办大学所需的比较高的学费。

Many Chinese families are able to afford higher tuition fee needed to go to a private college.

(6) 民办大学为大量年轻人提供了受高等教育的机会

Private colleges have provided a large number of young people with access to higher education.

(7) 从某种意义上说，民办大学正在为文明进步做出贡献并将取得长足发展。

They are, in a sense, doing a great favor to the improvement of civilization, and will move towards greater prosperity.

有了上述的练习作为铺垫，再以适当的扩展方法进行组段连篇，就不难写出如下一篇合乎要求的短文。

Private Colleges

With the steady development of higher education in China, thousands of middle-school graduates are admitted by hundreds of privately-funded colleges each year. The rapid growth of these schools has its own social roots.

The reasons lie in many ways. Firstly, state-owned universities are not sufficient to take in all the high-school graduates, and therefore a great number of students are denied the chance to go to college. The rapid economic growth creates a huge demand for well-educated people. To meet the social needs, our government encourages the establishment of new colleges with individual or collective funds. Many Chinese families are able to afford higher tuition fee needed to go to a private college. The expense of about 5,000 yuan each year is not beyond the income of most families.

Private colleges have provided a large number of young people with access to higher education. They are, in a sense, doing a great favor to the improvement of civilization, and will move towards greater prosperity.

三、段落的写作方法

一本专供美国大学新生写作课用的教材《写作手册》(*The Bedford Handbook for Writers*,Diana Hacher,1991)讲,要想写好一篇文章,先要学会写好一个段落。一个好的段落结构和内在逻辑要严谨,段落的第一部分必须是主题句(topic sentence),点出全段要表达的主要思想(central idea);第二部分应由几个支持句(supporting sentences)组成,说明、解释、论证或发展主题句所提出的论点(developing the idea);最后一部分是结论句(concluding sentence)或称"总结句"。

可以说，这些"洋教条"或 format 正是对上述应试作文的基本要求，也是作文的基本写法。简而言之，是就某一问题表达思想的基本方法，即提出观点，围绕该观点展开讨论，最后下一个结论。

从下面的例子可以清楚地看出如何写好一个段落。

[例 A]

The Elderly

Although old people in the United States and in my country, Japan, are treated the same in some ways, in other ways they are treated differently. In both countries the elderly are shown respect. Young people will give them a seat on a bus or train or will open a door for them. In both countries older people may ride the bus or go to a show for less money than the young have to pay. Nevertheless, in Japan the elderly have the highest respect. Grandparents live with their families all their lives. They help to raise the grandchildren. If anyone needs advice, the first person to be asked is the grandfather, because he is the wisest. In the United States, the grandparents live with other old people in the "senior citizen" places. They see their grandchildren only on holidays or special occasions. I think it is better for families to live together in companionship.

本段一开始就给了一个非常明确的主题句，其题目实际是"treatment of the elderly"；其中心思想（controlling idea）是"both similar and different in two countries"。作者举了三个例子说明 similarities，即 giving the elderly seats, opening doors, charging them less money。然后作者用了一个过渡词 nevertheless 把文章转向 the main difference，即 living with the family 和 in the senior citizen places。最后以个人的观点作为该段的结论（或总结）。注意作者用了三个例子说明相似之处，写了一种情况说明不同。

该段落可列成如下提纲：

Title: The Elderly

Topic sentence: Old people are treated similarly and differently in Japan and the United States.

Supporting Sentences:

Ⅰ. Similarities

    A. Giving seats on buses, trains

    B. Opening doors

    C. Lowered costs

        (1) Transportation

        (2) Entertainment

Ⅱ. Differences

    A. In Japan the elderly live with family.

        (1) Help raise children

        (2) Get more respect

    B. In the United States the elderly live with other elderly.

Conclusion: Japanese treatment is better.

下面的图解会使该段的结构更加一目了然：

Topic sentence
Supporting Sentences
Similarities:
Comparison 1
Comparison 2
Comparison 3
Differences:
Contrast 1
Contrast 2
Concluding sentence

从图解中可以清楚地看到，作者用了比较（comparison）和对比（contrast）作为段落的扩展手段。实际上，议论文中一个十分重

要的写作手段就是比较和对比。比较(包括比拟)常指两种事物相同点的比较,而对比则常指两种事物差异的比较。因此,比较和对比泛指人或事物之间相同点和差异的比较。通过比较和对比的手段,作者可使文章不空洞抽象。具体地说,使用比较和对比起码可以达到两个目的:第一,进一步阐述清楚论点;第二,引导、得出某种合乎逻辑的结论。

[例 B]

Gold

Gold, a precious metal, is prized for two important characteristics. First of all, gold has a lustrous beauty that is resistant to corrosion. Therefore, it is suitable for jewelry, coins, and ornamental purposes. Gold never needs to be polished and will remain beautiful forever. Another important character of gold is its usefulness to industry and science. For many years, it has been used in hundreds of industrial applications. The most recent use of gold is in astronauts' suits. Astronauts wear gold-plated shields for protection outside the spaceship. In conclusion, gold is treasured not only for its beauty, but also for its utility.

本段的主题句不仅概括了段落的观点,而且以 for two important characteristics 限定了该主题在本段落详细论述的范围。第二句 First of all, gold has a lustrous beauty that is resistant to corrosion 和第五句 Another important characteristic of gold is its usefulness to industry and science 是第一层次上的说明句,分别说明主题句中的 two characteristics,可称之为 supporting sentence A。第三、四句和第六、七、八句则通过给出一些事实和例子分别对第二句和第五句,即对 two characteristics 进行解释说明,是第二层次上的说明句,可称之为 supporting sentence B. 作为结论句的第九句...gold is treasured not only for its beauty, but also for its utility 与主题句首尾呼应,回到主题,但又不重复主题句。各句之

间的彼此关系,可用下图示意:

Topic sentence
Supporting sentence A (1)
Supporting sentence B (1)
Supporting sentence B (2)
Supporting sentence A (2)
Supporting sentence B (1)
Supporting sentence B (2)
Supporting sentence B (3)
Concluding sentence

例 A 和例 B 除了具有上述结构的三大组成部分之外,还具备了使段落内在逻辑严谨的两个基本要素:统一性(unity)和连贯性(coherence)。统一性就是一个段落的各个句子都旨在清楚地表达一个思想内容。该思想内容由主题句概括叙述,然后通过各支持句逐一阐述。在例 A 中,通过对相似处和不同点举例,分述老人在美国和日本的生活处境,把主题句点明的思想内容说得清清楚楚,并得出合乎逻辑的结论。在例 B 中,主题句言明黄金由于具有两个特性而贵重,下文紧接着就这两个方面进行论述,对有关黄金的其他问题则不予讨论。简而言之,在论述中句句都要紧扣主题,不可东扯西拉,横生枝节。

连贯性指为使段落便于阅读和理解,支持句应按某种逻辑顺序排;各部分内容用适当的过渡词语连接起来。例 A 中有两个主要论述部分:相似处和不同点;例 B 中也有两个主要论述部分:黄金美观,黄金有用。两大部分依次进行论述,且举例说明,这就是一种逻辑顺序。各部分之间用适当的过渡词或短语,如 nevertheless, first of all, in conclusion 等紧密地联结在一起。

综上所述,我们可以清楚地看到,好的段落要包含主题句、支持句、总结句三大组成部分以及统一性和连贯性两个基本要素。通过这样的分析,相信学习者必定能够对短文写作的篇章布局、上下呼应、前后连接等有所体悟。

应当说明的是,段落本身还具有完整性。它既可以是文章的一个组成部分,又可以是一篇独立的短文(例 A 和例 B 均可视为独立成篇的短文),因为段落的结构和短文的结构是基本相似的。每个好的段落都具备了文章最基本的结构和要素。如果我们在写作实践中能够练习写作多种体裁和主题的段落,那么写出好的短文就是水到渠成的事了。

四、各种文体的基本写作技巧

根据不同的写作目的,英语作文体裁一般可分为本书所包括的议论文、记叙文、描写文、说明文及应用文五种类型。议论文(亦称为"论说文")以议论为主,通过摆事实讲道理来阐述作者的观点。记叙文(亦称为"叙述文")泛指记人叙事,即记录和叙述人物的行为或事件的发生、发展和变化。描写文用来描述情景、事件、人物和气氛。说明文是用解释的方式来解说事物,阐明事理。应用文是在实际应用和交际中使用的一种文体。初学写作时,文章的目的和内容比较单纯,可自始至终采用一种文体。若文章较长,表达的思想内容比较丰富,在写作上往往以一种文体为主,兼用其他文体。

1. 议论文(Argumentation)

议论文就是说理,通过摆事实讲道理和逻辑推理来阐述作者的观点。通过分析事物、发表意见来论证一个看法、主张或现象。议论的目的在于表明自己观点的正确。一段完整的议论,总是由论点、论据和论证组成。论点就是作者的观点和主张。多数议论文只有一个论点,叫做中心论点。有的议论文除了中心论点外,还有几个从属的分论点。论据就是用来证明论点的理由或者事实,可以是事例、理由,也可以是数据。各种形式的考试中大多采用议论文形式,即要求考生针对某一问题或某种现象进行议论,谈自己的看法,并说明理由。议论文就其种类来说可分为四类:

1) 解释性议论文(Cause-and-Effect Essay)

解释性议论文一般用于解释和分析社会现象或社会问题。要求考生对某种社会现象产生的原因及其可能造成的种种影响进行分析。请看下列参考范文：

Generation Gap

The younger generation is essentially different from the older generation. The world of older people has vanished, and they do not understand all of the problems of the modern world. On the other hand, the younger people have grown up with these problems, and they are deeply concerned about them. The older generation still controls the power in business organizations, government, and education. The young people want to make changes in these areas to fit the needs of modern society. In order to reconcile their differences, both generations must realize that the world has changed, and that new responses are necessary for many of the problems of society. However, generation gap is unavoidable.

Generation gap refers to the distance and contradiction between the old and the young. As a social phenomenon, it results from the different psychological qualities of the two age groups. For example, having had varied experiences, the older generation tends to be conservative, while the younger generation, fresh and energetic, tends to be liberal. Generation gap exists in all times and in all cultures, and affects a wide range of aspects of life, from attitudes about social events to choices of clothes and foods.

Traffic and Population

At 7 a.m. and 5 p.m. everyday, the rush hours, traffic is very crowded. People go to work on foot, by bus, or by bicycle in a hurry.

This is a photograph we often see in big cities. Because the traffic is crowded, people have to waste more time on their way home or to work and even might be involved in an accident. If you want to cross the street, you must be very careful and calm, or you will be in danger. The reason why the traffic is crowded is that the population increases too quickly. On the other hand, the building of cities increases too slowly and the transportation is poor. Also the limitation of land is a disadvantage for the development of cities. People need land enough to work and live, and they also need enough land to grow food. This is the dilemma facing us.

In a word, if we want to have orderly traffic and a comfortable life, we must control the population increase and solve traffic problems.

2) 比较性议论文（Analyzing-Alternatives Essay）

比较性议论文用比较两种或几种类似的事物，要求考生通过比较它们各自的优点或缺点，说明自己的看法，并加以论证。这是认识和说明事物特征的基本方法。可以先讲出两种或几种类似事物的共同之处，再说明不同之处；或两者逐项对比；或先说明某一种事物再说另一种；或将这几种方法灵活地综合运用。请看下列参考范文：

Country Life versus City Life

I have always found country life most enjoyable.

The city is only a place for business, to be visited occasionally; it is not an ideal place for permanent residence. People may say that the city can provide you with the best that life can offer. Your friends are always available for an informal chat or an evening's entertainment. The latest exhibitions, films or plays are always within easy reach. Shopping, too, is always a pleasure. But what about the hustle and bustle of city life? The city dweller never has a moment of peace; he is always in a hurry. And what about the noise and pollution of the city? Day and night the city is in an uproar with its unceasing traffic. The air is polluted with poisonous gases emitted by the smokestacks of factories. The water supply is tainted with impurities that are harmful to the human body. The city is indeed not a place to live in.

  Country life is in many respects superior to city life. For one thing, the people there are friendly. People are acquainted with one another. You can never fail to receive a friendly nod or a kind word from anyone you chance to meet. In the city people who live in the same apartment are often strangers to one another. The air in the country is fresh and pure. Air pollution is a thing unheard of there. You live a healthy life in the open air. Life goes on in a leisurely way and you don't have to hurry to catch a bus or travel in a crowded bus with people packed like sardines. Gardening and fishing will be pleasant pastimes. Reading a book by the warm fireside will be another pleasant pastime on a cold winter night. Life in the country is indeed simple and pleasant.

Science: Good or Evil

  The debate regarding the good and evil effects of modern science has gained wide attention.

  Science has brought about several outstanding advantages to mankind. The vast improvements made in the field of medicine have served to lengthen our life expectancy and to reduce the rate of infant mortality. The discovery of mechanization, better seeds, better techniques of irrigation and pest control has worked to increase productivity levels on farms. In transportation, the railway, modern ocean liner, jet plane, and motor vehicle have made our lives more comfortable and provided great possibilities for modern commercial development and industrialization. The invention of the computer has assisted the process of calculation in laboratories.

However, science has been responsible for pollution and has given us the nuclear bomb which threatens our very existence. But in this instance the fault lies not with science, but rather with man's intention to misuse the discoveries of science.

3) 阐述性议论文 (Inductive/Deductive Essay)

阐述性议论文要求考生针对某一问题，正面阐述自己的观点，并说明自己的理由。请看下列参考范文：

The Importance of Praise

Praise is very useful and important to a person. When a person has done something good and is praised, he feels good. Praise may bring his initiative into full play, so he can do better and contribute more in the future. On the contrary, a person may feel upset and down-hearted when he has done something good and not received praise.

The effect of praise is even greater on children. Studies have revealed that a child will become more active when he is praised. He instinctively turns against a person who continually criticizes him. A child's efforts should never be satirized even if you are attempting to make fun of him.

Try to praise others in your everyday life. Praise functions as lubrication oil. It can promote understanding between leaders and the masses. It can ease the tension among colleagues and neighbors. Too much complaining and criticism will do the opposite. So we should learn to praise others and help to create a light, pleasant atmosphere in which to live.

Advertisements

Advertisements appear everywhere in modern society. For example, when you walk along the streets, you can see large advertisement boards with pretty girls smiling at you. In newspapers, for another example, you often see half of the pages covered with advertisements. As still another example, you turn on the TV set and you see advertisements again. Whether you like it or not, they are pouring into your life.

In order to attract more customers, advertisers will go to extremes. They have adopted every possible simulative means in making advertisements, such as sound, light, colours, cartoon films, and human performance. For instance, to advertise a certain food, advertisers will ask an actor to sit at a table and enjoy the seemingly delicious food while they film him. Later this advertisement will be shown on TV.

Although advertisements enable you to make decisions quickly, sometimes they can cause trouble. The most unbearable thing is to watch the advertisements before and during the films on TV. There are always so many of them that they make you forget what you are sitting there for. The ironical thing is that the advertisements of the same type of things are often shown one after another so that you are confused as to which product you should choose.

4) 驳斥性议论文 (Pro-and-Con Essay)

这种议论文要求考生就有争议性的问题发表议论，针对在这一问题上反映出的某一观点进行驳斥，提出自己的看法并加以论证。请看下列参考范文：

Should Men and Women Be Equal

Should men and women be equal? This is a question much talked about by many people. Some hold the opinion that men are superior to women in many ways. For one thing, many a job men do can hardly be done by women, who are not physically strong enough; and for another, most of the world-famous scientists or statesmen are found to be males. Moreover, the whole human society seems to have all along been dominated by men only. Isn't it evident enough to show that men are a lot stronger than women? Hence, the former should enjoy more rights than the latter.

Other people, however, think quite differently on this question. They firmly believe that men and women are born equal. And women are certainly as talented as men if they are given equal opportunities of education. Isn't it a fact known to us all that women have been working side by side with men in China and elsewhere in the world? Like their men folks, they have been distinguishing themselves not only in research institutions, but in government bodies and other organizations as well.

Personally, I am firmly standing on the side of those women's rights defenders. Since men and women are playing an equally important role in all human activities, why should not they be on an equal footing? Furthermore, from time immemorial, there have been two sex groups, namely, men and women. Our society could definitely not have existed or advanced without either of them. Is it any wonder that men and women ought to be equal and enjoy equal rights accordingly?

上述四种议论文只是议论的方法有所不同,并无本质的区别。同样的主题,由于题型和要求不同,可以有不同的议论方法,从而形成不同的议论文。

2. 记叙文(Narration)

记叙文主要是指以叙述的方法来记人、叙事,即叙述人物的行为或事件的发生、发展和变化。以写人为主的记叙文,把人物作为主要记述对象,可通过一件完整的事来写,也可以写人物行为、活动的几个片断或几个不同侧面。以写事为主的记叙文则把事件作为主要记叙对象,文章着眼于事件的发展和变化。

为叙述清楚,记叙文的写作需采用直接或间接说明的方法,清楚地叙述以下几个内容:时间(when),地点(where),人物(who),事件(what),原因(why)和过程(how)。这六点构成记叙文的"六要素"。但在写作中不一定要把六要素一条不漏地全部摆出来。有些文章作者故意省略何因、何果,目的在于给读者留有思考、想象的余地;有些在上下文中不言自明的"要素",可以省略。

记叙文不论是以写人为主,还是以记事为主,一般是按时间先后顺序把文章自始至终地连贯起来。有时也可用插叙或倒叙的方式。插叙,是指文章在叙事的过程中由于发展的需要,中断原来情节的叙述线索,插入另一个有关事情的叙述。倒叙,是把事情的结局或某个突出的重要片段提到前面,然后再从事件的开头叙述;这种方式可引起悬念,激发读者的阅读兴趣。

在叙事过程中,写作角度常用第一人称或第三人称。第一人称的叙事角度是作者以当事人的口吻记叙事件或人物,会使读者感到作者是在讲述自己的经历和感受,给人以直接感、真实感,加强故事的感染力。第三人称的叙事角度灵活,可不受空间限制,使人物和事件得到最广泛的表现,并使文章头绪清楚,结构完整。请看下列参考范文:

An Autumn Excursion

Last autumn, we took a trip to Tiger Hill. It is about thirty Li from the city. When we walked along the road, we saw many farms and the leaves on the trees with yellow or red hues.

After we had arrived at our destination, we tried to climb up the hill. Though it is not a very high mountain, the view from the summit is very nice. Upon it there are many wonderful rocks. Most of them are like tigers. This is the reason why the hill is named "Tiger". On the southern side of the hill is an old temple. In the temple there is a famous cave with a stone niche and a table inside. A small hut stands in front of its door. When we sat in it, we could hear the sonorous sound of the bell struck by the monks. Sometimes the sweet songs of the birds came to our ears, mingled with the wind from pine trees. Hunters were running down hares and other small wild animals. There is, too, a stream

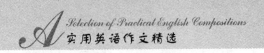

around the hill. Fishermen were paddling their boats with great joy. We took delight in their easygoing life.

On our return, the sun was nearly set. I should say that we had gained much knowledge from nature; at least we were made happier.

My First Class at College

My first class at college was quite dramatic.

It was an English lesson that morning. Though in a front seat listening to the teacher very attentively, I could understand only a few separate words she spoke. Her English seemed to be quite different from what I had learned at high school. I was wondering about this when she pointed at me, saying something. I figured that she was asking me a question on the text. Trying to find a way out, I ventured to say, "Yes, it is." This sent the whole class into roaring laughter. The teacher stared at me in surprise. Then she nodded and said, "Thank you." Now it was my turn to be surprised: what did she thank me for? My neighbour pulled me by the sleeve and whispered, "'Thank you' means sit down!"

3. 描写文(Description)

描写文就是用生动的语言文字对人物、事件、环境、气氛等进行细节上的描写。描写文一般都是从某个观察角度出发，抓住要描写的对象的特点，按一定的顺序进行描述。一般说来，描写文没有主题句，但作者往往通过客观的描述来表达主观的印象，告诉读者所描绘的事物看起来、听起来或感觉起来怎样。这种文体主要对人物、事件、场景、动物及产生的印象和心理活动进行描写、刻画，旨在通过描写使内容具体、生动、形象，给人留下难忘的印象。最常见的描写有景物描写、空间位置的描写与人物的描写。请看下列参考范文：

At the Seaside

Along the very long seashore, there lie the town near the water and the village midway on the mountain. The numerous villas scattered in the green leaves look like so many white eggs laid on the sand, the rock, and in the pine forest. The sea strikes the beach with short and monotonous waves. Small white clouds are carried along quickly by a strong wind like birds across the wide blue sky. The village is flooded with sunshine and embraced by a valley that projects into the sea.

A Talkative Person

He is so talkative that whenever he chooses you as his listener, whether you are willing or not, you cannot escape from him without helplessly giving up two or three hours of your precious time. He is a frequent visitor to others' houses. Once he has settled himself comfortably on your sofa, he will remain there rooted, talking on and on except for a few intervals of filling his tea cup and lighting his cigarettes. He is extremely insensitive to others' attitude; while his victims keep silent, desperately giving him hints to stop, he takes their silence as admiration of his eloquence. He is really a great talker and able to seize on any chance to begin his constant flow of words whenever he sees you.

People are fed up with him, afraid of him, and yet unable to get rid of him. He is a terror. Whenever they catch sight of his short figure, they immediately turn back and flee in panic.

就描写文的写作技巧而言,要注意两个方面:(1)事物描写要遵循一定的、符合人们观察、思维规律的描写顺序,比如由外到内、由远及近,从一般到具体等。在人物描写中,可从外表到内心,从大处到小处等等;(2)描写要生动具体,这是描写文的特点。在描写人或事物时,不能只用概括性的词语,诸如"很美、很丑、很坏、很

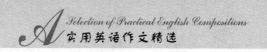

好"之类,要具体描写美在哪里,丑在哪里,怎么坏,怎么好。要精细入微,把特征精细地描写出来,达到生动具体的效果。

4. 说明文(Exposition)

说明文与议论文关系密切,有人将其统称为论说文。但在写作目的和方法上两者是有区别的。说明文主要是通过事实客观地解释或说明事物本身;而议论文则如前所述,是以事实、数据作为根据,表明主观见解,使读者信服、赞同某一观点。

具体地说,说明文是用来说明、解释某一客观事物的特点、某种工作程序、工作原理、生产过程,以及解释某种抽象概念、科学原理、自然现象等阐明事理的文章。说明文以介绍知识为目的,完全是客观描述,不带任何感情色彩。要使读者对所说明的事物有一个明确、完整的了解和认识。写说明文常采用的方法是解释、分类、举例、比较、对比和比喻等。请看下列参考范文:

How to Make Dumplings

Chinese boiled dumplings are not only delicious to eat but also easy to make.

First, make the filling. You can choose your favorite meat, say pork, beef, or mutton, chop it up and mix it with chopped yellow scallions or cabbage. Meanwhile you had better put in seasoning such as salt, soy sauce, pepper, sesame oil, chopped green onion and ginger to get your favorite flavor. Stir the ingredients in a container well to make them evenly mixed.

Second, make the dough. You should measure your wheat flour to go with the filling, put it in a container, pour water bit by bit, stir it strenuously to make it sticky, then let it rest for about 20 minutes. After that you can cut part if the dough and put it on pastry board, knead it and cut it into small pieces. You press each piece with the palm of your hand slightly and then roll it with a rolling pin into a round piece.

Finally comes the stage of folding the dough to make

dumplings. You should hold a dough piece horizontally in your left hand, put a suitable amount of filling onto the central part, fold the side around the filling, press the upper-central part of it firmly and make firm and nice lace from left to right around the fold edge to make your finished product better-looking and free from leakage.

The Chinese make dumplings when family or friends are together on holidays. You just imagine the heartening talk and intimate atmosphere created while people are sitting together to make dumplings!

Different Ways of Living

For Americans, nineteen is not considered too young to leave home. Many American families do support their children through college, but quite often the students do not live at home. They live in a dormitory or an apartment. After graduation, even if they have been living at home, they are usually expected to move out and begin making their own living. They must go to work to support themselves. Some American parents expect their children to be financially independent immediately after high school.

However, Chinese families are different from American families. Chinese children are expected to live with their parents until a much later age. If we go to college, we usually live at home unless the school is in another town. Independence from parents is not encouraged in our country as it is in America. When we are young, parents take care of us. In fact, Chinese people would like their sons and daughters to stay with them forever.

写说明文要注意写作顺序和写作层次。写作顺序是指写作时采用的空间顺序、时间顺序、逻辑顺序或认识顺序；写作层次是指说明文应由浅入深，由易到难，由外到里，由始及末。依这样的层次写就的文章,读起来思路清楚,条理分明。

5. 应用文(Practical Writing)

应用文主要包括各种书信、通知及便条等。

1) 书信(Letters)

书信是人们进行书面交流的重要形式,用英文写信是学习者必备的一种基本写作技能,也是四、六级作文考试中测试的形式之一。

英文书信通常由六部分组成,即信头(Heading)、信内地址(Inside Address)、称呼(Salutation)、信的正文(Body of the Letter)、结束语(Complementary Close)、签名(Signature)。有时私人信件和非正式信件常把信内的寄信人地址和收信人的地址省略。一般书信规则如下:(1)发信人的地址、日期,位于信纸的右上方。先写地址,后写日期。(2)收信人姓名、职务和地址写在信纸的左上方,略低于寄信人的地址和日期下两行处。(3)称呼写在收信人职务、地址下面两行处。称呼是对收信人的尊称语,通常在收信人的名字或尊称前加"Dear"。对不熟悉的男士可称 Dear Sir,对熟悉的男士称 Dear Mr.,对不熟悉的女士称 Dear Madam(不论婚否),对熟悉的则称 Dear Miss 或 Dear Mrs.。如是同辈和小辈可直呼其名,如"Dear Tom"等。事务书信的称呼后一般要用冒号,个人书信的称呼后一般用逗号。(4)正文在称呼下方隔行写。必要时要分段写,每段有一个中心思想,表达要清楚,语言要简明。考试时,会要求考生把规定的内容写进信中。(5)结束语写在正文之下两三行偏右的地方或左边与正文对齐。第一个词的开头字母大写,末尾用逗号。给机关团体或不相识的人可用 Yours truly 或 Truly yours,Yours sincerely 或 Sincerely yours;给上级或长者的信可用 Yours respectfully 或 Respectfully yours,Yours gratefully 或 Gratefully yours;给一般熟人或朋友的信可用 Yours,Your Ever,Ever yours,As ever 或 Yours sincerely;给亲属或挚友写信可用 Lovingly yours,With love,Your loving son 或 Your devoted friend 等。(6)署名写在结束语下面,用手写也可以打印,如打印应在打印的姓名下再亲自签名。请看下列参考范文:

A Letter of Inquiry about Admission to an English Course

May 10, 1995

Dear Sirs,

  I have heard from a friend of mine that your language center will run a three-month English course this summer vacation. I am planning to apply for admission to it. Now I should like to obtain a booklet, an application form and some information about your entrance requirements and costs. I'll be very grateful for your kindness if you send them to me.

  I have been accepted as an entering student for the fall of 1995 by Smith College. So I wish to reach your country a bit earlier and get a chance to enter your course which will be of great help for my further studies at Smith College. Also, may I inquire about any possibility of a spare time job from your center? I hope you will kindly do what you can do for me and give me a reply at your convenience.

Yours sincerely
Zhang Ping

A Letter of Invitation to a Weekend House Party

July 16, 1993

Dear Bob and Janis,

  We are hoping that you have not yet arranged to do anything on the weekend of July 24, and will come to spend this weekend here, at our university. It's beautiful here now, with everything in bloom!

  We have also invited the Smiths, so if you can make it, bring your tennis rackets and we can enjoy some good tennis together.

There's a very good train Friday afternoon. We've marked it in red on the timetable. It gets you here about seven thirty, which is just in time for dinner. You can get a late train back to Cheng-du on Sunday night, or there's an early express that we usually take on Monday morning.

We hope nothing will prevent you from coming. Please let us know what train you are taking so that we can meet you at Emei Station.

With love
Wu Dan and Xiao Lin

2）通知和便条（Notices and Notes）

通知和便条是日常生活中最常见、常用的应用文形式，用来传递简短信息。写作格式与信函不同，语言要简练、明确。

便条内容包括日期、称呼、正文和署名。

通知是上级对下级部署工作或召开会议用的一种文体，同级之间有事商议，也可发送通知。通知有两种形式：一种是以布告（Bulletin）的形式，把内容传达给有关人员；另一种是便条或启示（Notice）的形式，把事情传达给有关人员。海报在形式上与通知有相类似之处。请看下列参考范文：

Asking for Sick Leave

Dear Mr. Fang,

Please excuse my absence from class today. I had a cold yesterday evening and could not fall asleep until late in the night. I'll go and consult the doctor today, and will resume my study if I feel better tomorrow.

Very truly yours,
Liu Wen

Transmitting a Telephone Message

Dear Lin,

  Mr. Cheng of Hebei University has just rung you up saying that he will be expecting you in his office about ten tomorrow morning.

  Please give him a ring if the time does not suit you.

Xiao Wang

Talk

  Speaker: Professor Frank Edward of the University of Southern California, U. S. A.

  Subject: Contemporary American Literature

Time: October 28, 1994, at 2:00. p. m.

Place: Room 108, the Teaching Building.

All Are Welcome

The Foreign Affairs Office

Notice of the President's Office

  Tomorrow being New Year's Day, there will be no class. All classes will be resumed as usual on the 2nd.

The President's Office

December 31, 1994

五、培养挖掘写作内容的能力

  作文是一种传达思想、见解的行为。作文的过程是思考、组织、表达的智力活动过程，需要除语言知识之外的其他诸方面的知识。不少学生对作文题目望而生畏，思路不通畅，不知从何处下笔。有的学生甚至说，汉语文章都写不出，更不用说英语文章，可以说写好英语作文的一个关键环节或困难所在就是挖掘写作内容,即通过各种可能的方式打开思路,确定写作的基本内容。这便是作文的第一步——审题构思。

审题就是对所给定的作文题目进行仔细的分析、揣摩,准确地把握题目所要求写出的内容。构思则是指谋篇布局,是在仔细分析题目含义的基础上,按照题目的要求确定短文的内容和范围。这是短文写作的首要环节,是成功写作的先决条件。

在确定短文的内容和范围时,可以从不同的角度去思考事物。这里的角度,是指思考问题的出发点、立场、需求、目的、观念、经验等思维背景。通过多角度、多侧面的思考去挖掘写作内容,就有可能写出切题且言之有物的短文。

培养挖掘写作内容的能力,自然要靠学习者持之以恒,坚持不懈的实践,养成勤于动脑、勤于动笔的好习惯。就具体学习方法而言,可以从认真分析某一类良好的语篇着手。下面数例,在切题的前提下,从不同的角度完成了短文写作,语言规范,表达准确,其中遣词造句中使用的句型、词语,都是大学英语中学到且常用的表达方法。其中一些使短文清晰连贯地展开的衔接手段,也是常用模式。这对已具有一定英语应用能力而在写作方面仍处于入门阶段的学习者说来,无疑具有十分明显而积极的启迪作用。

What Electives to Choose

①

Nowadays, there usually exists a wide selection of electives for college students to choose from. However, students have quite different plans for their future, so they always end up learning courses based on their own idea.

Some students may choose to learn a certain course in order to obtain an extra certificate for their job hunting after graduation, because they assume that some more knowledge could ensure more chances of winning in finding a good job. Others may have their choice made just for fun. They tend to hold the idea that college life could be more colorful if they could widen their knowledge through elective courses.

As far as I'm concerned, I'm inclined to choose electives based on both the value of the courses and the interest of my own.

②

Nowadays many college students prefer to have electives in their spare time because the courses can offer a variety of skills and abundant knowledge apart from what they learn in the daily courses. There are many factors that may account for it, and the following are the most conspicuous aspects.

To start with, many students want to get another degree besides their own, so that they can have more competence when they seek a job. Furthermore, as for me, I don't care about degree or job. I just want to obtain some necessary skills to make my college life worthwhile. What I'm concerned most is how to own more skills that may be necessary for my future. Finally, some students want to learn anything that is different from what they are learning now. The science students, for example, want to know about Shakespeare while the art students want to tell how a vehicle works and how to deal with it when it breaks down. So, they can all get what they think is useful to their college life.

On the whole, the phenomenon is one of the results of multi-demand of the employment market. There is still a long way for us to improve the elective itself, but as a student myself, I find it rewarding and interesting.

③

Nowadays, more and more universities are opening more

opportunities for their students to choose from various optional courses in their spare time. This is, in fact, not a new phenomenon, but presently, it is of different implications to the students who want to or need to improve themselves.

There can be a great many different reasons for students to choose their optional courses. For example, some of them may choose some courses on practical skills so that it will be more likely for them to get a good job after graduation, because nowadays companies are placing emphasis on a candidate's working experience, an inseparable part of which is practical skills. However, some others may choose to learn some courses, like literature, philosophy, etc., to broaden their view and find a different way of looking at things. And still some others may choose the electives just in that they are interested in the courses.

Personally, I prefer to choose courses which can enrich my knowledge of science and society, and even of ourselves as human beings; whether the courses can be of any practical uses does not make any big difference to me, because I think "To learn is fun."

④

With the reform of Chinese higher education, more and more colleges and universities put emphasis on nurturing students' abilities. As a result, elective courses are available not only for excellent academic performers but also for students about the average level.

Certainly, students have different reasons to choose their own electives. For some, practical skills are the essence of college education, and therefore, courses on computer science, marketing, and finance are highly preferred. On the other hand, others may hold the idea of liberal education and electives concerning literature, history, and philosophy are the most welcome.

　　Take me as an example: being a disciple of free education, I stand for the notion that university is not a place for survival skills, but a palace of knowledge and critical reasoning. Although my major is chemistry, the electives I attend most frequently are English Literature, an Introduction to Classical Music, and Different Schools of Western Painting. They really widen my horizon.

Spring Festival Gala on CCTV

①

　　Some people are in favor of the CCTV Spring Festival Gala. Those who like it have their reasons. First, they think that the gala is of tradition to us. What's more, some feel that they can find nothing to do except watching this on the eve of the Lunar New Year. Besides, it is said that this is a good chance for a family to have a rest happily.

　　But others do not agree. People who dislike it have their reasons. Firstly, they say that they can find something else to do. Moreover, they argue that the spring festival gala on CCTV should not have been the most powerful program in this day.

　　There is some truth in both arguments. But it is likely to do more harm than good, if you maintain that it is the only thing to do at that night. Some more meaningful things can be found easily, such as parties, sharing views with families, etc.. Obviously, there is little doubt that further attention will be paid on this issue.

②

　　The approach of the Chinese Lunar New Year poses a

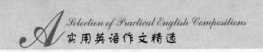

national issue concerning the necessity of holding the CCTV Spring Festival Gala. Its established status is being challenged by a growing number of people, especially by younger generations. It is increasingly difficult to cater for all tastes.

Some individuals deem that it should be canceled or replaced by other programs. These young people focus their attention on other forms of celebration instead of immersing themselves in TV. Despite that, the majority of mid-aged people and senior citizens uphold the importance of the traditional performance. The most striking feature of this gala is its traditionally close link with ordinary people's lives. Most of people view this gala as an annual staple on the traditional Chinese Spring Festival Eve. They all have a restless night and glue their eyes on the television.

I am not supportive of the view that the grand gala should be abandoned. Undoubtedly, it plays a vital role in the celebration of Chinese New Year. To increase its appeal and meet young adults' need, the upcoming performance should invite some big names including super stars from Hongkong and Taiwan. We are all eagerly anticipating this unforgettable evening show.

③

It has been a hot topic for a long time whether the CCTV Spring Festival Gala should be cancelled or not. Many people advocate that CCTV Spring Festival Gala offers a wonderful opportunity to celebrate this traditional festival, for the Chinese all over the world can share the same happiness and excitement brought by the TV program. In addition, many performances are very impressive, and some can even positively affect our life value.

However, every coin has two sides. Some people hold that CCTV Spring Festival Gala should be cancelled. One of the most significant reasons may be that this form of celebration forces people to spend the eve more passively. What's more, a great proportion of the programs are not attractive enough.

As to me, my favor goes to the former opinion, because CCTV Spring Festival Gala gives us another option to celebrate this important moment. But it is really essential to improve the quality of the programs. And I hope some better forms of celebration will be created in the near future.

④

The Spring Festival Gala performed on CCTV on New Year's Eve, as a form of celebration of Chinese lunar New Year, has been considered indispensable by all Chinese people for over two decades. People are accustomed to enjoying the grand sight and sound it presents as a brilliant feast.

However, there are more and more people claiming to cancel it in recent years. With the roaring development of economy, various mass media come out like the bamboo shoots after spring rain. As a result, more fascinating programs are available in the daily life. Moreover, the program at Spring Festival Gala has remained nearly the same form since it was born.

As far as I am concerned, I prefer the program to stay, because it serves not only as entertainment but an occasion for the families to gather, chat and laugh. Of course it is supposed to be improved to draw attention, with more diverse forms. In a word, the Spring Festival Gala is a tradition and treasure of the Chinese people, and we still need it, maybe a better one.

国外学者 Liz 等人指出:"……一个成长中的作者,倘能从一个作者的立场出发去学习范文,那么,他便能从范文中获取大量有益的东西。"(Liz Hamp-Lyons & Ben Heasley, 1989:2)这些话简明易懂,颇有见地。上述几篇谈及"春晚"和"选修课"的同类短文,从不同的角度挖掘写作内容,均言之有物,思路清晰,内容连贯,总体水平较高。通过这些示例,我们可以体味、熟悉进而运用所学的基本写作技巧,感知、领悟写作过程中如何挖掘写作内容。我们还可以找出其中的衔接手段(如 however, moreover, as a result, as far as I am concerned, in a word),准确理解这些衔接手段怎样清晰连贯地展开语篇,并学着依照相应衔接手段模式在类似的短文写作中谋篇构架,就会写出一篇头绪清楚、结构完整、文字通顺连贯的作文。

值得注意的是,在构思短文段落的同时,学习者必须考虑自己的英语表达能力能否胜任自己所构思的内容。一定要从自己的实际水平出发,不可好高骛远。有些人在中文思维的支配下,阐述一些哲理性强的思想和复杂的句子,然而他们的英语表达能力却无法使他们自由驰骋,勉强写出的话也是诘屈聱牙,不伦不类,语不成篇,错误百出,甚至通篇都是残句,让人连猜带估也难解其意。因此,在构思时,切忌天马行空,一定要选择一些既切题,又能用浅显规范的英语表达出来的内容去写。

六、作文考试的命题形式

1. 根据给出的段首句续写短文

该形式也称主题句作文。其特点是,以题目为中心,分为若干分支,从不同的角度,用不同的事实予以说明。一般情况下是将文章分为三个段落,每段的提示即为该段的主题句(Topic Sentence)。考生要按主题句的要求去组织材料,提出论据,讲事实或摆道理,也就是以主题句为中心,写出几句说明主题句的支持句(Supporting Sentences)。例如,大学英语四级考试(CET4)大纲中的样题,其中作文部分的题目、提示和段首句如下:

Directions: For this part, you are allowed 30 minutes to write a composition about Television in three paragraphs.

You are given the first sentence of each paragraph and are required to develop its idea in completing the paragraph. Write about 35 words for each paragraph, not including the words given. Therefore, your part of the composition should be about 100 words. Remember to write clearly.

You should write this composition on the Answer Sheet.

Television

(1) Television presents a vivid world in front of us. _____

_____

(2) Television can also play an educational role in our daily life.

_____

(3) However, television can also be harmful. _____

_____

范文：

Television

(1) Television presents a vivid world in front of us. By means of TV, we can know the events that happened or are happening in the world. We can see sports, listen to concerts and enjoy other entertainment. For example, in bed we can see the World Cup Football Championship being held on the other continent on TV.

(2) Television can also play an educational role in our daily life. TV has made education easier and less costly. Some special courses can be given through TV. For example, we can learn English courses without a step outside our rooms. We can also learn a lot of other things by watching TV.

(3) However, television can also be harmful. It can be harmful to

one's body and to one's mind as well. If people, especially the young, sit in front of TV for too long a day, their eyesight and bodies may be hurt and their study and work may be affected. Moreover, the influence of some bad programs is extremely strong On the youth.

2. 按所给的关键词（key words）写短文

给出的关键词可以是单词也可以是短语，一般按一定顺序或逻辑关系排列。这种作文是一种限制性作文，要求考生根据所指定的关键词语，在理解词语的基础上，扩展思路，写出内容切题，表达合乎逻辑的文章，并且能通顺地将所给的关键词语全部用到文章中去。关键词在某种程度上也起路标的作用，能向考生提示文章主旨和展开的方向，作文的内容和思路，帮助考生弄明写作对象、文章中心思想和写作重点。例如，一篇为"News Media"的作文，根据题目，可以确定文章的中心思想是写有关"新闻媒体"的。而从哪些方面着手去写，则需认真审阅指定的关键词语，通过文字加工，将具体内容写进去。

例：News Media

Directions: *Write a composition on the topic given, in which the following key words and expressions should be included.*

Key words and expressions:

(1) consist of; radio; television; newspaper; oldest; major source

(2) the invention of radio; influence; up-to-the-minute; seconds

(3) television; most recently; advantage; see; hear

范文：

News Media

News media consist of radio, television and newspapers. Newspapers are the oldest forms for communicating news. Today many people still begin their day by reading the morning paper while having breakfast. Having a long history, newspapers continue to serve as a major source of information.

The invention of the radio had a tremendous influence on the world. It is able to bring up-to-the-minute news to distant places in a matter of seconds. Thus, the development of radio as a means, of communication has made the world a smaller place.

Television is the most recently developed device for communication. The greatest advantage of television is to allow us to see as well as to hear the news. The fact that it enables people to see visual images has had a considerable effect on our perceptions of the world events.

3. 看图作文

该形式是以一幅或一组图为命题方式，让考生在看懂画面内容的前提下，正确理解图画所反映的事实、包含的思想内容或象征意义，把图中所提供的信息转化为文字形式。既要写出从图中直接观察到的情况，又要根据合乎逻辑的想象和推理展开议论，写出图画所包含的思想内容。看图作文是一种比较灵活的出题方式，突破了命题作文的局限性。它不仅测试考生对画面的观察力和想象力，而且测试考生的辨析能力。因而，写好看图作文的关键是仔细观察、体味画面内容，揭示画面内容的内在涵义，紧扣主题展开描述或议论。2001年考研英语作文就是一个非常典型的范例。

Directions: *Among all the worthy feelings of mankind, love is probably the noblest, but everyone has his/her own understanding of it. There has been a discussion recently on the issue in a newspaper. Write an essay to the newspaper to*

(1) show your understanding of the symbolic meaning of the picture below,

(2) give a specific example, and

(3) give your suggestion as to the best way to show love.

范文：

Among all the worthy feelings of mankind, love is probably the noblest. It is of the utmost importance to human beings. Everybody not only needs love, but should also give love.

As is described in the picture, "Love is a lamp which is brighter in darker places." This is indeed true. People in darker places need more light. Even dim light can give them much hope for a better life and progress. And just a thread of light will call forth their strength and courage to step out of their difficulties.

For instance, when someone is starving to death, just a little food and water from you may save his life. Or when a little girl in a poor rural area drops out of school because of poverty, just a small sum of money from you may support her to finish her schooling and change her life. By doing so, you are giving love which is like a lamp in a dark place where light is most needed.

To sum up, we should offer our help to all who are in need. We expect to get love from others and we also give love to others. As a matter of fact, everybody can be a bridge for others, and it is only by helping others can you get other' help. So when you see someone in difficulty or in distress and in need of help, don't hesitate to give your love to him. I believe the relationship between people will then be harmonious and our society will then be a better place for us to live in.

　　此范文分四段,第一段使用了一句试题指令中的话,点明了主题,然后用自己的语言阐述一个重要观点:每个人都需要爱,也要付出爱,深化了主题。第二段体现了第一条提纲的内容,阐明了自己对图画象征意义(symbolic meaning)的理解,强调了"爱"的重要性,即"爱"对在困境中的人们所起的重大作用。第三段体现了第二条提纲的内容,用实例说明自己对"爱"的理解,具有说服力。第四段体现了第三条提纲的内容,提出了个人的观点并得出合乎逻辑的结论:有了爱,人与人会和睦相处,社会将变得更美好。

　　4. 根据图表作文

　　要求考生根据所给的图表进行描述和议论。一般是通过统计图表(Table)、曲线坐标图表(Graph)或圆形结构图(Pie Chart,也称"饼图")等提供一组或几组数据,来反映某个趋势、某一问题、某种现象或社会问题。图表作文也是一种控制性作文,利用图形、表格和曲线图作为作文提示,要求考生对图表中的相关数据进行描述、分析和评论,并得出合乎逻辑的结论。这种作文形式是一种把数据、形象信息转化为文字信息的过程。在写作时,图表上表明的主要信息不要遗漏,与图表无关的内容不要涉及。在具体写作方法上可以采用先描述后议论或夹叙夹议的方法。叙述是为议论打基础。除了直接引用图表中所给的主要数据外,还有必要做一些简单计算,如指出增加的百分比、倍数或绝对数字。不可单纯地对图表进行描述或把全部的数据都变成文字。一般说来,图表作文可分下述两类:

　　(1)客观解释图表中所传达的信息,对所提供的数据之间通过比较分析,找出产生变化的原因,指出某种规律或发展趋势。

例：

Changes in Chinese Diet

food \ Year	1986	1987	1988	1989	1990
Grain	49%	47%	46.5%	45%	45%
Milk	10%	11%	11%	12%	13%
Meat	17%	20%	22.5%	23%	21%
Fruit and Vegetable	24%	22%	20%	20%	21%
Total	1000%	100%	100%	100%	100%

范文：

Changes in Chinese Diet

According to the above table, we can see that some changes have taken place in people's diet since 1986.

One of the big changes is the decrease of grain consumption with 49 percent in 1986 and 45 percent in 1990. On people's dinner tables the traditional dominant food-grain has given some way to milk and meat, which were seldom seen on dinner tables before. This phenomenon clearly indicates the improvement of people's living standard. Since the economic reform in 1978, various kinds of food have become popular in Chinese families.

However, there is a steady reduction of fruit and vegetables with 24 percent in 1986 and a three-point drop by 1990. But this is not the main trend. As the living standard of the Chinese people is rising, we look forward to further changes in people's diet. The proportion of fruit and vegetables as well as milk and meat will definitely increase in the coming years.

作者首先根据1986—1990年中国人的饮食结构图,说明人们的饮食结构发生的变化,然后分析表中数据的含义:粮食消费下降,肉奶类食品消费上升,说明人们的生活水平提高了。

(2) 写出看完图表后的想法和评论。即对其中趋势或问题进行分析,分析问题产生的原因或造成的后果,得出自己的结论或表明自己的看法。

例：

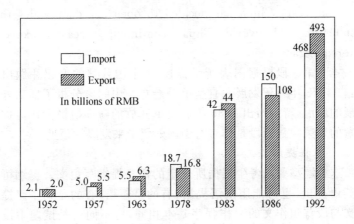

Changes in China's Foreign Trade

范文：

Spurred by the fast growing economy, China has witnessed booming foreign trade in the last decade. As is shown in the chart, before 1978, the foreign trade increased but slowly. China then followed a policy of "self-reliance" and mainly traded raw materials and traditional goods for industrial equipment. After 1978, the rapid economic growth demanded importation of high technology, which in turn boosted its development. China is now capable of providing the world market with a variety of high quality products. Foreign trade, being of increasing importance, has been spiraling upward.

It is the open policy that has brought about the prosperity. Especially after 1986, China made quite a few big decisions, which included opening up many cities to overseas investors, encouraging private business and promoting foreign trade. Foreign investment and advanced technology flowed in. China has made continuous progress in productivity, which is now higher than ever before. The Chinese people are confident that the more open China has a brighter future.

  This year, China has decided to open her door wider than ever before to the world. Thus a continuing increase is expected in foreign trade.

  本文第一段根据图表所示描述了中国外贸的变化并做出评论:自1978年外贸发展一直呈上升趋势。中间段分析了推动外贸发展的原因,特别指出1986年后改革开放的新举措极大地促进了外贸的繁荣。最后段是作者对中国外贸未来发展的预见。

  5. 根据提纲作文

  这种题型要求考生根据所规定的情景提纲写短文。提纲可能用英语提出,也可能用汉语提出,有的是短语,有的是句子。提纲作文与段首句作文的写作程序基本相同,所不同的是试题中没有给出主题句。考生需要结合题目和提纲所给的信息自己写出主题句。提纲中的每一条都限定了文章某部分(例如某一段)的中心和内容范围,写作时不可偏离,不可任意增加或删减。

  例:

Importance of Developing Listening Ability

Outline

(1) Some students' attitude towards the development of listening ability
(2) The importance of developing listening ability
(3) Comments

范文:

  In learning a foreign language, some students do not pay

much attention to the development of their listening ability. They tend to think that listening practice is of little use and they would rather do more reading to improve their language proficiency. This is because they do not understand the importance of listening ability in language learning.

In fact, listening is one of the most important ways to learn a language. How a child learns his mother tongue is a case in point. Much of our knowledge comes to us through our ears. Moreover, listening is an essential means of communication, If we are faced with a situation where a great deal depends on our ability to listen and we cannot understand what is being said, communication will be interrupted.

Clearly, listening skills are very important in learning and communication. How can we expect to learn a foreign language well without practising listening? Therefore, a college student must consciously improve his listening skills in order to make great progress in language learning.

本文紧扣标题,围绕提纲所规定的内容和提供的思路写作。第一段写了某些学生对提高听力所持的不正确的态度并说明其原因;第二段论证了听力的重要,言之成理,持之有据;第三段给予简短评说并得出合乎逻辑的结论。

6. 托福作文

托福作文的考试是以 essay question 的形式出现。其命题手法一般有以下三类。

(1) 给出对立的两个事物或一个事物对立的两个方面,要求考生支持一方并给予说明。例如:

对立的两个事物:

Some people think that parents should plan their children's leisure time carefully. Other people believe that children should decide for themselves how to spend their free time. Which idea do you agree with? Give reasons for your choice.

一个事物对立的两个方面:

Some people like to communicate by telephone. Other people like to communicate by letter. Which do you prefer to communicate—by phone or by letter? Use specific reasons and details to explain your answer.

(2) 只给一个论点,要求用具体理由证明其正确或予以反对。例如:

Someone thinks that playing a game is fun only when you win. Do you agree or disagree? Use specific reasons to support your answer.

(3) 给出若干选项,要求选择一项予以支持。例如:

Newspapers contain many information topics such as sports, current events, business and entertainment. Which topic do you like to read most often? Give reasons to explain your answer.

显然,此类作文均属议论文,即讨论某种观点或方法,以具体理由加以论证。

上述种种不同的题型只是作文要求的不同形式,是不同的外包装,里面所含的内容是一样的,所考的作文体裁是一致的。若用四、六级命题形式来包装,就成了四、六级题目,若用托福题型来包装,就成了托福型题目。再者,有图表形式的作文题型实际上和一般作文的题型也没有本质的区别。只不过一个是在指示中把作文要讨论的问题或现象用文字表达出来,而另一个是把问题或现象用图表的形式反映出来,让考生看懂后用文字表达出来,再针对该问题或现象展开议论。

7. 写概要作文

写概要作文就是把长文章压缩成短文章,而又使文章意思保持不变的写作。换句话说,概要是对文章中所传达的主要信息和主要论据、例证的总结。概要作文是比较正式的使用性文体。英文中常见的与概要对应的词语有 summary, precis, abstract 和

synopsis 等。

　　summary 是大学英语四、六级要求掌握的写作方法。论文或文献所附的 summary 通常放在后面，告诉或提醒读者原作的要点和结论，以供读者复习、参考或记忆。通常 summary 不包含原作的某些细节过程、程序、方法、写作目的或其有关的写作背景。summary 不同于提纲，必须用完整的句子和连贯或过渡词语使之自成一篇独立的短文。

　　summary 短小精悍，具有高度的概括性。长度一般不超过原文的 1/3 或 1/4，有的甚至短至一二句话（见本节范例）。summary 必须忠实于原作，对原文做客观的概括，不可添枝加叶。写概要的方法有以下几点：

　　(1) 认真阅读原作，充分理解中心思想的要点，弄清原作的篇章结构，判明哪些重点应该写入概要，哪些次要材料应该删减。

　　(2) 在阅读原文的过程中，可随手在你认为重要的句子下面画线，也可以在页边做记号或批注。如原文较长，每隔七八行做一个批注，最后对画线部分和批注做一番加工，就可成为概要。

　　(3) 概要的基本结构大多取决于原文的特点和结构。文章中的论述、记叙、描写或说明均有清楚的逻辑关系，如时间先后顺序、空间位置顺序、先具体描写或说明后归纳总结，或者先一段概括后具体描写、说明、分析、论证等等。只要删除次要的细节、铺叙、补充说明、大量的例证而将主题句和表达中心思想的句子组织在一起，就可写出与原文基本结构相同的概要。

　　(4) 为了压缩原文，可用短语替换原文中的句子或从句；用小词代替大词；用概括性的词代替具体细致的说明和描述。有人编了写概要的 32 字口诀，可帮助考生掌握写概要的基本方法："抓住要点，略去细节；减少例子，压缩描写；掌握比例，注意层次；长句变短，大词变小。"所谓"比例"是指文章各部分的篇幅，即重要部分多着笔，次要部分少写或略去。

　　下面是一篇题为 THE FIFTH FREEDOM 的文章的全文及其三个不同层次的概要。值得一提的是该文是一篇文质兼美的文章，常见于国内外英语材料中（如美国教材 *Assignments in Exposition*，*Sixth Edition*，Copyright 1979 by Louise E. Rorabacher and Georgia Dunbar,p.294,以及上海外语教育出版社出版的《大学英语》（修订本）第五册,第二课）。

The Fifth Freedom
Seymour St. John

  More than three centuries ago a handful pioneers crossed the ocean to Jamestown and Plymouth in search of freedoms they were unable to find in their own country, the freedoms we still cherish today;freedom from want, freedom from fear, freedom of speech, freedom of religion. Today the descendants of the early settlers, and those who have joined them since, are fighting to protect these freedoms at homes and throughout the world.

  And yet there is a fifth freedom—basic to those four—that we are in danger of losing: the freedom to be one's best. St. Exupery describes a ragged, sensitive-faced Arab child, haunting the street of a North African town, as a lost Mozart: he would never be trained or developed. Was he free? "No one grasped you by the shoulder while there was still time;and nought will awaken in you the sleeping poet or musician or astronomer that possibly inhabited you from the beginning." The freedom to be one's best is the chance for the development of each person to his highest power.

  How is it that we in America have begun to lose this freedom, and how can we regain it for our nation's youth? I believe it has started slipping away from us because of three misunderstandings.

  First, the misunderstanding of the meaning of democracy. The principle of a great Philadelphia high school is driven to cry for help in combating the notion that it is undemocratic to run a special program of studies for outstanding boys and girls. Again, when a good independent school in Memphis recently closed, some thoughtful citizens urged that it be taken over by the public—system and used for boys and girls of high ability, that it have entrance requirements and give an advanced program of studies to superior students who were interested and able to take it. The proposal was rejected because it was undemocratic! Thus, courses are geared to the middle of the class. The good students are unchallenged, bored. The loafer receives his passing grade. And the lack of an outstanding course for the outstanding student, the lack of a standard which a boy or girl must meet, passes for democracy.

The second misunderstanding concerns what makes for happiness. The aims of our present-day culture are avowedly ease and material well-being: shorter hours; a shorter week; more return for less accomplishment; more soft-soap excuses and fewer honest, realistic demands. In our schools this is reflected by the vanishing hickory stick and the emerging psychiatrist. The hickory had its fault, and the psychiatrist has his strengths. But the trend is clear: *tout Comprendre c'est tout pardonner* [To understand everything is to forgive everything]. Do we really believe that our softening standards bring happiness? Is it our sound and considered judgment that the tougher subjects of the classics and mathematics should be thrown aside, as suggested by some educators, for dull-playing? Small wonder that Charles Malik, Lebanese delegate at the U. N., writes: "There is in the West"—in the United States—"a general weakening of moral fiber. [Our] leadership does not seem to be adequate to the unprecedented challenges of the age."

The last misunderstanding is in the area of values. Here are some of the most influential tenets of teacher education over the past fifty years: there is no eternal truth; there is no absolute moral law; there is no God. Yet all of history has taught us that the denial of these ultimate, the placement of man or states at the core of the universe, results in a paralyzing mass selfishness; and the first sight of it are already frighteningly evident.

Arnold Toynbee has said that all progress, all development come from challenge and a consequent response. Without challenge there is no response, no development, no freedom. So first we owe to our children the most demanding, challenging curriculum that is within their capabilities. Michelangelo did not learn to paint by spending his time doodling. Mozart was not an accomplished pianist at the age of eight as the result of spending his days in front of a television set. Like Eve Curie, like Helen Keller, they responded to the challenges of their lives by a disciplined training and they gained a new freedom.

The second opportunity we can give our boys and girls is the right to fail. "Freedom is not only a privilege, it is a test." writes De Nouy. What kind of freedom where no one can fail? The day is past when the United States can afford to give high school diplomas to all who sit through four years of instruction, regardless of whether any visible results can be discerned. We live in a narrowed world where we must be alert, awake to realism, and realism demands a standard which either must be met or result in failure. These are hard words, but they are brutally true. If we deprive our children of the right to fail we deprive them of their knowledge of the world as it is.

Finally, we can expose our Children to the best values, we have found. By relating our lives to the evidences of the ages, by judging our philosophy in the light of values that history has proven truest, perhaps we shall be able to produce that "ringing message, full of content and truth, satisfying the mind, appealing to the heart, firing the will, a message on which one can stake his whole life."This is the message that could mean joy and strength and leadership, freedom as opposed to serfdom.

SUMMARY OF "THE FIFTH FREEDOM"

概要(1)：较长文字写出的概要

More than three centuries ago a few pioneers came to America in search of the freedoms we still cherish: freedom from want, freedom from fear, freedom of speech and freedom of religion. Today their descendants and others are fighting to protect these freedoms everywhere. But there is a fifth freedom, basic to the four, which we are in danger of losing-the freedom to be one's best through the opportunity of developing to one's highest power. (1—2 段)

This freedom is in danger because of three misunderstandings. The first is about the meaning of democracy. This misunderstanding has defeated attempts to give special opportunities to superior students. The second is about what makes for happiness. Our culture's stress on material well-being has been reflected in the school by too little discipline and too easy subjects. The third is about the importance of values. The recent denial of such ultimate as eternal truth, absolute moral law, and the existence of God are already reflected in increasing mass selfishness. (3—6 段)

To preserve the fifth freedom, we need do three things. First, we must give our children the most challenging curriculum, of which they are capable, for only a disciplined training produces great people. Second, we must give them the right to fail, for only through standards which make for success or failure can they learn what real life is like. Third, we must give them the best values that history has given us; these will assure them of freedom. (7—9 段)

原文是一篇长达 1000 个词左右的文章。用的是说明加议论的方法。文章的中心思想是人应该争取"第五自由",即达到自己最佳水平的自由(the freedom to be one's best)。文章概要用 250 个词左右,但抓住了原文的中心思想,保持了原文的结构,分清了主次,以压缩、归纳手法讲明了造成失去"第五自由"的危险性的原因及如何保住"第五自由"。

概要(2):以一段文字写出的概要

We are still fighting today to protect what the pioneers sought in America three centuries ago: freedom from want and fear, and of speech and religion. Basic to these, a fifth freedom—to be one's best by developing to one's highest power—is now endangered by three misunderstandings: of the meaning of democracy, the nature of happiness, and the importance of moral values. As a result, all our standards have deteriorated alarmingly. To preserve this freedom we must give our children the most challenging curriculum possible, the right to fail, and exposure to the highest moral values.

概要(3):以一句话写出的概要

To preserve the traditional four freedoms for our children, we must also preserve a fifth, freedom to be one's best through full development, which can be safeguard by intellectual challenges, realistic testing, and high moral standards.

概要(2)和(3)在文字上高度精练,高度概括,在内容上仍保持了原文的意思。

七、口头作文提示

口头作文,也称"讲话题"(Talk on the topic),要求学生围绕话题组织语言,实际上就像写作一样,要学会选材、安排结构、层次、段落,充分地就每一要点或某一方面进行连贯清晰的叙述、说明、分析、推理、评述和判断。因此,讲话题的基本模式和具体方法完全可以参照写作的基本模式和具体方法。下述常用的具体方法简明易学,以实例阐明了讲话题如何开头,如何展开话题,怎样结尾,最终使三者有机地结合起来,融为一体。

1. 启动话题

话题开头可根据不同的内容和类型,采用以下几种方式:

- 直接点明主题(**Begin with direct announcement**)

开门见山点出主题是最常见的,也是最重要的启动话题的方法。主题句(或主题段)所表达的思想要尽量涵盖话题的中心思想和内容。这种方法可用于多种类型的口头作文。

例1. Science and technology have contributed in several important ways to the improvement of agricultural production. (主题句)

这是"Impact of Science on Agriculture"的第一句话,它概括了整个话题的中心思想,它既是话题内容的浓缩,也是话题展开的铺垫。

例2. Nowadays, when one applies for a job, he will be interviewed before he can be employed. This practice is advantageous to both the interviewer and the interviewee. (主题段)

这是话题"Advantages of a Job Interview"的主题段。主题句在段落的末尾,指出就业面试对面试者和被面试者都是有利的。其前面的句子是说明主题句的。

例3. With the increase of population, housing shortage is becoming a more and more serious problem in large cities. Some people have no rooms of their own to live in and have to spend a lot of money renting a room; some families have to crowd in a very small room, and what's more, in some families, three or four generations live in the same room. (主题段)

这是"Housing Shortage in Large Cities"的主题段。主题句是"随着人口的增长,大城市的住房短缺问题越来越严重。"其他句子说明住房短缺的现状。

- 定义法(**Begin with definition**)

为了把内容表达清楚,可首先给要说明的某个词或短语下个定义。这种方法多用于类似说明文或议论文的话题中。

例1. Teenage crime, also known as juvenile delinquency, is crime committed by young people and it has been on the rise and has become a serious social problem. (主题句)

这是话题"Teenage Crime"的主题段,以定义法引出青少年犯罪这一个严重的社会问题。

例2. Soap operas are serial dramatizations of domestic conflicts between married men and women. Soap operas derive their name from the fact that in the early days most of them were sponsored by manufactures of soaps and detergents. (主题段)

这是话题"Soap Opera"的主题段。第一句首先确定肥皂剧属系列剧,顺便提到它的主要表现内容和剧名的由来。

例3. Lucky numbers are numbers which sound like some Chinese characters meaning good fortune. For example, 8 is associated with wealth or fortune making, 6 with smoothness and success, and 9 with a long life. (主题段)

这是话题"Do 'Lucky Numbers' Really Bring Good Luck?"的主题段。第一句通过定义引入主题,指出迷信幸运数字的人的观点,随之举例说明各种表现。

- 数据法(**Begin with statistics**)

在开头第一句或开头的几句话中提供一个数据,然后据此引出一个话题。

例 1. By the year of 2000 there will be ten million Americans over the age of eighty. Can we expect these people to be cared for by their relatives, who are themselves in their sixties? ……（主题段）

这是话题"The Problem of Old Age"的主题段。文中第一句以"到 2000 年美国将有一千万人的年龄在 80 岁以上"为数据式开篇，并进而谈到这些人由谁来照料。

例 2. The number of students enrolled in college and universities was 0.2 million and rose 1.2 million in 1998…（主题句）

这是话题"Colleges Open Their Doors Wider"的开篇第一句，以数据为证指出大学招生人数越来越多的现状。

例 3. A recent survey of people out of work analyzed the type of worker who is unemployed. Out of the one million registered as unemployed one in five were women. 60% of men who were unemployed were to be found in services and engineering. However, there was a one in eight chance of being unemployed in the construction industry. One in twenty were unemployed in industries such as metal goods and textiles.（主题段）

这是话题"Unemployment"的开篇，用了若干具体的数据说明失业现状，使话语有理有据。

● 问题法（**Begin with a question**）

以提问的方式引出话题，然后以回答问题的方式对所提出的问题进行解释或说明。

例 1. Do you ever think you have to pay the tuition and fees yourself? Now that more than two-thirds of the high school graduates can go to colleges and universities, the government can no longer provide all the money for higher education…（主题段）

这是话题"Tuition"的主题段。第一句便以提问的方式引出话题。

例 2. In recent years, college students find it necessary to hunt jobs long before their graduation, some even in their third year. How come college students who are intelligent, ambitious and knowledgeable need to go job-hunting so early? There are several reasons for this new development. (主题段)

这是话题"College Students' Job-hunting"的主题段。它先阐述现状后发出疑问。

例3. Why are bicycles so popular in China? There are three reasons ... (主题段)

这是话题"Bicycle—an Important Means of Transport in China"的主题段。首先以问句形式指出现状,而后罗列理由。

● 引语法(**Begin with quotation**)

引用名人名言或成语、谚语来支撑自己要阐明的观点,使论说更具有说服力。

例1. Everyone who aims high wants to be successful. But what is the key to success? Einstein, the great scientific genius, gave us a formula about how to succeed: success = hard work + right direction + seldom indulging in idle talk. But I believe that there is at least one more thing worth mentioning—never being satisfied with the existing state of affairs and always trying to do better. (主题段)

这是话题"You Can Never Try Too Hard"的主题段。首先引用爱因斯坦的名言,而后导出自己的观点:永不满足,不断尝试。

例2. As the proverb says, "well begun is half done," it is clear that a good beginning is the foundation of our future success. A tall building, as everybody knows, must be built on the solid foundation. A good beginning is the same as the base of a tall building. When we begin to do something, we should lay a solid foundation. Otherwise, we would fail in the end. (主题段)

这是话题"Well Begun Is Half Done"的主题段。首先引用谚语并加以解释,略述"好的开端"的重要性。

例3. Some people often fail to finish their work on time.

They say that there is much time awaiting them and so they always leave the work of today until tomorrow. This habit is not advisable. We should always remember the famous maxim, "today's work must be done today" and never go to sleep before our day's work is completed.(主题段)

这是话题"Today's Work Must Be Done Today"的主题段。首先从解释现象入手,而后引用格言"今日事今日毕",说明不可蹉跎时日。

2. 展开话题

通常可用下述5种手段展开话题。

● 例证法(Exemplification)

例证法是用实例证明或解释主题句的观点。广为流传的《新概念英语》第三册中的许多课文都是采用这种方法发展段落的。选例要具有代表性,能明确地支撑主题句中的观点。

例1. Scientifically compounded fertilizers make the land more productive, chemical insecticides and pesticides, applied periodically to growing crops, selectively destroy a wide range of insects and pests. The numerous herbicides now available eliminate unwanted grasses and weeds, freeing field crops for more abundant growth. Research in plant sciences has produced higher-yielding plant strains and seeds. Moreover, technology has developed various kinds of machines such as tractors and combines, which perform many heavy tasks that once required a great deal of manual labor. Advanced irrigation techniques supply water and power for the complex needs of the modern farm.(扩展段)

这是话题"Impact of Science on Agriculture"的扩展段。它通过化肥、农药、农业机械等实际事例对主题句予以论证或阐述。

例2. First, the interviewer can get the first direct impression of the interviewee, such as his appearance and personality. Second, he can inform the interviewee of the working conditions in his company or institution as well as the salary of the job. Finally, he can get some idea of the interviewee's interest through the interview.

The interview is also advantageous to the interviewee. To begin with, the interviewee can introduce to the interviewer his education background and working experience. Besides, if the interviewee is good-mannered, decently-dressed or has a good appearance, he will make a good impression on the interviewer. Most important of all, the interviewee can demonstrate his ability while talking with the interviewer.（扩展段）

这是"Advantages of a Job Interview"扩展段，分别从面试者、被面试者两个角度举例说明面试的种种益处。

例3. There are various reasons for the housing shortages in large cities, but I think the main reasons for it are as follows. Firstly, the urban population increases so fast that the speed of house building can't meet the need of city dwellers. Secondly, the government or large companies invest in commercial and recreational buildings, but ignore the building for residence. Thirdly, with the development of industry, more and more factories take up so large area that there is not enough area to build residential houses.（扩展段）

这是"Housing Shortage in Large Cities"的扩展段，列举了造成大城市房屋短缺的种种原因。

● 比较与对照法(**Comparison and Contrast**)

比较法是把两个事物的相同之处进行对比，对照法是对两个事物的不同之处进行对比，依此展示出各自的特点、差异、优劣势等。出于对不同话题的需要，有时只用比较法，有时只用对照法，有时两者并用。这是展开话题最常用的方法之一。

例1. Although there are some similarities between the city and the countryside, there still exist great differences. In our country, most people like to live in the city, because life in the city is more convenient. There are more kinds of goods, various entertainment as well as better health service. Children can get better education. But it is nosy and crowded in the city. Life in the countryside, on the other hand, is much simpler and comparatively dull. Transportation is not convenient, and the chances of education are limited. But anyhow, there much less noise there, and the air is cleaner. (扩展段)

这是话题"City Life versus Country Life"的扩展段。本段从交通、娱乐、教育和环境四个方面论述了城乡生活的差异，采用的是先城市后乡村的集中对照手法。

例 2. Although old people in the United States and in my country, Japan, are treated the same in some ways, in other ways they are treated differently. In both countries the elderly are shown respect. Young people will give them a seat on a bus or train or will open a door for them. In both countries older people may ride the bus or go to a sow for less money than the young have to pay. Nevertheless, in Japan the elderly have the highest respect. Grandparents live with their families all their lives. They help to raise the grandchildren. If anyone needs advice, the first person to be asked is the grandfather, because he is the wisest. In the United States, the grandparents live with other old people in the "senior citizen" places. They see their grandchildren only on holidays or special occasions. (扩展段)

这是话题"Treatment of the Elderly"的扩展段。本段用比较法说了三例相同之处，又用对照法说了一种不同的情况。

例 3. Although mysteries and science fiction may seem very different kinds of writing, the two forms share some basic similarities. First of all, both are action-oriented, emphasizing plot at the expense of character development. Possibly for this reason, both types of literature have been scorned by critics as being "mere entertainment" rather than "literature". But this attack is unjustified, for both mysteries and science fiction share a concern with moral issues. Science fiction often raises the question of whether or not scientific advances are beneficial to humanity. And a mysteries story rarely ends without the guilty person being brought to justice.(扩展段)

这是话题"Science Fiction and Mysteries Story"扩展段。第一句表明中心话题是关于神秘小说和科幻小说的相似之处。其一,它们都以对人物动作的描写为主展开情节;其二,它们关心的都是道德问题——科幻小说常常提出的问题是科学的进步是否有益于人类,而神秘小说差不多都是以坏人受到惩罚而结局。

● 过程描述法(**Process and Procedure Description**)

这种方法通常用来客观的描述一件事物的进行过程或操作程序。它不同与表达说话者的主观意愿,而常用于说明做某事的过程,或提供一些常识性的东西,例如怎样做某种食物、如何照相等等,很像一纸简单的说明书。

例1.(略:参见36页说明文"How to Make Dumplings"中间三段。)

这三段话叙述了包饺子的程序,把做馅儿、和面、擀饺子皮和包饺子的具体步骤说得清清楚楚。

例2. How to Take Photographs

First, take the film cassette out of its packet, and insert it into the back of the camera. Wind the film on until a number 1 appears in the film window at the back of the camera.

Now set the aperture(光圈孔径) to one of the five positions, marked by the sun or cloud signs, according to the lighting conditions. Look through the view finder(取景器) and move the camera until what you want to photograph appears between the white lens. Hold the camera steady and press the shutter release button slow. That's all you have to do to get perfect pictures!

上述两段话叙述了照相的步骤,用了一系列的动词和动词短语排列出动作的顺序:take→insert→wind→set→look through→hold→press

● 因果关系法(Cause and Effect)

此法用于说明事情发生的原因和由此原因而引出的结果,也就是叙述发生的事情及其之所以发生的原因。一般用来解释和分析社会现象或社会问题。以因果方式扩展段落时可采用先因后果或先果后因两种模式。

例1. One reason, perhaps, is that it is getting more and more difficult for an average college graduate to get a good a job. With the restructuring of the state-enterprises, job vacancies become less available and the requirements for jobs are becoming more and more challenging. So further study seems to be a better choice for most college graduates. Another reason is that some young workers want to improve their education in order to hop to better jobs. To them an MA degree will certainly attract the employer's interest and become a favorable means in their fierce competition with their peers. Still another reason is that some young people feel the need of renewing their knowledge. They have found that, with the rapid development of hi-technology, their former knowledge and skills can't meet the requirements of some demanding jobs. (扩展段)

这是话题"A Boom in the Number of MA Candidates"的扩展段。主题段指出近年来研究生报名人数剧增,扩展段详尽阐述了造成这种现象的三个原因,是先果后因的模式。

例2. There are several reasons why their burden will not be easily lifted in spite of repeated social protests. For one thing, parents have a strong desire for the early intellectual achievement of their children. They believe that if they don't force them to read more, a golden opportunity for success will be lost and the chances of their being admitted to key schools, and then to famous universities will be slim. So children are under constant pressure to score high, be among the best or get a first. For another, our teachers ally themselves with parents in applying pressure. Since scores are not only the mark of success or failure for a particular student, but also a measurement of a teacher's performance, and failure on the part of his students in school examinations is often seen as evidence of bad teaching, it is natural for a teacher to assign more homework for his own sake as well as to the liking of the students' parents. (扩展段)

这是话题"Children's Schoolbags are Getting Heavier"的扩展段,从家长和教师两个方面分析了造成学生书包越来越重的原因。

● 驳斥法(Pro and Con)

用于就有争议性的问题发表议论,针对在这一问题上反映出的某一观点进行驳斥,提出自己的看法并加以论证。

例 1. There is a deep-rooted concept in the minds of many people that money is the only yardstick for success. What they do not realize, however, is that there are many types of success, and that some are associated with wealth but others not. It is high time for these people to open their eyes and take a fresh look at the world around them.

While it is true that a successful businessman or inventor will usually become rich, many other people who are outstanding in their fields do not reap monetary rewards. One example is the rocket scientist who makes great achievements in the field of astronautics. While doing credit to his country, he usually draws only a modest salary. Another example is Lei Feng, who has marked his name in history with his lifetime devotion to helping and serving the people, although he lived a short life and owned almost nothing.（扩展段）

这是话题"Can Success Be Measured in Term of Money ?"的主题段和扩展段。首先指出一部分人深信金钱是衡量成功的标志,并加以批驳,然后举例论证成功是多种多样的,进一步有理有据地驳斥了错误论点。

例 2. In my opinion, if you are not satisfied with your present job, you certainly have the right to replace it with a more challenging and better-paid one. Every change is a step to further success.

So, it is reasonable to change your job if you have a better opportunity. But once you have found a position where you can fully display your ability, it is advisable to settle down to it and put all your efforts into it. Only in this way can you get the true joy of achieving your goal.（扩展段）

这是话题"Is Job-Hopping Preferable ?"的扩展段。前面的主题段提出一种观点:成功之道在于终生守候一种工作。本段论述了赞成跳槽的观点和根据并提出建议。

3. 话题收尾

常用的话题收尾有如下 5 种方法。

● 概括总结整个话题,提出解决方法(**Summary and Solution**)

例 1. In a word, large-scale agricultural production in the modern times benefits greatly from the developments in science and technology.（终结段）

这是话题"Impact of Science on Agriculture"的收尾。由于该话题的扩展部分已通过例证法明确地说明了科技对农业的重要作用,收尾部分只简单地对整个话题予以概括总结。

例 2. Therefore, an interview during the job hunting should not be regarded as a nightmare, but rather something welcome. （终结段）

这是话题"Advantages of a Job Interview"的收尾。它对前文做出总结，纠正了错误的看法。

例 3. Although housing shortage is a serious problem in large cities, there are still many possible ways to solve it. First of all, the government can take stricter measures to slow down the population growth. And at the same time, the governments should invest more money on residential houses. Besides, multi-storied residential buildings can be built to accommodate more people. In a word, as long as the whole society takes the housing shortage seriously, this problem will be solved sooner or later. (终结段)

这是话题"Housing Shortage in Large Cities"的收尾。它总结了全文(In a word, ...)，提出了解决办法。

● 回答题目或开头段所提出的问题(**Answer to a Question**)

例 1. I believe it is of great importance for every foreign-language-learner to speak the language with fluency. A test of spoken English will stimulate students to improve their oral English. So such a test is necessary. And I intend to take it if possible. (终结段)

这是话题"Is a Test of Spoken English Necessary?"的终结段，它阐述了口语的重要性，明确地回答了题目所提出的问题——口语考试是必要的。

例 2. In my opinion, there is an undying hunger for improvement and advancement in human nature. So dissatisfaction makes us feel challenged and stimulates us to further efforts in building a better world both for ourselves and our children. (终结段)

这是话题"Is Content Happiness?"的终结段。它指出人们该永不知足，只有这样，才能建设一个更好的社会，从而对题目"知足常乐吗?"做出回答。

● 提出解决问题的建议(**Recommendation and Suggestion**)

例 1. So the secret of coping with stress is not to avoid it but to do what you like to do and what you should do, at you own rate. For most people, it is really a matter of learning how to behave in various situations. The most important thing is to have a code of life, to know how to live. (终结段)

这是话题"Is Stress a Bad Thing?"的终结段,它提出了如何对付压力的建议。

例 2. Therefore, it is time for us to take this problem into consideration. First, we should take some measures to control the world's population. Then the rising demand for energy by industry should be reduced. Most important of all, the public should be educated about the scarcity of energy and urged to conserve the actually limited resources. And meanwhile great efforts should also be made to find new energy resources. (终结段)

这是话题"Global Shortage of Energy Resources"的终结段。它提出了解决全球能源危机的办法。

- 给出预见(**Prediction**)

例 1. Personally, I firmly believe in the magic force of the new education policy, and eagerly look forward to enjoying the great benefits the program will bring about. I can see in my mind's eye the more colorful life, the more cheerful environment, and the more creative minds of the future students. Our education, so to speak, will not be making a "robot" or "computer" out of the students, but bring up a new generation that are masters of the robot and the computer. (终结段)

这是话题"Education: Exam-Oriented or Quality-Oriented"的终结段。它肯定了素质教育并展望素质教育的美好前景。

例 2. With the development of modern science and technology, there will be no limit to the application of computers to our lives.

In the future, computers will be made small enough to enable people to carry in their pocket and they can serve as language interpreters so that those who do not share a common language can talk to each other freely without any difficulty. By providing a computer with a patient's symptoms, a doctor will be able to diagnose the nature of the illness as well. (终结段)

这是话题"Computers"的终结段。它对计算机未来无穷无尽的应用做出预见且给出具体例证。

● 提出要采取的行动或措施(Call for Action)

例 1. In order to protect non-smokers from the harm of smoke and prevent them from becoming smokers, measures should be taken to educate the public about the harmfulness of smoking. And cigarette companies should not be allowed to advertise their products on television or radio, in newspapers or magazines. And again, the smokers should refrain from smoking in public places and places where there are non-smokers, especially women and children. (终结段)

这是话题"Stop Smoking"的终结段。它提出了为消除吸烟陋习应采取的措施。

例 2. This population explosion has brought a severe threat to man's survival on this planet, because many people are already suffering from food shortage and overcrowded housing conditions, and lack of clean fresh drinking water. This high rate of population growth has to be brought under control and birth control has to be practiced and more severe laws have to be put into effect in order to ensure a better environment for people. And finally, pollution has to be kept in check so that the health of living species can be secured. (终结段)

这是话题"The Problem of Human Population"的终结段。它分析了"人口爆炸"的危害性,提出必须诉诸行动,采取更为严格的法规,以控制生育。

在初学阶段,可依照上述方法模拟有关话题,言之有物地、简单地讲清一件事,以避免东一榔头西一棒子地拼凑句子。经过一段的实践有所提高后,可以综合性地、创造性地运用上述方法,"长篇大论"地谈一个话题。比如,下面是一篇谈论 money 的常见话题:

Money: Slave or Master?

No one would argue, I suppose, against the fact that money is necessary. Without money, even a hero will be driven against the wall. In a way or to a certain extent, money is the source of all happiness, at least material happiness. There are certain things that we need: food, housing, clothing, medical care and other basic necessities, all of these things cost money. If you want to get a little pleasure out of life or a little fun from time to time, you have to pay some money. If you want to buy a big house, a private car, or just have a holiday by the sea, you will have to be rich by our standard.

While we are in a market economy, people can buy whatever they enjoy, and do whatever they like to do. Many people appear to be hungry for money. They bow to it, they scramble for it. Some of them even sell their souls for it or risk their lives in the pursuit of it. Money is firmly in control of man. The relationship between man and money has been reversed. Money talks; man listens. Money has become his master. Then, is money the key to happiness?

Not really!

Why? because money is not everything. In other words, with money you can have a very comfortable life. However there are still a lot of things that cannot be bought with money. For example, pleasure in spirit, true love, sincere friendship, ability and intelligence. These things are invaluable and can never be measured by wealth. Even if you were born with a silver spoon in your mouth, it doesn't follow that you are intelligent or you can be happy all through your life. Even if you have accumulated heaps of money, it is still not enough to make you a happy person if you have no one to laugh with, or no one to cry for.

However, we cannot go to another extreme that money is the root of all evil. Money itself is neither good nor bad. It is just a tool of society. It depends on whether we have a correct attitude towards it or not. Man needs money, but should not be its slave; on the contrary, be. the master of money.

All in all, the uses of money are beyond comprehension. However, we must bear in mind that money has only as much value as we give it. In the pursuit of money, we must be careful not to let it corrupt us. Money is nothing more than a tool to a successful life. Perhaps we should remember the saying: money is the best of slaves but the worst of masters.

这席话含有三个要点：

1. Money is necessary.（金钱是必要的）作为话题，是以比较口语化的形式表达的。

若从"启动话题"的方法看，用的是"直接点明主题法"，然后用"举例法"证明、解释"money is necessary"这一观点，并进而指出一些人不惜一切追求金钱的倾向。

2. Money is not everything.（金钱不是万能的）在讲述这一要点时，以提问的方式引出话题：

Then, is money the key to happiness?

Not really!

Why? because money is not everything.

在展开话题时，使用举例法说明人生中许多珍贵的东西是金钱买不到的。

3. Don't go to extreme.（别走极端）

这一段开头直接点明有一种认为"金钱是万恶之源"的极端看法，然后用驳斥法进行反驳，指出金钱只是社会的工具，人们对之应有一个正确的态度。

最后一段可视为全篇的收尾，它回答了题目所提出的问题：钱是最听话的奴仆，最恶毒的主子（或：钱可为奴，不可为主），意指人要支配金钱，不要金钱支配人。这正好也是一句英语谚语，用在这里恰如其分，很有说服力。

No.1 Our School
我们的学校

(1) Our College

Our college is situated in the northern suburbs. But the transportation is convenient and the environment is pleasing. A hill lies in the back of the college campus. Not far away before the campus is a great lake, where we often go swimming on Sundays.

There are four classroom buildings and five dining-halls on the campus. The classrooms are big and bright. And each of them is large enough for sixty students to study in comfort. Behind the main classroom building stands the college library, where both the teachers and students are busy borrowing and returning books every day. I usually go there once a week for borrowing and returning books.

Our college life is rich and interesting. Not only have we many experienced teachers, sufficient books, scientific *apparatus*① and instruments to help our studies, but we are also encouraged to take part in many college activities such as seminars, parties, talks, sports, visiting factories, etc. Basketball and volleyball matches are held almost weekly.

All in all, studying in our college is a great privilege, so students always remember their *Alma Mater*② after their graduation.

---

① 仪器；设备
② （拉丁文）母校

(2) Our College Campus

Our college is situated in the west of Beijing. Although our campus is not big, all the *facilities*① needed for college study and life are concentrated here.

As you enter the college, you can see the reception office just inside the school gate on the left, and the office for incoming and outgoing mails on the right. If you go along one of the campus passages eastwards, you are greeted by flowerbeds and a rockery. You will see a bicycle park and a garage on one side, and an office building on the opposite. At the end of the passage there's an apartment building, north of which are two classroom buildings. Two of the students' dormitories are located in the eastern part of the campus. In the northern part of the campus there are buildings occupied by the general affairs department, the clinic, the bathhouse, and dining halls. Our sportsground is located in the northwestern corner of the campus. From there another campus passage leads to the college gate. Going down this passage you will see the club on the left and our newly built library on the right. In the centre of our campus there is a flag pole surrounded by flowerbeds. Following this route, you can easily find every place you want to go to on our campus.

(3) Our Library

Our university boasts a big, well-equipped library which has earned enduring fame throughout the country. It has a huge collection of books and many modern facilities under the supervision of many librarians. It is made up of many sections,

---

① 设备；设施

including "Collection and Purchase," "Cataloguing," "Periodicals," etc., It is accessible to all the students of the university, who can borrow as many as three books at a time and keep them for any length of time up to a fortnight. They have to renew or return the books they have borrowed by the end of this period. Otherwise they would have to be fined as a penalty, or refused permission to borrow any more.

There are a number of rules for behavior in the library. The students are supposed to put back the books of the reference room in their original places on the shelves. They ought to leave the magazines and newspapers in good order and treat the books carefully and keep them in good condition. The students are not allowed to talk in the library or disturb others. They are also supposed to keep reasonably quiet when they are passing along outside the library.

Our university library plays an important role in teaching, academic studies and cultivation of talented people. As a centre of books, reference materials and information, it is one of the "human's treasure-houses of spiritual wealth." It is a scholarly institution which offers services for teaching, studies and scientific research. Like a cradle, our library has *nurtured*① a great number of learned people, experts and *star professors*②, who were previously enthusiastic *patrons*③ of the library and have made great achievements in all walks of life.

(4) Our Classroom

Our classroom is on the third floor of the Teaching Building.

---

① 培养
② 著名教授
③ 惠顾者

我们的学校
Our School "No.1"

It is a large room about twenty feet long and ten feet wide. The walls are light green and the ceiling is white. Under the windows there are two painted radiators for heating the room in the winter time. On the opposite wall, near one end there is a brown door.

There is a large blackboard on the front wall of the room with chalk and erasers on the ledge. The teacher's desk is in front of this blackboard. In the back of the room there is a row of hooks on the wall for students' coats and jackets. There are about thirty light-colored chairs in the room for the students. Each chair has a flat right arm, which serves as student's desk. On the whole, it is a pleasant and comfortable room.

(5) My Bedroom

My bedroom is on the second floor, facing the north. It is small, crowded, but neat.

As you enter the room you are stopped short by four bunks which occupy much space of the room. On your left, against the wall, there are two *bunks*[①], one for two students, the other served as a closet for suitcases and handbags. Close to the door, pushed into corner, there is a large bookcase which is packed with papers and books. A map of the world is on this side of the wall.

At the centre stand two big writing desks, with not a speck of dust but many *odds and ends*[②] on them. They, in fact, serve as dinner tables, too.

On your right, there are two bunks for four students, while near the door is a stand for basins. The old wooden floor has lost its *luster*[③] but it is clean. Every corner, even every crack, has

---

① 双层床
② 零星杂物
③ 光泽；光彩

been carefully swept.

This is the place which has been home to me and will continue to be all through my college life.

(6) A Teacher's Lounge

On every floor of the main classroom building there are two teacher's *lounges*①, where teachers can take a rest between classes.

The one on the third floor is a room of 20 square meters. Its large *arch-framed*② window, facing south, with curtains of light blue cloth held back by strings, *commands a broad view of the city*③.

The left-hand wall is covered with a well-copied *motto*④ "Teachers are the engineers of the men's souls," under which squats a radiator. On the right-hand wall is a large-sized oil painting "Huang Shan," under which lies a couch with imitation leather cover. In one corner is a wash-stand with a basin of water on it and in the center a long table is *flanked by two rattan chairs*⑤. A white cloth covers the table with two ashtrays on it.

When the teachers come in, the room *beams with*⑥ an atmosphere of *restful merriness*⑦.

(7) A Major Problem in My College

The biggest problem in my college is the lack of space in the library. The reading rooms are packed with students and it is

---

① 休息室
② 拱形框架的
③ (从这扇窗户)可一览大片市容
④ 格言
⑤ 两把藤椅置于(桌子)两侧
⑥ 充满
⑦ 轻松愉快

impossible to find seats after classes. The total enrollment is three thousand, excluding the special students. The rooms can contain only one third of the students.

The hours of the library are not flexible enough to accommodate the students. Most students have classes in the morning and early afternoon. So all of them *swarm into*① the library. The hours should be extended. Some may sacrifice their lunch breaks and do some reading there.

Do all students study there? No, some of them talk. As the students are closely seated, their talk disturbs those serious students who want and need a quiet place to study. I often feel frustrated as I can not concentrate on my studies in the library.

---

① 涌进

No.2 Life at School
学校生活

(1) My View on Elective Courses

Elective courses have been part of university education for many years. After *careful observation*①, we can find that they are more complicated than we thought of.

On the whole, I should say elective courses are necessary for our education system. On one hand, students can choose courses of their special interest and make further explorations. On the other hand, elective courses can be informative, instructive and inspiring because different teachers, subjects, classmates and environment will never fail to sparkle new thoughts.

To make elective courses do the job, however, we have to make sure of several points below. For one thing, we should not only increase the quantity but also improve the quality of elective courses. For another, the university should make a careful arrangement of selective courses so that they can facilitate instead of hindering normal study.

The elective courses are an important part of college education. Only by planning it wisely and conducting it reasonably can we make best use of it.

---

① 仔细观察

学校生活
Life at School

(2) How to Eliminate Cheating on Campus

Nowadays, instead of listening attentively in class and working hard after class, a number of students adopt all kinds of dishonest methods to get high scores in examinations. It has become such a serious problem that it has aroused the concern from the whole society.

To put such a serious problem to an end, in my mind, calls for the efforts from all sides. First of all, the university authority should make it clear that any cheating behaviors in the examination, from whispering and copying, receiving answers via mobile phones to asking ringers for help, will be severely punished with no exception. Moreover, teachers of all subjects should go all the way to restore honesty by setting an example for the youth through speaking sincerely and behaving truthfully. Last but not least, young students, the future of our nation, should view *integrity*① as the *prerequisite*② to an upright and responsible citizen so as to learn to despise and fight dishonest behaviors throughout the life.

How can anybody expect to lead a meaningful life until he is far from any kind of cheating behaviors? Only when all of us join in the efforts of eliminating cheating at all levels can we expect to have a cleaner society and a more beautiful future.

(3) Living a Colorful Life on Campus

It is necessary that university students make life on campus as colorful as possible. On the one hand, only when university

---

① 正直
② 先决条件

life is colorful can it be meaningful and fruitful. On the other hand, *monotonous*① and lonely life is not healthy — the university should be a place where students can share opinions, display talents or study a subject thoroughly, and a place where students play leading roles.

There are many ways to live a colorful life on campus, among which joining various bands is the easiest one. By attending musical bands, literary communities and sports clubs college students can share their hobbies with a lot of friends. In addition, social investigation is also a good choice. Through various activities, the students will not only get to know the outside world but also become more responsible, reasonable and realistic.

As far as I am concerned, I will combine the two methods mentioned above. I enjoy jazz music and took part in the music band of our college last year. I will forget about my unhappiness and sorrow whenever I start playing my beloved *saxophone*②. Moreover, I will take an active part in social practice, which is most helpful for our personality development.

(4) Does College Life Simply Mean Getting a Degree?

Going to college is considered one of the most important and valuable experiences in one's life. In our culture, the most commonly recognized criterion of a student's academic achievement is the degree. A good degree means a decent and well-paid job. Admittedly, the degree is essential for students who want a promising future, but it is by no means the only reward college life grants us.

First of all, college life provides you with an enjoyable

---

① 单调的
② 萨克斯管

atmosphere of study and of other activities, which can greatly enrich your life, nurture your thoughts, and *widen your horizon*①. College life will reward the students not only with degrees, but also with a comprehensive cultivation.

Although it is generally believed that the higher degree the better the job, it is not necessarily the case. Many successful men *made their debut*② without a good degree or even without a good schooling. For example, Einstein got many poor grades in college and sometimes he even thought the exams as intolerable. But he turned out to be one of the most brilliant scientists in history. From this, we can see the degree isn't everything.

All in all, the degree does play an important role in one's future career, but it cannot cover all that college life offers. To succeed, we need many other qualities. Therefore, we should take full advantage of college study and try to be our best through the opportunity for the development of ourselves in an all-round way.

(5) How to Improve Students' Mental Health

College is a critical period in one's life in which a higher level of maturity is reached. Therefore, being healthy mentally is a matter of the first importance for a student's personal development. Mental health can be attained effectively through two channels: the school and the student himself.

What the school can do is to inform the students of the significance of mental health. Psychologists can be invited to give lectures on how to stay healthy mentally, how to always be one's own best friend. Furthermore, it may establish consulting center

---

① 开阔视野
② 初次登台,初露头角

with experts who are able to work with students individually. For example, a student who is heart-broken because he or she is *disappointed in love*① can go to the consulting center and have a talk with an expert in order to feel better and get some practical advice to solve the problem.

Meanwhile, no one can be more helpful to the students to maintain mental health than the students themselves. The psychological issues that students are frequently faced with are minor. In other words, they can be settled through self adjustment. For instance, students *are prone to*② feeling tired due to daily routine, stressed out because of exams and uncertainty towards the future. When you have those feelings, you should try to calm yourself down by telling yourself that you are not alone in feeling these and many others feel the same. And then you can find some *solace*③ and have a clear mind to think whether you need to carry out actions or simply change your view to get yourself out of the bad mood.

(6) Reduce the Negative Effect of Online Games on Campus

Online games are very popular now on campus. We can hear lots of students talking about their experience of playing online games. We can get access to various kinds of information concerning online games on newspapers and magazines. Some students even *burn themselves out*④ to play online games all night long.

Online games exert several unfavorable effects on college students. Some youngsters are not mature enough to restrict

---

① 失恋
② 易于
③ 安慰
④ 使……疲惫不堪

themselves and tend to *be indulged in*① the games, which will be bound to influence their daily study. Moreover, staying up late at night and too much exposure to the computer will surely *undermine*② young people's eye-sight and healthy condition. Indulgence into the visional world will make the students hard to be adjusted to their real life.

It comes undoubtedly that it is of great importance for us college students to balance the time attributed to study and online games. Treated appropriately, the latter will certainly lessen the strains of study and stimulate our inspiration as a means of entertainment.

(7) How to Relieve Pressures

University students of the 21st century *are confronted with*③ various pressures: the academic pressure to achieve high marks, the employment pressure due to the fierce competition on the tight job market, and the pressure coming from the preparation for postgraduate or overseas study.

There are many ways to relieve these pressures. Firstly, it is *advisable*④ to go in for proper outdoor activities, such as jogging and football. Exercises will help students refresh their mind and thus lessen the burden of study. Secondly, associating themselves with different kinds of friends will also *do the trick*⑤, because chatting and communication will make students more open-minded. On the other hand, isolation will do no good to them.

As for me, the best way to do away with stress is to enjoy

---

① 沉湎于
② 损害,削弱
③ 面临
④ 可取的,明智的
⑤ 取得效果,达到目的

music. When listening to different kinds of music or going for a walk, I'm always relieved and refreshed, leaving all distresses and tensions behind.

(8) Should Class Attendance Be Rigidly Required?

It is generally believed that required class attendance is necessary at colleges. Many teachers, and students as well, assume that it is a basic requirement for teaching and learning to take place. However, quite a few students maintain that college students are adults; they go to university to *acquire a broader perspective of life*①, to enlarge their ideas and to learn to think for themselves, so it is up to the students, not the professors, to decide whether to attend class regularly or not.

Personally I agree with the second group of students. As a matter of fact, rigid class attendance policy does not inevitably guarantee that students get the best out of the higher education. A student may not miss a single attendance in a course, but God knows whether he is just sitting there daydreaming all the time. Another student, more inclined by nature to teach himself, will benefit more from his or her own studies. This shows that class attendance does not necessarily result in brilliant performance in a course. Then why not allow the students to stay away or to skip classes to study in a quieter environment to teach themselves?

To conclude, required class attendance, though it may secure 100% attendance for a course, does not necessarily benefit students all the time. Students should be granted some freedom in deciding whether to attend a certain class, and they can leave a teacher's class if they don't like what they are being taught.

---

① 获得一个更广阔的生活前景

(9) On Your Own

Moving away from home and going to college is an experience that teaches a person how to become independent and do particular tasks on his own.

When I lived at home with my parents, everything was easy under their guidance. My mother would put warm, delicious food on the table for me three times a day. I could thoroughly enjoy my meals in the comfort of my own home. Now that I am in college, I have to walk across the courtyard at three specific times each day to eat reheated food. Handling my own money can be a difficult task too. When I was at home, I always had my parents help me with my money problems. Now that I'm on my own, I have to learn how to do this by myself. I am now teaching myself how to use a checkbook and *balance*① it diligently. A great luxury at home that I have to give up when I went away to school was having my mother do my laundry. Every week at home, I had no problem at all finding a clean shirt or an unused pair of underwear. At college, I realized that this was now my job.

In the last two months I have learned how to do many different tasks and handle different circumstances on my own. I have become used to living away from home, and that has made me more independent than I have ever been.

(10) University Life

Our university life is both *strenuous*② and pleasant.
In the university curriculum are listed various courses,

---

① 使收支平衡
② 紧张艰巨的

obligatory and optional.① Only when adequate credits have been achieved can students gain the qualification for graduation. *Tense and arduous exertion is the order of the day.*② Students are busy with preparing their lessons, and are burdened with doing exercises. When the examination draws near, *they are often so pressed as to resort to cramming*③.

But what has been mentioned is only one side of students' life. After class some students go to the playground, which is alive with a variety of sports games. Others go to the library to enjoy reading books and magazines. Still others attend all kinds of *forums*④ and *symposiums*⑤, which *get the campus permeated with academic atmosphere*⑥. At the weekend, there are always intersting entertainments to keep students occupied: going to cinema, taking a stroll and going to dancing party. *Equally enjoyable is the time students spend in their dormitories where they play chess and music instruments, or have cheerful random talks.*⑦

(11) My First Day on Campus

I still remember the day when I first came to the college. Being a boy of 17, I was longing for a new life as a college student; but, at the same time, I had no idea what college life would be like.

That morning when the bus carried me to the gate of the

---

① 大学课程表上有各种必修和选修课。
② 奋发与努力学习蔚然成风。
③ 由于压力重他们采取死记硬背的方式
④ 专题讨论会
⑤ 学术报告会
⑥ 使校园充满学术气氛
⑦ 倒装句。在寝室渡过的时光也同样愉快,同学们下棋,弹奏乐器或兴致勃勃地聊天。

college, I was so excited that my heart was beating very fast as if it would leap out of my mouth. From then on, I would be a student of this college. After *registration*①, we were led by an instructor to the dormitory, where, for the first time, we were going to live without our parents but with roommates. I was so clumsy that I did not know how to make the bed or fix the mosquito net.

In the afternoon, I took a walk around the campus together with my roommates. To think of studying in such a beautiful place made me feel quite proud of myself. As we were walking along, talking and laughing, a voice came into our ears, "Oh, look at these freshmen!" It was our middle-school-students' looks that *gave us away*②. We continued our tour of the college, inspecting every building and every garden until the sun began to set.

In the evening, we sat together, talking about the past and the future. We were so excited that no one wanted to go to bed.

(12) My First Year at College

My first year at college opened a new chapter in my life. It was a year of great changes. At the beginning, I found it difficult to adapt to things which were strange to me.

From the very first day, I had to take care of myself. I must not leave my things about as I had done at home. Fortunately, soon I found a place for everything and a time for every task. I wrote to tell my parents that they did not have to *worry themselves to death*③.

---

① 报到
② 暴露了我们的身份
③ 过于担忧

Classes were conducted quite differently from those at high school. There were plenty of discussions. The lectures were designed mainly to *usher us to*① new worlds of knowledge. I worked very hard after class so as to keep up with reading and writing assignments. Later, as I learned to plan my time, I did even better.

I think my most important *attainment*② during that first year was that I discovered new worlds of wonders and *developed a passion for*③ learning, learning for a rich, useful life.

(13) My Opinion of Students Taking a Part-time Job

Everything has two sides to it. College students taking a part-time job is not an exception. It has advantages and disadvantages.

There are many advantages for a student to have a part-time job. For instance, it helps him to realise that *no success comes from nothing*④. It enables him to be more independent. It also serves to build up his self-confidence. In a word, work will give the student an opportunity to know more of himself and of his personal value in society.

Of course, the disadvantages cannot be ignored. As is well known, a person's energy is limited. As a student, his main task is to study. If he spends too much time on his part-time job, he may find it hard to get along. Not only may he fail in his part-time job, but he may even be unable to continue with his study.

Personally, I don't think we should encourage a student to take a part-time job or discourage him from doing so. It is up to

---

① 将我们带入
② 收获
③ 产生了对……热情
④ 没有天上掉馅饼的事

each individual to decide. The most important thing is for him to keep a good balance, put his study on top of the list and assign an adequate amount of time to it.

(14) Should College Students Do Part-time Job?

With the economic development of our country, more and more college students are engaged in the activities of doing part-time jobs. People wonder whether it is good or bad for students to do so.

*It goes without saying that*① working part-time in school has some advantages. First, a part-time job brings students more money and helps them to reduce their parents' economic burdens. Second, it offers them a chance to demonstrate their ability and to apply what they have learned in school. Third, it helps them to gain some social and economic knowledge and to practise their *sociable abilities*②, which are of great help to their future careers. Finally, it enriches their school life.

But this activity may also bring some disadvantages to the students. First, too much part-time working may lose their time needed for sleep, rest, study and recreation. Secondly, it may affect their studies if they come back with tiredness. And as a result, their studies are going down. Finally, more money may bring bad effects on some of the students who spend it smoking, drinking, dressing rather than studying.

In my opinion, those students should keep a balance between study and the job. As a student, acquiring more knowledge, especially more useful knowledge from books, is the main task.

---

① 不用说；不言自明
② 社交能力

Although a part-time job can do you *a world of*① good, you should not spend too much time on it.

(15) The Students' Associations

The history of *students' associations*② is long. They were established in the last century. The main purposes are to promote friendship and cooperation among students and to arouse interest in schools.

A students' association is *self-explanatory*③ in that it should include every single student of the school. Thereby, everyone has the sense of belonging and sense of responsibility toward his own association. Besides, he will *take an active part in*④ improving the association or union.

The students' association provides students with chances for social training. They can prepare themselves to be leaders and able to look after their own affairs *in their own sphere*⑤. In future, when they step into society they will contribute more.

To conclude, students should participate in the activities of the association to train themselves to be sociable and useful to the society.

(16) A Sports Meet

The sports meet of our university was held on a charming spring day. *The stand around the playground was packed with*

---

① 很多的
② 学生会
③ 不言自明的
④ 积极参加
⑤ 他们自身范围内的

spectators.① First came the *parade of the opening ceremony*②. Athletes walked into the field in orderly arrays. *After the opening address was delivered*, *the athletes withdrew*.③ Then there was a performance of *group callisthenics*④.

The contests and races of track and field events were exciting. The runners of 100-metre race dashed to the terminal point. The winner *took the lead only by a small fraction of second*⑤. A boy athlete gave a *javelin*⑥ a forceful throw. It shot across the sky and arrived at a point far ahead of the former record. A girl athlete, in a long-distance race, *stumbled over the foot of another athlete*⑦ and fell down. She rose to her feet, *clenched her teeth*⑧, and continued her running. The most attractive is the *relay race*⑨ that was so intense that all spectators cheered, hailed and applauded.

The sports meet was over. Our athletes not only gained a good harvest of prizes, but also strengthened their body and tempered their will.

（17）What Do You Think about Grades?

Grades are really important things for most students. Schools and the society as a whole often *evaluate*⑩ a student just by his or her performance in the subjects. Students with higher

---

① 操场周围的看台上坐满了观众。
② 开幕式的列队行进式
③ 开幕式致词完毕,运动员退场。
④ 团体操
⑤ 仅领先零点零几秒
⑥ 标枪
⑦ 绊到了另一名运动员的脚
⑧ 咬紧牙关
⑨ 接力赛
⑩ 评估

grades are considered as winners. On the other hand, those with lower grades are, unfortunately, looked on as losers. Forced by this expectation, students *try as they might*① to get higher grades no matter how they like the courses.

  Last year, when I entered this college and took the regular courses, I found the competition here was even harder. All the courses were new and demanding. For example, in the English classes, the teacher spoke too fast, and I often felt like a dumb elementary school kid. Though I worked harder than anyone else did in my class, I had no expectation that I would be a winner.

  I believe that a grading system is good for a school, but it is not the only measure of a person's ability. Schools should set up more elective courses, for instance, to train the students to solve practical problems. Or they can give more thought to some varieties which can arouse the learning interest instead of just giving grades.

---

① 尽可能地

No.3 | Teachers and Students
老师·学生

(1) Our English Teacher

Miss Brown is our teacher this term. She has been here for two years but I have never attended her classes before as she teaches only in the Senior Middle School. I have, however, seen her very often and heard a great deal about her. She is known to be a teacher of considerable ability and author of a number of books, among which, *The Country Doctor* is one of the few English novels I have read. I am really fortunate to have been able to attend her lectures this term.

She is of medium height, about twenty five years of age. Though young and attractive in appearance she is *dignified and reserved*[①]. She is somewhat strict at times but never severe or stern. Her patience is really wonderful. She will never give up explaining until everyone understands. As she does not speak Chinese she has to draw pictures sometimes, and I think she draws unusually well.

Her method of teaching differs somewhat with that of our former teacher. Instead of explaining fully every new lesson beforehand she just gives us assignments and lets us work out ourselves. She explains only during the time of *recitation*[②] when

---

① 沉稳持重
② 背诵,详述

she will explain and correct mistakes. Her method means more work for us to do outside of class, as we have to consult the dictionary again and again, but we feel that we have been making a rapid progress. She really deserves our love and respect.

(2) Teacher's Social Status

Teaching is a *sacred*① profession. Teachers are usually compared to be engineers of human soul. They not only impart their knowledge to the students but also train their moral character. Yet because of historical factors, in the past years teachers were usually looked down upon and as a result, though they were asked to do too much, they were paid too little. With the rapid development of our society, people begin to realize the vital importance of education. Many works have been done to improve teachers' living conditions and to raise their salary. Now people pay more respect to teachers.

The celebration of Teachers' Day reflects that teacher's social status has become much higher than ever before. In honor of teachers' noble responsibility, the Standing Committee of National People's Congress passed a resolution that September 10 be the national Teacher's Day. The celebration includes congratulations from students, commending outstanding teachers, etc. This festival certainly helps bring about a social atmosphere, in which teachers are esteemed and knowledge is valued.

Teachers devote their lives to education and contribute much to the development of our country. Therefore, we should attach more importance to their works and show more respect to them.

---

① 神圣的

(3) The Most Desirable Personal Qualities in a Teacher

Probably no two people would draw up exactly similar lists about the most desirable qualities in a teacher, but I think the following would be generally accepted.

First, the teacher's personality should be lively and attractive. This doesn't *rule out*① people who are physically plain, *homely*② or even ugly, because many such people have great personal charm. But it does rule out those who are *sarcastic*③, unfriendly or bossy. Second, it's not only desirable but essential for a teacher to have a capacity for sympathy — that is, a capacity to understand the feelings of students and a capacity to tolerate mistakes. Third, teachers must be intellectually honest — that is, they should *admit openly what they know and what they don't know*④. Fourth, every teacher should be a bit of an actor. They should be able to enliven the classes with imaginative performances that keep the students interested. Fifth, teachers must remain mentally alert to develop their "*teachership*⑤". They must be quick to adapt to any situation and be able to make improvement. Finally, a teacher should always go on learning. A teacher who has lost his true thirst for knowledge will never inspire his students to learn effectively.

(4) My View on Teacher-Student Relationship

Teacher-student relationship plays a significant role in school

---

① 排除在外
② 容貌不好看的
③ 讽刺的,挖苦的
④ 知之为知之,不知为不知
⑤ 教师的职业性;此处指作为教师应具有的创意、洞察力和分析力

life. A good relationship will make learning interesting and teaching enjoyable. On the contrary, a bad relationship can make learning dull and teaching unpleasant.

To have a good teacher-student relationship, it is important that the teacher and the student understand each other and respect each other. The teacher must know that he should be neither too tough nor too permissive. If he is too tough, the students may get frightened and discouraged. If he is too permissive, the students may become lazy and careless. As a student, he should know that what the teacher does is for the benefit of his students. He should always show his respect to the teacher. However, he should always be eager to learn and willing to work hard.

In one word, a good teacher-student relationship can be mutually helpful and beneficial. The student may find the learning process enjoyable and productive while the teacher may find his teaching satisfactory and rewarding.

(5) An Angel on the Platform

Of all the teachers I have met since the day I started my long school years, Ms. Yu is the most impressive one. It is no *exaggeration*① to call her an angel on the platform.

As a teacher, she is *competent*② and strict. She arranges her class teaching-activity wonderfully and the students never feel bored in her class. Of course, she is also known for her strictness on students; once she catches your making a mistake, I'm sure you will not make the same mistake again. I do not mean she is a terrible punisher who would strike or scold the students. She does have a magic power to make students behave themselves —

---

① 夸大，夸张
② 能干的

she has a pair of bright eyes that can detect the wandering minds on class and a marvelous memory that can warn the careless guys of the possible pits in study.

She is more a friend than a teacher and there's no generation gap between us. In her class, her passion can easily take you to her world. She makes wonderful *elaboration*① on the texts and usually she blends the explanation with her own personal experience. Always, we enjoy her outright laughter and pleasant mood.

With the angel-like Ms. Yu teaching us, taking classes becomes our greatest enjoyment.

(6) Changing Criteria for Good Students

Years ago, good college students simply meant students good at academic work. On being admitted into a college, students usually work very hard just to be "*at the top*"②. Most of their campus time was spent in classrooms, reading-rooms and laboratories.

But the criteria for good students are changing now. True, good marks continue to be some students' dream, yet there is a growing number of students who are concerned much more about community activities, art, music and sports. Some students even become campus "businessmen" or "businesswomen" by starting or serving in self-supporting business.

The changes are for the better. Times are different, and the job market demands personnel with varied skills. Therefore, the students today are, in a sense, better prepared for challenge and competition upon graduation — even if academic excellence has to

---

① 详尽解释,说明
② 当尖子生,名列前茅

suffer a little on that account.

(7) My Favorite Teacher

Perhaps the most interesting person I have ever met is a Chinese professor who teaches *Contemporary Chinese Literature* at my university. Although I last met this man ten years ago, I have not forgotten the qualities that make him one of my favorite people.

I was most impressed by his devotion to teaching. Because his lectures were always well-prepared and clearly delivered, students *swarmed into*① his classroom. His followers appreciated the fact that he knew well what he taught and he was intellectually stimulating. Furthermore, he could be *counted on*② to explain his ideas in an imaginative way, introducing such aids to understanding as paintings, recordings, pieces of sculpture, and guest lecturers. Once he even sang a song in class to *illustrate*③ a point.

I also admire the fact that he would *confer with*④ students outside of the classroom or talk with them on the telephone. He would join groups to discuss subjects ranging from astronomy to diving. Many young people visited him in his office for academic advice; others came to his home for social evening.

Finally, I was attracted by his lively wit. He believed that no class hour is a success unless the students and the professor share several chuckles and at least one loud laugh. Through his sense of humor, he made learning more enjoyable and more lasting.

If it is true that life makes a wise man smile and a foolish man

---

① 大群地涌入
② 依靠,依赖,指望
③ 说明,阐明
④ 探讨,讨论

cry, and my teacher is truly a wise man.

(8) Confucius as a Teacher

Confucius (551BC-479BC) was a great philosopher, statesman, and educator of the late Spring and Autumn period. He occupies a unique place in the intellectual history of China.

Confucius devoted nearly 50 years to teaching and formulated a systematic and profound theory of education. He was the first public teacher in history who made teaching a profession, and thus he popularized education. He was the first in China who openly declared that "*in teaching there should be no class distinction*"①, and opened the doors of education to all.

In his long career of teaching, Confucius believed that learning should be a process of exploring and understanding of one's own initiative, so it was very important for the students to learn by themselves. What is more, Confucius was also skillful in arousing students' interest and eagerness in study. It was his opinion that only by making students interested in what they were learning, only when they were eager to learn, could they study on their own initiative. If so, there would be no barrier between their minds and the knowledge to be acquired. Confucius' instructions were always interesting, and they attracted and held the attention of his students.

To sum up, in Confucius' opinion, the teacher's role of guiding was twofold. One was guiding the students to do better in the process of learning, and the other was developing in them an interest and eagerness in study.

---

① 有教无类

(9) An Ideal Teacher

An ideal teacher is a friend as well as a teacher to his pupils. He will pardon anything except bad work and bad conduct. He explains the lessons in much detail and does his best to answer questions. He takes great trouble in correcting papers, and is very strict in giving marks, not willing either to give one mark more or one mark less than the pupils deserve. In the classroom he always keeps the dignity of a teacher.

But as soon as school is over, he becomes the pupils' friend. He visits the pupils' dormitory to have a chat with them. He goes to the playground to play with the pupils. When a pupil is in trouble, he comforts him. He helps to solve any problem that may trouble any pupil. He keeps in constant touch with his pupils and *induces*[①] them to study hard and behave well. He always sets a good example himself so as to influence his pupils.

He keeps in touch with not only his pupils but his pupils' families. His purpose in so doing is to obtain the assistance of parents in educating the pupils. He tries to learn about the family conditions of the pupils. Those whose family conditions are good he urges to study hard. Those whose family conditions are bad he warns to avoid being influenced by them. He thus increases the efficiency of his work.

(10) A True, Good Student

What is meant by a true, good student? A true, good student is one who possesses good morality, sound health, perfect

---

① 劝导

knowledge and various abilities. *To attain this end*①, I shall give a few suggestions as follows:

First, cultivate good morality. One of the best qualities of a student is good behaviour. Bad character is easily *scorned*② and *disdained*③. Polite manners and noble ideas make up a true man, whereas evil habits such as smoking, drinking, gambling, etc. should be got rid of. Whenever you find something wrong, correct it boldly. You should examine yourself frequently as to whether you are honest to your friends, sincere to your teachers and the like. In short, you should do everything right.

Second, study diligently and put your knowledge to practical use. "Knowledge is power," said *Francis Bacon*④. One will not reach *the rich storehouse of knowledge*⑤ unless he studies carefully: no diligence, no accomplishment. To apply knowledge to practical use is, however, more important. Students ought to apply their learning to something practical to benefit the people.

Third, make your body strong and healthy. Health is the key to success. Broken in health, one can do nothing. A sound mind is found only in a sound body. The healthier your body is, the brighter your mind will be, and the higher learning you can attain. So you should never neglect your health. "Work while you work; play while you play" is a good way for everybody to observe.

With the foregoing three points in mind, you may be "a truly good student."

---

① 为达到这个目标
② 蔑视
③ 轻视；鄙弃
④ 弗朗西斯·培根(1561—1626)，英国政治家、哲学家、英语语言大师
⑤ 丰富的知识宝库

No.4 Schoolmates and Friends
同窗好友

(1) My Best Friend

Of all the friends I have, I think Li Quan is my best friend. He used to be my classmate and a good neighbor as well. So from elementary school to senior middle school, we pledged ourselves to be great friends and were really as good as our word. For many years we remained true to each other in times of difficulty.

Li Quan and I had much in common. We were both rather fond of sports. Hardly did we spend a day without playing ball or swimming in the sea. Once I was ill for a couple of weeks and could not play games with him. He came to see me every day. I could feel he was as miserable as I was. Another interest we share is poetry. The word "sea" always reminds me of those days when we lay on the beach reciting poems and talking about Li Bai and Su Dongpo.

After graduation from senior middle school, Li Quan joined the army and I went to college. We have not seen each other for two years but we are as close and friendly as we used to be. This is because we have been writing to each other ever since our parting. We are so trustworthy as to share our every secret. We cherish our friendship and want to be good friends forever.

(2) How to Get on Well with Our Classmates

Learning to get on well with others should be an important

part of our school education. We are often told that personal relationship is even more important than our professional skills or knowledge for our future career. Although the modern society is filled with competition, yet, cooperation with others is absolutely indispensable if we want to be successful.

Getting on well with our classmates is not difficult if we can observe the following rules. First of all, we should learn to respect our classmates and not to make fool of them. By so doing, we can win respect from them. Besides, we should always be ready to help our classmates whenever they are in difficulty. A friend in need is a friend indeed, and it is only by helping others in need that we can get others' help in the end. Finally, we should never talk bad things about others behind their backs. We should always remember the saying, "*Never do to others what you would not like them to do to you.*①"

If we can follow the suggestions mentioned above in our everyday life at college, I am sure we will get on well with our classmates and win ourselves a lot of life-long friends.

(3) A Friend in My Memory

I had a great many friends in my childhood, but one of them I can never forget. Her name was Susan and she lived next door to me. Although she was five years older than I, we grew fond of each other. She had many qualities that appealed to me then and have since been a great image in my memory.

In school, Susan was *a star pupil*②. She *excelled in*③ every subject, but she never seemed to be proud of her achievement.

---

① 己所不欲,勿施于人
② 尖子生
③ 在……方面出色的

She was quiet, diligent, and a big sister to the students of lower grades. Being the protector of the little ones, she would not let anyone *bully*① them, was quick to dry their tears when they cried, and helped them up when they stumbled and fell.

Susan had a big kind heart. Although she was the only child of her family, she was not spoilt. She was polite to the elders, generous to her friends, and kind to the poor. She had never hesitated in giving her pocket money to *the needy*②.

Susan did not like to argue with others, but she *could not bear injustice*③. If someone had wrongly accused her, she would write a letter to protest, for she thought it would be better to write than to argue and confuse the facts. She might be quiet, full of sympathy, and modest, but she was *far from*④ weak. She might seem *fragile physically*⑤, yet behind her soft face was *a strong will of her own*⑥. Therefore, no one would take her as a weak person.

After her graduation from middle school, she went to England with her family. For quite a long time, I missed her very much. Though I have never seen her again, what she did and said left on me a very deep impression. I will always remember her.

(4) My Friend

My friend's name is Tom. He is five feet tall, weighs 175 pounds, is twenty years old. His eyes are brown, his hair is black, and his skin is light brown. His father is a teacher and his mother, an

---

① 欺负
② 这里指"需要钱的同学"
③ 不能容忍不公正的行为
④ 远远不；完全不
⑤ 体质弱的
⑥ 她特有的坚强意志

accountant①. He majors in English at University of California. He is usually dressed in a light-colored shirt or sweater.

  Tom is an interesting man, with a delightful sense of humor. Most importantly, he *is* very *thoughtful of others*②. His humor and thoughtfulness cheered me up last Saturday. Tom and I waited for a bus for over half an hour on a cold street corner. We could do nothing but wait. Both of us at that time, dreamed of having a car of our own, so that we would not have to wait for a bus like that. When we finally got home, he handed me a small paper bag. Inside was a little model car, with a note saying, "Now you won't ever have to wait for a bus again."

(5) Mary and Jane

  Mary and Jane are classmates who have many things in common. First of all, both girls have the same background. Mary lives in China with her parents, who are foreign experts in a certain factory, and so does Jane. Next, both girls are very friendly to people around them. Mary likes practising her Chinese with her Chinese classmates and makes friends with them. In the same way, Jane also has many Chinese friends and her Chinese is even better. *What is more*③, they have the same kind of interests in school, and are often seen together. Finally, both of them want to remain in China after school. Mary plans to be a teacher. But Jane likes to become a journalist. As you can see, the two girls are almost like twins.

---

① 会计
② 体贴别人
③ 更重要的是

No.5 Extracurricular Activities
课外活动

(1) After-class Activities on Campus

At 4 o'clock in the afternoon, when classes are over, students *swarm out of*① the classroom buildings. Tired after a whole day of serious study, they mostly spend one or two hours before supper to relax and to refresh themselves before a long evening of hard work. If you take a walk on campus around this time, you will *get an idea about*② what students do after class.

On the sports ground, various kinds of sports activities are going on. You will see students jogging or playing ball games. Some of them may only be practising, some are competing seriously against each other. If you are lucky, you may get a chance to watch a football game between *the host and a visiting team*③.

The Students Activities Center becomes the busiest place on campus. Members of various clubs meet at this time. You will find some students learning dancing or enjoying a game of chess while others simply sit around and talk. Perhaps this is the only time during the day that they can afford to talk with fellow students and to make friends. And they learn a lot from one another in this way.

---

① 蜂拥而出
② 了解有关……情况
③ 主队和客队

(2) A Basketball Match

Yesterday afternoon, a basketball match was played between our university and the city police. The policemen, well-built and skillful, claimed that they would certainly *carry the day*①. But the first half of the game turned out to be *an even one*②, with a score of 30 : 30. When I got there, our coach was talking excitedly with the players. Clearly both sides had a hard time striving to win.

After a short rest, the whistle blew for the second half to begin. Both sides *went all out*③. One goal was scored after another. Again and again the audience cheered the players on. Soon the score came to 36 : 30 *in our favour*④. However, the policemen managed to catch up and even *to turn the tables*⑤. In the last second their *center forward*⑥ shot the decisive ball. The final score was 42 : 40 in favour of the visiting team!

Though we had lost the game, the coach said that he was satisfied because, as the term was coming to an end, the students were busy preparing for exams and had not had enough practice.

(3) A Basketball Game

The basketball game began with the referee's whistle — a championship match between the team of the Agriculture College and ours on our playground. Every student of our college crowded

---

① 获胜
② 平局
③ 全力以赴
④ 对我们有利
⑤ 扭转局面
⑥ （篮球等的）中锋

around the court, cheering for us.

  I played the *left forward*① position. Like the other boys of our team, I was nervous because our coach had ordered us to defeat this guest team, the champion team for so many years.

  We all played desperately on the court but we were three points behind *at the half*②. After fifteen minutes in the second half we had made four more points. Then thirty seconds before the game was over, *the scores of the two teams were tied*③. Now the ball was in my hands. Hurriedly I *dribbled forward*④. *Personal foul*⑤! How happy we were! I got two *penalty shots*⑥. Unfortunately, the first shot failed. My heart nearly leaped out of my chest and my hands were trembling. The spectators seethed with excitement. Soon after my second shot fell into the basket, the referee whistled the end of the game. We were wild with joy. I was tossed into the air many times by my team members. That night I couldn't get a wink of sleep!

(4) Visiting a Museum

  One Saturday afternoon the lecturer who taught us *Chinese General History*⑦ took us to visit a museum.

  The exhibition hall was decorated *in an antique mode*⑧. Charts and pictures were hung on the walls. Many *ancient*

---

 ① 左锋
 ② 半场时
 ③ 双方打成平局
 ④ 向前运球
 ⑤ 撞人犯规
 ⑥ （篮球的）罚球
 ⑦ 中国通史
 ⑧ 以陈列古文物的方式

utensils①, curios②, weapons and arms, robes, crowns, coins, ornaments, books and farm tools as well as recently *unearthed relics*③ were exhibited. Each dynasty was presented in a separate room along with written and pictorial descriptions. Our teacher now served as the narrator, giving us a detailed lecture on the development of Chinese history, and explained his new viewpoint on how to divide Chinese history into different stages.

We were happy to have such a vivid lesson, one that made us not only review what we had learnt in class but also feel proud of our motherland's great and glorious historical culture of more than five thousand years.

---

① 古代器皿
② 古玩
③ 出土文物

No.6 Vacation 假期生活

(1) How I Spent My Summer

As it became hotter and hotter, I went together with my family to my uncle's farmhouse, which lay in the country a hundred miles away, to spend the summer. Obviously, life in the country is very different from that in the city. People who have lived long in the city often wish for that calm, pure, and beautiful rural life.

Early in the morning I took a stroll along the field side. The air was so fresh and pure that I breathed and breathed, deeply and fully. With a dog following sometimes I ran a race in the meadows, covered with tall grass. Sometimes I climbed up the hill to see the sun slowly yet steadily emerge out of the eastern horizon. The birds also seemed to have awakened from their dreams, twittering restlessly among the bushes. I fixed my eyes upon the smooth, clear, and bright surface of the murmuring stream to see the fish swimming. In order to appreciate the quietness of the country, I *gave myself up* entirely *to*[①] nature, with a light heart and a happy mind.

At noon I dared not go out of doors, when the sun was at its height. Instead of rice and meat, we took much ice-cream, water-

---

[①] 使自己沉湎于；使自己纵情于

melon, and fruit for lunch. It was my habit to take a nap in some windy, cool places. In the evening, I always talked with my uncle and my aunt and even forgot to go to sleep. Besides these, I was often attracted by the mysterious night scenes when the moon shone through the willows and the fireflies wandered above the dark green corns.

(2) Summer Memories

How time flies! It seems as if it was only yesterday when I had just finished my examination. The heavy load of intense study had been lifted, and I was free. I started to enjoy the wonderful summer time.

Swimming is my favorite pastime. I often went to the swimming pool with my friends to escape the heat and to soak in the cool clean water. On other days, I stayed at home. I turned on the electric fan and curled up in an armchair, reading a novel *in cool comfort*[①]. My teachers had given us a reading list of titles to read during the holidays. Unfortunately, I had lost it, so I had to read what I myself *fancied*[②].

I had also spent quite a good time watching television shows. Though it is good for the relaxation of our brains, we must not indulge in it excessively, for it is very tiring to our eyes.

Cold drinks, ice-creams, water-melons, etc., all these indispensable constituents of the holidays *faded*[③] into the past as the long hot summer passed away, and we now turn towards the path that leads to school once more. With the new term coming ahead, the end of summertime announces the approach of another

---

① 凉爽、舒适地
② 喜爱
③ 消失

year of hard work.

(3) How I Passed My Summer Vacation

In the summer I got up early in the morning and amused myself in reading. I was delighted in perusing *Washington Irving's*① writings. When the clock struck ten, I began my daily lesson in drawing pictures till twelve. After taking lunch, I retired for rest. I usually passed the first two hours in reading newspapers and some of the noted novels. After that, I took a bath and spent the rest of the day *rambling about*② the surrounding villages. There we could see a beautiful lake. Many ducks floated on its surface and many fishes swam under it. We could also see the fields, *teeming with*③ wild *fertility*④; the boundless plains, waving with *spontaneous*⑤ *verdure*⑥, the clean and blue *streamlets*⑦, *gurgling*⑧ their sweet tones and murmurings to lull one *to repose*⑨, and the skies, *kindling*⑩ with the magic of summer clouds and glorious sunshine.

Sometimes, I, in company with a number of friends, took a rod and went to the river and sat down fishing. It made the *household*⑪ happy when they saw me returning with a basketful of large and fresh fish. When we were *filled with good cheer*⑫, we

---

① 华盛顿·欧文(1783 — 1859),美国散文家、小说家及历史学家
② 漫步
③ 充满;富于
④ 这里意指"野花、野草"等
⑤ 自然的;自然产生的
⑥ 青翠的草木
⑦ 小溪
⑧ 作汩汩声
⑨ 休息
⑩ 发亮
⑪ 全家人
⑫ 充满欢乐;充满喜悦

would declare that there was nothing on earth so happy as our family meeting.

When night came, I would sit at the door and tell the most marvellous and interesting stories to my younger sisters and brothers, who listened to the tales of wonder with open eyes and mouths. They would be very frightened if they heard a *spectre*[①] killing a man in a most fearful manner.

(4) My Summer Vacation

After the final examination, I received a letter from my aunt and uncle who live in the countryside. They invited me to stay with them for a *fortnight*[②]. The news brought me a *restless night*[③]. When I reached their home after a long journey, I was kindly received. They prepared a very nice and airy room for me.

I enjoyed the life there very much. Every morning we took a walk in the neighboring hills where we could enjoy the fresh air and sweet songs of the birds. We gathered wild flowers here and there among the bushes, and I found it full of fun.

In the afternoon I mostly spent my time reading and writing, for I was shut in the house by the terrible heat. The evening was the only time we could go to swim together. I improved my swimming during those two weeks.

Though the fortnight passed away at lightning speed, the memory of it will last forever.

(5) The Happy Vacation Life

This year's summer vacation was most enjoyable. I spent ten

---

① 鬼怪
② 两星期;半个月
③ 不眠之夜

days in the countryside with my uncle *making a social investigation*① on rural life, and another ten days absorbed in a book that I had long planned to read.

In the countryside, as I saw the boundless green *croplands*② under the *gentle breeze*③, I became carefree and happy. The hard farm work, the simple life led by farmers and the backward *mode of farming*④ aroused in my mind a serious *concern*⑤: what should we youth do for the modernization of agriculture in our country? The ten days were short but the experience was unforgettable.

Coming back home I used another ten days reading the book, *The History of Chinese Literature*. I was deeply fascinated by the works of ancient poets. Reading and reciting their poems helped me see how great the *treasury*⑥ of Chinese literature was.

It is *regrettable*⑦ that the summer vacation is so short, and after some days school will begin. When I think of all our classmates meeting together, my heart begins to leap happily again.

(6) How to Spend Sundays

A great pity it is indeed that we always spend our Sundays aimlessly. We generally derive no profit from the invaluable hours of Sunday. Though Sunday is set aside as a day for rest, we ought to devise some good ways of spending it.

---

① 进行社会调查
② 庄稼地
③ 微风
④ 耕作方式
⑤ 令人关切的事
⑥ 财富
⑦ 令人遗憾的

First, we should review what we have learned during the past week. "*One will get something new in looking over one's old studies*"① is a very wise saying. If we do not fully understand what we have been taught in the week, how can we expect to understand next week's lesson?

Secondly, to increase our knowledge, we should read on Sundays those books, newspapers and magazines that are not in our regular *curriculum*②. We have to attend to our daily lessons on weekdays; hence the utilization of Sunday hours for improvement is highly advisable.

Thirdly, we should organize ourselves into a party or a club for travelling or debating, which is very beneficial to our health and speaking faculty.

The three ways of spending Sundays will surely do anyone good if he will carry them out faithfully and persistently.

(7) During the Summer Holidays

Every student has a long vacation in the summer. But not everyone knows how to spend it meaningfully. I am glad to have spent a most meaningful summer vacation last year.

I went back to my hometown, Wuxi, after the school was closed. I found a job in a restaurant and began my work as a waitress there. The job made great demands on my energy and *endurance*③. From 9:30 in the morning until 10:00 in the evening, I spent most of my time on my feet waiting on customers, walking from counter to kitchen to table, and carrying trays heavy with plates of food. The restaurant was popular in

---

① 温故而知新
② 学校的课程
③ 耐久力；忍耐力

the street, and the *streams of customers*① kept me in almost constant motion. Even in the rare moments when business slowed down, I was expected to mop the floor and to clean the wall. My hands and arms ached by the end of the work. I worked there for almost a month.

  I spent my wages on a bookcase and some interesting books which I had been wanting to have. I also bought a pair of *ivory*② chopsticks as a birthday present for my mother.

  I benefited a lot from my experience as a waitress in the summer holidays. I'll remember all my life that life is not easy, and one will not succeed unless he works hard.

---

① 客流；川流不息的顾客
② 象牙制成的

No.7 | Way of Study
学习之道

(1) Why Do We Attend College?

Most of us assume that we go to college in order to be well educated. Of course, this is true, but there is something more than that. We go to college not only to acquire knowledge, but to prepare ourselves for the real world, to get a broader perspective of life, to enlarge our ideas, and to learn to think for ourselves.

While we are at college, we should have as frequent contacts with our teachers as possible. They are as human as we are but with a wider range of knowledge and can help us in more ways than just teaching us school subjects.

As college students, some of us tend to go to extremes. We are either too fond of studies and become bookworms or too much occupied by off-campus activities. The former can be *straight-A*① students at college but not likely to be successful in their career because they lack the knowledge of real human things and their range of interests is too narrow. The latter, since they neglect the basic knowledge of science and humanities, are not likely to succeed, either. Thus we must steer the middle course between these two extremes in order to become all-round development talents.

---

① 所有学科均最佳的

(2) Reading Selectively or Extensively?

Now, it is generally accepted that reading is very important. But when it comes to how to read, there has *sprung up*① a heated discussion as to whether we should read selectively or we should read extensively.

Those who are in favor of the idea of reading selectively believe that it is not how much one reads but what he reads that really counts. For one thing, living in an age when much time has to be taken up by work and other activities, people are unable to find enough time to read extensively even if they intend to. For another, some books are harmful, such as *pornographic*② books and magazines sold by the street book vendors. Lack of intelligent discrimination in this matter may cultivate one's bad, indecent taste to such a degree that his mind might be corrupted. Therefore, the choice of books can never be overlooked.

However, those who insist on reading extensively argue that it is through reading extensively that we obtain most of our knowledge. Now branches of knowledge diverge into each other. Only when one goes beyond his own field and reads widely can he really make remarkable achievements in his study. In addition, the most valuable gifts bestowed by books are experience, broad view and wisdom. Thus a man who reads extensively live many lives while a man who does not read or read only a selected number of books *walks this earth with a blindfold*③.

In my opinion, we should read both selectively and extensively. That is to say, upon reading, we have to exercise

---

① 出现
② 色情的
③ 犹如蒙着眼睛在世上走

extreme care in distinguishing good books from indecent and *vulgar*① books. The latter should never be touched, but the significance of good reading cannot be overvalued. Whatever the purpose in reading, our contact with good books should never fail to give us enjoyment and satisfaction and there is no such thing as "too many" in reading good books.

(3) Book Knowledge or Practical Experience?

Which is more important in life, knowledge from the books you read, or personal experience you gain in reality? The answer may vary from person to person. But in my opinion, they are of the same importance.

Experience is priceless for it helps one deal with the problems with ease and confidence. Experience, however, is limited in terms of time and space. For one thing, it is impossible for anyone to experience all the important events. For another, as the speed with which skills are *obsolete*② and new problems *crop up*③ is unprecedented because of the fast development of society, experience is far less adequate.

One way to *compensate for*④ it is to read books. Books of various kinds can bring us almost unlimited additional experience. To be sure, it's secondhand experience. But it is the ideal supplement to our own limited experience. Few of us can travel around the world, or live long beyond one hundred years, but all of us can live many lives by reading books.

Both book knowledge and personal experience are essential. While experience makes one more resourceful, book knowledge

---

① 粗俗的
② 过时的,陈旧的
③ 突然出现
④ 补偿,弥补

makes one more learned.

(4) Should Students Be Skeptical about What's Taught?

Most Chinese students are used to believing that teachers are truth-holders in class and their authority is unquestionable. They are afraid of voicing their own opinions, *let alone*① defying the authority of teachers.

As for me, skepticism is a valuable spirit in academic life. For one thing, teachers, as human beings, are not perfect and do make mistakes. So unquestioning acceptance does great harm. For another, when doubting what is taught, students will be eager to seek the truth, either by *resorting to*② reference books or by turning to teachers for further arguments. Undoubtedly, students will benefit greatly from the truth-seeking process. What's more, when they have fun in learning, their interest in what is taught will grow and interest is the best teacher.

Therefore, students should be encouraged to adopt a *skeptical*③ attitude in class or, in other words, we must learn *with an analytical and critical eye*④, not blindly. Only by *challenging*⑤ the authority and generating their own ideas can students develop their creativity and gain academic independence.

(5) Good Study Habits

Good study habits are based on two things: a mature mental attitude and appropriate physical techniques.

---

① 更不用提,更别说
② 求助,诉诸
③ 怀疑的
④ 以分析批判的眼光
⑤ 质疑

Required courses provide general knowledge expected of every college graduate. Those who neglect these courses are limiting their intellectual growth. Students should spend about forty-five or more hours a week studying them.

Full concentration is essential. While studying, many students just inattentively run their eyes over a page between frequent distractions from the radio and conversations. Five hours of this kind of study are worth less than an hour of uninterrupted concentration.

Students should not delay course *assignments*① to the moment just before an examination. Students with poor study habits often *frantically*② do all their reviewing just in a day or two. The result usually is that they come to the examination not only exhausted but also confused by a mass of unrelated facts. They could have avoided all this by keeping up with their assignments, making orderly notes, and reviewing their notes regularly. Students with good study habits can obtain a lot more in their *scholastic achievements*③ than those without.

(6) Self-study

Self-study is far more important than schooling. It runs from cradle to tomb; it covers a much wider range; it *caters* more directly *to*④ our needs. We learn in every possible way, and we also discover new ways for ourselves.

The discovery of new knowledge is most essential to mankind because it carries society forward. And it is mainly self-study that enables us to do this. We may well ask: Who taught Edison to

---

① 指定的(课外)作业
② 发狂似地;狂乱地
③ 学业成绩
④ 适合;满足

make over one thousand inventions? Wasn't it self-study?

  In our times, though educational facilities are much better than those in the past, self-study remains as important as before. Many electronics experts are brilliant examples to us. People who are *in the forefront*① of progress are always those self-taught.

---

  ① 居首；在前面

No.8 Language Learning
语言学习

(1) Writing an Essay

Writing an essay, while easy for a fortunate few, can be *sheer*① *torture*② for others. It involves an *interplay*③ of ideas, a good command of grammar and vocabulary, and some knowledge of writing skills.

One must have some ideas to write about. Without relevant ideas, the essay would be meaningless. A person's rich experience and wide range of knowledge is the source of ideas upon which he must draw while writing.

Given adequate ideas, one needs to write them down by the correct use of grammar and words. An essay full of grammar and spelling mistakes is not readable at all.

Furthermore, one must master certain writing skills, otherwise his pen would be *awkward*④. Writing skills enable one to write an essay with *unity*⑤ and *coherence*⑥. They can also help him *drive his ideas home*⑦ in simple and clear language.

---

① 十足的;全然的
② 苦恼的事
③ 相互影响;相互作用
④ 笨拙的;不熟练的
⑤ (文章)统一性
⑥ 连贯性
⑦ 使人理解、接受

So if one tries to achieve *an easy pen*①, he must develop his writing ability *in terms of*② these three aspects.

(2) Foreign Language Learning

Learning foreign languages is of great significance today. The mastery of foreign languages enables us to communicate with people from other countries, achieve mutual understandings, and further our trade contacts, economic cooperations, and cultural and academic exchanges with other countries. *By means of*③ foreign languages, we can read foreign books, documents and data in original, draw new ideas and fresh thoughts, and introduce advanced science and technology into our country. So foreign languages are playing an important role in our efforts to enlarge China's influence and make greater contribution to mankind.

There is great popular interest in foreign language learning in our country. More and more people start to learn foreign languages. Everywhere we can see people reading aloud English and listening to a tape-recorder. And there are English corners where language learners seize the chance to practise speaking. To satisfy people's needs, many foreign textbooks and references have been introduced into our country. *Equally remarkable are foreign language programmes on the TV screen that attract a large audience.*④

The mastery of a foreign language needs painstaking efforts. One can never have a good command of it overnight. On the

---

① 文笔流畅
② 根据；按照
③ 通过
④ 本句为倒装句。同样引人注目的是电视屏幕上的外语节目,这些节目吸引了为数众多的观众。

contrary, he has to spend enough time and take great pains before he can make real progress. It is not unusual that in the face of difficulties, *a person gets so frustrated as to give in*①. But where there is a will, there is a way. So long as you persevere in your learning and practise hard, you will surely *bring your study to fruition*②.

(3) Gateway to the World

The various traditions of education have always *placed an importance on*③ the learning of other languages. There are many practical reasons that students of any nation should learn foreign languages. The knowledge of one more language has *distinct*④ effects on an indivdual.

One effect of learning a second language is that a person can experience at *frist hand*⑤ the great literature of another people. One can experience directly the power and the *subtleties*⑥ of the *original*⑦, which are often lost in translation. One can feel the *flow of the language*⑧, the combinations of sound and word order, all of which combine to bring the work alive — alive as the artists have *intentionally*⑨ planned.

Learning another language *reinforces*⑩ a second effect: the gaining of knowledge about another culture. When one learns a

---

① 一个人受到挫折而放弃
② 你会学有成效
③ 重视
④ 明显的；显而易见的
⑤ 直接地
⑥ 微妙(之处)
⑦ 原著
⑧ 流畅的语言
⑨ 有意地
⑩ 加强

second language, one sees that there are other ways to see how men are related to the environment. Every country has different customs and cultures.

Perhaps the most powerful effect of learning another language is communication. With a second, or third, or fourth language, one can make contact with a fellow human being. Through communication, one see that the human mind, whether of the east or the west, is basically similar.

Many people study foreign languages because of *school requirements*①. Others learn a second language because of more practical reasons. *Regardless of*② the reasons for acquiring another language, however, the effects are *considerable*③. Since greater understanding of other cultures and better communication with other peoples can promote world peace, learning at least one more language will certainly contribute a part to the promotion.

(4) Successful Language Learners

Some people seem to have a *knack*④ in learning languages. They can pick up new vocabulary, master rules of grammar, and learn to write in the new language more quickly than others. Perhaps if we take a close look at these successful language learners, we may discover a few techniques which make language learning easier for them.

First of all, successful language learners are independent learners. Instead of waiting for the teacher to explain, they try to find the patterns and the rules for themselves. They are good guessers who look for clues and form their own conclusions.

---

① 学校的规定、要求
② 不管
③ 相当大的或多的
④ 诀窍；技巧

When they guess wrong, they guess again. They try to learn from their mistakes.

Successful language learning is active learning. Therefore, successful learners do not wait for a chance to use the language; they look for such a chance. They are not afraid to repeat what they hear or to say strange things; they are willing to make mistakes and try again. It is more important for them to think in the language than to know the meaning for every word.

Finally, successful language learners are learners *with a purpose*①. They want to learn the language because they are interested in the language and the people who speak it. It is necessary for them to learn the language in order to communicate with these people and to learn from them.

What kind of language learner are you? If you are successful, you have probably been learning independently, actively, and purposefully. On the other hand, if your language learning has been *less than*② successful, you *might as well*③ try some of the techniques *outlined above*④.

(5) Learning English at College

Learning English at a college is different from learning English at a middle school. In a middle school, we learn English mainly for college entrance examination, while the purpose of learning English at a college is quite different. We study a foreign language to improve our ability to work well in the future and, especially to communicate with foreigners.

Having been studying in college for nearly two years, I have

---

① 具有(明确)目的的
② 不那么
③ 不妨
④ 以上概述的

come to some conclusion① about how to learn English well. Firstly, you should try your best to enlarge your vocabulary, only in this way can you read more and understand others better. Secondly, listening and speaking *plays important roles*② in learning English. While talking with foreigners, if you can't understand them, how can you express your ideas? And the last point is that you should improve your English whenever you can.

However, there is still a long way to go to learn English well. As people usually say, "There is no end in learning." There are so many methods to learn English. So long as you keep studying, you will surely make progress.

(6) Advantages and Disadvantages of *Electronic Dictionary*③

The discussion about electronic dictionaries has never stopped in the past few years. Let's have a look at advantages and disadvantages before drawing the final conclusion.

The biggest advantage of an electronic dictionary is its convenience. Whenever you meet new words or expressions, you can know the meaning quickly. What's more, with the development of science and technology, electronic dictionaries are becoming more and more advanced: they can pronounce the words clearly, provide sample sentences to illustrate word usage and store difficult words for special memorization. Last but by no means the least, electronic dictionaries are becoming cheaper and cheaper, and more and more students can afford them.

However, the negative effects are also obvious. To begin with, some students rely too much on the electronic

---

① 得出一些结论
② 起很重要的作用
③ 电子词典

dictionary — they can hardly fix in mind the new words and expressions. In the second place, some explanations are neither complete nor accurate, which are quite misleading. Finally, new technical inventions do not necessarily lead to progress in learning. Diligence is always the decisive factor, because *"there is no royal road to learning①"*.

Up until now, we can see it clearly that electronic dictionary is neither beneficial nor harmful in itself. The key lies in the user — so long as we can make proper use of it, it can be most helpful study aid to us in many respects.

(7) How I Overcome Difficulties in Learning English

Like any other English learner, I met a lot of difficulties in learning English. The learning process was one of the most difficult yet most rewarding experiences of my life. Although at times, learning English was frustrating, it was well worth the effort.

First, I found it difficult to understand what I read because most English words have more than one meaning. Besides, I found it difficult to write in *idiomatic②* English or put Chinese into idiomatic English. Finally, I could not express myself because I had no opportunity to communicate with English speakers. Although I often read aloud, this didn't prove to be an effective way to improve my spoken English.

But I didn't lose heart in removing these obstacles. I tackled English vocabulary in two ways. First, I tried to understand and memorize the specific meaning of a word that appeared in the context. Second, I enlarged my vocabulary by breaking them up

---

① 学无坦途
② 地道的

into roots or *affixes*①. To overcome Chinese English, I tried to think in English directly. Although I didn't have any opportunity to communicate with native speakers, I tried to improve my spoken English by listening to the English broadcast and writing English compositions.

These experiences turned out to be effective. I am now feeling very confident in myself while sitting here for the CET-6 and I am even sure I will pass it with excellent marks and I am prepared to enter my name for the CET Spoken English.

(8) *Worldwide Fervor in Learning Chinese*②

It is reported that currently 25 million people in the countries other than China are learning Chinese language and culture. In the United States alone, over 80 universities offer programs in Chinese. People are becoming more and more interested in Chinese language and culture. There is every indication that a worldwide fervor in learning Chinese is rising.

Chinese is a language used by people of all ethnic groups of China and is one of the official and working languages in United Nations. It is also among the world's most highly developed languages with the longest history, a recorded history of at least 6,000 years. Whether in the past or at present, the Chinese language has had great influence both at home and abroad and occupied a prominent position.

The current worldwide interest in learning Chinese is *attributable*③ to the long history of the Chinese nation, its glorious and magnificent culture and its tremendous contribution

---

① 词缀
② 世界兴起"汉语热"
③ 可归因于

to human progress. More importantly, as China's overall national strength has grown in the course of reform and opening-up over the last three decades, more and more countries, international organizations and people come into contact with China and take interest in Chinese culture. For them, learning the Chinese language has become the only road to a profound understanding of China.

(9) The Use of Dictionary in Language Learning

The dictionary is a living teacher. Whenever you come across an unfamiliar word, you can consult it and get a clear definition. Every student, whether attending school or studying by himself at home, is likely to have one at hand. Being convenient, inexpensive and full of information, the dictionary is indeed a good study aid.

The constant use of various dictionaries will develop your skill. The more you use them, the more familiar you will become with them. Sooner or later, you will be so skilled in using dictionaries that, for an unfamiliar word, you can find the page, *scan*[①] the *entry*[②] and *locate*[③] the exact information within a few seconds.

But as a language student, you should not become too much *attached to*[④] dictionaries. Basic language skills do not come from dictionaries, but from your practice. Only through sufficient practice in listening, speaking, reading, and writing can you master the language.

---

① 粗略地看;浏览
② 条目;词条
③ 找出
④ 使依附于

(10) On Developing Speaking Ability

In teaching a foreign language, most of the Chinese instructors *give priority to*[①] the development of reading skills. They tend to think that speaking practice is of no use because most Chinese students have few opportunities to talk with foreigners. That is the reason why the importance of speaking has not been understood and emphasized properly.

In fact, speaking is one of the most important means of communication. Much of our information goes to other people through speaking. Practically, we are often faced with situations where a great deal depends on our ability to speak. *In such cases*[②] if we can't make ourselves understood in a foreign language, *communication will be cut short*[③]. Therefore, it is extremely important to develop speaking skills in learning a foreign language.

In my opinion, one can't learn a foreign language well without practicing speaking. Hence, we need to give serious attention to the development of speaking ability in language study.

---

① 以……为先
② 在这样的情况下
③ 交流就会短路

No.9 Language and Communication
语言与交流

(1) Means of Communication

One of the first things we think about when we hear the word "communication" is language. There are thousands of languages spoken around the world today. In fact, *linguists*① say that there may be as many as 10,000.

Speaking with others is an important means of communication, but we can also communicate without using words, that is, by *nonverbal communication*②. Nonverbal communication includes voice note, eye movement, facial expression, and body movements, such as gestures and changes in body position. But many people do not realize that everyone uses nonverbal communication. Sometimes, we "say" more with our faces and gestures than we do with our voices.

Books, magazines, newspapers, radio, television, and telephone are other means of communication. Today we can also communicate over long distance with the help of communications satellites. Some scientists say that soon machines will be developed for sending messages through the earth. The technology necessary to build these machines is very *complex*③. But the language we speak every day is much more complex than

---

① 语言学家
② 非语言交际；无需用语言来表达的交流
③ 复杂的

the most modern communications technology.

(2) The Gift of Conversation

Good conversation opens the door to friendship. It is the quickest way to make a friend. You can make a new friend with a bright smile and a warm handshake, but it takes good conversation to keep him.

One suggestion is to let the other person talk about himself. It is easy to begin a conversation by asking what sports a person likes, what TV program he enjoys watching, or what he thinks about this or that. If you are truly interested in knowing him and being his friend, then your interest will be sincere and honest.

Suppose you are in America. If you don't talk, nobody will know how nice you are, so don't let shyness keep you silent. You may *be very conscious of*① not being able to speak English well or not wearing nice clothes. Things like that make you self-conscious. Consequently, you find *words catch in your throat*②. All of this is caused by the *spotlight*③ you put on yourself. But if you put the spotlight on the other fellow or on the situation as a whole, you will forget yourself and not feel nervous any more.

Another suggestion is to enjoy listening to other people's talking. A good listener is *popular*④. People like his company. You should listen attentively while another person is talking. You may respond with a smile or something interesting on your own to let him know you are interested in what he is talking about. This well-balanced give-and-take makes conversation lots of fun.

These simple rules work for everybody. If you make them an

---

① 此处指"很在意……"
② 此处指"有话说不出来,似乎被卡在了喉咙里"
③ 大家的注意
④ 受众人喜爱的,受欢迎的

everyday habit, you can carry interesting conversations and make a large circle of friends.

(3) The Charm of the Chinese Language

Extensive research has revealed that Chinese possesses many advantages over other languages. Written Chinese is based on a set of *ideogram characters*①. From a simple word one may obtain a wealth of information about its hidden meaning, *evolution history*②, and related phrases. Historians can *decipher*③ the damaged ancient characters carved on ox bones, but no such achievement could be obtained with Latin-based languages. To express a given idea, the Chinese version is always the shortest, the most accurate, and the most effective.

Moreover, Chinese kids learn Chinese by memorizing patterns or funny pictures which stimulate curiosity and imagination. It is well recognized that human brains work well with patterns and that *pattern recognition*④ in turn promotes brain development. What's more, Chinese is also easy to learn. Many foreigners speak Chinese fluently after a few years of learning. Recently, several word processing programs have been successfully developed for the Chinese language and turned out to be better than those designed for English.

Chinese is *the crystallization of the splendid culture*⑤ developed continuously for over 5,000 years. Many treasures remain to be explored. As China grows stronger, more and more foreigners will learn Chinese and share the invaluable treasure.

① 表意文字
② 演变历史
③ 辨认
④ 图案辨认
⑤ 灿烂文化的结晶

(4) **Advantages of Written Communication**

Written communication has advantages. First, it is *permanent*①. Most members of organizations file all *correspondence*②, which means record of your message exists. Listeners might forget three of the five reasons outlined in your oral presentation, but with a written document they have a record of your ideas.

Written records also prevent *distortion*③ of your ideas. A letter or *memo*④ can guarantee that what you say is what they will receive. Then, if someone makes an unfair *accusation*⑤, a record of your message is available: "Sure I told you about the problem. Here's a copy of my March 15 memo to you."

Written messages also have the advantage of being most easily planned in advance. You can take all the time you want to shape their content and tone. You can test out several versions on sample audiences to predict the response of your real audience, and you can *make modifications*⑥ until you get the desired result.

(5) **Advantages of Oral Communication**

The biggest advantage of oral communication — both face-to-face and by telephone — is its speed. Once you have made contact with your receiver, the message is *conveyed*⑦ instantly. This

---

① 此处指"可长期保存而不被改变的"
② 信件;函件
③ 曲解;歪曲
④ 备忘录
⑤ 指责;控告
⑥ 进行修改或润饰
⑦ 传递

speed is especially valuble when time is of the essence. Should a customer's check be approved? Are the parts you desperately need available? An oral response can answer questions like these *in a timely manner*①.

A second advantage of oral communication is the instant feedback it provides. Do your listeners have any questions? Did you forget to say anything? A conversation can let you know. Nonverbal reactions are just as *revealing*② as the words your receiver speaks. Does the other person look bored? Do your remarks get enthusiastic nods and smiles or frowns and head shaking? You can even get valuable feedback in telephone conversations from the speaker's tone of voice.

Finally, oral communication gives you control of the situation — far more than you have with written messages. Your receivers might briefly scan the letter you worked so hard on and *toss it aside*③. Even worse, they might not read it at all. In a conversation, however, the audience has to, at least, pretend to pay attention. Your message ought to be clear and effective enough to be well received.

(6) Key Differences in the Communication Patterns of Men and Women

*Anthropologists*④ have summarized three key differences in the communication patterns of men and women:

The first difference is in asking questions. In conversations, women see questions as a way to maintain a conversation, while men view them as requests for information. Men are, therefore,

---

① 及时地
② 此处指"表达真情的"或"反映问题的"
③ 扔、丢在一边
④ 人类学家

less likely to ask personal questions. They think, if she wants to tell me something, she'll tell me. A woman thinks, if I don't ask, he'll think I don't care. For men, questions may represent *meddling*①, while for women, they express *intimacy and caring*②.

The second difference is in interrupting the other person. Men are more likely to make negative comments than women. Women are often troubled by these, hearing them as interruptions, to which they may respond with *"silent protest"*③. While women see negative comments as an attack, men view them simply as a form of conversation.

The third difference lies in deciding what's important. Women discuss problems with one another, share experiences, and *offer reassurances*④. Men tend to hear women who discuss problems with them as requesting solutions, rather than simply *looking for a sympathetic ear*⑤.

Learning to recognize these differences can *provide a safeguard against*⑥ misunderstanding between men and women.

(7) Face-to-face Communication

There are many different ways of communications, such as letters, emails, or telephone calls. However, face-to-face communication still remains the most efficient way of communication between people.

Firstly, in face-to-face communication we can get direct

---

① 干预;管闲事
② 亲密关系和关心
③ 此处指"以沉默来表示反对或抗议"
④ 消除恐惧;恢复信心
⑤ 寻求同情和怜悯
⑥ 此处指"防止"

response from the other party. When we talk with our friends, we can get feedback immediately from their verbal response, body language and facial expressions. Based on these responses, we can know how to carry on the conversation, and change the direction or finish the conversation if necessary. Sometimes, speaking words and body languages may not mean the same thing. Although we can hear words from a telephone conversation from our friends but we do not always know if they really mean it. Thus, face-to-face communication is more *perceptible*[①] and can help us understand a speaker's true feeling better than other ways of communication.

Secondly, face-to-face communication is the most helpful way to express ourselves. In communication, it is just not enough for us to say the words; we need eye contact, body language to express our feelings. Sometimes we are so happy or angry that we are out of words. In these cases, there is nothing more efficient than a big hug or turn our face to another side.

In brief, face-to-face communication is a very important way for us. It is good for better understanding. It is more visible, direct and more effective than any other ways.

---

① 易感知的

No.10 Examination 考试

(1) On Examinations

In our system of education today, examinations are a common feature. Our present education system has often been criticized as too *examination-oriented*①. However, one must remember that in offices and other areas of work, examinations still feature clearly. So it therefore appears that examinations whether considered good or bad would stay for a while as a test of human knowledge.

Examinations are meant to test the intellect of a person — how much he knows or how much he has learnt from a particular course. It is designed to make students study diligently, which should be their immediate mission in life. In our competitive world of today, examinations have a highly selecting or *filtering*② role. In the university, students have to pass annual examinations before they are allowed to continue, or study a harder *syllabus*③. Moreover, for entrance into a university, preuniversity examination results would provide a guide as to whether a student has the minimum qualifications necessary.

In offices, whether government or private ones, examination

---

① 以应试为主导的
② 筛选，过滤
③ 教学大纲

results show clearly whether a person is fit for promotion. The results indicate how much he knows about the work.

In all these cases, examinations *inculcate*① a spirit of hard work and competition. Students or office workers can refresh their mind again and again on what they have learnt. This maintains a certain individual and overall standard of knowledge.

(2) Examination

There are many arguments about the advantages and disadvantages of examination. Some people think examination is the only way to test how much examinees have mastered what they have studied and the only measurement for examiners to select the persons they need. On the other hand, some object that examination can't measure how well the students have really studied. They say it can do nothing but burden the students.

As for me, I take both examinees and examiners into account. The examination can show what and how much the examinees have mastered. The results of examinations are just like mirrors for both examiners and examinees. Through examination the examiners can check their work and become aware of which aspects they have not done well, so that they'll make much improvement in their work. *As far as examinees are concerned*②, they can not only know how well they have studied but also find out what they still don't know or what they haven't mastered well. Thus they will be inspired to greater efforts to improve their studying method so as to make greater progress. Of course, too many examinations are burdens to both examiners and examinees.

In summary, the examination does more good than harm for

---

① 灌输
② 就被考者、考生而言

both examiners and examinees. We must take a positive attitude towards examination. We should take full advantage of it and avoid its disadvantages.

(3) Some Disadvantages of Examination

We might *marvel at*① the progress made in every field of study, but the methods of testing a person's knowledge and ability remain as old as ever. Examinations may be a good way of testing memory and cleverness of working rapidly under pressure. They can, however, tell you little about a person's ability.

Very often, examinations are nothing but anxiety makers, because they tend to be considered as marks of success and failure. Your whole future may be decided on one *fateful*② day, when nobody would care whether you were ill or not. What's more, teachers' judgements may, sometimes, be unfair, for they may get tired and make mistakes.

In short, examinations motivate passive memorizing instead of creative thinking. We are looking forward to a simpler but more effective way of judging a person's true ability.

(4) The Negative Sides of Closed-book Exams

As a college senior, I *went through*③ numerous closed-book exams, and survived. But I still feel that these exams, like a slave owner's whip, drive students crazy.

We often emphasize the strengths of these exams but overlook their weaknesses. To begin with, these exams inevitably

---

① 惊叹
② 与命运有关的；重大的
③ 经历

result in *a test-oriented force-feeding teaching method*①, which seriously hinder the development of students' creativity. To get better scores, students *are tied to*② homework and problems. Consequently, many students have poor health. Moreover, they don't have time to learn the practical things they need most. What is worse, exams are terrible even to the well-prepared. Many students fail in important exams just because of being too nervous. The great pressure and anxiety often *adversely*③ affect the final score and a dumb mistake may ruin everything. *Ironically*④, quite a few top college graduates with almost perfect scores often fail in their careers.

There are better alternatives available: for instance, open book exams, term paper writing, research projects. These alternatives are likely to encourage students to *have initiative in*⑤ *giving full play*⑥ to their talents. As students, we must not *be too fussy about*⑦ scores. After all, we are not the slaves of books.

(5) Is the Test of Spoken English Necessary?

A test of spoken English will be included as an *optional*⑧ component of the College English Test. Many people think that it is definitely necessary to have spoken English test because spoken English is one of the indispensable qualities of a learner's overall English proficiency. A test of spoken English will effectively motivate an English learner in his/her training in spoken English.

---

① 此处意为"应试型、填鸭式的教学方法"
② 此处指"忙于做;埋头做"
③ 不利地
④ 令人哭笑不得地
⑤ 有积极性;主动去做……
⑥ 充分发挥
⑦ 此处指"重视"
⑧ 可选择的;非强迫的

But there are some people who have different opinions on this issue. They argue that they learn English mostly to obtain useful written information from English sources, and thus they do not need to spend much time on spoken English. In addition, they think that the test of spoken English cannot be as fair as the written test since every examiner could have his/her own standards of evaluation as to pronunciation, intonation, and fluency.

As for my opinion on this subject, I think the test of spoken English is necessary as the purpose of a language is to communicate. And now China has entered WTO. We have more and more chances to speak with foreigners. So the test of spoken English can be *a stimulus*① for us to learn to speak the language.

(6) About Examinations

There are two kinds of examinations: objective and subjective. Questions in an objective test, like the multiple-choice test, have only one right answer for each. A subjective test, like an essay exam, has many possible responses.

Here are some *hints*② on taking an examination. First look through the test to see how long it is, what kind of questions there are, and which subjects are included. Then go back to the beginning and answer the questions in order. If you do not work in this way, you may forget to answer some important questions. When you come across a question which is very hard for you, go on to something you can answer easily, then come back to the hard questions. And, finally, before you hand in your paper, check your work. You may find some errors which you can correct before the teacher marks your paper.

---

① 鼓励因素;促进因素
② 提示

When the teacher gives you your score on the exam, compare your score with the class *average*①. You did well if you are in the top third of your class. Be realistic about your grades. You have to face the fact that some exams are harder than others and that you may not always get high marks. It is also necessary for you to keep a record of your mistakes. The important thing is that you do not repeat your mistakes. Always try not to make new mistakes.

(7) The Night Before Examination

The clock struck eleven at night. The whole house was quiet. Everyone was in bed except me. Under the strong light, I looked gloomily before a huge pile of disgusting stuff — books.

I was going to have my examination the next day. "When can I go to bed?" I asked myself. I did not answer. In fact, I dared not.

The clock struck 12. "Oh, dear!" I cried. "Ten more books to read before I can go to bed!" We students are the most *wretched*② creatures in the world. Dad does not agree with me on this. He did not have to work so hard when he was a boy.

The clock struck one. I was quite desperated. I forgot all I had learnt. "Who wrote David Copperfield?" I asked myself. I scratched my head. For a moment, I could not answer.

The clock struck two. I was too tired to go on. I did the only thing I could — I prayed. "Our Father who are in Heaven have mercy on a sinner. Please let me pass my exam tomorrow. I shall be grateful to you all my life, and I promise you I will work hard afterwards. Amen."

I yawned. My eyes were heavy, so heavy that I could hardly open them. A few minutes later, with my head on the desk, I fell asleep.

---

① 平均数;平均分
② 可怜的

No.11 Way to Success
成功之路

(1) *Pride Goes before a Fall*[①]

"Pride goes before a fall" is a well-known proverb which all of us have been familiar with. I fully agree to it and its implication, in my mind, can be justified in three respects.

First, if you are proud of your success, you may stop working hard and no longer make progress. In this case you will probably fail the next time. Second, *modesty is the color of virtue*[②], which, in my mind, is vital to their success. Third, looking at the matter from another perspective, we will find that our achievement is nothing to be proud of when compared to the fantastic dream in our heart — if we want to realize our life's ultimate goal, we can never stop pursuing.

Living in an age when most people are hard working, modesty seems more than necessary. As the modern competition becomes more and more fierce, we should realize the importance of modesty. If we can be modest all the time, we can make progress constantly, and life will be more meaningful.

(2) No Pains, No Gains

The well-known proverb "No Pains, no gains" has long been

---

① 骄傲在前,失败在后
② 谦虚是有德行的表现

accepted by all of us. It tells us that we have to make strenuous efforts whenever we want to be successful in a certain field, and we can never wait for gains without pains.

Let's take English study for an example, if we want to improve our listening ability, we have to keep on listening to different materials and make records from time to time. It is also true with spoken English. Listening to teachers attentively in class and reading books are far from enough — you should practice talking with anybody who knows English on all possible occasions.

Another good case in point is *acrobatics*①. Nobody is born a good acrobat, and one can only become a skilled one after countless failures. All of us feel excited when they win grand prizes in international competitions, but who knows how many hardships they have endured?

From the examples given above, we may have a better understanding of the proverb "No pains, no gains." So why not try our best to learn our specialty well? I am sure we will become experienced and proficient if we keep on making painstaking efforts.

(3) Is Failure a Bad Thing?

Failure is what often happens. It is everywhere in our life. Students may fail in exams, scientists may fail in their research work, and athletes may fail in competitions.

Although failure happens to everyone, attitudes towards failure are various. Some people don't think their failure is a very important thing at all. So they pay no attention to it. As a result, they will have the same failure later. Some people think

---

① 杂技

themselves are fools and lose their hearts in everything after they get a failure. Consequently, they spend their time and energy on useless things and they may really be fools as they have thought.

Other people are quite different from the two kinds of people mentioned above. Instead of being distressed and lost, they draw a lesson from every failure and become more experienced. Just as a Chinese proverb says: *a fall into the pit, a gain into your wit*[①]. After hard work, they will be successful in the end. It is said that failure is the mother of success. Success will be gained after times of failures so long as we are good at drawing lessons from our failures.

In my opinion, failure is not a bad thing; the really bad thing is taking a failure as failure or even feel depressed after failure.

(4) Competition

Competition makes people original and creative. It is very necessary to compete if human society wants to advance. (Even animals compete for survival.) Without it, we would become lazy and nobody would take any responsibility. When three monks live together, there will be no drinking water. This Chinese proverb vividly describes why China's productivity was so low before Mr. Deng came to power. At that time, we had the so-called planned economy. There was no competition at all. So neither farmers nor workers worked hard. China was on the edge of collapse.

Competition can stimulate people to try their best to do anything. For example, in 100-meter race, each sportsman runs as quickly as possible, trying to win the champion. The same things happen in our society and in our daily life. If a company wants to surpass others, it must compete with them. It must

---

① 吃一堑,长一智

raise its efficiency. All the companies doing this will no doubt benefit the whole society and the whole human race.

Being a student, I must compete with other students in our studies. I must study hard in all the fields so that I can be a useful man when I enter the society after graduation.

(5) How to Achieve Success

Some people say the key to success is good luck, while others claim it is hard work that really counts. There is no doubt that successful people do take the advantage of opportunities. But if they do not work hard, they can only wait to see opportunities pass by. So in my opinion, *diligence*[①], *devotion*[②] and *perseverance*[③] are three fundamental factors in success.

Diligence is the first key to success, which simply means to work persistently without any waste of time. Diligence makes a fool wise and a poor rich. If we work hard now we could expect a success later on. And if we don't, our future life will probably be *gloomy*[④].

Devotion, which means the concentration of our mind on doing things, is another key factor to success. Only when we focus our minds on the job can we do it well.

Perseverance is also *indispensable*[⑤] for success, without which we can hardly overcome the difficulties and will have nothing accomplished.

To conclude, success is not something easy to achieve, and it is based on diligence, devotion and perseverance. Just as the

---

① 勤奋
② 投入,热爱
③ 坚持,毅力,恒心
④ 黑暗的,阴沉的
⑤ 不可或缺的

famous sayings go, "No pains, no gains," and "Where there is a will, there is a way."

(6) Opportunity or Determination

It is an *undeniable*① fact that opportunity is indispensable to one's success; however, the way to success is like a zigzag path to the mountain peak. Faced with *frustrations*② and setbacks, only those who have a *dogged*③ determination can stick to their cause to the end and *stand a chance*④ of success.

Admittedly, opportunity is vital to one's success. Without opportunities, one can hardly display his talents, competence and abilities. Without opportunities, one can seldom get access to further education to arm himself with the latest knowledge in his field.

However, "Opportunity knocks but once", and it promptly slips away when people are frustrated by hardships. Moreover, opportunities seem to favor those who have *inflexible*⑤ determination and resolute perseverance. Whether one is able to utilize every opportunity well or not depends largely on the attitude he is to adopt towards difficulties or even failures.

In a word, determination is the key to success. With a strong determination, one can not only bring his opportunities into full play, but conquer whatever hardships or dangers he may face.

① 不可否认的
② 挫折
③ 顽强的
④ 有机会
⑤ 不屈不挠的

(7) Opportunity and Success

Opportunities do not come often. They come *every once in a while*①. Very often, they come quietly or go by without being noticed. Therefore, it is advisable that you shall value and treat them with care.

When an opportunity comes, it brings *promise*② but never realizes it *on its own*③. If you mean to achieve something or intend to fulfil one of your ambitions, you must work hard, make efforts and get prepared. Otherwise, you will *take* no *advantage of*④ opportunities when they come to visit you.

The difference between a person who succeeds and one who does not *lies* only *in*⑤ the way each treats opportunities. The successful person always makes much preparation to meet opportunities as they arrive. The less successful person, on the other hand, works little and just waits to see them pass by.

(8) My View on Opportunity

There is no *consensus*⑥ of opinions among people as to the view of opportunity. Some people suggest that opportunities are rare and only the luckiest persons can obtain them, while some other people argue that *in a sense*⑦ everyone has opportunity from time to time.

---

① 偶而;间或
② 希望;可能
③ 自动地;独自地
④ 利用
⑤ 在于
⑥ (意见等的)一致
⑦ 在一定意义上

As far as I am concerned①, I agree with the latter opinion *to some extent*②. I think that various kinds of opportunities are around us all the time. However, the opportunities will not *run into*③ you voluntarily. You must try your best to find them and make full use of them. For example, when I was studying in high school there was a national chemistry competition. Most of my classmates thought that we had *virtually*④ no *chance*⑤ of winning the competition since we were studying in high school. But I felt that it was a good chance and I must grasp it. So I prepared for it thoroughly and finally I won the first prize.

In conclusion. I believe that opportunities are *abundant*⑥ in our society and everyone is equal for them. We can acquire them only if we are prepared and qualified, just as a proverb says, "*Opportunities are only for the prepared minds.*"⑦

(9) On Work Efficiency

More and more people have become aware of the significance of *work efficiency*⑧. What does work efficiency mean? First of all, it means working without any waste of time. A person with efficiency can produce more things in less time. In addition, work efficiency is closely linked with better quality of work results.

Many people are interested in improving their work efficiency because it can bring a lot of benefits both to an individual and to the society.

---

① 就我而言
② 在某种程度上
③ 跑进
④ 实际上
⑤ 可能性
⑥ 充分的
⑦ "机遇属于有准备的人"
⑧ 工作效率

The most obvious benefit of work efficiency is that a person can use the time saved to do a lot of other valuable things. For example, a student who studies with high efficiency can win time to read more books and to be engaged in more activities. Another benefit is that a person who works efficiently can have more leisure time to enjoy life. He can do whatever he likes to do in his leisure time, such as listening to music, going to movies, shopping, and touring.

High efficiency in work will undoubtedly lead to the great increase of output and the improvement of the quality of products, which will, *in turn*①, *contribute to*② the development and the *prosperity*③ of the society.

(10) The Importance of Confidence

Whatever one does, one should do it with confidence. If one had no confidence, there is little possibility that one would ever achieve anything. This truth seems to be *self-evident*④, especially for those who are faced with *drawbacks*⑤ or hardships. For those people, confidence keeps their spirits up whenever times or things are hard for them.

However, in reality we do see a lot of people who complain that their difficulties are too great to overcome. For some, this might be true, but for many others, this only shows that they lack confidence. There are two main reasons why those people often feel frustrated even though they are capable of doing

---

① 反过来
② 起一份作用；有助于
③ 繁荣
④ 不言自明
⑤ 障碍；不利条件

something. First, they do not have a *correct estimate*① of themselves, and second, they overestimate the difficulties.

It is possible to build up confidence in oneself by having the right attitude toward one's own abilities. We should never *underestimate*② our abilities but should believe in the proverb: "Where there is a will, there is a way." Confidence is the *premise*③ for fulfilling a task successfully.

---

① 正确的估计
② 低估
③ 前提条件

No.12 | Make Full Use of Time 爱惜光阴

(1) Time

Time is invaluable as everyone of us *is endowed with*① life only once, and the life span is limited. Time is money. It should be the thing we most *cherish*②. Time passed will never return. That means we can hardly afford wasting time, *indulging in fantasy and living in idleness*③. On the contrary, we should devote our time to a noble cause and live a meaningful life.

To save time means lengthening one's life. To make the best of time, the following points are important: Never delay or postpone to tomorrow what should be done today; make a proper schedule and stick to it; raise the working efficiency so as to achieve the desired result at half cost of time.

We students are *in the prime time of life*④. We must seize the golden hour to master knowledge and develop abilities. Laziness is a thief of time. Time lost in youth cannot *be compensated*⑤ in age when one will *remorse*⑥ for the early meaningless life. So there is no room for idleness. Nor can we

---

① 被赋予……
② 珍惜
③ 沉湎于幻想和无所事事
④ 一生中精力盛时期
⑤ 补偿
⑥ 后悔；悔恨

allow *dilatoriness*① and delay.

(2) Make Full Use of Time

Nowadays, there are a few students who waste time *casually*②. Some of them pass much of their time in front of telescreen; others *while the time away*③ on cards and the like; still others kill time by eating, drinking and *making merry*④, and so on. *At* these we must *let out a mighty roar*⑤. Stop wasting time, lads!

Mind you, time is the most precious thing in the world; just as the saying goes: "Time is money." Furthermore, time flies; and as soon as it is gone, it never returns. How long *on earth*⑥ can one's life be? It will end before you know. Therefore, we must value time and make full use of it to do something usefull.

How do you make full use of time? First, *seize* it *firmly*⑦. In this respect, we should do as Lu Xun did, who *utilized*⑧ the time when others had coffee. We should also follow the example of Lei Feng, who displayed the spirit of the nail — snatching every available minute.

Second, use time scientifically. Make a list of what to do in your mind, and then *make a rational disposition of*⑨ a timetable. Of course, we should *strike a proper balance between work and*

---

① 拖延；迟缓
② 随便地
③ 消磨时间
④ 尽情欢乐；作乐
⑤ 对……大喊一声。本句中 at 提前以强调宾语。
⑥ 究竟；到底
⑦ 牢牢地抓住
⑧ 利用
⑨ 合理安排……

rest① to raise our working efficiency.

(3) Youth

Youth is a precious gift and a golden time in our life. It will not last forever. When we are young, we are strong and healthy. Learning comes easily. It is the time for us to prepare ourselves to become responsible citizens.

Youth comes only once in a lifetime. It is important that we do not waste those years in idleness and dissolute living. Youth is also the time when our memories are best. We are better able to learn more during this time than when we are older. Since learning is easy, the young person should try his hardest to learn as much as he or she can. The knowledge will be useful in later years. During our younger years, we have the *enthusiasm*② and the *vitality*③ to *set high goals*④ for ourselves. We also try to overcome obstacles which may be placed *in our way*⑤ in order to achieve *a large measure*⑥ of success in whatever we *set out*⑦ to do.

If we realize how precious youth is, we will be fulfilled when we are young as well as when we are older. If we waste our youth, we will spend the rest of our lives wishing we were young again.

---

① 劳逸结合
② 热情
③ 活力
④ 制定崇高的目标
⑤ 妨碍
⑥ 大部分
⑦ 打算

(4) Spending Our Leisure to the Best Advantage

Most of us are apt to feel that it is difficult to spend our leisure properly. When we are busy with one thing or another, we *are* usually wholly *occupied with*① it, thinking of nothing else. When we are free or on holiday, we often feel bored and do not know what to do.

Actually, having this feeling is quite natural since, in our daily life, we do things more or less *in accordance with*② an unwritten *daily routine*③ in our mind. For example, a student goes to school in the morning, takes lunch at noon, goes home in the evening and does homework at night. Gradually we get used to the *regular procedure*④ in our mind. And once we have holidays we need not carry out this routine. So we are at a loss what to do.

Then, how should we spend our free time? Here are some suggestions which may be of some help to you. If you are an active person, you can go on a picnic or play some ball games. If you are not so active and like to stay at home, you may turn on the radio to enjoy the light music or read a few *best-sellers*⑤ instead. You can also visit different sorts of exhibitions and attend all kinds of lectures when you are free. After having relaxed with such activities, you will feel much happier and more energetic, and you will be able to study and work still more efficiently.

---

① 使忙碌；使从事……
② 与……一致；按照
③ 惯例；日常程序
④ 有规律的程序或做法
⑤ 畅销书

(5) The Value of Time

What is life? Life is nothing more than the time we have. To kill time is therefore a form of suicide. We are shocked when we think of death, and we spare no pains, no trouble, and no expense to preserve life. But we are too often indifferent to the loss of an hour or of a day, forgetting that our life is the sum total of the days and of the hours we live. A day or an hour wasted is therefore so much life *forfeited*①. Our life is a brief span measuring some seventy or eighty years in all. But nearly one third of this has to be spent in sleep; some years have to be spent over our meals; some in making journeys on land and voyages by sea; some in merry-making; some in watching over the sick-beds of our nearest and dearest relatives. Now if all these years were to be deducted from the term over which our life extends, we shall find about twenty or thirty years at our disposal for active work. Whoever remembers this can never willingly waste a single moment of his life.

All time is precious, but the time of our childhood and of our youth is more precious than any other portion of our existence. For those are the periods when alone we can acquire knowledge and develop our capacities. If we allow these morning hours of life to slip away, we shall never be able to *recoup*② the loss. Just as money laid out at interest doubles and trebles itself in time, so the precious hours of childhood and youth, if properly used, will yield us incalculable advantages.

---

① 丧失
② 重新获得

No.13 On Books
书籍与读书

(1) *Companionship of Books*[①]

A man may usually be known by the books he reads as well as by the *company*[②] he keeps, for there is a companionship of books as well as of people, and one should always live in the best company, *whether it be of books or of people*[③].

A good book may be among the best of friends. It is the same today as it always was, and it will never change. It is the most patient and cheerful of all companions. It does not *turn its back upon*[④] us *in times of difficulty or distress*[⑤]. It always receives us with the same kindness, *amusing and instructing us in youth, and comforting and consoling us in age.*[⑥]

Books introduce us into the best *society*[⑦]. They bring us into the presence of the greatest minds that have ever lived. We hear what they said and did; we see them as if they were really alive; we sympathize with them, enjoy with them; their experience

---

① 以书为友
② 朋友;常共处的人
③ 无论是人还是书籍
④ 背弃
⑤ 在困难或痛苦的时候
⑥ 在我们年轻时给我们愉悦和教导,在我们年老时给我们以安适和慰藉。
⑦ 社交圈

becomes ours, and we feel as if we were *in a measure*① actors with them in the scenes described.

Men often discover their *liking*② for each other by the love they have each for a book — just as two persons sometimes discover a friend by the admiration which both have for a third. There is a proverb, "*Love me, love my dog.*③" But there is more wisdom in this: "Love me, love my book."

(2) Reading Makes a Full Man

"*Reading makes a full man*"④ is a saying of the famous English philosopher Francis Bacon. It means that anyone who wants to be a full man must keep on reading.

A full man may *be defined as*⑤ one who has a mind filled with ideas, or one who *is stocked with*⑥ knowledge. Certainly school education can fill the young minds with a certain amount of ideas and knowledge. But to think that the ideas and knowledge thus taught make a full man is a mistake. Evidently, no one can say that he is a full man because he is a graduate of a middle school or even a university.

Then can such ideas and knowledge be obtained through experience? Indeed, from experience we get new ideas and knowledge. But to suppose that ideas and knowledge thus acquired make a full man is also a mistake. A carpenter's experience is different from a smith's and a smith's is different from a barber's. Obviously, the statement that experience can

---

① 在一定程度上
② 喜爱
③ 爱屋及乌
④ 读书使人充实
⑤ 定义为……
⑥ 贮备有;备有

make a full man does not *hold water*①, either.

Thus, we see that the real factor by which a full man is made includes not only education and experience, but also reading. By reading scientific books, we *are informed of*② many facts; by reading geography, we know the earth's surface, *forms*③, *physical features*④, etc.; by reading history, we are told of the growth of the nations. It is by reading that we can learn many things without actually seeing or hearing them.

Therefore, no matter how high our education may be or how much experience we may have, we cannot become a full man unless we keep reading.

(3) The Choice of Books

If we make the right choice of books, reading can offer us the greatest pleasure. Some books like interesting novels, for example, are simply for amusement and fun. Novels should have their place in our shelves. When we get tired or weary, it is healthy to read some *fascinating*⑤ stories by great writers.

But to read nothing except books of *fiction*⑥ is just like eating only cakes and sweets and not tasting other nice things. As a matter of fact, as *serious reading*⑦ is to the mind, so is *plain*⑧ food to the body. There are many good books on history, philosophy, travel and science. We must read these kinds of books because they give us not only joy but also education. We

---

① (论点等)站得住脚;说得通
② 对……知晓,了解
③ 结构
④ 地形;地貌特点
⑤ 极具吸引力的;令人着迷的
⑥ 小说
⑦ 严肃读物
⑧ 家常的

can develop a taste for serious reading which will give us more knowledge than novels.

(4) Books for Recreation

Students must keep some books for the recreation of their minds. Some people think that books not used in the classroom are a *hindrance*① to a student's career. This is a wrong idea.

The three main classes of books for recreation are books of biography, of travel, and of fiction.

We should read the biographies of heroes and statesmen. They *stimulate*② our minds to an *industrious*③ and productive career. Worthless biographies should *be discarded*④.

Nothing is so helpful in developing our minds as books of travel, which tell us the customs, politics, and social conditions abroad. Morever, from them we may *gain an insight into*⑤ the geography of another country.

Fiction can enlarge our sympathies and extend our knowledge of mankind. But students are *apt to*⑥ read too much fiction. Care must be taken that the mind is provided with a variety of *intellectual nourishment*⑦.

Men's characters are *revealed*⑧ by the books they read. Books exercise much influence on men's lives.

---

① 障碍;妨碍
② 激励;促进
③ 勤奋的
④ 被抛弃
⑤ 洞悉……;洞察……
⑥ 有……倾向的;易于……的
⑦ 精神食粮
⑧ 揭示

(5) Novel Reading

Besides reading our textbooks, most of us like to spend our leisure reading novels. It is very hard to answer the question: "Is novel reading a waste of time?" The answer may be yes or no. Some people agree that novel reading is a waste of time, for they think that our textbooks are already a heavy burden, and we should not waste our time on those "useless" novels. In my opinion, novel reading is not a waste of time, for we may obtain knowledge which we cannot gain from textbooks. Of course, it depends on the type of the novel we read.

Novels may be classified into four kinds, namely, the romantic, the historic, the ethical, and the artistic. The romantic novel gives us a vivid picture upon the author's imagination about some mysterious things or events, which often arouse our deep interest and curiosity. The historic novel records certain past events. It appeals to our critical mind and enables us to form our own opinions regarding men and events. The ethical novel teaches us some moral lessons. In this kind of novel, the author often writes from the standpoint of an abserver, and pictures some social evils or government corruption so vivid and striking that they often stimulate a reformation. The last or the artistic novel appears to our senst of beauty. It is the highest form of novels.

On the other hand, there are many bad novels. They *advocate*① wrong ideas and *superstitious*② beliefs. There are immoral books which even cause social disease. We waste our time if we read these novels. They act as poison to our minds. What is worse is that we cannot resist those wrong ideas, which

---

① 提倡
② 迷信的

may lead us to do very foolish things.

(6) Advantages of *Marking*① Books

So far as I am concerned, marking books is quite right. To begin with, the *mere*② act of underlining and *making brief marginal notes*③ *keep us alert*④. We cannot glance through the lines of a great book and *come up with*⑤ *a sure grasp*⑥ of what we have read. To absorb the ideas of a great book, we have to *keep wide awake*⑦ while reading. Furthermore, active reading is thinking, and thinking *tends to*⑧ express itself in words. A marked book is a kind of intellectual diary, *so to speak*⑨. Finally, the physical act of writing help fix words and sentences much more firmly in the memory than does an inactive *scanning*⑩. We may be able to preserve the thoughts we have and the thoughts the author expresses only when we let our pencils work along with our eyes.

(7) Reading the Classics

Reading the classics benefits us in many ways. Classics refer to those pieces of literature that have been accepted and recommended by many generations. Their value is universally

---

① 在书上做标记
② 仅仅的
③ 做简短的眉批
④ 使我们保持警醒
⑤ 得出
⑥ 准确的掌握
⑦ 保持头脑清醒
⑧ 倾向于；往往……
⑨ 可以这样说
⑩ 浏览

acknowledged. Unlike those informative newspapers and popular magazines filled with advertisements and articles of low quality, the classics can best evoke people's feeling, urging us to use our brains, and thus, serving as a good means if enjoyment.

Reading the classics is also helpful in language learning. Many classics *outshine*[①] the non-classics in language, style and organization. Classic Chinese is well known for its *conciseness*[②]. The poems and novels are very beautiful and elegant, serving as excellent examples of language use. As for learners of English, reading English classics can be both interesting and instructive.

Moreover, reading the classics is of particular significance to self-cultivation. As a famous saying goes, "A nation without literature is a nation without soul." The reason is that literature, especially those classics, *manifests*[③] people's ability and readiness to express, to think and to act. In the process of reading, we improve our intellect of the universe and sensitivity to beauty. Besides, the *comprehensiveness*[④] of classics makes it possible for us to acquire a vast range of knowledge.

Reading the classics is great for entertainment, language learning, and self-cultivation. The more we read, the more benefits we get. Pull a classic off the shelf for a good read!

(8) The Pleasure of Reading

Though modern times has made it available for people to be informed in many ways, such as listening to the radio, watching TV, and even having access to the Internet, reading books is still a substantial way of acquiring knowledge, because reading books

---

① 胜过，优于
② 简洁，简明
③ 显示，证明
④ 广泛

is the most flexible and consistent way of getting knowledge. People can read as long as they like and as many times as they like.

English philosopher *Francis Bacon*① once said, "*Reading makes a full man.*②" Reading good books can enrich one's mind, broaden one's scope, sharpen one's insight, and develop one's sense of beauty. Through reading good books we can increase our contentment when we are cheerful and lessen our pain when we are sad. In a word, people can derive pleasure, enjoyment, inspiration and encouragement from reading good books.

No reader has ever *run short of*③ good books to read. The pleasures of reading are indeed pleasures. In fact, the word should be changed. The true name is happiness. You can live longest and best and most *rewardingly*④ by attaining the pleasures of reading.

（9）Will E-books Replace Traditional Books?

A new era has come. With the mass production of electronic devices and application of new technologies, mankind has entered an "E" age. Nowadays, we have e-mails, e-tickets, e-tests, and e-books, and consequently, paper-based materials gradually vanish. Nowadays, e-books become extremely popular among youngsters, while traditional ones seem to suffer a great loss of their readers. For some people, electronic and internet based books are convenient and accessible. Environmentalists advocate the benefit of e-books on the ground of forest protection. E-books lovers even assert that traditional books will disappear in the near

---

① 弗朗西斯·培根(1561-1626,英国哲学家,语言大师,提出知识就是力量)
② 读书使人充实
③ 缺少
④ 有益地

future.

I have been a book worm for a long time. For me, reading experience is unique and rewarding. Nothing can be more *thought-provoking*[①] than thumbing through a book bought years ago under a table lamp in a dark night. As to note-taking, scanning and skimming, and portability, traditional books have advantages. Just as the invention of camera didn't put an end to the history of painting, traditional books are, and will still be, an intimate friend of readers.

---

① 令人深思的 发人深省的

No.14 Happiness
幸福观

(1) How to Obtain Happiness

Happiness is something which all men want and everyone seeks for, and yet few find true happiness. Then, how to obtain it? I think true happiness can only be obtained by proper means.

In the first place, true happiness comes from hard work. How happy a student is when he has passed through his examinations successfully, but his happiness is the result of his hard and patient study. Those who are idle and lazy and seek only for momentary pleasures will fail in the long run. Therefore, it is hard work that makes a student successful and happy.

In society, the same principle *holds true*①. It is those who toil and struggle hard, not those who stint their strength, that get the reward of life in the end.

In the second place, happiness comes from frugality. We often see many men spend their money *lavishly*②. They *squander*③ what they have for the satisfaction of their low desires. Consequently, they may find themselves unable to support their life style. As the family cannot get along, it has to suffer the consequences of poverty. Therefore to live a simple and contented

---

① 适用
② 大手大脚地；浪费地
③ 挥霍；浪费

life makes us happy and comfortable.

Thirdly, happiness can also be obtained through *will power*①. From history we learn that a truly great ruler enjoys a peaceful and happy *reign*② by the *exertion*③ of his will power. A *man of wavering mind*④ and *feeble*⑤ determination can accomplish nothing and his moral weakness is a frequent cause of sorrow to him. Will power, therefore, is essential to the obtaining of happiness.

(2) How to Be Happy

Happiness is the most precious thing in life. Without it, a man feels that his ill fate has *taken charge of*⑥ him and the world is utterly dark and dreadful to him. *On that account*⑦ his body grows weak, his work *slackens*⑧, and above all things, he thinks he would rather be dead than living.

"How to be happy, then?" you may ask. Now, this is the very puzzle that we are going to solve. First, do things right *in accordance with*⑨ the moral feelings of your own *conscience*⑩, that is, do to others as you would others do to you. Then you are on the main road of life. Second, pay more attention to your health which is the *root*⑪ of success. A *sound constitution*⑫

---

① 意志力
② 统治
③ 发挥
④ 犹豫不决的人
⑤ 微弱；薄弱
⑥ 掌管；操纵
⑦ 由于这个原因
⑧ 松懈
⑨ 按照，与……一致
⑩ 良心；道德心
⑪ 根基
⑫ 健康的体质或体格

enables you to succeed. Third, worry and sorrow are of no use at all! *In case*① you meet with some hard situation, you must try to overcome it without any hesitation. And last, but not least, adopt an optimistic attitude toward life, for the world is still in the *making*② and you can *have a share*③ in it.

(3) Work and Happiness

Happiness is dependent upon work. Work can make a man whose life is dull happier than a man who has no work at all. Sometimes we complain that we have too much work, but we fail to realize that it's our work that keeps us *alert*④ and growing, and helps us to *maintain our dignity*⑤.

Last year I visited my relatives in the small villages in my hometown. It was apparent that work played a necessary part in their lives. Aunts, uncles, cousins — all rose at dawn and went out into the fields, raking, plowing and planting, sometimes late into the evening. They worked hard and there was always something which needed doing. But on their faces there were such smiles as I had never seen.

It is also the case with us all. Work of any kind offers many rewards. Work is more than a necessity for most human beings. If we have no work to do, spending every day idly, we'll begin to lose interest in everything. Maybe we'll have no *incentive*⑥ for getting out of bed in the morning. Our lives will seem *out of*

---

① 假如
② 形成;发展
③ 有份儿;此处意为"贡献自己的一份力量"
④ 机灵的;活跃的
⑤ 保持尊严
⑥ 动机

focus①.

(4) Wealth and Happiness

Can wealth bring happiness? Different people have different opinions about this. Some people *take it for granted*② that wealth is the source of happiness. Money means everything to these people. But other people think that wealth is the root of all evil. *It can bring one misery.*③

There is no doubt that wealth brings happiness. One can buy modern *conveniences*④, new fashions and entertainments with money, which can make life more comfortable and colourful. But there are exceptions when wealth does not go hand in hand with happiness. If a person is devoted to seeking wealth, he may *go astray*⑤ to make dirty money by illegal means. Wealth may also encourage those *weak-willed*⑥ persons to *be addicted to*⑦ such harmful habits as drugtaking or gambling.

Therefore, whether wealth can bring happiness depends on how one earns money and how he spends it. Moreover, many invaluable things such as devoted friendship, real honour, which is important in one's life, can't be bought with money. Only when wealth is *acquired*⑧ by means of honest labour and spent for the benefit of not only oneself but also his people and country, can it bring happiness.

---

① 焦点没有对准;模糊不清;此处意为"没有明确目标"
② 认为……是理所当然
③ 它会给一个人带来不幸。
④ 可提供方便的设施
⑤ 走歧路
⑥ 意志薄弱的
⑦ 上瘾;染上……的癖好
⑧ 得到

幸福观
Happiness
"No.14"

(5) Life Can Be Happy and Meaningful

Not long ago, a *poll*① was conducted among students in a middle school. They were asked to make a choice between these two sentences — "No one can be happy," and "One can be happy." Shockingly enough, about 40 percent of the students agreed to the first statement. Some of them said, "Frankly speaking, life is bitter and meaningless. But to live on, we'd better say to ourselves that there is happiness in life."

It is true that all people have some bitter experiences. But it is through overcoming hardship that our happiness emerges. Many students admire *Madam Curie*②, and say with a sigh, "If I could live like her, I would be the happiest person in the world." But if we take a close look at her life, we will find her happiness is closely connected with her misfortune. She did not have a happy childhood. In her research work, she had to sit up late night after night. She experienced many losses, too — she lost her beloved father, her dear husband, and later her sight. But she never complained and never stopped working. That is why her life was happy and meaningful. She fought against life's bitterness and difficulties and conquered them all.

Some people complain that their work is dull and insignificant and thus their lives are meaningless. But what kind of work is significant? Workers, farmers, teachers and scientists are all working for the welfare of mankind, themselves included. That is, many people believe, where the meaning of life lies.

Different people may think of life differently. But one thing is certain: happiness never favors those who merely care about

---

① 民意测验
② 居里夫人

themselves, and the meaning of life can not be understood by those who refuse to sacrifice anything for others or fail to do anything for the betterment of society.

(6) We Need Humor in Our Life

Our world should be colorful. Humor is the paintbrush creating the picture of our world. Without humor, our life would be monotonous, as though all movies made use of the same background music.

Humor serves as lubricating oil, making the machine of human society run smoothly. Appropriate use of humor can ease embarrassment and settle family quarrels and conflicts.

Life is not always like sunny days, bright and comfortable. In our life there are ups and downs. In trouble, we should try to pull ourselves together, instead of crying over spilt milk. To stay quiet and think about the situation is one way, but to read some humorous stories so as to come up with solutions consequently is another way. If you are trying to make your friends feel better when they are *not in the mood*①, you may try to be humorous. Humor works better than any persuasion or consolation if it is applied properly and intelligently.

The lessons given by a teacher with a good sense of humor can often be very impressing. Learning through laughter becomes light and easy, and memorization will be strengthened in a light environment. Humor, a wonderful drug for various diseases, exerts great influence on the function of one's body, as is demonstrated scientifically. A TV program spiced with humorous interlude will attract a greater audience if the host is up to it. Using humor helps a man work more successfully and live a happy life.

---

① 心情不好

No.15 | Ideals and Wishes
理想与愿望

（1）Wishes

Everybody has his wishes, whether ambitious or modest. Parents wish their children would grow up healthy and wise; farmers wish to *reap bumper harvests*[①]; businessmen wish to make greater profits. One who had no wish would be *a gone case*[②], or *at the end of his journey*[③]! Practically, all people live on wishes, in hopes of something.

If wishes were horses, beggars might ride.[④] We cannot stay just wishing all the time. Without proper action, wishes will remain *castles in the air*[⑤].

Most of us strive to realize our wishes. Usually, those who persist in their efforts *systematically*[⑥] will succeed sooner or later. These people are skillful in finding out *how the wind blows*[⑦]. They readily *adapt themselves to new situations*[⑧] and are *smart*[⑨] at making decisions.

---

① 获得大丰收
② 不可救药的人
③ 穷途末路
④ （英谚）要是愿望等于事实,乞丐也早就发财了。
⑤ 空中楼阁
⑥ 有计划地
⑦ 发展的趋势
⑧ 使自己适应新的形势
⑨ 机敏的;聪明的

The realization of a *sound*① wish not only is in the interest of the person who cherishes it but also is beneficial to many others. It is desirable for the more able to help the less able in realizing their wishes. And the realization of a common wish requires the common efforts of *all concerned*②. In such a case, co-operation and *mutual*③ help are *all the more*④ necessary.

(2) Ideals

Everyone cherishes his ideals, fanciful or substantial. We dreamed of becoming scientists when we were school boys and girls; now we hope for a better society and are determined to work for it. And we strive, in one way or another, to realize our ideals.

One should be *sensible*⑤ whether one's ideal is *well-founded*⑥ or not. If it is, one has to plan and work hard for its realization. Effort, skill and *persistence*⑦ are all necessary. And very often, one has to get help from others, including advice and support in different forms.

In most cases, the realization of personal ideals is in the interest of society. Meanwhile, social ideals — such as the *preservation*⑧ of natural environment for the improvement of human living conditions and the production of sufficent material wealth for the world's population — concern the whole of society

---

① 合理的;正确的
② 有关的各方
③ 相互的
④ 更加
⑤ 明智的;头脑清醒的
⑥ 基础牢固的;有充分根据的;切合实际的
⑦ 毅力
⑧ 保护

and their realization *calls for*① contribution by all. We should always try our best to help such ideals come true.

(3) Young People Should Have Ideals

To different people, the word "ideal" may mean different things. To some, it may mean *success and fame in their career*②; to others, a peaceful life. Very often, we have ideals for the "SELF" and no ideal for society, *not to mention*③ the people of the world. Is it a sound attitude toward life?

In my opinion, a youth should have ideals. But it is more important that these ideals *are* not merely *centred on*④ the "self." They should be also the ideals of the majority of people. Then you would get strength and confidence toward life for you are striving for the *betterment*⑤ of your fellowmen.

The setting up of an ideal does not merely mean to *go without doing anything*⑥. Real and concrete action should be taken. For us students, the most important thing to do is to study both inside and outside school. We study not to become *bookworms*⑦ but to be well-equipped and prepared for the pursuit of our ideals.

Sometimes, in striving toward our ideals, we may encounter certain difficulties and failures. But we should not give up or lose hope, for as long as we try, there is always a way out. We will not lose heart if our ideals are the wish of the many!

---

① 需要;要求
② 在他们的事业中功成名就
③ 更不必说;更谈不上
④ 集中在……上;围绕着
⑤ 改善;此处指"生活得更好"
⑥ 此处指"只说不做;停留在口头上"
⑦ 书呆子

(4) The Aim of a Young Man

It is not wise for a young man to expect only to be rich, nor is it good for him to direct his attention solely to power and fame. The *mark*① that is set before every young man to aim at is this — *Be Somebody*②.

A young man who expects to be somebody often turns out to be one. The story told of *Disraeli*③ is *illustrative of the case*④. On entering public life, Disraeli aspired to be both scholar and orator. He succeeded better in his literary work than in his oratorical efforts. He was at first a total failure as a public speaker. However, he felt sure that he could overcome every obstacle, and devoted himself *with an invincible will*⑤ to the *trial*⑥. Some of his friends thought he was foolish and even *cranky*⑦. But he *stuck to*⑧ his purpose, and finally accomplished it. He became one of the *ripest scholars*⑨ and most eloquent public speakers that Great Britain has ever produced.

This story is not cited to show that to be somebody is to be a great scholar or a public speaker, or both. Besides a scholar and a speaker there are many *callings*⑩ which are as noble and as respectable. But a young man must aim high, as the proverb says

---

① 目标
② 成为一个有出息的人
③ 迪斯累里(1804 — 1881),英国著名政治家和小说家
④ 说明这一情况
⑤ 坚强的意志
⑥ 磨炼;考验
⑦ 古怪的
⑧ 坚持
⑨ 最成熟的、最具学识的学者
⑩ 职业;行业

"It is much better to aim high and not *hit the mark*① than to aim low and hit it".

(5) If I Were a Boy Again

If I were a boy again, I would practise *perseverance*② oftener and never give up a thing because it was hard or inconvenient. If we want light, we must conquer darkness.

Perseverance can sometimes equal *genius*③ in its results. "There are only two creatures," says a proverb, "who can *surmount*④ the pyramids — the eagle and the snail."

If I were a boy again, I would *school myself into*⑤ a habit of attention. I would let nothing come between me and the subject in hand. I would remember that a good skater never tries to skate in two directions at once.

If I were a boy again, I would cultivate courage. "Nothing is so mild and gentle as courage; nothing is so cruel and pitiless as *cowardice*⑥," says a wise author.

We too often borrow trouble, and anticipate evils that may never appear. "The fear of ill exceeds the ill we fear." Dangers will arise in any career, but *presence of mind*⑦ will often conquer the worst of them. Be prepared for any fate, and there is no harm to fear.

If I were a boy again, I would look on the cheerful side. Life is very much like a mirror; if you smile upon it, it smiles back

---

① 击中目标;达到目的
② 恒心;毅力
③ 创造能力
④ 登上
⑤ 使自己养成
⑥ 懦弱
⑦ 镇定;沉着

upon you; if you frown and look doubtfully on it, you will have a similar look *in return*①.

Finally, instead of trying hard to be happy, as if that were the sole purpose of life, I would, if I were a boy again, try still harder to make others happy.

(6) Where to Go after My Graduation

After they complete their university studies, some students prefer to live in their hometowns while others choose to live in different towns or cities. Everybody has his own reasons for his *preference*②. After my graduation, I will go back and live in my home city. I have made this decision because of the following reasons.

Firstly, my home city is a big city that can offer a lot. There are plenty of opportunities for work, many big libraries for studies, several different museums for visit, and *numerous*③ cinemas, theatres and centers for entertainment. When I go back there, I will have no difficulties in finding a job suitable for me and I can make use of all the facilities available there.

Secondly, if I go back to my home city, I can look after my parents. I *take this into consideration*④ because I am their only child and they are now weak and getting on in age. If I live in the same city with them, I can visit them very often and help them whenever it is necessary.

Thirdly, if I live in my home city, I will have a lot of friends, schoolmates and relatives to visit and to turn to for help when I

---

① 作为回报
② 喜好;选择
③ 很多;数不清的
④ 把这一点考虑在内

need. Of course, I could *get acquainted with*① many people and make many friends if I were to go to live in a strange place, but that *takes time*②. If I go back to my home city, everybody will be waiting for me and I will be able to settle down comfortably without any trouble and waste of time.

*In short*③, my choice is based on a careful consideration of the conditions of my home city and my family. I think it is a better and sensible choice; in a certain sense, it is a "must".

(7) On Faith

Life is a journey from cradle to the grave. In this sense, man is the same as any animals. What is different is that man is endowed with the ability of thinking, which makes man superior to other animals and determines that man will suffer more in life. So human life, in a way, is to suffer. But we have to live on and the only way out is to hold faith to support us through the long journey.

Faith is powerful, which can work miracle. It has inspired the great scientist Deng Jiaxian and his colleagues to succeed in making the atom-bomb and H-bomb under *impossible*④ conditions. Their living and working conditions were extremely poor, and sometimes they even had to bear the torture of hunger, but the faith that we Chinese are not inferior and we must depend on ourselves to develop our science and technology was so strong that they faced the hardship optimistically.

In a word, a person with strong faith is happy no matter how many difficulties waiting for him to overcome. Even if we are not

---

① 认识
② 需要花费时间
③ 简而言之
④ 难以忍受的

able to achieve as much as Mr. Deng Jiaxian, faith is indispensable to us — we must have belief in the English proverb: "*Faith can remove mountains.*①"

(8) Beliefs

Your beliefs are very powerful and have the power to create or to destroy your life. In most cases, whatever you believe is what you will become. If you believe that you are loser, that you never *get the breaks*② in life, that you can't accomplish anything, these things will be your reality. Believe that you are unlimited, that you can do anything you commit to doing, and when you do, your accomplishments will know no bounds.

You control your beliefs, and that is how you ultimately control your life. This is a very important point. So how do you develop beliefs that will *empower*③ you? Many of our beliefs come from our environment, the world we live in on a daily basis. If your environment is limiting your beliefs, then work very hard on changing it. Beliefs also come from past experience. That is why it is so important to experience success on a regular basis. Set small, achievable goals, and then try your best to reach them. Beliefs come from knowledge. The more you learn, the more things you will know to be possible or attainable.

Most importantly, you can develop new beliefs by setting and visualizing goals for your life. Define your goals clearly and with precision. Your nurtured beliefs will lead you to their reality.

---

① 诚能移山(≈精诚所至,金石为开。)
② 交好运,碰到有利的机会
③ 使能够,使具有能力

No.16 On Will
立志

(1) Where There Is a Will, There Is a Way

There is nothing hard in this world for people who have a strong will. A task, no matter how difficult it is, can be accomplished, provided that one makes up one's mind to do it. Many a great hero performs excellent service to his country and is deservedly respected by his countrymen, simply because he possesses an iron will and steady effort. We know that Rome was not built in a day. Before she was built, her founders had suffered a great deal from severe and almost unendurable *distress*[①], but they never lost their faith.

Another example is that a person of great reputation, Columbus, who discovered America, owed his success to his *singleness of purpose*[②] and perseverance. For, on the ocean, hundreds of times he suffered the *affliction*[③] of storms and tempests. However, instead of admitting defeat, he went forward.

A student who has no resolution will never succeed in his studies. We must always remember the old saying that "where there is a will, there is a way."

---

① 危难；忧伤
② 专心致志
③ 折磨；磨难

(2) Perseverance

Perseverance means *steadfastness*① in purpose. It is perseverance that keeps us continually doing something valuable and admirable in spite of difficulties and discouragement. And it is perseverance that makes us renowned *in due course*②. Therefore, perseverance is *momentous*③ and fundamental to anyone who undertakes great deeds.

It *admits of*④ no doubt that in doing things, whether great or small, there are more or less difficulties, and the greater the thing is, the more numerous the difficulties will come forth. But it is much better for one to persevere than to despair. Mencius said, "When heaven is about to confer a great office on any man, it first exercises his mind with suffering, and his sinews and bones with toil. It exposes his body to hunger, and subjects him to extreme poverty. It confounds all his undertakings. By all these methods, it stimulates his mind, consolidates his character, and increases his efficiency."⑤ So let us be patient. Indeed, if we do a thing without perseverance, nothing will be done in the end.

(3) Rome Was Not Built in a Day

The good old proverb, "Rome was not built in a day," reminds us that great things are never done without much time

---

① 坚定不移
② 在一定的时候
③ 极重要的
④ 容许(有)
⑤ 孟子说:"天将降大任于斯人也,必先苦其心志,劳其筋骨,饿其体肤,空乏其身,行拂乱其所为,所以动心养性,曾益其所不能。"

立志
On Will "No.16"

and labour. It takes us back to Rome, the capital of the greatest empire of the ancient world and the most brilliant city of ancient times. Indeed, Rome was built through the labours of many a great man who had been striving against difficulties.

As human beings, we are eager to *win merits*[①] for ourselves. It is, however, only patience as well as endurance that can help us to succeed in performing great deeds, for difficulties are, in fact, unavoidable, unless we do not engage in anything at all.

Young people are, however, mostly impatient. Brave as they may be in the beginning, they often give up halfway in the face of what seems to be *insurmountable*[②]. Men of such a type can hardly expect to succeed.

(4) Don't Stop Halfway

When a man does a piece of work, he hopes *to derive*[③] some benefit from it. In order to get this benefit, he must hold the work to the end and completely finish it.

A piece of work, whether hard or not, requires patience and firmness for completion. Therefore, when you have some work to do, you must do it faithfully, not caring about the difficulty. Difficulties and obstacles are unavoidable. If you turn back on meeting them, you will succeed in nothing, but if you can overcome them, you will accomplish something.

To stop halfway in doing something is very bad. Suppose that a precious stone is at a great distance from you and you want to obtain it, you must reach for it; you must not stop halfway. If you stop halfway, you will not only get nothing, but also lose

---

① 立功
② 不可克服的;难以制胜的
③ 获得

something, because your time and strengh will be wasted.

I have heard of many students who failed because they stopped halfway. Some of them did not continue their course till completion for fear of difficulties, while others, having studied for some years, grew tired of their lessons, and tried to pursue some new studies. *To put it in nutshell*① they did not endeavour to reach their destination, but stopped halfway. Their time and strength were thus wasted. So, when of middle age, they were as ignorant as when they were children, and could hardly support themselves, let alone *render*② valuable service to their country.

It is a good thing for one to do one thing at a time, and never stop halfway.

(5) Discontent

The advice given to young men or women by most people is this: "Be content." Doubtless there is truth and strength in this. But *one man's meat may be poison for another*③. There are people who, progressive in spirit, are always discontented, yet they are happy and *are* highly *revered*④. To this group belong discoverers, scientists, and people doing research work. It is this spirit, the spirit of being unsatisfied with the existing state of things, that is responsible for improvements. If our forefathers had been content with wheelbarrows, there would never have been trains and motor cars. It is due to being discontented with gestures to express thoughts and feelings that a language develops. Thus, discontent is really a progressive force. It is

---

① 简而言之
② 给予
③ 对甲有利的未必对乙也有利
④ 受到尊敬

wrong to *preach*① to everybody against discontent. Those who can only *grumble at*② things, but cannot think of means of *bettering*③ them, should *be censured*④ as severely as possible. But those who are willing to labour hard for betterment ought to be encouraged in every way. Their discontent *bears good fruit*⑤.

(6) Man's Strong Will

Strong will is universally regarded as a very praisable quality. It is neither *genius*⑥ nor *extraordinary*⑦ ability that gives us power to deal with and *overcome whatever hardship that befalls*⑧. It is strong will that enables us to endure the trying situation and to attain our goals. Strong will gives us light when we are in the dark, and encouragement when we *are frustrated*⑨. With this praisable quality, no enemy can *overwhelm*⑩ us, and no obstacles can stand in our way. So the saying where there is a will, there is a way.

There have been many examples that success can be achieved by strong will. During the Long March, the Red Army soldiers met with the greatest hardship man has ever experienced. They had nothing to eat but grass roots and barks of trees. It was their strong will that made them weather the hardship. Helen Keller, a strong-willed American blind woman, mastered the English

---

① 说教；劝戒
② 抱怨；发牢骚
③ 改善
④ 受到指责
⑤ 结出丰硕的果实
⑥ 天才
⑦ 非凡的
⑧ 克服所发生的任何艰难险阻
⑨ 受挫
⑩ 压倒

language and became a well-known educator.

It is not easy to cultivate a strong will. First of all, we must set up a firm faith in our cause and be ready to devote our lives to it. Secondly, we must learn from strong-willed persons. Finally, we should boldly go through trials and hardships to train our will so as to get rid of the weak points of our moral character.

(7) Self-reliance

Self-reliance means depending on one's own power or judgment. A self-reliant person forms his own judgment and carries out his own determination. When he encounters difficulty, he solves it by himself instead of turning to others for help. He believes in the old saying, "*God helps those who help themselves.*"①

However, it doesn't follow that one can manage without others' help. Self-reliance is no equivalent to self-will or conceit. Good suggestions and timely help are of great value to one's success. *Thomas Jefferson*② was a versatile and self-reliant person, and yet he had a lot of friends of artists, and he often talked with them and listened to their advice. Likewise, one should not *echo*③ the views of others and do what he believes is right.

As college students, we should have a sense of self-reliance. Having got used to working under strict control from our middle school teachers and parents, we have to adjust ourselves to a new life style with more freedom and responsibilities. Under such circumstances, self-reliance becomes essential to our success.

---

① 天助自助者。
② 托马斯·杰斐逊,美国第三任总统,《独立宣言》的主要起草人
③ 附和,摹仿

First of all, we must learn to study by ourselves and to take care of ourselves. Besides, we should decide what kind of friends to make and what kind of activities to participate in. Furthermore, we should even find some part-time jobs to help earn our own bread. In a word, only those who are reliant and dependent on themselves can turn out to be the most promising.

(8) Making Decision

Growing up means making one's own decisions. In my opinion, it's a shame to turn to others for help all the time. Seeing that we have grown up, we should be independent of our parents; that is, we must be our own masters. For example, we can make decisions to do anything right. To my regret, quite a few people have been spoilt since they were children. When they grow up, they are still dependent on their parents to do anything. As result, they are often despised by people around them. For this reason, they are always the losers in the competitive society. In order to be winner, I often make decisions for myself.

The hardest decision that I ever made was to work hard. Since I was a lazy boy in my childhood, I used to delay handing in assignment as an elementary schoolboy. Therefore I was often punished by the teacher. Indeed I often wanted to have got out of the bad habit, but it was hard to make such a decision. Once I was caught dozing in class by the headmaster. He called me out and taught me a good lesson. That incident made me firmly make a decision to be diligent. Till now I often think of the man, my headmaster, who made me make a hardest decision to work hard.

(9) Enjoy Challenges

For thousands of years, people have accepted challenges in

different fields. There are not only physical challenges, but also social and intellectual challenges. Some people risk their lives in playing sports to see how well they can do. Others try to make and invent something to make life easier. They all enjoy challenges.

Why do people enjoy these challenges? There are probably many reasons. One is curiosity. The other is the personal feeling of success, of achievement. And nowadays, for some people, it is a business.

Today, we still have many challenges before us. Medical science faces the challenges of conquering many diseases which still attack human beings. Engineers and planners must build new cities and design and produce new kinds of transportation. Scientists must develop new forms of energy. In short, we live in an age of challenge, and so let us exert our utmost to meet challenges and render meritorious service.

No.17　Self-cultivation
道德修养

(1) On Selfishness

　　Selfishness or egoism, is by no means rare today. In workplaces, in public places, and in our colleges, it is really sad for us to see some people trying to gain their own interests at the cost of their grace and dignity.

　　What are the effects of selfishness on a person? First, I think, a selfish person is unable to make true friends. He doesn't understand that friendship is based on mutual respect and mutual help. It is something of "*give-and-take*①". Second, a selfish person can never be really happy. Stingy with his time, energy and money, unwilling to help others, and eager to profit at other people's expense, a selfish person constantly finds himself despised and lonely. He can never share other people's joy, nor will others share his. Third, selfishness may very well lead a person to destruction. A selfish person's desire to get something for nothing is *insatiable*②. He will shamelessly steal a book from the library and keep it for his own use even though he knows his fellow students are in desperate need of it. Once he succeeds in stealing something petty, his selfish desire will drive him to steal

---

① 平等交换，互让
② 不知足的，贪得无厌的

something big and expensive until he ends up in prison.

Selfishness poisons people's minds and runs counter to the basic values of the society. It should have no place in our country today.

(2) On the Misbehaviors of Chinese Tourists Abroad

With the rapid development of economy in China, the majority of Chinese people now enjoy a higher income than ever before. This makes it possible for some of them to go abroad for a visit. However, according to a recent survey, a handful of Chinese tourists abroad have been blamed for their misbehaviors such as spitting, shouting and *jumping the queue*[①]. This phenomenon, as far as I see it, *can be ascribed to*[②] the following causes.

First, some of the tourists, though having a large sum of money, are not well educated. In the past two decades, some Chinese people have made a lot of money in their business. However, not all of them have received enough education to realize spitting, shouting and jumping the queue are uncivilized behaviors. Second, little attention has been paid to the proper behavior of tourists in the domestic tourist industry. In China, a customer is treated as a God if he has a large purchase to make. And it is no exception at all in tourism. A tourist can do almost all he likes if he has a deep pocket, and he is seldom criticized for his misbehavior.

In view of the above, some urgent measures should be taken to solve the problem. In the first place, some training programs should be offered to those who plan to visit overseas. In the

---

① 不按次序排队,插队
② 可归因于,可归结于

second place, those who have been found behaving inappropriately during an overseas visit should be prohibited from going abroad for a visit before they get to know what good manners and good behaviour mean.

(3) How to Prevent Cheating in Exams

It is said that many college students cheat in their examinations and *they don't believe that cheating on examinations is reprehensible*①. This is a serious problem affecting all aspects of education. Therefore, how to solve the problem deserves more attention. The following suggestions may help prevent cheating.

First, honesty is the best policy. Both teachers and parents should care more about the students' moral development. The most effective way to prevent cheating is to *promote academic integrity*②. Second, strict regulations or rules should be established so that those who are discovered cheating in exams could be punished severely, namely, *the cheater could be expelled from school by way of disciplinary punishment*③. Third, students should be strict with themselves and realize that cheating is harmful to society as well as to themselves in the long run.

To sum up, we should help college students realize that it is honesty, respect, rigor, and fairness that lead to an effective study.

(4) Sense of Independence

Independence is of great significance in our life. To an adult

---

① 而且他们认为考试作弊无可厚非
② 提升学业诚信
③ 开除学籍，以示训诫

student, it means to be confident and able to do things by himself in his own way without relying on parents or others for support.

People are born to work, to create and to be happy. In part, happiness is to be found in independence. We have no right to live in this world without doing any work. To wish to live on the labor of others is to *contemplate a fraud*①. Independence is a cornerstone of our strength that *boosts*② our freedom, courage and self-confidence. Besides, independence is the greatest security against slavery and inspires creativity. In the long journey of our life we should depend solely on our own merit and our own *exertion*③ as did many great men and women in the history. Perhaps this is why Americans emphasize independence in children's education.

Unfortunately, lack of independence is our common weakness. As compared with American youngsters, we are *vulnerable*④ in social competition. Therefore, we have to redouble our efforts in building up our sense of independence to meet the challenges in life.

(5) On Virtues

Virtues are any good qualities of one's character or behavior, such as temperance, prudence, modesty, fortitude, justice, cleanliness, chastity and so on. Of the numerous virtues, some are indispensable, without which one couldn't survive, not mention success. They are industry and perseverance.

Industry means losing no time, being always employed in something useful, and cutting all unnecessary actions. With

---

① 意图欺诈
② 提升,促进
③ 努力,尽力
④ 脆弱的

industry, one can always *start from scratch*① without fear of any difficulties. With industry, one can create wealth, succeed in almost everything, and without industry, one can have nothing accomplished.

Perseverance is to resolve to perform what one ought to perform without fail. It is one of the most important factors in achieving success. Without perseverance, one will lose his bearings, give up half way when facing hardship and difficulties.

In short, industry and perseverance contribute a lot for a person to live a meaningful life and to make achievements. So it may be safe to say that it is the two virtues — industry and perseverance — that will make you a true man.

(6) *Patriotism*②

Patriotism is love of one's country. It is an essential element of the existence of a nation, and yet it is one of the most sacred emotions.

Patriotism, in other words, is the fulfillment of one's duty. The readiness to die in the cause of the nation is patriotism for soldiers. The working for the good of the country is patriotism for statesmen and good citizens. Generally speaking, patriotism for everybody is to maintain the honor and integrity of the motherland. It is the easiest and most effective measure for the people to take to make one's country strong and prosperous, with advanced industry, agriculture and national defense. In short, the true patriot desires *righteousness*③ and uprightness for one's own land. He puts love of country before love of oneself, and is

---

① 从零开始;从头做起
② 爱国主义
③ 正义,正直

willing to make any sacrifice for the betterment of one's country.

(7) Honesty

What is honesty? Honesty means speaking the truth and being fair and upright in act. Considered a virtue, it is admired in every country and every culture. He who lies and cheats is dishonest. Dishonesty is generally regarded as an evil, and is *despised*① and *condemned*② by the society.

As the English proverb goes, "honesty is the best policy." For one thing, if you want to be trusted and respected by your friends, you must be honest. A liar is always looked down upon and avoided by the people around him. For another, if you want to succeed in your work, the first qualification you should have is honesty. It is through honest efforts that Newton and Einstein became great figures in history. Therefore, whatever your aim is, you must work honestly to attain it.

However, there are people who try to get benefits by dishonest means. For example, some students copy the exercises done by others or cheat in examinations in order to get good marks. The same thing may be said of a merchant who tries to get rich by deceiving customers. Those people may succeed *for a time*③, but sooner or later, they will *be caught*④. In the end, dishonesty will bring them nothing but troubles.

(8) Bravery

Bravery does not require us to hurt and kill. If it requires us

---

① 鄙视；看不起
②．谴责
③ 暂时；一度
④ 被发觉

to hurt and kill it would be a terrible thing. Is it not brave to try to save life?

Thousands of brave men are risking their lives every day to help men and to save them all from harm. Brave doctors and nurses go where deadly disease is and are not afraid to help save the sick. Brave students are trying *perilous*① experiments so as to find out better knowledge for human race. Brave engineers on thousands of *locomotives*② are not afraid of sudden death if they can save their passengers from harmful accidents. Brave sailors are always facing the sea and the storm. Brave firemen stand ready to die to bring little children safely out of burning buildings. Brave boys every summer risk their lives to save their comrades from drowning. Brave fellows *hold in check*③ *maddened*④ horses and prevent them from running into any children. Brave women risk their own lives daily for the sake of others. Indeed, all these are brave actions and it is brave to try to save life.

(9) Thrift Is Always a Good Virture

Waste has been a serious problem in China. Large amounts of *manpower*⑤, energy, farm land, materials, money and other state properties are wasted every day. People *junk*⑥ furniture, cars, equipment in *chasing the latest fashion*⑦. What is worse, our youths feel ashamed to be thrifty.

---

① 冒险的;危险的
② 机车
③ 制止;控制
④ 发狂的
⑤ 人力;劳动力
⑥ 扔掉;废弃不用
⑦ 赶时髦

Thrift is a good virture. We now have an *unprecedented*① power of production side by side with unprecedented shortages. We have invented machines to work for us, but have less natural resources than ever before for human, even for such essential things as water to drink and fresh air to breathe. "To live upon little" is the great security against slavery; and this principle extends to clothes and other things besides food and drink. Moreover, extravagance may lead to either disgrace or *degradation*② and wastes may result in pollution. China is a developing country and there are millions of people living in *dire*③ poverty. We cannot afford such *reckless*④ waste. Even in advanced countries, waste is considered sinful. Making the best use of anything is an ultimate goal for everyone.

High living standards don't necessarily mean to waste. The question is not to give up modern comfort; the question is how to *enhance*⑤ efficiency. In fact, economic growth depends strongly on saving. We have only one Earth to live on; we should leave behind nothing but footprints.

(10) To Be Patient

Everybody must be patient. In the way of living, to be patient is always safe; for it can *bestow*⑥ on us, at least, two great gifts: happiness and success.

As we know, it is easy to lose one's temper. To be patient is, indeed, very hard. Men, especially young men, easily become

---

① 史无前例的
② 堕落
③ 可怕的
④ 不顾后果的
⑤ 提高
⑥ 把……赠与;给与

*peevish*①. When we get into trouble with sombody, we always want to be winners and wish our opponents to be defeated. The feelings on both sides, then, will become more than unpleasant. If we are patient, we are happy. Whenever we meet any trouble, we may safely *smooth it over*②. This is the first gift bestowed on us by patience.

The second gift patience will bring is success. Any work we undertake will be successful if we go on *with no regard to*③ difficulties. For example, *Han Xin of the Han Dynasty*④ is typical of those who had patience. He was patient even when he *was humiliated*⑤ by a person of the lower class. So finally he became the greatest general of that dynasty. We admire him and ought to imitate him. In short, if we want to be happy and successful, we must be patient.

(11) Our Responsibility

We Chinese *place a high value on*⑥ responsibility. It is traditional for us Chinese to take care of our parents. We *owe*⑦ them a great deal for the love they gave us while we were growing up. It is right then, when they are getting older with each passing day, that we help them and *see that*⑧ they *are well cared for*⑨. In this way, we give back some of the love and care they gave to us.

---

① 易怒的；暴躁的
② 消除（障碍、困难等）
③ 不考虑；无视
④ 汉朝的韩信
⑤ 受到羞辱
⑥ 重视
⑦ 亏欠
⑧ 保证；注意做到
⑨ 得到很好的照料

As loyal Chinese citizens, we must have a strong sense of responsibility to our country. It is our duty to keep China strong in the eyes of the world. Therefore, we should obey the laws and the government. We should study and work hard for China's *prosperity*① which also depends on advanced science and technology. We must be willing to join the Army and defend our country, should we be threatened by an invader. In short, to be a responsible citizen, we must put our country's welfare above our own needs.

Finally, we must remember that we have a responsibility to the world we live in. It is important that we learn to live in peace with the other nations of the world, and to protect our environment. If we carry out these responsibilities, we will be respected citizens of our country.

---

① 繁荣

No.18 Good Manners
文明礼貌

(1) Good Manners (Ⅰ)

People all over the world set great regard on good manners. To certain degree, good manners indicate a person's good education and *breeding*[①]. In schools, it is part of students' moral training to develop good manners. A person with good manners always wins praise. On the contrary, *people will frown on him if he behaves roughly and impolitely*[②].

There are good manners in which we behave in public places. It is a good manner to offer help to the young, the old and *the handicapped*[③] when they are in need of it. So is it to conduct ourselves politely and keep away from foul language. Besides, we should guard against such *minor offences*[④] as making a loud noise, casting peels and shells, smoking, and spitting.

If everyone has developed good manners, people will form a more *harmonious relationship*[⑤]. If everyone behaves considerately towards others and follows the *social ethics*[⑥], people will live in a better world. With *the general mood of*

---

① 教养
② 如果一个人行为举止粗鲁无礼,人们便会皱眉蹙额对他表示不满
③ 残疾人
④ 小的不良之举
⑤ 融洽的关系,和睦的关系
⑥ 社会准则

society① improved, there will be a progress of civilization.

(2) Good Manners (Ⅱ)

"Good manners" mean good behaviour in *social intercourse*②. It is an *interchangeable*③ term with "politeness", the art of pleasing.

A person with good manners is always an *agreeable*④ companion. He is agreeable because he is always thinking of others. He does not interrupt people when they are talking. He is careful not to say anything to hurt other people's feelings. He does not push in a crowd, but waits quietly until it is his turn to pass. All such are called good manners and show that the possessor is *a man of high standing*⑤.

However, good manners *take a variety of forms*⑥. First, they vary from country to country. What is considered as *refined*⑦ and *courteous*⑧ in one country may not be considered so in another. This difference is especially *noticeable*⑨ in the manners of Westerners and the Chinese. Secondly, manners vary from time to time. Our ancestors who lived a century ago must have thought that their *stately*⑩ *usages*⑪ were the most perfect forms *adapted to*⑫ a civilized nation. But modern people look

---

① 整个社会风气
② 社交(活动)
③ 可以互换的
④ 令人愉快的；令人惬意的
⑤ 有身份的人
⑥ 此处意为"有各种各样的表现形式"
⑦ 文雅的
⑧ 有礼貌的
⑨ 显而易见的；明显的
⑩ 庄重的
⑪ 习俗
⑫ 适应于

upon these forms as empty and *absurd*①, and think their own behaviour more appropriate to a gentleman's *station*②. If the ancients *came to life*③ again, our manners would seem rash in their eyes; though in our eyes theirs would seem very tedious.

So far we have discussed the difference of good manners between one place or one time and another. But no matter what age or what country it is, there must be a kind of politeness which is *sanctioned*④ by the *community*⑤ of that country and that age. By acting *in accordance with*⑥ the *prevailing*⑦ custom, one is considered a member of polite society. Otherwise, he is looked upon as a *knave*⑧, and will be *shunned*⑨ by those who are of high breeding. Politeness is truly a valuable *asset*⑩!

(3) Voluntary Blood Donation

Voluntary Blood Donation is becoming more and more popular in our country. Not only the youth but also the aged are ready to donate their blood voluntarily. Some young people even do so twice a year, for they believe such donation benefits society as well as themselves.

However, not all of the people think so. There are two different attitudes. One group insist voluntary blood donation should be called on and carried out by the public, and they regard

① 荒谬的;可笑的
② 身份;地位
③ 苏醒过来;此处指"复活"
④ 支持;鼓励
⑤ 社会
⑥ 按照;与……一致
⑦ 流行的;通行的
⑧ 无赖;恶棍
⑨ 避开
⑩ 宝贵的财富

it as a kind of civil duty. The other group think blood donation should be paid and only those who lack money are willing to do so. They believe the loss of blood will do harm to health.

In my opinion blood donation is a virtue. We Chinese look up to those who are always ready to help others in difficulties. If there is no such donation, the price of blood will be higher and the hospitals will be subject to lack of blood. Therefore, those who donate their blood voluntarily are actually doing something great for the betterment of society and should be highly respected.

(4) Politeness

It is hard to *define*① politeness but it is easy to tell politeness from impoliteness. Politeness is *abstract*②. No one can give an exact definition. In practice, any good manners, kind words, and courteous behavior are willingly accepted and *appreciated*③ by the public, while bad manners, rude speech, and crude and rash behavior are disliked.

Politeness, to some extent, is like a mirror reflecting one's *self-cultivation*④. Rude words, face-to-face quarrelling, unreasonable fighting, *turning a deaf ear to*⑤ lectures, no thanks for others' help, etc. could mean nothing but *ignorance or ill behavior*⑥. A friendly greeting, a keen invitation, or a short "thank you" reveals one's *internal*⑦ spiritual world.

---

① 给……下定义
② 抽象的
③ 赞赏；正确评价
④ 自我修养
⑤ 不听；对……充耳不闻
⑥ 无知或粗鲁
⑦ 内在的

文明礼貌 Good Manners "No.18"

A friendly nod and a nice smile can break the ice in human contact and win the world. They are, sometimes, more powerful than *gun barrels*①. Politeness, which is like sunshine, warms another's heart and win friendship, while impoliteness *offends*② others and *isolates*③ oneself. So, always follow the golden rule: *Do as you would be done by.*④ Be polite.

(5) *Punctuality*⑤

Punctuality is the main *constituent*⑥ of good character. A punctual person is in the habit of doing a thing at the proper time, and is never late in keeping an appointment. An unpunctual man, whether wearing a watch or using an alarm clock, never does what he has to do at the proper time. He is always in a hurry and in the end loses both time and his name. There is a proverb which says, "Time flies never to be recalled." This is very true. A lost thing may be found again, but the lost time can never be regained. Time is more valuable than material things. In fact, time is life itself, and an unpunctual man is wasting and mismanaging his most valuable *asset*⑦ as well as others'.

Failure to be punctual in keeping one's appointment is a sign of disrespect towards others. If a person is invited to a dinner and arrives later than the appointed time, he keeps all the other guests waiting for him. This is a great *discourtesy*⑧ towards both the host and the other guests.

Unpunctuality, moreover, is very harmful to one's duty.

---

① 枪筒
② 冒犯；伤害……感情
③ 使孤立
④ "你愿意别人如何待你，你就应该如何待别人。"（源出基督教《圣经》）
⑤ 守时
⑥ 要素
⑦ 财产
⑧ 失礼

Imagine how it would be if those who are entrusted with important tasks failed to be at their proper place at the appointed time. A man who is known to be habitually unpunctual is seldom trusted by others. As time passes, it will spoil friendship.

  To be or not to be punctual is a habit. So when we are young, we should try to be punctual every time and never be late, for punctuality is much more easily acquired in youth than when we are older.

No.19 | Friendship 友谊

(1) Friendship

Friendship is important to us. Everyone needs friendship. In all our lives, we cannot live without friendship just as we cannot survive without air and water. Friendship gives us a feeling of security and warmth; friendship encourages us to *go ahead*① all the time.

But real friendship is not easy to *come by*②. True friendship must be sincere and unconditional. It is based on mutual understanding, not on mutual benefit. Some people try to get something from their friends, and their friends also try to make use of them. If such a relationship can be called friendship, we need no friends at all.

The mutual understanding between two friends means both of them have similar ideas and trust each other. Otherwise, it is impossible for them to help each other and to make their friendship last long. As an old saying goes, "A friend in need is a friend indeed," so real friendship should be able to *stand all sorts of tests*③.

---

① 前进
② 获得
③ 经得起各种考验

However, *it is advisable*① to have as many good friends as we can. A good friend can always be a good teacher to us. By his advice, we are persuaded to go the right way; by his help, we can be free from many difficulties; by his warning, we are aware of the danger of doing wrongs. The more friends we have, the more help we can expect from them, the more pleasure we can share with them and the more beautiful a life we will live.

(2) Making Friends

A person cannot live alone in this society because there are many different kinds of work that requires cooperation. Man's life depends upon each man *pooling*② his individual ability with others.

Our society has become more and more complicated. No matter where we live and work, we cannot stand *aloof*③ from the people around us. Sometimes, we might need their help. Of course, we will also *lend* them *a hand*④ whenever one is needed. Our lives are established upon a relationship of *mutual*⑤ help. This means that we should be friendly with each other.

When you have many friends, you will find that they can not only give you the aid you need but also make you feel the pleasure of living. They may be your good teachers who teach you many things about life and the world. They may help you solve many problems. You may also enjoy going out with them and doing things together with them. With them, you will find life worth living.

---

① ……是可取的；最好……
② 集中(智慧等)
③ 远离；避开
④ 帮助
⑤ 相互的；彼此的

(3) How to Make Friends

Every one of us needs to have friends. However, making friends is not easy. If we feel shy, we may hesitate to *make the first move*①. It is also difficult at times to keep the friends we already have. The following points, in my opinion, seem to be essential to making more and better friends.

Firstly, be polite. Always greet people in a friendly and enthusiastic manner. Begin your requests with little phrases like "Would you please," "Would you mind," or "Excuse me." Remember to say "Thank you" when anyone has done you a favour.

Secondly, be *tolerant*②. Listen carefully when others are talking to you, whether it is interesting or not. Don't constantly interrupt or *contradict*③ other people. What is more, never lose your temper, even if you *are offended*④. If you do feel offended, try to talk to your friend *frankly*⑤ and *earnestly*⑥.

Thirdly, be *considerate*⑦. Be ready to help your classmates, roommates, even strangers you happen to run across, whenever they are in trouble. Making an extra cup of soup for a sick neighbour may seem like a little thing to do, but it will make your neighbour feel much better.

Lastly, remember names. *Concentrate*⑧ when you are introduced to someone, and remember the person's name. They

---

① 迈出第一步;主动做某事
② 容忍的
③ 反驳
④ 被冒犯;被伤(感情)
⑤ 直率地;真诚地
⑥ 认真地;诚挚地
⑦ 体谅的;体谅别人的
⑧ 集中;全神贯注

say that the sweetest music to a person's ears is the sound of his or her own name.

If you can follow these suggestions, I am sure you will succeed in making many good friends.

(4) My Ideal Friend

My ideal friend is of course a good friend whose goodness is shown below. He has no bad likings like smoking or drinking. He lives in frugality. He studies diligently so as not to waste his golden time. At home he honors his parents and loves his brothers; at school he *venerates*[①] his teachers and sympathizes with his schoolmates. He treats those truely who are true to him. He never speaks of others' evils nor boasts of his own merits. Most of all, the good characters he has should be better than mine and he can try his best to make me follow him as a model. Especially, when I am in danger of doing something wrong, he can give me warnings and persuade me to go the right way. Indeed, if I have such a person as my friend, I shall never fear difficulty and I shall never know the existance of the word "failure."

(5) On Making Friends

As a human being, one can hardly do without a friend. We need friends to share our joy and sorrow; we consult with friends if there are problems we cannot handle alone; we go to friends for help when we are in trouble; and we sometimes *confide in*[②] our friends what we are reluctant to reveal to our family. In a sense,

---

① 尊敬;崇拜
② 信任

friends are often more important to us than relatives.

But not all who are friendly to each other and enjoy each other's company in the social gatherings can be called true friends. True friendship *consists in*[①] sincerity, mutual trust, and *self-sacrifice*[②], both in times of happiness and at moments of crisis. A true friend does not just tell us what we want to hear but will do what he thinks is the best for us *in the long run*[③].

When I choose friends, I do not care what work they do or what social background they are from, but I do notice those little things which reveal one's characters. I would make sure that we really care for each other, so that no matter how much time goes by without our seeing each other, I know my friends will always be there, ready to help if I need them. And I know we are true friends indeed.

(6) On Friendship

Friends similar to you and friends different from you are both beneficial for each kind has its advantages.

The first kind of friend is sure to have the similar ideas and interests in life and in work. If you are conservative, they may accompany you to enjoy some classical theatre or opera or go to a department store to pick up a dark Sunday suit. At work you get on smoothly with them, as the research project they have chosen is to your taste; the way they solve problems and the steps they take in doing experiments accord with your preferences or vice versa. Whenever there is an argument you can definitely obtain their support.

---

① 包括
② 自我牺牲
③ 从长远角度考虑

Your life is colourful. Different tastes and conceptions may bring an entirely new world to your small region. With friends different from you, you may find the *exuberance*① of popular songs and rock music irresistible, and a fashionable cowboy suit rather smart and comfortable. The advice and suggestion, opposite to your own, may help set you on the path to exploration. Diverse ways of tackling problems just demonstrate other versatile and skillful aspects of human beings. Thus your vision is extended and your mind is expanded.

I like them both as I need them both, for the world is made up of two parts — similarity and diversity.

---

① 丰富多彩

No.20 Habit and Hobby
习惯和爱好

(1) Habit

One of the things that we often fail to *appreciate*① is the power that habit has in our life. Habit is working for or against us every minute of the day. We are constantly forming new habits, and constantly giving up old ones. Our future is with us now and we can make it whatever we wish. We must *resolve*② right now to be all that we wish to be. We must be careful about our actions *all the while*③.

In one word, we must *cultivate*④ good habits. When we repeat any one of our actions often enough, it will become a part of our character permanently. Honesty is a habit, *loyalty*⑤ is a habit, *temperance*⑥ is a habit. We should know that a man with good habits always *wins popularity*⑦ while one who has bad habits is everywhere despised. What pleasure can a man find if he is despised wherever he goes? So let us cultivate good habits if we want to lead a happy and successful life.

---

① 意识到；懂得
② 决心
③ 一直；始终
④ 培养
⑤ 忠诚
⑥ 节制；自我克制
⑦ 得众望；受欢迎

(2) Good Habits Affect People

Having read a *self-development*① book *Harvard Girl Named Liu Yiting*②, I then *self-evaluated*③ my achievement in life and my future goals. This book has really stimulated a passion for cultivating good habits in life.

Liu Yiting was admitted to Harvard University, a top university in the world. Her story sets me thinking a lot. Liu Yiting has formed good habits since she was a young girl. She has always studied earnestly and handed matters seriously. Good habits play an important part in her achievements. Following Liu Yiting's example, we should spend more time on managing important activities and not ignore renewing the body and mind, which are two main bases of our make-up. We should also form good habits even in trivial things because they can affect our attitude towards our studies.

So *Liu has set a standard for us college students to emulate*④. I suppose we can also do what she has done and achieve our goal by making painstaking efforts.

(3) To Rise Early

*At the peep of day*⑤, nothing is more enjoyable than a walk along *the bank of a river fringed with trees*⑥. With fresh air and

---

① 自我发展
② 此处指《哈佛女孩刘亦婷》一书
③ 自我评估
④ 刘亦婷给我们树立了一个学习的榜样
⑤ 在黎明时分
⑥ 树木成行的河岸

*a sober mind*①, we can see the universe full of calm and mystery. The rising sun *bursts into view*②, and millions of golden rays shine everywhere. Wet with pearls of morning dew, the grass smiles at us, flowers nod to welcome us, and *chirping*③ birds sing their merry songs. All these can be enjoyed only by those who get up early.

To rise early is a good habit which young men ought to cultivate. To get up late can never make our mind sober and our body strong. Most of the young men, *to our deep regret*④, have the bad habit of rising late.

Morning is the best time in a day just as "spring is the year's pleasant king." Only in the morning can we remind ourselves of our life's *mission*⑤. As *promising*⑥ youths, therefore, we should cultivate good habits and do something useful, great and noble.

(4) My View on *Burning Night Oil*⑦

Today more and more people stay up late or all the night. They argue that this practice has several advantages. First, it is quiet at night and they can concentrate on what they are doing and increase efficiency. Second, some people say they are more creative during the night, because they are not disturbed by others, or just they have formed the habit. For example, when the noises of TV and telephone are not there, they can do a better job.

---

① 清醒的头脑
② 闯入视野
③ （鸟）吱吱地叫
④ 使我们深感遗憾
⑤ 任务；使命
⑥ 有希望的；有前途的
⑦ 熬夜

I am afraid I cannot agree to their opinion. To begin with, although you may feel absorbed in your subject at night, it doesn't mean you cannot do a better job at other times. In the second place, a wise man will not always burn the night oil because it is extremely harmful to his health. A German proverb says a sleeping hour before midnight is worth two after it, which means we should follow *body clock*① that regulates our physical and mental functions with normal daily activities. Finally, as to the people burning night oil playing video games online or chatting online, I myself see no reason in doing so at the price of precious time and personal health.

From the above analysis, we may arrive at the conclusion that burning the night oil is not a wise choice.

(5) Bad Habits

It is easier to go down than to climb up hill, so it is easier to *fall into*② bad habits than to *get into*③ good ones.

Bad habits don't come suddenly. They come little by little when one doesn't realize their danger. Schoolboys often *pick up*④ little bad habits at school or in the streets. When they can't do their exercises, they copy from their deskmates. If they see bigger boys smoking, they also want to learn to smoke. If they see their friends *acting a lie*⑤, they learn to do the same soon.

When they get bigger, the bad habits become stronger and stronger, so that they cannot easily get rid of their bad habits. From copying, they learn to steal. From acting a lie, they learn

---

① 生物钟
② 开始(某事);陷入(某状态)
③ 形成;染上
④ (偶然地;无意地)学会
⑤ 用行动骗人;撒谎

to cheat. At last, no one will believe them and no one will trust them. If the bad habits become still stronger, they may be put into prison. How dangerous bad habits are!

It is quite necessary for us to get rid of bad habits in the beginning so that they cannot *conquer*① us in the end.

(6) Hobbies

Almost everyone has a hobby. A hobby can be anything a person likes to do in his spare time. A hobby can provide us with interest, enjoyment, friendship, knowledge and relaxation. It can be something from which we learn more about ourselves or about the world. It may introduce us to friends who share our enthusiasm and from whom we can also learn. It helps both *manual*② and *mental*③ workers relax after periods of hard work. It also offers interesting and enjoyable activities for *retirees*④. Moreover, it can help a person's mental and physical health.

Different people have different hobbies. People who *take up*⑤ hobbies are hobbyists. Some paint pictures, sing pop songs, perform on musical instruments and enjoy collecting coins or stamps, others raise flowers, go fishing, hunt animals or spend their time on sports: climbing mountains, swimming, skating and playing football. Anyone, rich or poor, old or young, sick or well, can follow a satisfying hobby, regardless of his age, position, or income.

As for me, I like sports very much. Sometimes I play tennis

---

① 征服
② 体力的
③ 脑力的
④ 退休者
⑤ 开始(从事于)

or *badminton*① or go swimming. Sometimes I exercise alone and go running regularly in the morning. Whatever I choose, if I exercise regularly, I will be sure to maintain and improve my health throughout my life.

(7) **Philately**②

Philately is a very sound and interesting hobby that attracts more and more people. *Philatelists*③ are spending much of their spare time dealing with stamps. So great is their passion that they would *grudge*④ no pains and money for their favorites. They take pride in producing an *album*⑤ containing a large collection. They take delight in appreciating the varied designs — Chinese and foreign, old and new. Surely, there is nothing that can satisfy their thirst and appetite for stamps.

Philately has the advantage of enriching our knowledge and broadening our vision. On many stamps are printed drawings or pictures of rare birds, animals or flowers. On others there are portraits of historical figures such as Qu Yuan, Lu Sun and George Washington. Moreover, some stamps present before our eyes historical sites and famous scenic spots, not to mention the latest developments in science and technology. So in the course of time, philatelists will gain a good harvest of common sense and a large store of knowledge.

Philately can also function as a good means of improving our character. It can increase our imaginative power, enhance our

---

① 羽毛球
② 集邮
③ 集邮家；集邮者
④ 吝惜
⑤ 集邮册

*esthetic sensibility*①, or raise our *connoisseurship*②. By engaging in such a sound and interesting hobby, we keep ourselves occupied in the spare time, never feeling bored. And we maintain an *animated*③ and optimistic mind, never getting depressed. *To crown it all*④, through exchanging stamps with other persons, we develop our relationship with them so as to widen the circle of our friends.

---

① 对美的识别力
② 鉴赏力
③ 活跃的
④ 更好的是……;更令人高兴的是……

No.21 Education
教育

(1) Online Education

To some degree, being online has become part of our daily life. We can do a lot of things online, such as searching for information and communicating with friends far and near. But recently another helpful online activity has become very *in*[①]. That is online education.

Why could online education be so popular within such a short period of time? Among other reasons, the quick development of the internet should be an essential one, which makes all our dreams of attending class in the distance possible. Another underlying reason is the quick development of both society and technology.

Today, modern science and technology is developing with lightening speed. To catch up with this development we all feel an urgent and strong desire to study. However, due to the great pace of modern society, many people are too busy to study full time at school. Online education just comes to their aid.

Personally, I appreciate this new form of education. It's indeed a helpful complement to the traditional educational means. It can provide different learners with more flexible and versatile

---

① 流行的

ways of learning. Most of all, with online education, we can stick to our jobs and at the same time study and absorb the latest knowledge.

(2) Attend a College Abroad

Some people think that attending a college in a foreign country has many disadvantages. It seems to them that students in a foreign country will meet many difficulties both in life and in study. For example, they may not understand thoroughly what the teachers say just because of the language barrier, unfamiliar culture background and social custom. So if they are not flexible and determined, they are likely to fail in their study. Besides, costs and expenditure there are much higher than those in their native country, so most overseas students have to work for a living, and they can't devote all their attention to study.

But some people don't agree with them. They believe that attending a college abroad has many advantages. They think that studying abroad will enable them to learn more than they do in their own country. Besides, they can develop their ability to cope with the routine matters such as finding a part-time job, to "*work their way through college*"[①]. Moreover, they can make friends with foreigners and learn many new things to broaden their horizons and enrich their minds.

In my opinion, by attending a college abroad we can learn not only the useful knowledge of science but also the culture and customs of other nations. And what's more, the experience of foreign countries in how to develop their national economy, science and technology is of great value to our own country.

---

① 打工挣钱读完大学

(3) Are Children Overburdened?

Nowadays many people argue that children are overburdened, and that educators should find out ways to rescue them. But I do not think so.

It is true that today's children learn more than we did in our childhood, which conforms to the objective laws of child development and accords with the demands of our society. Education in the early childhood is an indispensable task in the whole world because this period is a golden age in children's mental as well as physical development. Grasping the fine chance to educate children can *get twice the result with half the effort*①. The so-called genius is the result of proper education at early stages. In addition, the whole world is full of competition, and we do need gifted successors to build our country.

In summary, I believe that children are not overburdened and that pressure impels them to study hard continuously. This is good for our society as well as for themselves. We should remember the old Chinese saying, "*If one does not exert oneself in youth, one will regret it in old age.*②"

(4) On Students Choosing Lecturers

Nowadays, some universities give students the right to decide who are to teach some of their classes. This has led to some debates over whether students should be given this much power.

There are several factors that students consider when

---

① 事半功倍
② 少壮不努力,老大徒伤悲

choosing a lecturer, including the teaching style of the lecturer, the lecturer's academic background, and the lecturer's reputation among students. The ideal lecturer is one who has an interesting teaching style, a diverse academic background, and a good reputation among students.

There are both positive and negative aspects to allowing students to choose their lecturers. Giving students the choice encourages them to take ownership for their classes, and also puts pressure on teachers to improve their teaching quality. However, the factors that students consider might not be the ones that lead to the highest quality of education. Schools might *end up with*① lecturers who teach some interesting classes without much substantive content.

(5) Quality Education

Nowadays, educationalists advocate that Quality Education should be *promoted*② in the country. But the situation worries them a lot. Students are being burdened with countless homework and various examinations, and their development of other important nonacademic qualities is *hindered*③ or totally overlooked.

It is obvious that Quality Education is beneficial to students. First, it will, to some extent, free them from homework and tests. Second, it can broaden students' horizon and enhance their capacities. What's more, it values ability more than memory, so students will develop their abilities in an all-round manner.

But how can Quality Education be enforced? First, the

---

① 结果得到，最后获得
② 提倡，促进
③ 受阻

education system should be reformed by changing the educational objectives, revising the *syllabuses*① and so on. Second, the workforce of teachers should be trained and new teachers with more innovative ideas and higher qualifications should be employed. Third, new advanced practices and teaching materials should be introduced from countries with developed education system. In this way, a new educational prospect will be in sight in the near future.

(6) Is Study Pressure Good for University Students?

As regards the study pressure in universities, students vary in their opinions. Some argue that too much pressure is harmful to their academic life; while others regard pressure as a driving force that encourages them to work hard and be top students.

As far as I am concerned, too much pressure from study will do harm to the academic life. First and foremost, being overburdened by study, students will be exhausted and become less creative. Moreover, excessive tension will do no good to their physical health. Only a sound body could guarantee long-term efficient academic study and research.

As the proverb goes, "All work and no play makes Jack a dull boy", so the university students should balance their work and leisure by putting aside enough time for relaxation. Only in this way could higher efficiency in academic study be ensured.

(7) Does Higher Education Cease to Be Useful?

Disappointment is *prevailing*② among Chinese university

---

① 课程大纲
② 流行

graduates. In spite of four-year diligent study, some of them still have difficulty in landing a decent job on today's tight job market. Doubts about the function of higher education arise among youngsters.

What does higher education bring to us? First of all, academic lectures and research *endow* students *with*① more insights into the nature of the world and society, and nurture good methods of dealing with problems they would encounter anytime in the future. Moreover, social activities and *field trips*② are necessary preparations for future careers. In this way, youngsters will learn to regard highly the value of cooperation and interpersonal skills. Lastly, the *climate*③ of freedom at college *facilitates*④ the cultivation of independence, which will doubtlessly be of help to career success.

All in all, a good command of foreign languages, or if possible, a minor degree in other fields would make Chinese university graduates more marketable on the job market.

(8) Graduate School Rush

Recently, all kinds of graduate schools have become more and more popular. A large number of college seniors spend their summer vacation and the whole fall semester preparing for the graduate school entrance examination, and an increasing number of those who have already got a job are also considering entering their names. The picture vividly shows that the suspension bridge leading to the castle, graduate school, is becoming more and more crowded though the planned enrollment figure has been growing

---

① 赋予
② 实地考察
③ 氛围
④ 促进

rather quickly.

There are several reasons for this phenomenon. First of all, many college graduates have realized that postgraduates *have superiority over*① them in the job market. They would rather spend two or three more years at university in order to find a more satisfactory job. Moreover, their interests also play a role in this trend. A considerable number of students have chosen their undergraduate programs *at random*②, or they were too young to make a proper decision at that time. Later they may find they are not interested at all in what they have learned. Entering a graduate school provides the best opportunity for them to change their field of specialization. Apart from those, many people who have jobs find it helpful to continue their study at graduate school. Their purpose is to learn more about their subject. People rush into graduate schools out of pragmatic and academic reasons.

The trend shows that people value education more and more. This will inevitably further raise the level of our national education and, as a result, speed up the economic development of our country. Therefore, let's *cheer for*③ the "graduate school rush", which, to some extent, provides even grander prospects for China's economic development.

(9) Active Classes or Passive Classes?

Although classes often seem outwardly alike, the differences between passive and active classes are *enormous*④.

The passive kind of class usually has a teacher who lectures,

---

① 比……有优势
② 随意地
③ 支持,呐喊助威
④ 巨大的

puts outlines and terms on the blackboard and *dispenses*① information to the students. For example, my *sophomore*② biology teacher, Mr. Li, rarely looked up from his notebook in which he had carefully written all his lectures. Teachers in a passive classroom simply dictate information and answers. *They pour facts into the students like water into a sieve.*③ The students are usually forced to sit, listen, take notes, and do only what the teacher has required.

The other kind of class, the active kind, usually has a teacher who *stimulates*④ the students to learn for themselves by asking questions, by *posing problems*⑤, and most of all, by being a student, too. Such a teacher might plan the outline of a course, but doesn't force the class in only one direction. Students in active classes become more involved in their learning; they ask questions and read books to search for some answers themselves, then discuss what they have found in class.

I prefer active classes because learning becomes fun. Although students may not care much about the facts taught in classes, their attitudes toward learning and their excitement in developing answers for themselves don't end with the class.

(10) The "Hope Project"

Education plays a very important role in the modernization of our country. Without a well-educated population, China will not be able to achieve its planned economic growth, to catch up with the more developed nations technologically, or to greatly improve

---

① 发送
② （大学或高中）二年级
③ 他们把信息一股脑儿地灌给学生，就像把水灌进过滤器一样。
④ 激发
⑤ 提问

the living standard of its people. Yet according to recent statistics, there are over two million school-age children who have dropped out of school in the *poverty-stricken areas*[①] of the countryside.

To help those poor kids go back to school, the lack of money seems to be the biggest problem. As there are thousands of things to be done in the *full-scale*[②] reconstruction of our economy, our government simply does not have enough money to help all those poor kids in time. And most parents of the school drop-outs are unable to raise the money needed to give their children a decent education. So a nationwide *drive*[③] called the "Hope Project" has been launched to rescue those children from a life of illiteracy and ignorance.

The "Hope Project" is both necessary and timely to *alleviate*[④] the government part of its financial problem. It also brings hope to the *deprived children*[⑤]. But we need more than the "Hope Project" based on the love and generosity of ordinary citizens. Only by *laying* greater *emphasis on*[⑥] the importance of learning and knowledge and establishing a better funded public education system can we guarantee the realization of the hopes cherished by all the children in China.

(11) The Reform of the College Curricula

Nowadays some college graduates complain that what they learned at college is not much helpful to them in their work. They

---

① 贫困地区
② 全面的;大规模的
③ 运动
④ 减轻
⑤ 被剥夺了入学机会的孩子
⑥ 强调

find most of the knowledge they acquired in class is *out-dated*①, impractical and even *inapplicable*② to their work.

*It is high time*③ for colleges to advance a revised teaching program and *adapt* its curricula *to*④ the new economic system. In the past decades, the teaching goals have been closely connected with the planned economy and great importance was attached to pure theory. However, now that *a market-oriented economy*⑤ has been adopted, one can hardly imagine that a student of arts focusing on pure theory will be competent for any career in the future.

In a word, the *shift*⑥ of the economic system requires a corresponding change in our college curricula. It is essential to make adjustment and catch up with new developments. Our limited time of college studies should not be wasted on certificates and degrees.

(12) Hard Life Is Good for Children

There is an old English saying:"*Spare the rod and spoil the child.*"⑦ Beethoven's father made a very strict demand on his son and struck him hard or *scolded*⑧ him *bitterly*⑨ whenever he was lazy or *disobedient*⑩. In order to make a child grow healthily, we

---

① 过时的
② 无法应用的
③ ……是非常必要的了
④ 使……适应
⑤ 市场经济
⑥ 变化;转变
⑦ (谚)孩子不打不成器。
⑧ 申斥;怒骂
⑨ 严厉地
⑩ 不听话;不顺从的

must let him eat bitter foods, do hard work and *plunge into*① such places where he can get the fullest training and knowledge.

To begin with, eating bitter foods is necessary for a child, which are generally easier *to digest*② than sugary or oily foods. Moreover, giving a child poor food to eat can help *cultivate*③ in him the *frugal habit*④ and make him realize that what we eat daily is the fruit of the sweat of the labouring people. As a result, he will not be wasteful when he grows up.

We should also let a child do hard work. Doing hard work will give him an opportunity to taste the bitterness of *arduous*⑤ labour and get him highly trained so that he will make progress quickly. Besides, hard work may enable him to cherish the fruit of the labour of others. Children who live luxuriously and comfortably can never *become somebody*⑥ in the future.

Lastly, children should be sent to some places where life is hard if possible. Human society is full of tests and *trials*⑦. Flowers from a *greenhouse*⑧ can never *withstand*⑨ a storm. Therefore, we must let a child face the world and *brave the storm*⑩. It is in difficult conditions that young people can get the most training and learn how to solve problems *in various circumstances*⑪.

If we fail to follow the three points discussed above, we will

---

① 投入;置身于
② 消化
③ 培养
④ 节俭的习惯
⑤ 艰巨的;艰苦的
⑥ 有出息
⑦ 考验;磨炼;艰苦
⑧ 温室
⑨ 经受住;顶住
⑩ 冒风雨
⑪ 在各种情况下

only harm the child and make him an ordinary man incapable of accomplishing anything in his life.

(13) The Advantages and Disadvantages of Private Tutoring

A recent investigation shows that about 70 percent of pupils in cities have private tutors. While private tutoring has both advantages and disadvantages, I feel the disadvantages are greater.

Such a popular practice indicates that people are *attaching greater importance to*① education. Many parents, *for various reasons*②, missed the chance of obtaining a good education. When their children meet with difficulties in study, they are helpless. Private tutoring is the only solution. As private tutoring is usually one-to-one, the teacher knows the weak points as well as strong points of the pupil, and teaching is, in most cases, directly *to the point*③. Private tutoring thus benefits a lot of pupils.

On the other hand, private tutoring has its own disadvantages. For one thing, it *takes up*④ so much of the pupil's time that they can hardly find enough time for rest and entertainment, which are essential for their physical and mental health. For another, some tutors, busy "*shuttling*"⑤ from one family to another, tend to neglect their regular teaching duties. What is more, some tutors are eager to help pupils to do well on the test, offering the so-called *tips*⑥ for test-taking rather than

---

① 给……以更多的重视
② 由于各种各样的原因
③ 切中要害；针对问题
④ 占用
⑤ 穿梭往返于
⑥ 窍门

help them acquire what is most needed.

  Generally speaking, the disadvantages *outweigh*① the advantages. Greater emphasis should be laid on classroom teaching and practice, on the improvement of teaching quality and on the *tapping*② of the pupil's potential. Only in this way can a new generation be healthily brought up.

① 超过
② 开发

No.22 Children and Childhood
儿童与童年

(1) When I Was a Child

When I was a child, I could not wait to become an adult. I wanted very badly to be independent and to live alone so that I did not have to do what my parents wanted me to do. I could leave my dirty clothes on the floor if I wanted to or leave the dirty dishes in the *sink*① for a week if I so wished.

I did not want to have to rely on anybody. I wanted a job so that I did not have to depend on my parents for money. I also did not want to rely on anyone for a place to live. I wanted my own apartment so that my parents could not disapprove if I came home too late or had *loud*② parties. Also, with my own apartment, no one could get angry at me if I shut the door too loudly, forgot to turn the lights off, or stood with the refrigerator door open. If I lived alone, no longer would there be long discussions about who I was going out with, when I would return, and other typical questions my parents asked. Everything in the apartment would be my own belongings, my things — life would be excellent.

Now that I am an adult, I look back and laugh. I can see how *infantile*③ my thoughts about adulthood really were.

---

① （厨房内洗菜、碟等的）洗涤槽
② 吵闹的，喧噪的
③ 幼稚的，孩子气的

Independence is a very difficult *situation*①, with a lot of responsibilities and *emotional stress*②. I sometimes want to be a dependent child again.

(2) My Childhood

I was born in a village, which was *semicircular in shape*③, with a large sea in front, and many kinds of trees planted on all sides. About a mile from the left side of the village, there stood *a seven-storied pagoda*④, built more than a thousand years ago and about three hundred feet in height.

In spring, some of my classmates and I always climbed up to the top of the pagoda to see the *budding*⑤ beautiful flowers.

In summer, we spent most of the time in the forests, picking wild flowers and fruits to eat. I seldom went to swim because twice I nearly drowned myself.

Autumn was the kite flying season. Every one of my *pals*⑥ went to the hill with me to fly kites. Kite flying was not the only sport, and *cricket fighting*⑦ was another popular one. We always went to all places to catch as many crickets as we could. When we caught them, we brought them home and *sorted out*⑧ the best ones. We took good care of them and trained them to be good fighters.

In winter, though the weather was cold, we seldom stayed at home. We used to go to other places to engage in *pebble-throwing*

---

① 境遇,处境
② 情感方面的压力
③ 半圆形
④ 七层高的塔
⑤ 含苞待放
⑥ 伙伴
⑦ 斗蟋蟀
⑧ 拣选出

battles[①]. This battle was fought between two groups of boys from two villages, and we just threw pebbles at each other. When most of the boys had left a certain side, that side was defeated and they had to *pay tribute to*[②] the winners.

As time sped rapidly on, those childish habits or pastimes seem like an empty dream, and they have become a historical page of my life.

(3) My Boyhood Days

Whenever I recall my boyhood days, I often have a mixed feeling of regret and happiness. In fact, there is more regret than happiness. For if there were any past happy moments, they are gone and can not be recovered.

I am the only boy of my parents' three children. As boys are prized more than girls in a Chinese family, I received more care than my sisters in my boyhood days. My parents were ready to buy me anything that I wanted. But also I was more strictly educated as boys are regarded as the pillar of a family. They sent me to the best school in town.

The happiest moments which are still vivid to me are those past evenings. After supper, my father used to tell us stories of brave and honest boys. He always ended his story-telling by patting on my shoulders and said, "My son, I hope you will grow up like the hero in the story." My mother and my sisters never failed to echo the expectations with applause as if I had already been a hero.

Now I am already a young man. I regret that their hope is still a dream. However, there is no use regretting. I will make good use of

---

① 扔石头玩打仗的游戏
② 进贡

the present and try my best to *live up to*① their expectation.

(4) A Better Understanding Between Parents and Children

There is often a lack of understanding between parents and children. Children often complain that their parents cannot understand them, while parents feel sorry that their children seldom listen to them. Why?

First of all, owing to their different ages, experiences and ways of thinking, they have different likes and dislikes. Children are energetic and curious. They are eager to learn. Meanwhile, they are active. They enjoy a lot from taking part in all kinds of activities. On the contrary, parents are practical and realistic. They prefer a peaceful and smooth environment, especially when they are at home. After housework, they like watching TV, reading newspapers or having conversations with their family members.

Misunderstanding is another reason. Children regard their parents' concern for them as a burden. They ask for independence. However, in the parents' eyes, their children are still young and need to be taken care of under their wings. When children *turn a deaf ear to*② their *well-intentioned*③ advice, they feel angry and sad.

To solve this, for parents, they should treat their children as friends rather than small babies and try to understand the feelings and thoughts of the young. For children, they should respect their parents and be aware that what their parents do is just for their good. The problem will be solved if parents and children both make their efforts.

---

① 不辜负;实践(誓言)
② 听而不闻;一耳朵进,一耳朵出
③ 好意的

No.23 | Recollections of the Past
往事的回忆

(1) My Days in the Middle School

My middle school life was the best part of my life. The school was in Hangzhou, Zhejiang, situated near the beautiful West Lake. On Sundays, I used to visit the lake with three or four schoolmates, cycling or walking along its bank; we would not stop until we were perfectly tired. But after a night of sound sleep, I got up the next morning with *renewed vigour*① and could study with more than *ordinary efficiency*②.

But this is not the reason why I consider my middle school life the best part of my life. The real reason is that all my teachers at the middle school were respectable men. In the classroom they were never *negligent*③, they were strict both in teaching and in giving marks. But after school the serious faces became smiling ones. They came into our bedrooms and chatted with us, and came to our playground and played with us. They were all young men. A stranger would not take them to be teachers for they were quite like us students, and we considered them to be our schoolmates.

I wish I could become a boy of sixteen or seventeen again and

---

① 恢复的精力
② 通常的效率
③ 不负责任的

enjoy middle school life once more.

(2) Farewell to My Middle School Life

Six years of happy middle school life was about to end. Our class held a farewell party and all of us had a photo taken as a memory. We were all sad to think that we were going to part from each other soon.

At the party, some classmates said that they would do their best to pass the entrance exam to enter a college; others stated that they would *take up an occupation*① to help their family; and still others, including me, felt at a loss concerning the future. In tears our monitor recited a poem to say "Goodbye" to all of us. Our teacher made a final speech to encourage us to go forward and *treasure*② our friendship forever. With a song of farewell the party ended. On leaving I looked for the last time at the *deserted classroom*③, and at my empty seat. A strange feeling of sorrow flowed in my heart. In the school yard I could see my footprints everywhere — on the paths, beside the flowerbeds, on the playground, around the trees and in front of the houses.

Farewell to my school, where I studied hard and played pleasantly, where I was educated and brought up, and where I passed six years of my golden youth! Farewell to my unforgettable middle school life!

(3) A Terrifying Experience

I was spending the night in my uncle's village one summer.

---

① 参加工作
② 珍重;珍视
③ 无人的;空荡荡的教室

"往事的回忆 Recollections of the Past No.23"

At bedtime, being in a different bed and feeling excited, I was unable to get asleep. The quiet and peaceful moonlight was so attractive that I *slipped out of my bed*① and went to the garden. My cousin Wen Ping was there. We soon started a conversation in front of the garden fence. Suddenly, I heard a strange noise coming from behind.

Turning around, I saw, creeping just behind my heels, a snake of a considerable length. "Ah," cried I, frightened *out of my wits*②. "Stand still, Wen Qing! Don't move," my cousin shouted.

The snake crept slowly under my feet. My heart beat fast, and my brow was covered with sweat. I *stood rooted to the ground*③. Luckily, the snake crept away without taking any notice of me.

After the danger had passed, I managed to turn to Wen Ping and say, "Let's go." This was easier said than done, for it was almost impossible for us to move our *limbs*④, which had turned stone-stiff.

(4) A Meaningful Day to Remember

Last Tuesday was the most meaningful day I have ever had, because I not only had a good time, but also made others happy. I will always remember that day. In the morning, our *mixed chorus*⑤ of ten went to the huge *auditorium*⑥ of Yangzhou City and gave a successful performance. We sang in front of thousands

---

① 悄悄地下床
② 不知所措
③ 站着发呆;呆若木鸡
④ 肢体;四肢
⑤ 男女声合唱团
⑥ 礼堂

of people. We were on TV, too. When we finished, everyone stood up and cheered and threw flowers at us. Mr. Jim, the mayor of the city, gave a short speech to praise us and also had a photo with us. And then we were invited to a famous Chinese restaurant. The food was rich and delicious, much better than my mom's cooking. So everyone of us had a big meal. After lunch, we *went sightseeing*① around the city. To end our day, we went out dancing at a disco until midnight. That day I had a good time although my feet were killing me!

(5) My Surprise Birthday Party

Last Tuesday turned out to be a different and special day — the first time *anybody*② gave me a surprise birthday party!

It started out for me like any other day. When I first arrived at the office, the boss sent me to the bank to *cash a check*③. I worked at my desk from the time I returned until lunch, when I went out to our usual "*hangout*④" to meet some friends. Instead of continuing the work on my desk when I got back, I was surprised to see my boss carrying a birthday cake with my name on it and leading everybody into my office. Someone had told her that it was my birthday and they all arranged for a surprise party. Sending me to bank was how she got me out of the way so the people could bring in the cake and party trimmings without me seeing anything.

That birthday party is an event I know I will never forget because it was really so unexpected.

---

① 观光游览
② 此处用作名词，意为"重要人物"
③ 兑现一张支票
④ 经常去的地方

(6) Farewell to Home-village

Up to now, I still vividly remember the time when I left my beloved family and that small home-village. It is a piece of memory that can never be brushed off my mind.

Years ago, at a sunset when all birds were flying to their nests, I was leaving my home all alone on a *creaking*① oxcart. My parents and my younger brothers and sisters saw me off to the tall *pagoda tree* ② at the entrance of the village. The gentle advice and concerns they repeatedly expressed, along with the sight of looking at me and waving at me under the tree in the distance, *faded away*③ soon, as the oxcart was *rattling*④ along with the tardy sound of trampling hoofs.

A long way off, when I turned and looked back at the tranquil village my eyes blurred with tears. I saw the village now immersed in the *serenity*⑤ of the dusk. And the top of the old pagoda tree towering over the village, was nodding in the breeze of the twilight. It was just like mom's wrinkled hands, waving at me forever with expectation, with melancholy, and with a subtle tinge of sadness that shook my resolutions to leave.

---

① 吱吱作响
② 槐树
③ 慢慢减弱
④ 发出卡嗒卡嗒声
⑤ 平静

No.24 Profession 职业与择业

(1) College Students' Job Hunting

In recent years, college students find it increasingly difficult to get a job. It sounds strange since young college students are usually intelligent, well-educated, *aspirant*① and eager to bring their talent into full play. Then, what *underlines*② this phenomenon?

There are several reasons for this. To begin with, nowadays college students aim too high. What they want are "good" jobs which could offer good salary, comfortable working conditions and high social status. Consequently, most college students are unwilling to accept vacant jobs that they consider not "good" enough. Another reason is that there is a big gap between the majors some students study in school and the demands of vacant jobs.

Solution to the problem requires efforts on both the society and the students. The companies should value the students' talent and knowledge while the latter should not merely aim at material gains. They should be *down-to-earth*③ in building up their career. Furthermore, they should learn to identify their

---

① 胸怀大志
② 加强，加剧
③ 脚踏实地

weak points so as to improve themselves and be more competent.

(2) How to Succeed in a Job Interview

A job interview is vital to the job-hunting process in that if you are successful in it, you stand a good chance of finally obtaining the ideal job. Then how can we succeed in a job interview?

In the first place, you should dress and behave properly in order to leave a good first impression on the interviewer. In the second place, when it comes to talking, you should speak of your *expertise*① and special abilities clearly and honestly. What's more, self-confidence is also an important factor. If necessary, just put confidence in yourself and tell the interviewer that you will face the challenge whenever you encounter difficulties.

You will succeed in a job interview as long as you put the above principles into practice. As a result, you will most probably obtain the job you have been dreaming of.

(3) Why Do Graduates Find Jobs Irrelevant to Their Majors?

As a latest survey shows, there are 45 percent of the graduates whose jobs are irrelevant to their majors in 2008 while there were only 30 percent in 2002, excluding those who continue to study. People may wonder what makes it increasingly difficult for college graduates to find a rewarding desirable job.

A number of reasons might contribute to the phenomenon. On the one hand, many colleges and universities fail to adapt the courses to the development of the economy. On the other hand, there is an oversupply of college graduates in some specialties,

---

① 专业技术

and it keeps increasing. Therefore, many of them have to take other jobs which are not relevant to their majors.

The problems that most of the college students encountered in job hunting begin to invite the attention of the whole society. First of all, the colleges and universities should make their courses meet the needs of the society and follow the on-going development of national economy. Besides, the government should provide college graduates with more opportunities to display their skills.

(4) Suitability Is the Key to a Good Job

What is a good job? Different people may have different answers: good salary, light workload, and high social status, etc. Yet then why are some people still unhappy even if they are privileged to all these? As I see it, the best job should be the one that suits your personality and interest.

For one thing, a good job is not only the means of "*making a living*①", but is a career that can "*make a life*②". High salary is desirable, nevertheless it does not automatically lead to happiness if one does not love the work; light workload is attractive, but it equals idleness if one does not engage in the work; high status is enviable, but it does not produce respect if one does not do the job well. Doing something that interests you turns work into a kind of enjoyment.

For another thing, a suitable job is the best in the long run. It is able to tap people's enthusiasm and initiative, so that they can constantly improve themselves. A motivated worker can acquire knowledge and skills more willingly, and hence foster the

---

① 维持生计
② 过有意义的生活

capability to do the job better in the future. What's more, with good performance, pay will raise and promotion may follow.

A suitable job provides a platform for workers to develop themselves. Therefore, I believe suitability is the key to a good job.

(5) Choosing the Right Careers

We often talk about what we want to be after graduation. Some want to be teachers, some want to be film stars. A few young people simply don't know what should be their right career.

Choosing the right career is very important, however, as it often decides whether a person can be a successful one or a failure in life. Before you choose a career, first you must know the nature of the career, its advantages and disadvantages, and whether it suits your own character or not. If you don't have an ear for music, never dream to be a singer; suppose you are not good at maths, give up the hope of becoming an astronaut. We should keep in mind what *Lao Tze*① said, "*He who knows himself is wise.*"②

You needn't feel disheartened for that. Try to find out your own talent and get yourself well trained. Teaching, newspaper work, medicine, engineering—these and many other fields offer *fascinating*③ careers to persons with talent and training.

(6) On College Students Supporting Rural Construction

Nowadays, college graduates are encouraged to find jobs in

---

① 老子
② 自知者明
③ 吸引人的

rural area to support its construction, such as village officials, agriculture technicians, teachers, etc. According to statistics, the number of students who have got jobs in rural area is on the rise.

Several factors lead to the phenomenon. Firstly, there is an urgent need of brains in the countryside. Actually, the root of poverty in those regions is the lack of knowledge. Therefore, talents importing is the first step to the success of the development. Secondly, with the expansion of college enrollment, the job market becomes more and more competitive. Graduates find themselves difficult to get a satisfactory job in urban area, especially in big cities. Thirdly, government's call arouses many graduates' patriotism and enthusiasm to join the rural construction.

As for me, I am proud of those students who have devoted themselves to the rural construction. I firmly believe that with the great effort of the government and the student workers, the rural region will be well developed and become better off in near future.

(7) My View on *Job-hopping*①

Many people are inclined to do one job in their lives. In their opinions, people who change their jobs frequently are *superficial*② and *tactless*③. They believe that the only way to success is to stick to one job, for constant practice in a professional field helps make an expert.

But there are still many people who don't agree. They argue that change means progress. If you are not satisfied with your

---
① 此处指"跳槽;不停地换工作"
② 肤浅的;浅薄的
③ 得罪人的;言行不得体的

present job, of course you have the right to replace it with a more challenging and better-paid one. Every change is a step to further success. This idea may be the reason why they change their jobs so often.

For my part, I think it reasonable to change your job if you have a better opportunity. But once you have found a position where you can fully display your ability, it is advisable to settle down to it and put all your efforts into it. Only in this way can you get the true joy of achieving your goal.

(8) Teaching — My Profession

Teaching is a noble profession. Many people like to engage in it, and so do I. To me, no profession under the sun is more glorious than the profession of teaching.

Teaching is a significant job. Through my work, I will pass knowledge from one generation to another; through my work, I'll teach my students to be real and useful men to the society and people.

But teaching is also a very demanding job. Teachers need to have a wide range of knowledge. Therefore, I must work hard in all subjects. I should always remember that knowledge is a matter of science, and no dishonesty or *conceit*① is permissible. What it requires is definitely the opposite — honesty and modesty.

I hope I can become a successful teacher. I often tell myself that I should always think of the interest of the students. I'll try my best to be their good teacher and helpful friend.

---

① 骄傲;自负

No.25 | Health
健康

(1) How to Keep Healthy

Nowadays more and more people are concerned about their health. If you happen to be in one of the city parks in the early morning, you will see lots of people there. Some are practicing *taijiquan* and sword-play and others are either running, walking, or exercising through dance. Research shows that getting plenty of exercise makes the heart beat faster and the lung work harder, thus strengthening the heart and reducing the chance of heart attack, and helping to lower blood pressure.

Medical researchers have proved that what people eat affects their health. They advise people to eat more fruits and vegetables and less red meat like beef and pork because red meats contain more fat than poultry and fish. Fats can *build up*[①] in the *arteries*[②], *block*[③] the flow of blood, and cause a heart attack or stroke.

Getting rid of bad habits like smoking and drinking alcohol is also an important way to keep healthy, but it still fails to *draw enough people's attention*[④]. If people pay equal attention to the

---

① 聚集
② 动脉
③ 堵塞
④ 引起人们足够的注意

above mentioned three ways of keeping fit, they will greatly improve their health.

(2) Staying Healthy

Good health is the most valuable possession a person can have. There are three things that a person can do to stay in good shape. He should eat the right foods, get enough rest, and exercise regularly.

Proper nutrition is important for good health. Avoid foods with lots of sugar and fat. Eat plenty of high *protein*[①] foods, vegetables, and fruits. Do not overeat. It is not healthful to be overweight.

Getting the proper amount of sleep is also important. Without enough sleep, you feel tired and *irritable*[②]. Allow yourself eight hours' sleep each night.

Finally, get plenty of exercise. Exercise improves your heart and lungs, and prevents you from gaining weight. Swimming, basketball, bicycling, and running all provide good exercise.

If everybody were to eat the right foods, get plenty of sleep, and exercise regularly, there would be much less complaining about poor health.

(3) Health Improvements in Developing Countries

In the past three decades, developing countries have made great progress in many aspects, among which are the improvements in health *domain*[③].

---

① 蛋白质
② 脾气躁的;易恼怒的
③ 领域

Such improvement can be seen clearly in the *chart*① that the *life expectancy*② in 1960 in developing countries was only 40 years old, while by 1990 it reached about 60 years old. On the other hand, the *infant mortality*③ dropped from 20 precent to 10 percent in the same period.

Obviously, it is not difficult to find reasons for these changes. First, people's living conditions are much better than before. With nutritious food, spacious rooms, a longer life is the definite result. Moreover, good medical technology provides better medical care to both the aged and the newly-born, either at home or in hospital. With further development of society, we can hopefully expect that a much higher *life expectancy*④ and a lower rate of infant mortality will appear in the future.

(4) How to Lose Weight

A beautiful and healthy figure is everyone's dream. However, not everyone can fulfill this dream. Overweight people often have to find ways to lose weight.

For normal healthy people, weight is gained by taking in more calories than the body needs. Therefore, if you want to lose weight, you either have to eat fewer calories or find ways to use up more calories than you take in. *Dieting*⑤ is probably the most popular way of losing weight, because when on a diet, you are taking fewer calories.

However, the body needs many chemicals in order to stay

---

① 图表
② 寿命
③ 婴儿死亡率
④ 预期寿命
⑤ 节食

healthy, and "*fad*"① or starvation diets are bad because they are not nutritiously balanced. A better way of dieting is to *keep track of*② everything you eat, either by your own careful choices or buying, for a week at a time, the packaged meals sold by some diet companies. If you do not exercise normally, you should also begin doing exercises sensible for your age and life style to help your body use up calories.

In short, a combined effort of reducing the calories you eat and using up more calories than usual through exercises should help you lose part of your weight.

(5) Health and Life

It is a common saying that we do not fully learn the value of a thing until we lose it; we don't know what health is until we are ill. "Health is of vital importance to life" sounds like a *cliché*③ to everyone, but it is absolutely true.

The negligence of the delicate balance of your body and soul, the harmful habits such as smoking, excessive drinking and *burning mid-night oil*④ will impair one's health. How many big plans are interrupted by poor health! Even a normal life is unimaginable without the guarantee of health.

How to keep fit is an eternal topic of diversity and controversy. Regardless of all the different suggestions poured from all kinds of sources, one should do at least two things for himself. First, hold an active and optimistic attitude toward life and maintain a mental well being. Second, live a regular life and keep a balanced diet. Anyway, a healthy life is within reach when

---

① 一时的风尚
② 计算,记录
③ 陈词滥调
④ 熬夜

you begin to adjust your mind and body.

(6) People's Knowledge of AIDS in China

Since the first reported case of AIDS in China in 1985, the number of both those who *develop AIDS*① and those who carry AIDS has been increasing rapidly. The serious situation has attracted more and more attention. However, surveys indicate that the Chinese people's knowledge of AIDS is scanty.

In cities, more residents know about AIDS than people in suburban or rural areas. According to a *random survey*② conducted in big cities such as Beijing, Shanghai and Guangzhou, 6.82% of the inhabitants had heard of AIDS, 15.48% knew about it, 77.70% knew little about it.

When asked how AIDS is spread, those who claimed to know a lot about AIDS gave various answers. 16% of them believed that external contact would lead to the spread of AIDS; half of them mentioned sexual relationship and mother-baby channel; 34% included sexual behavior, blood transfusions and *needle sharing*③. The survey also revealed that the younger and the better educated a person was, the more likely he or she was to be aware of the threat of this disease.

Regarding the seriousness of AIDS, 1% of those who replied believed that there was no need to worry; 56% held that the AIDS problem was not serious; 8.59% recognized that the problem was serious but only in some areas; 13.77% advocated more efforts; 8% were uncertain.

It is evident that AIDS education needs to be enhanced here

---

① 患艾滋病
② 随机调查
③ 共用针头

in China. The more people who understand how the disease is spread and what they can do to lessen their risk of getting AIDS, the better. Public awareness about AIDS and the resulting social issues need to be brought to the attention of all Chinese, not just the young and the educated.

No.26 My Parents
我的父母

(1) Motherly Love

Only motherly love is true love. You must have seen how sincerely mothers love their children. When you were a baby, your mother protected you as best as she could. In your waking hours she held you in her arms. Whenever you made the least noise, she stopped her work *to attend to*[①] you. Sometimes, when she slept at night, the least *stir*[②] on your part would awake her. She *set her whole heart on*[③] you, so much that she even forgot her own sleep. She protected you *without hoping for any reward*[④]. Your natural growing was the only reward she expected — her only source of *consolation*[⑤].

When you were old enough to go to school, you might not feel anything. But your mother never forgot you. When it grew a little colder, she would think that you might be wearing too little clothing. When it grew a little warmer, she would think that you were wearing too much clothing. When there was anything nice to eat in the family, she would wish you were at home to eat it.

① 照顾
② 骚动
③ 一心扑在……上
④ 不求任何回报
⑤ 慰藉

When she heard of your good health and good work at school, she would feel as happy as though the good health and good work were hers. *In case*① your health and work were not very good, she would feel sorry for you — even more sorry than you felt yourself. When you went home for a vacation, she would make your bed and prepare foods for you, as she would do when she was about to receive some guests. When you were about to start for your school at the end of a vacation, she *fixed up*② your things for you and told you where to find your *wadded clothing*③, where to find your shirts and where to find your money. If you searched your trunk carefully, you might find some tears in a corner, which your mother had shed because she could not bear the thought of separating from you.

When you have grown up and married, your thoughts will turn to your wife. At that time your mother will not blame you, but feel very happy instead. She does not hope for a reward from you, but only hopes for your happiness. Moreover, she is willing to *sacrifice*④ her own happiness for yours. What *sacred love*⑤ this is!

(2) My Beloved Mother

If you ask me whom I love best in the world, I'll say *without the slightest hesitation*⑥: my mother. Like many other Chinese women, my mother is diligent. She works in a primary school. In order to teach well, she prepares her lectures very carefully and

---

① 如果；假使
② 整理好
③ 棉衣
④ 牺牲
⑤ 神圣的爱
⑥ 毫不犹豫地

often works very late at night.

Mother is very kind and sincere. She gets along well with her neighbours and colleagues. When they have difficulties, she is always ready to *lend them a helpful hand*①. Therefore, she is loved and respected in our neighbourhood.

Mother often tells me to be honest and upright. She expects me to be useful to the people in the future. Up till now, I still remember her saying, "Do as much as you can and you'll succeed."

(3) My Mother

My mother is an educated lady — a lady of the new type. She treats my father kindly. She cares for her children willingly. She treats my grandmother as if she were her own mother, so my grandmother loves her.

When my mother has spare time, she reads books and newspapers. She knows many stories. After supper, we often sit in our sitting-room hearing her tell stories. As she was once a teacher she can tell stories very interestingly. When we find any difficulty in our lessons, we *consult*② our mother. Her explanation is very helpful; so she is not only our mother but also our teacher.

She takes us out of doors on Sundays. She wants us to study hard, but does not want us to study too hard. She never allows us to study late at night. On the other hand, when we are playing, she often warns us not to waste time so as to fail in the examination. Therefore, we always prepare our lessons very

---

① 帮助他们
② 请教

well, and do not need to *cram*① when an examination approaches.

She loves us very much, but does not allow us to do anything wrong, such as smoking, drinking alcohol, or gambling. Of course, she does not do such things herself; she sets us a good example herself.

(4) The Busiest Person in My Family

In my opinion, my father is the busiest person in the family. He works at a university. Besides giving lectures, he does most of the housework. Almost every day he *has a full schedule*② and can't afford much leisure.

Yesterday, for example, he had to get up very early. He did some shopping, prepared our breakfast, and went to work in a hurry, because he had to go to the classroom before 8 o'clock. Right after the first two classes, he went to his office to prepare his lessons for the next day. He came back home at 12. He cooked our lunch and wrote a letter. After lunch he went out to mail the letter. Afterward, he had an appointment with his friend to talk over some important things. On the way to work, he had his hair cut and shoes repaired. Then he went to the lab to do experiments. In the evening, he corrected students' reports until 11.

Although my father is a very busy person, he feels happy. He often says: "Being idle will make me ill." So he often finds something to do to keep himself busy.

---

① 赶功课;考前突击
② 时间安排得很紧

(5) Parents Are the Best Teachers

Who teaches you to walk? Who teaches you to speak? It is your parents who teach you to do these basic things in your life. So don't you think that parents are the best teachers!

Firstly, parents know us very much. Parents give us life, and I think that we will spend large amount of time with them. So they know our *merit and demerit*① in details. Meanwhile, they will help us to get rid of our demerit.

Furthermore, parents possess many experiences. Since they are older than us, they have experienced many things. Sometimes, they are just like our models. And as the saying goes, "Example is better than precept,"② so we will unconsciously copy some of our parents' habits and styles of behavior, i. e., we can learn many things from them.

Finally, parents will teach us everything. Since school teachers can just teach us knowledge from the books, our parents can teach us everything. For example, I learn knitting, cooking and make-up from my mother, while learn *fixing leaky faucet*③ from my father. They are the persons who love me most, so they will teach me everything *without reservations*④.

Just as the saying goes, "There is no place like home," and I think there is no teacher like our parents. They are the best teachers in our life.

---

① 优缺点
② 身教胜于言传
③ 修理漏水的龙头
④ 毫无保留地

No.27 My Hometown
我的家乡

(1) My Hometown (Ⅰ)

My hometown is a beautiful scenic spot with a population of 200 thousand. It is situated at the foot of a hill, beside a river. The railway runs on its north side where trains *carry away*① the agricultural products and *bring back*② *manufactured goods*③ for daily use.

Its streets, though narrow, are straight and clean with shady trees on both sides. Stores, banks, a theatre and a cinema are in the shopping centre. Schools, a library and factories *are scattered*④ in the outer areas. Among the small old houses new *multi-storey*⑤ buildings are rising, creating *ornaments*⑥ of modernity for the city. Of course, in a wooded area there is a large park where a playground, *pavilions*⑦ and gardens are located around the banks of a large lake. Here people enjoy holidays with their families.

Like other villages and towns of our country, my hometown is becoming rich and prosperous. I love it very much because it is

---

① 运走
② 运进
③ 商品
④ 分散
⑤ 多层楼的
⑥ 装饰品，此处指"(现代化的)风采"
⑦ 亭阁

the place where I was born and brought up, and because I have numerous schoolmates, friends and relatives there.

(2) My Hometown (Ⅱ)

There is some very beautiful scenery near my hometown. Just to the west lies a small, *tranquil*① lake whose surface is as smooth as glass. The lake *is fed by*② an ice-cold stream, which *tumbles*③ down a nearby mountainside and *winds through*④ a number of apple and pear orchards.

However, the best thing about my hometown is the people. They are kind and hospitable and happily welcome visitors in for tea. They try to *help each other in hard times*⑤ and *share happiness in good times*⑥. Sometimes it feels like we are all one big happy family.

Though I am far from it now, I often miss my hometown. This is particularly true when my day has been very busy, tiring, or worrisome. I like to sit back in the evening and *take comfort and strength*⑦ from the land and people of my hometown.

(3) My Birthplace

In the western suburb of the city stands a small village. That is my birthplace. My birthplace is full of beauty. A green hill is behind it, and a wide field in front. Around the village, there is a

---

① 平静的
② ……汇入；……流入
③ 翻腾；滚动
④ 蜿蜒流过
⑤ 有难同当
⑥ 有福同享
⑦ 寻求安慰和力量

我的家乡
My Hometown No.27

little stream in which fishes are swimming *to and fro*①. The most *populous*② part of the village is in the west. There are many *stone cottages*③ *clustering*④ among the green trees. In the east of the village there is *a Tai Wang Temple*⑤, which *was converted into*⑥ a primary school. If one stands on the hill, one is sure to *command a perfect and distinct view*⑦ of the village.

(4) Home Sickness

Only a person far away from home knows what homesickness is.

It is the impatience, anxiety, misery, fear, and wild guesses when you are waiting for a letter from home. It is the never fading joy of reading it again and again in bed.

It is the sudden delight of closeness that strikes you when you meet a person from the same town, or even a stranger who has just been there. It is the eagerness to ask about everything, the trees, the hills, and your dear old folks. It is the sparkling eyes when you come upon a few words about your hometown in one corner of a newspaper.

It is the silent sign and faint pain in your heart when you begin reading the story, "That spring forty years ago, I waved farewell to my village and my dear parents..."

So warm a word is home, and such a sweet sadness is homesickness.

---

① 来来回回地
② 稠密的；挤满的
③ 石屋
④ 成群、成片地出现；聚集
⑤ 太王庙
⑥ 改变成；改建成
⑦ 可以清楚地看到

265

No.28 Love and Marriage
爱情与婚姻

(1) Love

Love is a very important part in this world today. With the growing modernization of the society, the relationships between people are becoming looser and looser. They will feel more isolated than ever if there is no love for each other. Love is the caring and concern for, and understanding of other people and the acceptance of their strengths and weakness. To love and to be loved is the one true happiness in life.

The love for your parents is exceptionally special love. This love, as any other sincere love, must be honest and be shared by both parents and children. Children can always share their happiness and sadness with their parents. The love of parents is a great support in children's life. It will remain with them and help them overcome all difficulties and make them *feel secure*[①]. The children's love for their parents is the parents' best reward.

The love of friends is always important to us. There is hardly anyone who can live without friends. When we grow up and leave home, friends take the place of parents. The love of friendship may also *endure*[②] all of our lives. Even though we may not have the opportunity to visit each other, it may be kept alive over many

---

① 感到安全的
② 持续

years only by *correspondence*①.

(2) International Marriages

Today people don't marry just for tradition's sake. Many young people seek adventure, romance and emotional fulfillment in marriage.

It has been really interesting for us to come across marriages in which people of different colors join together — black with white, black with yellow, and white with yellow. More and more people have, in choosing a partner, stepped out of their own culture and with *unbridled emotion*② date with people from other culture.

International marriages are full of adventure but really are not easy. When two people of different cultures want to become one, they need to overcome a language barrier and distinctively different ways of thinking. But what would a marriage be worth if we have no confidence in the love it carries? Perhaps we should remember the saying: *Love knows no obstacles and grows with them.*③

(3) Being Single

Many young people nowadays prefer to stay single instead of getting married. Single people have their own needs. Because single people usually live alone, they tend to rely on a network of friends for their social and emotional needs. Without the responsibility of raising children and feeding the family, single

---

① 通信
② 激情
③ 爱情不怕任何障碍,越有障碍增长的越快。

people have more freedom to pursue leisure-time activities such as parties and sports. Their most serious discussions tend to occur more frequently with friends rather than with family members.

Single people may also find being single sometimes results in loneliness. They may not be able to have someone beside them when they are not feeling well. Worse still is that when they *contract an acute disease*[①], they could not possibly get immediate help from their husband or wife as one who is married. When they meet with setbacks and do not want others to know their problems, they have no one to *turn to*[②]. This may lead to tension and stress which are very harmful to their health.

All in all, being single is far from being free from all troubles and worries.

(4) Marriage and Partner Relationship

Marriage is certainly one of the most beautiful dreams of life. The marriage license, though only a piece of paper, ensures the legitimacy of the relationship between a man and a woman. Families are also the cells of the whole society, whose health is much dependent upon that of husbands, wives, and children. What's more, the family is the harbor of grown-ups in this highly adventurous world.

But many people today prefer to live with a partner for the whole life or for a long time before marriage. The most visible benefit of this *stripped-down*[③] type of man-woman relationship is that life is much relaxing. For example, one doesn't need to take up the never-ending responsibilities or mind the chores of the

---

① 害急病
② 求助于(某人)
③ 简化的

family. Often both the man and the woman, believing that familiarity breeds contempt, meet only on weekends to enjoy the company of each other. People can therefore spare a lot of time and energy, precious in this competitive world, for an expected career.

Of course, both kinds of relationships have their weaknesses. Marriage could be time-consuming in *smoothing out*[①] all the *itches*[②], *seven-year ones*[③] or daily *skirmishes*[④]. Partnership, though pretty romantic, often produces an awful sense of imperfection.

As for me, I'd like to have a family when I am sufficiently prepared for pitfalls on the road of a successful marriage. Before that, I would choose to live with a partner, and then make the lifestyle of *Dinks*[⑤]. But as long as we love each other, life could be equally beautiful.

---

① 消除
② 此处指"烦恼"
③ 指 seven-year itch〈谑〉,七年之痒(指夫妇结婚七年后常会出现的相互厌倦的趋势)
④ 小争执,小冲突
⑤ Dink 是 Double income, no kids 的缩写,一般音译为"丁克"

No.29 Family 家庭

(1) The Chinese Family Structure

Chinese family structure has been changing in the past two decades, especially since the 1970's. Now in the cities in China, *the average size per family*① is three or four members though there are some families consisting of five or more. It is the *current trend*② that when the young people get to the age of marriage, they begin to consider their own future life — to build their own "small family". When they get married, many of them leave their *original home*③. Now in the countryside, many young people begin to *follow this pattern*④, too.

But things were quite different twenty years ago. At that time, most people followed the traditional Chinese idea that the younger generation had to *show filial obedience to the older generation*⑤. The old generation lived together with at least one of their children and *had a strong voice*⑥ in that family.

The reason for the change in the family structure is the rising

---

① 每个家庭的平均规模
② 流行趋势
③ 最初的家
④ 仿效这一模式
⑤ 表现出子女对长辈的服从；尽孝道
⑥ 有绝对的发言权；说了算

living standards and family planning. Because now every city woman has her job, because many nurseries have been set up, and because many older people have their *pensions*①, the two generations are not so dependent on each other. Each becomes relatively independent economically.

(2) Family and Personal Development

Family has a great influence on our *personal development*②. If we are from a happy family, we tend to be *cheerful*③ and *optimistic*④. If we are brought up in an unhappy family, we may grow *miserable*⑤ and *pessimistic*⑥. If we are not loved by our family, we may not learn to love others.

An ideal family should be a place where we can get warmth, help, comfort, and strength. It should also be a source of laughter, as laughter is a good means to *lessen the tension and pressure*⑦ we all face every day. A family should be where we cultivate our self-confidence, which is *crucial*⑧ to our further development and to our mental health.

Since family plays such an important role in our life, it is up to every family member to contribute to the building of an ideal family. We should be *considerate*⑨ and understanding. We should love and *show concern for one another*⑩. We should strive to

---

① 养老金;退休金
② 性格培养;个性发展
③ 快乐的
④ 乐观的
⑤ 痛苦的
⑥ 悲观的
⑦ 缓解紧张情绪和压力
⑧ 至关重要的;决定性的
⑨ 体谅别人的
⑩ 彼此关心

establish a happy family. After all, if every family is happy, the whole society will be stable.

(3) My Family

My family is rather small. There are only three persons: my parents and I. My parents work in a factory. My father is an engineer. His responsibility is designing new and better models of *electric appliances*① for daily use. Mother works on the *washing-machine assembly line*②. I am a physics student.

During the daytime, our apartment is locked, for we don't come home until late in the afternoon. When we are home, we have much to do. My mother does much of the housework and goes shopping twice a week. But my father seems *a better hand at cooking*③. I like to repair broken furniture and *household utensils*④. My parents also help me check my homework. We often discuss *current affairs*⑤ and technical problems. Though we read more than we watch TV, we have a family concert for half an hour or so every evening. We all like music.

(4) Is Family Influence Critical?

Family influence is of great importance in one's life. We cannot choose our family, but *taking advantage of it the right way*⑥ may give us great benefits.

It is lucky to be born in a "good family", but one can not rely

---

① 电器设备
② 洗衣机装配线
③ 更擅长烹调
④ 家用器具
⑤ 时事
⑥ 充分或恰当地利用家庭影响

on his family all his life. As we all know, many people from high ranking officials or rich families turned out to be failures, whereas many great men came from poor families. Such examples are numerous. *Ancestry*① is most important to those who can accomplish nothing themselves. However, it is one's talents, personality and dedication that really count.

I firmly believe in the *honest sweat*② of my own history. I came from a poor peasant family in a small mountainous village. When I struggled at the starting point of my long journey of life, others were already far ahead. However, I *hold dear*③ the many *good virtues*④ my parents taught me, such as courage, honesty, and independence, which turned out to be more valuable than money. Though I could hardly pay for my tuition, I worked harder than most students and became the first college student in my hometown. If I keep on earning my bread with my sweat, I will surely have a bright future.

(5) Honour Our Parents

Aunt Lee, a widow of 58, complained sadly that her only son did not call her even once when she was in hospital for three weeks. Now there is a *widespread concern*⑤ that many young couples are reluctant to support their old parents, especially in the countryside.

*Honouring one's elders*⑥, parents in particular, is one of the major virtues highly valued in China. The policy that every family

---

① 世系;此处指"家族的兴旺或衰败"
② 此处指"实实在在的或踏踏实实的艰苦努力"
③ 高度重视;此处指"珍惜或珍视"
④ 优良品性;美德
⑤ 广泛的关注
⑥ 尊重长辈、年迈的人

can have only one child, however, challenges this traditional virtue. The only child, often treated as the "Little Emperor" of the family, *lacks a sense of independence and family responsibility*①. Growing up as flowers in the "greenhouse", we young people tend to rely heavily on our parents. We often ask too much of them and think little of their practical difficulties.

Unlike our parents, we are more sensitive to social changes. We *appreciate*② privacy, freedom, and personal values but hate *blind obedience*③. We sometimes spend money freely on fashionable clothes, *fancy food*④, and "modern" things like Rock-and-rolls, disco and American movies. As *practical people*⑤, our parents may not like these. Thus, *on many occasions*⑥, we unintentionally hurt their feelings.

It is a fact that our parents are getting old and need our help and support. Aunt Lee's son was wrong whatever his excuses might be. My fellow young friends, ask not what our parents can do for us, but what we must do for them. If we do not honour our parents, how can we expect our children to respect us?

(6) Resist the DINK *Fad*⑦

Nowadays, one of the greatest changes in family life is that the 'DINK' (double income no kids) family structure is getting fashionable among many young couples. They decide not to have any children because they think that children bring more misery

---

① 缺乏独立性和家庭责任感
② 此处指"重视或追求"
③ 盲目服从、顺从
④ 精美可口的食品
⑤ 讲求实际的人
⑥ 在很多场合;在很多情况下
⑦ 一时的风尚

than joy. Does married couple without children really have a better life? I doubt about this point of view.

Though couples without children may enjoy the freedom from the worries for bringing up children and can spend all the money they earn for their own, they can never experience the pleasure brought by children. The process of giving birth to children, bringing them up and cultivating them is very interesting and enjoyable. Through observing the growing process of babies, couples can get conception about how they themselves grow up. What's more, the children's growing is full of magic and miracle. The experience of raising children is unique and can't be substituted by anything else in the world.

Besides the pleasure children bring, children can act as the most efficient *lubricant*[①] for a family. After the honeymoon of the first happy year, the affection between couples will become steady and the trivial family affairs are prominent in family, so family conflicts are unavoidable. With a child or children in a family, the common affection on child can promote the sentiment between couple. And for the sake of children, the two sides of the conflicts can easily reach a compromise or mutual understanding if there isn't something really serious. The children can bring more happiness for a family and reduce the frequency of quarrel.

From the viewpoint of society, those who choose to have no children are selfish and self-centered. Happy marriage doesn't mean the absence of the responsibility for both children and society. The development of society needs its members to bear, bring up and educate children in conformity with the requirements of society. If everybody escapes from the responsibilities, there will be no human beings on the planet of earth.

---

① 润滑剂

(7) A House Is Not a Home

Generally speaking, a house is a place where people live and the house is their home. In other words, a home always lies in a house. As a matter of fact, a house is different from a home in meaning. However, quite a few people often confuse house with home. For example, I have a sweet home, but we cannot say I have a sweet house. Likewise, I have a beautiful house, but it cannot be said that I have a beautiful home.

As the English folk song *Sweet Home* goes, "Be it ever so humble, there is no place like home." When one is depressed and experiences frustration, he always thinks of his home — his family. In the house are his parents, brothers, and sisters who can console or help him. In this manner, a home and a house always coexist and cannot be separated. The truth is that while there is no house, there is no home. To sum up, a house offers one a shelter and a home offers one the sweetness and security of family.

No.30 Festivals and Holidays
新年佳节

(1) Chinese New Year: Tradition in Change

Chinese lunar New Year, or the Spring Festival, has always been a time of joy and happiness, and a time of family reunion, fine *cuisine*①, new clothes, a sleepless night with carnivals, yet something has been changing in all these.

For the Chinese people, a big table of food in the house with a big family sitting around on the eve of the Spring Festival is what family reunion means. Yet, today more and more families are having their new year eve dinner in restaurants. Jiaozi, or dumpling, is what *turkey*② means for westerners on the eve of Christmas. Yet even for those who choose to have their dinner at home, they seem to have abandoned the pure joy of making Jiaozi. Fireworks are another must on the eve of spring festival. But most of the major cities have banned fireworks for safety and noise pollution concern. As a compromise, authorities in many cities have arranged for firework shows in public squares. Apparently, sending New Year greeting cards in the post office is no more *in vogue*③ People use more electronic cards on the internet to save forest.

With the rising of people's living standard, the celebration of

---

① 烹饪，菜肴
② 火鸡
③ 流行，风行，时髦

Chinese New Year has become more colorful and jubilant.

(2) The Chinese New Year

In our country men and women, boys and girls, all look forward to the Chinese New Year. It is a time for rest and *refreshment*①. Business *is suspended*② for a time. Young fellows *lay aside*③ their school work and *give themselves up to*④ merriment and joy. *Gaily dressed*⑤, children indulge themselves in games. Family members gather together to enjoy *a feast*⑥. It is indeed a delightful time for our fellow-countrymen.

When you take a walk in the street, you will *be much struck*⑦ at sight of rich and beautiful decorations. Some families have their new *scrolls*⑧ on the doors. Lanterns are hung in some shops. All these are welcome signs to a visitor. People are busy coming and going on a New Year's visit to their friends and relatives. "Happy New Year!" is the usual greeting you would hear them say to each other.

The Chinese new year lasts about a *fortnight*⑨. On the fifteenth day, *a lantern procession*⑩ is usually held. Lanterns are made in the likeness of different animals. All lamps are lit at night. After much recreation and enjoyment people *resume*⑪ their

---

① (精力或精神上的)恢复
② 暂停
③ 把……放在一边
④ 使(自己)沉溺于
⑤ 穿着鲜艳的服装
⑥ 盛宴
⑦ 被……打动;被……所迷住
⑧ 卷轴;这里指"对联"
⑨ 十四天;两星期
⑩ 灯会
⑪ 重新开始;(经打断后)再继续

normal work.

(3) The Lunar New Year's Celebration

The Lunar New Year is a great occasion to the Chinese people. They look forward to its celebration with excitement. Children, in particular, regard it as their favorite holiday of the year.

Several days before the New Year, people begin to prepare for its celebration. Houses are cleaned. *Couplets*[①] are pasted on doors. Colorful lanterns are hung at gates. Farmers kill pigs, sheep, cocks and hens, while *city-dwellers*[②] buy meat, fish and vegetables. Markets, stores and shops are always found crowded with people.

On the New Year's Eve, Family members gather together for *a family reunion dinner*[③]. After the meal, they watch TV until the clock strikes twelve. Then every family sets off long strings of *firecrackers*[④] and other *fireworks*[⑤] to welcome the New Year.

On the New Year's Day, almost everyone is dressed in his or her best. When people meet each other, they exchange New Year's greetings. Friends and relative *pay New Year calls*[⑥] and give presents to each other. Children often enjoy getting some *lucky money*[⑦]. There are also some parades in streets or at some big open space. People in costumes dance lion and dragon dances,

---

① 对联
② 城市居民
③ 团圆饭
④ 爆竹;鞭炮
⑤ 烟火
⑥ 拜年
⑦ 压岁钱

which is a typical Chinese tradition. It is also fun to take a walk in the streets, which *look gay*① with bright flags and colored lights. Everywhere people are enjoying themselves *to the full*.②

(4) The Mid-autumn Festival

The Mid-autumn Festival is celebrated on the night of the fifteenth day of the eighth lunar month. It is, in a sense, the Chinese moon festival.

On this night, people walk in the streets to enjoy themselves. They eat moon cakes, which are so called because they are shaped like the moon. These cakes are also set on a table *in the open air*③, meant to be eaten by the god or goddess of the moon.

It is generally believed that the moon is *at its brightest*④ on this night. Many poems have been written about it. Poets never tire of reading and writing such poems, in which the moon has been compared to a looking-glass, *a jade rabbit*⑤, etc. It seems that Chinese literature *is far more concerned with the moon than with the sun*⑥.

(5) The Miao Dragon-Boat Festival

The Dragon Boat Festival is the most important celebration of the Miao people, who live along *the Qingshui River in*

---

① 此处指"显出一派欢乐景象"
② 尽情地;充分地
③ 在户外
④ 最亮
⑤ 玉兔
⑥ 涉及月亮的内容比涉及太阳的要多

southeastern *Guizhou Province*①. Every year between 30,000 and 40,000 Miaos participate in the festivities.

In the eyes of the Miaos, the dragon is a symbol of good luck. Girls like to adorn their hair with silver ornaments shaped like dragons and wear clothes embroidered or woven with dragon patterns. The Miaos build exquisite dragon boats with carved dragon heads painted red, blue or yellow.

The Dragon Boat Festival is celebrated by the scores of Miao villages from the 24th to the 27th of the fifth lunar month. But according to local custom, people are allowed to send their dragon boats down the river after the 16th, provided that they have finished weeding their fields. The earlier appearance of the boats on the river testifies to the villagers' efficiency. *The hardworking Miaos consider it a shame not to finish weeding before the festivities begin*②.

(6) *Confucian Festival*③

Confucius, the philosopher, thinker and educator, was born on September 28, 551 BC. He can be called both the preserver and creator of Chinese Civilization. Confucianism has for more than 2,500 years summed up and included in its system all that is good in the original Chinese cultural heritage. In 1984, Qufu began offering the Confucius Home Tour, which has grown into an annual event and attracts some 100,000 visitors every year.

A variety of *commemorative activities*④ highlight the International Confucian Festival, to be held from Sep. 26 to Oct. 10 in Qufu, Shandong Province, Confucius' home.

---

① 黔东南清水江
② 勤劳的苗家人认为,龙船节到了,地里的秧还未薅完,这是莫大的耻辱。
③ 孔子文化节
④ 纪念活动

On the occasion, a *symposium*① attended by well-known scholars from both home and abroad will be held at the *Confucian Academic Hall*②. In addition to grand folk sacrificial rituals, the Confucian descendants, representatives from all walks of life of his hometown, as well as overseas Chinese, hold a large memorial ceremony. Moreover, a music and dance performance is also dedicated to Confucius.

---

① 研讨会
② 孔子礼学堂

No.31 | City Life and Country Life
城市与农村生活

(1) Living in a Big City

Most people love the advantages of city life, but big cities also have their serious problems.

There are many advantages of living in a big city. Big cities offer many of the good things in life. For example, people can buy all kinds of things at supermarkets or big stores, dine out in *exclusive*① restaurants, and go to first-class theatres and cinemas. Big cities provide excellent *transport facilities*②. Finally, the fact that *prestigious*③ universities, colleges, schools and modern factories are concentrated in big cities means that people have more educational and employment opportunities.

However, city life also has its disadvantages. In big cities the flow of people and traffic goes on unceasingly, and the noise never stops. During the rush hours streets are crowded with traffic; buses are *intolerably*④ full. Motor vehicle *exhaust*⑤ along with industrial activity pollutes the atmosphere, covering the cities and hiding the sun. Moreover, since the world population is fast becoming urban, there is an increasing demand for accommodation, and the cost

---

① 高级的
② 交通工具;交通设施
③ 有声望的;声誉好的
④ 过分地
⑤ 排出的废气

of living in big cities, in general, is very high. However, in spite of all these disadvantages, people are in favour of living in big cities, and they believe there will be a better environment to live in and to work in the future.

(2) How to Solve the Housing Problem in Big Cities

With the development of modern industry, more and more people are flowing into big cities. Accordingly, the housing problem in big cities is becoming more and more serious.

People have offered many solutions to this problem. I think building *satellite cities*① in the suburbs is more practical. The fresh air and beautiful scenery in the suburbs will be *appealing to*② the city citizens, who suffer from air pollution, noises, etc. in the overcrowded city. With more people leaving the city, more space will be available for those remaining. The housing problem in big cities will thus be solved.

In the meantime, I'm against the idea of utilizing the underground space to solve the problem. We can imagine how uncomfortable it will be to live under the ground, having to *probe*③ in the dark. The air there will be very *stuffy*④, and the cost of building underground houses will be *tremendous*⑤.

In brief, building satellite cities can not only improve the housing condition in big cities, but also provide a much better living environment. But the housing problem is very complicated. Perhaps people can hardly rely on only one way to solve the

---

① 卫星城（市）
② 对……有感染力的；吸引……的
③ 探索；摸索
④ 不通气的；令人窒息的
⑤ 极大的；惊人的

problem completely.

(3) Supermarkets

Since the first supermarket *emerged*① fifty years ago, it has become the most popular shopping center in many large cities around the world. In China, supermarkets enjoy an increasing *popularity*② among city-dwellers, especially the common people with low incomes.

Compared with other types of stores, supermarkets are getting popular for several reasons. First, fewer employees are required in supermarkets and management cost is reduced. Second, almost all goods are shipped directly from the producers and sold at considerably cheaper prices. Lastly, in supermarkets, almost every kind of daily necessity is available and placed on open shelves, so the customers can choose whatever they want on their shopping list and take the items to the checkout counter easily. As a result, instead of visiting many stores, customers can get the tiring shopping task done quickly and feel relaxed. What is more, many supermarkets stay open until late at night and provide large parking spaces.

In the last few years, supermarkets have *mushroomed*③ in Beijing and many other large cities in China. The comfort, economy and convenience of shopping in supermarkets have greatly pleased Chinese customers; and the supermarkets, steadily gaining popularity, are doing *booming*④ business in China.

---

① 出现
② 讨人喜欢；受欢迎
③ 涌现
④ 繁荣的；兴隆的

(4) Country Life

Country life has many advantages. First, country people are in close contact with nature. Living in peace and quiet, they can breathe fresh air and listen to the songs of birds. They need not worry about any pollution problems that always bother city-dwellers. Second, the people living in the country can enjoy many out-door activities. They can go fishing in rivers and hunting in forests. Another advantage that country people enjoy is that they can easily get fresh vegetables, fruits and milk at lower prices.

Country life, however, has some *inconveniences*[①]. The people living in the country cannot enjoy all the *miracles*[②] of the latest scientific achievements. Sometimes they have transportation or communications problems. Their daily life is not as easy as that of city people. For example, they cannot go shopping in big supermarkets. As for cultural *recreations*[③], as there are few cinemas or concerts halls in the country, people there cannot often see movies or plays.

People may have different opinions about country life. Some would think that country life is too hard and *tedious*[④], whereas others might enjoy it. It all depends on one's personal point of view and experiences. As for me, I was born and grew up in the country, and I am used to everything there. So I love country life.

(5) Pleasure of the Country

It is very pleasant in the country, especially during spring,

---

① 不方便
② 奇迹
③ 娱乐活动
④ 单调乏味的；沉闷的

summer and autumn.

In spring time the grass, the flowers, and the trees begin to look bright. The birds sing merrily, the sky is often clear and attractive, and as we *go about*① on a bright day we seem filled with new life and vigor. At this period, farmers are busy ploughing and in other ways attending to their land. It is very interesting to watch the plough turn up the earth with such evenness. The little lambs skipping about in the fields are always a welcome sight in spring.

In summer the country is still more attractive. The trees and the flowers are now *at their best*②, and the weather being warmer, we may lie in the fields, on the hilly slopes, or by the side of the brook, and enjoy the fresh air and the sights and the sound around. Driving in the country is very enjoyable, especially where the scenery is particularly fine.

In autumn the trees, the flowers, and the fruits *render*③ the country again attractive. The pleasures of summer-walking, driving, and harvesting are continued; and the rich brown *tints*④ of the leaves form a pleasing contrast to the brightness of spring and summer.

In winter the country is dreary and quiet, and hence its pleasures are few. But even then it is enjoyable to watch the farmer as he attends to his cattle, or to see the trees when the *twigs*⑤ are covered with snow.

---

① 到处走
② 处于最佳状态；此处为"树木和花草繁茂"之意
③ 使得
④ 色彩
⑤ 细枝

(6) A Rainy Day in the Countryside

It was raining. The earth was soft and wet beneath my feet as I made my way up the path which led to the house. Large *slabs of stone*① were arranged along the pathway, and as I stepped upon them, they *wobbled*② so beneath my feet that I was afraid I might fall. Little drops of rain *clung to*③ the grass which grew on both sides of the path.

The house, which needed to be white-washed, looked even more gray and *dreary*④ than it did in yesterday's sunlight. The light which shone through the front window, however, seemed to lend to the house a warm and inviting atmosphere.

Beyond the house there was a stream of water which was flowing rather quickly, and I watched the cool, clear water as it ran over the stones. A dog stood on the other side of the narrow stream, looking cold and wet as the raindrops sprayed from his *wagging*⑤ tail.

The entire countryside was indeed wet and dreary, and I was glad to go into the house from which shone the *inviting*⑥ light.

(7) Enjoyment of Country People

Let us *count up*⑦ some of the good things that the country people enjoy. They have the broad fields and the orchards and

---

① 一块一块的石板
② 晃动不稳
③ 粘着;依附
④ 沉闷的;阴郁的
⑤ 摇动、摆动着的
⑥ 诱人的;吸引人的
⑦ 把……加起来;数

woods, and maybe the ocean and an ample view of the great sky over them. They can *roam*① about freely. When the grass is *mown*② and the harvests are *in*③, they can go almost wherever they please, as if all the land were their own. The city boys and girls hardly ever see the cows that give them milk, or the lambs at play, or the young *colts*④ *frisking*⑤ in their *pastures*⑥. The country children can make friends with and *pet*⑦ all these creatures. They can hear the birds singing, and learn the secret of where they make their nests. The boys can also go fishing and swimming.

(8) Where to Live — In the City or the Country?

Many people appreciate the conveniences of the city. People can enjoy a colourful life there. They are *well-informed*⑧ because they have the access to news. They are well-paid because they have stable jobs. They are *well-fed*⑨ and well-dressed because there is an adequate supply of goods. They often have a wonderful time because there are many places for recreation and relaxation.

On the contrary, others are attracted by the country. They like clear streams, fresh air and high mountains. In the country, people feel closer to nature — the very nature that gives man life.

However, both the city and the country have their disadvantages. Air pollution is very serious in the city. Moreover, it is so crowded that many people don't want to go

---

① 漫步
② 割
③ （庄稼）已收进；此处 in 为副词
④ 小马（尤指"小雄马"）
⑤ 轻快活泼地跳跃；跳跳蹦蹦
⑥ 牧场
⑦ 宠爱；抚摸
⑧ 消息灵通的
⑨ 营养充足的

out. In the country, it is inconvenient to buy things. Besides, people can find no way to *kill*① the long and *tedious*② nights.

I prefer to live in the city for a time and then go to the country for a change.

(9) The Night Life in Dalian

Not so long ago, the nightlife in Dalian was no more than karaoke, local food and a walk along the seaside. But today if you spend a night in Dalian, you *are bound to*③ have a romantic time.

At nightfall, the city is *illuminated*④ by multi-colored neon lights. The garden lights and road lamps add radiance and beauty to the nocturnal views. Wandering in the street at that time, you may notice the bars and restaurants along the street are always packed. Here while appreciating the melodious music, patrons can ease back into the comfortable armchairs, enjoy drinks and try a vast variety of local specialties.

Dalian is famous for its plazas which serve as an outdoor playground for people at night. On Zhongshan Plaza, for example, lots of people dance the night away. It is also a great way to meet people and keep fit. *Shuttlecock kicking*⑤ is perhaps the most popular entertainment in Dalian. Every night the boys and girls are immersed in an exciting atmosphere.

Besides, you can also go to the concert hall beside Zhongshan Plaza, where classical music from around China and the world is frequently performed. Dalian has become a great international metropolis and a tourist attraction.

① 消磨
② 无聊的；乏味的
③ 注定的，肯定的
④ 照亮
⑤ 踢毽子

No.32 Sports
体育

(1) Sports in Our Country

Table-tennis is the most popular sport with the people in our country. School children start playing table-tennis when they are very young. Not only is it played at school but it is also a favourite game with workers and people *in other walks of life*①. In fact, it has become a sort of national game.

There are other popular sports. For example, badminton is another popular sport though it is not played as widely as table-tennis. Wushu and sword-play are both traditional forms of sport. *Mention should be made of*② such ball games as football, basketball, and volleyball which have become increasingly popular.

In order to keep fit and win honour for our motherland, men and women, young and old, take an active part in sports. And our government takes effective measures to promote physical culture and build up the people's health. You may see people enjoy different sports, either in or out of school. Many people are running, walking, or *shadow-boxing*③ in open spaces early in the

---

① 其他行业
② 还应提及,此处是被动式
③ 打拳

morning. Sports are *flourishing*① in our country now.

(2) Women in Sports

Women in the world participate in a growing number of sports and games.

Changes in both the view of women and the world of sports have allowed many more women to participate in sports. Women are no longer considered *delicate*②. People do not think it *unladylike*③ for women to compete in sports. Women who win in sports activities are highly regarded. Many women now take part in sports and games of many different kinds and enjoy doing so. This is partly the result of a change in the image of women in the modern world. Also, changes in the Olympics have encouraged many women to become more active in various Olympic activities. In the early twentieth century, women began to compete regularly in the Olympics and, the number of events for women in the Olympics has been growing steadily ever since.

Many women's competitions have been on TV, especially in recent years. Seeing women in professional sports on TV has made certain sports much more popular among women, *both as amateurs and as professionals*④.

In a word, women are more active in sports now than ever before because of the development in sports and in modern society, as well as in the Women's Liberation Movement in the world.

---

① 蓬勃发展
② 身体欠佳的;不强壮的
③ 欠文雅的;不适合淑女身份的
④ 无论作为业余选手还是职业选手

(3) Physical Exercise and Mental Advantages

Physical exercise develops will. None can succeed in doing anything if he does not put his will into it. A great many athletes *get a good reputation*① through nothing but a strong will which helps them succeed.

Physical exercise develops *judgment*②. There are many people who hesitate when matters come to them. This is because their judgment is not strong enough. An expert runner knows how much speed he should put into his first quarter and second quarter. When he is racing with *a green foot*③, he does not trouble himself no matter how fast the latter goes in the first *lap*④. He knows the situation. He knows when he should run faster and when slower.

Physical exercise develops self-confidence. Many people do not trust themselves. As things come before them, they usually pause, not knowing whether they have the ability to perform such things or not. So a great deal of time is usually wasted and matters are left unaccomplished. This is because these men have little self-confidence. An expert athlete believes that he has had sufficient practice in a certain *event*⑤, and most probably he wins the championship. Thus, we say that self-confidence can be developed through physical exercise.

---

① 赢得盛誉
② 判断力
③ 没有经验的长跑运动员
④ （跑道的）一圈
⑤ 比赛项目

(4) Physical Exercise and Social Advantages

From sports we can learn a very important lesson which tends to *inculcate*① cooperation and friendship. Various kinds of games are played by groups of men, and each group is divided into teams. In each team there is an organization or a system, in accordance with which every individual member should play his best. For example, in playing football, the player who is tall and sure in catching the ball is made the *goalkeeper*②, and those who are very *nimble*③ and sure in shooting the ball are always *forwards*④. Although their duties are not the same, they should always work together *in harmony*⑤. This is what we call "*team-work*"⑥.

From this, we see that the people of a country are much like the players of a football team. In playing football, "team-work" is important. In managing a country, "team-work" is important, too. In order that a country may be strong and wealthy, the people of the country must work together and cooperate with one another. In order to develop such cooperation, *athletics*⑦ is one of the best methods.

(5) Prize and Competition

There is no denying the fact that prize can *stimulate*

---

① 反复灌输(思想、原则等)
② 守门员
③ 灵活的;敏捷的
④ (足球的)前锋
⑤ 协调一致
⑥ 集体协作;团队配合
⑦ 体育运动

*competitors into full play*①. One will *go all out*② to seek his greatest success because of the prize *incentive*③ and the sense of superiority over others. Consequently, the highest achievement will be obtained in a fair play.

However, many competitors cannot overcome the temptation of the prize. They see nothing but the prize and may try to get it by improper means. As a result, we often hear of *scandals*④ in sports events.

I believe that the remedy lies in character education of the competitors. This helps them understand that prize are *a means to an end*⑤, but not the end itself. Meanwhile, we should enforce the law that no one should take improper actions before or at the competition. Then, prize will play a better part in any contest.

(6) The Importance of Physical Exercise

Everyone hopes to live happily in the world. Physical exercise is indispensable to a happy life. There is a famous saying: "Life lies on exercise." Although you will not necessarily die without regular physical exercises, they'll certainly help you live longer and more healthily.

Exercise is good for us to build our bodies. It helps coordinate the different parts of our bodies when we have sports. For example, we must try our best to coordinate the movements of the arms and legs when we play basketball, or we won't be able to shoot the basket. Exercise also benefits our organs. It lets the heart beat faster than usual, and then helps enlarge the blood

---

① 刺激竞赛者发挥最佳水平
② 全力以赴
③ 刺激；鼓励
④ 丑闻
⑤ 用以达到目的的手段、方法、事物或行动等（其本身并不重要）

vessels to protect us from heart attacks.

Exercise can also contribute to the development of our ability to response agilely. For instance, when you play table-tennis, you must try to reflect as quickly as you can so that you may fight back at the right position at the right moment.

Exercise will fill your life with various contents and make it more colorful. What's more, exercise will help you get rid of your *inertia*①. If you keep doing exercise regularly, you will never be a lazy person. Therefore, exercise has great effect on one's character.

In a word, exercise is helpful, important and absolutely necessary.

(7) Beijing Olympics Volunteer in My Eyes

As the 2008 Beijing Olympics drew near, China was also stepping up efforts in the *recruitment*② of volunteers. Applications came from people in all walks of life. Apart from enthusiasm and patience, a volunteer worker also needed other qualities, such as foreign language proficiency, driving skills, and first-aid knowledge, depending on the nature of the specific job.

Being a volunteer worker for the Beijing Olympic Games was very meaningful. For the country, it saved on operating costs for the Organizing Committee. Though pre-event training *entailed*③ a large investment, volunteers' contributions to the overall human resource requirement were invaluable. For the individuals, they could broaden their horizons through participating in this international event. For university students in particular,

---

① 惰性
② 征募,补充
③ 需要

Olympics volunteer work helped them gain life experience and cultivate social responsibility. What I can say about the above-mentioned facts is "Volunteerism works!"

To be sure, besides a sense of honor and achievement, volunteer work was both time and energy consuming. The training and rehearsal alone could last for months, and one may have to sacrifice leisure time for this unpaid work before, during and after the Olympics. However, to accomplish a successful *convening*① of the games, such sacrifice was worthwhile for students and adults alike.

(8) Chinese Basketball

With the rapid growing popularity of basketball, many Chinese love to watch games played by the *CBA professional clubs*②. However, unlike American *NBA*③ teams, CBA teams fail to attract young talents because few kids dream of being basketball stars.

Since basketball is a game of giants, people start to worry about the lack of young talents. In the 1970's, millions of high school teenagers were sent to remote rural areas to receive lifelong "re-education". Basketball had much attraction then because it could help some kids go back home. But now it is not so attractive any more. As a hobby it is OK, as a job — no. In fact, going to college has become more important than anything else in China.

What's more, since basketball stars have to be trained very hard at an early age, most Chinese parents often discourage their children to have such a training, which is considered as

---

① 聚集,集合
② CBA 职业俱乐部;CBA 为 China Basketball Association 之缩写
③ NBA 为美国 National Basketball Association 之缩写

unbearable and a waste of time. In addition to low pay, tough living conditions, and strict discipline, basketball players may easily get hurt. Besides, after retirement from the team, they can not get good jobs without higher education.

China has the potential to become a basketball superpower. However, if we fail to train *a galaxy of young stars*[①], the day will be remote when China can realize her dream of winning the world basketball championship.

(9) Swimming

Swimming is a very popular sport. People, old and young, men and women, all enjoy it. Not only is it a practical skill, but it also provides exercise for the heart, the lungs, and the limbs. In cold weather, swimming is especially *refreshing*[②]. It trains the skin to keep body warm more effectively. One who often swims is fit and *graceful in form*[③].

At times of emergency in a river or on the sea, a swimmer can save his life and even others'. It is true that a little skill may help one survive a serious accident. Yet it is also true that many good swimmers lose their lives because of too much self-confidence.

If estimates are correct, over half of the world's population are non-swimmers. Each year, thousands of people drown without realizing the importance of learning to swim. Unlike many animals, man has to learn to swim. But a few hours' practice is quite enough for the mastery of basic skills. If you cannot swim, why not learn?

---

① 一群杰出的年轻明星
② 使人重新振作的;使人恢复活力的
③ 体形优美的

(10) Mountain-climbing

Many people who were living comfortably in the town *civilisation*①　began to grow tired of it. One of the many *instincts*② of man is to *explore the unknown*③, and to look for things which the reason cannot explain and for sights and sounds which produce excitement.

People were no longer satisfied with a life in which everything is orderly, peaceful, and easily understood. They began to turn away from the man-made towns. Instead, they went to the untouched country. They even went to places where it was dangerous, *tough*④, and *disorderly*⑤.

It was then that mountain-climbing began to grow popular as a sport. To some people, there is something attractive about setting out to conquer a mountain. When you are finally at the top of a giant mountain after a long and tough climb, what a satisfactory reward it is to be able to look down at everything within sight!

(11) Skiing

Skiing is a *desirable*⑥ activity for young people. It provides the excitement that the youth is commonly seeking. The skiers can enjoy the *thrill*⑦ of gliding at a tremendous speed down a gleaming, white mountain slope. Often, *within split second*⑧,

---

① 文明；尤指城市的"现代生活的舒适环境"或"文明设施"
② 本能
③ 探索未知世界
④ 崎岖的
⑤ 杂乱无序的
⑥ 令人向往的
⑦ 兴奋；激动
⑧ 一瞬间；在刹那间

they must *dodge*① trees, *stumps*②, and rocks — or find themselves suddenly *sprawling*③ in the snow. If they have more than average skill, they can sail through the air in breath-taking leaps and jumps that bring excitement to the onlookers as well. True, there is danger in this excitement, but that is a risk the youth enjoys. Furthermore, skiing is *healthful*④. It provides exercise, often very strenuous, as the skiers *trudge up*⑤ a mountain path or *work their way*⑥ on skis up a slope of deep snow. The best of skiers know that they need strong muscles to successfully control their skis, so they exercise to keep themselves physically fit.

Another desirable feature is the companionship that usually develops wherever skiers gather. Friendships grow quickly on the slopes and in the usual nearby shelter where the skiers find food, warmth, and rest. Their experiences of the day and their youthfulness easily draw these people together in happy fellowship.

(12) Wake Up Your Life by Walking

It's a plain fact that exercise improves the quality of life. Studies have shown that people who exercise habitually are less likely to suffer from heart attacks but can enjoy better health and a longer life.

The most common form of exercise is walking. The benefits increase as you walk more. It has been found that men who walk

---

① 躲闪开；避开
② 树桩；树墩
③ 四肢摊开着倒下
④ 有益于健康的
⑤ （因疲惫等）缓慢或吃力地走上
⑥ 此处指"费力地走上"

nine miles a week have 21 percent lower risk of *premature death*① than those who walk less than three miles weekly. Another benefit of walking is reduced stress. After walking, you feel less anxious and think more clearly. Why this occurs isn't completely understood, but walking is, after all, an action that uses almost all of the body's bones and major muscles. And moderate exercise may change your mood and increase your *sense of well-being*②.

What's more, walking can help you lose weight. If you walk *briskly*③ 45 minutes a day, four times a week for a year, you could lose 10 pounds. In fact, walking is particularly good if you are very fat, because violent activities like running may be too hard on your bones and joints.

However, for any exercise, to increase long-term health benefits, it must be done consistently over a lifetime. This is where walking has distinct advantage over other activities. Walkers are rarely stopped by the injuries so common in other exercises. And walkers keep up walking, year after year, simply because it's so pleasurable.

---

① 过早死亡
② （身体或精神）健康的感觉
③ 轻快地

No.33 Recreations 消遣与娱乐

(1) Recreations

Recreation is an important part of people's life. For example, after hours of *attentive*① study students feel like having a football game to relax their nerves. Workers, too, find it very satisfying to sit in front of a TV set for an hour or two when they come back from a day's tiring work. Besides, recreation serves as a pleasing way for the retired people to pass their *leisure time*②. Everywhere you go, you will find that during their spare time, people are engaged in recreational activities of one kind or another.

Generally speaking, there are two kinds of recreation: physical activities and intellectual activities. Physical activities, on the one hand, keep one fit and *develop team spirit*③. Basketball is an example. One the other hand, intellectual activities such as playing chess and reading novels can train one's brains and provide *temporary*④ escape from one's troubles.

In my opinion, there should be a balance between the two forms of activities. This is because physical activities are

---

① 专心的
② 此处指"闲暇时光"
③ 培养合作精神
④ 暂时的

消遣与娱乐 Recreations No.33

necessary for good health while intellectual activities are *beneficial*① to one's mind. Therefore, in order to make his life enjoyable, one should go in for both kinds of recreation.

(2) Ways of Relaxing

"All work and no play makes Jack a dull boy" is a popular saying in English. There is much truth in this old saying. It means that in order to keep ourselves in good health, we must take sufficient recreation.

Everyone has his own way of relaxing. For people who sit much of the time at work cycling is said to be a *capital*② means of exercise. A good brisk walk is one of the finest forms of exercise, too. For people engaged in outdoor work, reading is an excellent change if suitable books are chosen.

I like sports and enjoy participating in them. My favourite sport is table-tennis because it brings the whole body into action. In fact, it doesn't matter whether I play a fast game of ping-pong or concentrate over the bridge table. It is important for me to relax from time to time.

(3) Music

Music is often divided into several *categories*③. Some of the categories are *classical*④ music, *traditional*⑤ music, *rock*⑥ music,

---

① 有益于……的
② 重要的
③ 种类
④ 古典的
⑤ 传统的
⑥ 摇滚乐

and *jazz*① music.

The first kind, classical music, *originated*② in Europe a few hundred years ago. Most of the original classical music was composed in Italy, Germany, Austria and Russia. *Beethoven*③ and *Bach*④ were two famous *composers*⑤ of classical music. It is usually played by a variety of *string instruments*⑥ and *wind instruments*⑦.

The second type of music is traditional music. It is the music that comes from a particular culture. Each culture has its own traditional music that is played by special instruments.

Another kind of music is rock music. It probably began in Europe about 30 or 40 years ago. Rock is generally a loud kind of music, played with a strong *beat*⑧. Rock musicians often use electric instruments, such as electric guitars and electric pianos, but other instruments can also be used.

The fourth kind of music is jazz. It probably comes from Africa originally. Jazz has a different kind of *rhythm*⑨ from other kinds of music. A variety of musical instruments are used to play this kind of music, especially wind instruments.

These are the four general types of music. Of course, these definitions are brief and general, and certainly there are other categories of music. In addition, many kinds of music are combinations of classical and traditional, or classical and Jazz, or rock and jazz, and so on.

---

① 爵士乐
② 起源于
③ 贝多芬
④ 巴赫(1685 — 1750),德国风琴家、作曲家
⑤ 作曲家
⑥ 弦乐器
⑦ 管乐器
⑧ 节拍;强节奏
⑨ 节奏

(4) A Kite

Last autumn, rediscovering my childhood interest in flying kites, I decided to build a *dragon*①. It had to be flexible and fly steadily. The design took me several days. When it was made, it measured six meters fifty in over twenty *sections*②, with head, tail and *paws*③.

One afternoon, I flew it with the help of my little friends. About ten children held different parts of the dragon while I took the *cord*④, standing some twenty meters away from the first boy. As the wind was quite strong, I feared my assistants might tear the dragon. But they cooperated perfectly.

I shouted, "Ready! Go!" and turned and ran *upwind*⑤. I heard the crowd cheering. Soon I stopped and looked back. The kite was fluttering *gracefully*⑥ as a real dragon would — if there were a real one.

The longer I *let go*⑦ the cord, the higher the dragon *soared into the sky*⑧. And so did my imagination.

(5) A Walk in the Rain

Getting up in the morning, I like to take a walk. One day it was raining. Drop by drop, the rain fell on my head. I was in high spirits. Along the path, there were many little red and

① 龙
② 节;段
③ 爪
④ 细绳
⑤ 顶风地
⑥ 优美地
⑦ 放开
⑧ 直上云霄

yellow flowers, which put their heads up to absorb their drinks. They had been completely washed. They appeared fresh and lively. How lovely they looked!

Whenever I was in these surroundings, I would forget all my troubles and unhappy events. To me this is a good *remedy*①. Many people do not like rain. They say that it is troublesome. I do not think so. Rain brings us water to drink and to *irrigate*② fields.

We keep breathing in unclean air in the city. But when it rains, we may take a walk in a park, and we can *taste*③ the fresh air which is good for our health.

Walking in the rain is an enjoyment to me. I do not know why, but I just like it.

(6) A Walk on the Seashore

Not very far from my house lies the seashore in the south. We can go there on foot in about ten minutes. On summer evenings when the sun is setting, my father likes to take me with my sisters to have a walk along the seashore. Though we do not like the loneliness of the place, we are glad to enjoy the coolness of sea breezes and the beautiful scenery of the nature.

The beach is rather rough with many big and small stones on the surface. The sand is also very big in form and brown in colour. At the time of low tide, we can see the *reefs*④ appearing out of the water. It is not fit for swimmers to come here to bathe, so it is quiet all the year round.

On the sea, we can see the distant fishing boats sailing back

---

① 治疗法；补救法
② 灌溉
③ 感受；此处为"呼吸"之意
④ 暗礁

to the harbour to anchor. The setting sun looks like an *immense yolk*①. The sky turns into orange red and the surface of the sea is glittering like a sheet of gold leaf. The waves beating at the rocks sound like music. All in all, a walk on the seashore is always enjoyable.

(7) An Art Exhibition

On the New Year's Day, the village people put on an art exhibition. As I had seen a lot in large cities with paintings by famous artists, I did not *feel like visiting*② it.

However, on a casual walk with my friends, I happened to notice the exhibition was just in front of us. So we *dropped in*③.

I discovered the objects painted familiar and dear to me: farmers harvesting rice, fighting cows on a hillside, sailing boats passing a rock in the middle of a river, the temple east of the village, huge old trees by a pond...

I *was amazed at*④ the artistic skill of the villagers. I *gathered*⑤ that their paintings were not famous just because they were not famous. If signed by an important artist and set in expensive frames, some of the exhibits might be worth thousands of yuan each.

(8) The Game I Like Best

I like Chinese chess best. It is my favourite indoor game. I play it in my spare time. After school, I always play it with my

---

① 大蛋黄
② (口语)想要参观……
③ 偶然进入(某地)
④ 对……感到惊愕；使惊奇
⑤ 得出(想法等)；推测

schoolmates. I am not very good at it because I am only a beginner.

Playing chess requires real skill. It requires thinking power to calculate each move. It is like a battle or a boxing match between two minds. It is an exciting mental combat. Of course, the cleverer man wins. It is, therefore, an amusing sort of game.

Playing chess trains my mind, and teaches me to think quickly, to see and find out what other people think and what they wish to do next. I like it best partly because it gives me real excitement and partly because it refreshes my mind. Whenever I play it, I think of nothing else except trying to win the game.

(9) Mountain Climbing

It was a day toward the end of August this year. About twenty of us had a picnic. The *drizzling rain*① which was falling in the morning could not prevent us from going, as we young men were not to be discouraged by such *trifling*② obstacles.

Along a straight narrow lane we went. On either side *stretched*③ the green *paddy-fields*④ *dotted* here and there *with*⑤ *cottages*⑥. On our way we could hear nothing except the *patter*⑦ of the rain and the sound of our footsteps. No sooner had we reached our *destination*⑧ than *it poured in torrents*⑨ that made us

---

① 蒙蒙细雨
② 无关紧要的
③ 延伸
④ 水稻田
⑤ 点缀着……
⑥ 农舍；乡间小屋
⑦ 雨点的嗒嗒声
⑧ 目的地
⑨ 倾盆大雨从天而降

消遣与娱乐 Recreations No.33

all *scatter in every direction*①.

When we had climbed to the top of a high mountain we found there was a white *villa*② of modern style *overlooking*③ the road below. The host invited us to his villa where we had a rest and heard the radio broadcasting that a *typhoon*④ was approaching from the east coast of Taiwan. Before long we all *did full justice to*⑤ the lunch which we had brought with us.

As we *plodded*⑥ our weary way homeward, we sang songs which *echoed*⑦ through the hills and *overwhelmed*⑧ the patter of the rain. It was already *candle-light*⑨ when we got home.

(10) Swimming in Winter

It was an afternoon late in the winter. Some friends and I were chatting in a restaurant, relaxing after a long examination. We talked and talked and soon swimming became the topic. Suddenly I had an idea: "Wouldn't it be funny if we went swimming?" They all agreed heartily. Soon we were planning for the swim.

Early in the morning three days later, we reached our destination. The sky was clear; the sun shining; but, all the same, it was very cold. There was not a soul on the beach. We were proud that we were the only ones that dared to challenge the weather. However, things were not going to be so ideal as we

---

① 四散开来
② 别墅
③ 俯瞰
④ 台风
⑤ 尽情享用;开怀大吃
⑥ 迈着沉重的脚步走
⑦ 发出回声
⑧ 淹没
⑨ 黄昏;掌灯时分

thought. The feeling I had when I jumped into the water I shall never forget. I was up instantly and rushed back to the shore. So did my friends. We put on our clothes as quickly as we could and went home.

We four did not attend school for the following three days, for we were all suffering from very bad colds. We missed the lesson, but we gained this unforgettable and amusing experience.

(11) Pet Dogs

City-dwellers have long been forbidden to keep domestic animals such as chickens and dogs, but now, we can see an increasing number of people walking their pet dogs on the pavements of Beijing nowadays. In the parks or shaded streets, they are seen side by side with the men and women who seem contented.

We are told that in some western countries where grown-up children live away from their parents, the old people keep pets for company. But in China, this doesn't seem to be the case. For one thing, it is mostly the young or middle-aged people who are seen walking and *fondling*① their expensively-bought and well-fed pet dogs. Some of them keep dogs to kill the time, to spend money, or to *show off their money*②. Like expensive cars in the western society, dogs now in China's cities could well be a symbol of wealth.

I think it is understandable for the retired elderly to desire pets as companions. As for the young and middle-aged, they should make better use of their time in the *prime life*③ instead of

---

① 抚弄
② 露富；显富
③ 风华正茂

spending so much time and money on pet dogs. What is more, one must know that social success should not be measured only by wealth.

(12) Pop Star as *Icon*① of Reform

Two years after she *shot to national fame*② by being popularly voted China's "super girl", *Li Yuchun*③ is once again at the center of attention. This time, she was selected as one of 100 candidates for the "icons of 30 years of reform" contest held by the *Southern Metropolis Daily*④.

The newspaper said on its website that Li was "a civilian icon by popular vote, whose rise to fame was regarded as a sign of the awakening of Chinese public awareness. However, not everyone was convinced by this explanation. Many challenged whether Li has the qualities to be an "icon of reform". Some were asking: "How great a contribution did she give to the country's reform and opening?" They argued that there are much more successful scientists and artists than her in this respect.

In my opinion, an "icon of reform" doesn't have to be a great scientist or artist. An ordinary person as pop singer Li Yuchun who by chance made a deep impression on the lives of millions of young people could also be such an icon. Li is just a good example of this.

(13) Why the Youngsters Like Popular Music

Of all the kinds of music, the youngsters like popular music

---

① 偶像
② 一举全国成名
③ 李宇春
④ 南方都市报

best. There are many kinds of popular music, such as rock'n'roll music and light music, which have much in common.

First, most pieces of popular music come from the real life, and are more accessible to the youngsters. People like things close to them because they feel at ease with them around. Classical music is a little far away and requires specialized knowledge of people to appreciate it. Second, many pieces of popular music are about love — a theme most youngsters care much for. They have many romantic dreams about love. When a popular song expresses what they feel and think, they will feel excited and encouraged. Third, some of the popular songs show much concern with social problems of all kinds. They arouse *resonance*[①] in the youngsters immediately. Having had their strong feelings released, they feel calm, and begin to do the constructive things.

For the above-mentioned reasons, no wonder the youngster *indulge themselves in popular music*[②].

---

① 共鸣
② 使他们自己沉迷于流行音乐之中

No.34 Excursion
郊游

(1) Our Spring Day Walk

One day in spring, I took a walk with some of my friends. As the day was bright and the air fresh, we were glad to be out. I thought it was much more pleasant to *ramble about*① through the woods and the fields than to study at home because knowledge can be obtained not only from books, but also from nature.

As we passed through a large meadow, we saw birds flying from tree to tree and singing their songs sweetly. The sky was blue and the trees were tall; the green grass and the little yellow flowers were quite soft beneath our feet. The stream flowed *serenely*②, the wind blew *gently*③, and *the scent of flowers stroked our noses*④. What a charming scene it was!

We sat on a meadow and chatted cheerfully for a while. Unexpectedly, the sun having set, it was growing dark everywhere. One by one the stars appeared in the sky, and the beautiful moon shone upon us.

People were all ready for supper with lamps lighted when we returned home.

---

① 漫步
② 平静地
③ 柔和地；轻轻地
④ 花香扑鼻

(2) An Excursion

One hot summer Sunday five roommates and I went on a holiday excursion to the North Mountain. At nine o'clock we came to its base. Oh, how beautiful the scenery was!

We followed other *sightseers*① and began to climb the mountain. Along the *rugged*② path rose *jagged*③ stones and rocks. Trees with *dense*④ foliage *sheltered*⑤ an ancient temple. Clean, clear water flowed from a nearby spring. Several *old trees towered grandly toward the blue sky*⑥. The melodious songs of birds continually pleased our ears. We felt very happy to *bathe*⑦ in the natural beauty.

At noon we picnicked on a spot of grass, then continued to climb until we reached the top. Below us we could see the open fields stretching far to the horizon with small houses and trees scattered here and there. Where was our city? It seemed to be hidden in the *mist*⑧ — now appearing, now disappearing.

In the late *twilight*⑨ we made our way down and *bid farewell to*⑩ the North Mountain, and returned to our college.

---

① 观光者
② 崎岖的
③ 参差不齐的
④ 茂密的
⑤ 遮蔽
⑥ 古木参天
⑦ 沉浸
⑧ 薄雾
⑨ 黄昏
⑩ 向……告别

(3) A Happy Outing

Last Sunday, my friends and I went for an outing. According to our plan, we met at eight o'clock and left for Pixia Dam by bicycle. We arrived at the foot of the Pixia Hill forty minutes later. Then all of us had a walk along the bank appreciating the magnificence of the great dam. At ten o'clock, we began to climb the hill.

The hill was not high and the slope was not very steep. We climbed slowly, picking up tiny wild flowers and sometimes we could even get a handful of wild dates. It wasn't long before we stood at the top of it.

How beautiful the scenery was! All the hill was covered with trees and wild flowers. High above us were the blue sky and the *brilliant*① sun. All of us could get a clear *bird's eye view*② of the vast dam lying at the foot like a huge dragon. Several pavilions were standing at the very summit to make the scene more splendid than ever!

We laughed and cheered, and had a nice picnic together around one flat big round stone. Later we took some pictures for remembrance.

It was about four o'clock when we returned home. Each of us wore a smiling face and carried a joyful heart.

(4) A Moonlight Picnic

It was at the close of a summer evening that I had a picnic with some friends of mine at a bay a few miles from my village.

---

① 灿烂的
② 鸟瞰

Being *noted for*① its *enchanting*② scenery, the bay was always *frequented*③ by visitors on Sundays and public holidays.

　　Five in number, we started in a boat when the moon, emerging from the eastern horizon, poured its bright rays upon the waves, forming thousands of *sparkling*④ mirrors.

　　Smoothly we *glided*⑤ over the *placid*⑥ surface, enjoying the cool air after the *glowing*⑦ heat of the day. *Harmonizing with*⑧ the playing of a *violin*⑨, we sang as we rowed on. Sometimes we chattered, and sometimes we ate the puddings we brought with us. The rowing was performed in turn by us; therefore, none of us felt the least *fatigue*⑩.

　　In about forty minutes, we were brought to our destination. Those who could swim left the boat to enjoy themselves in the shining water while others remained on board, amusing themselves with fishing and talking. The water, under the breeze, looked like a sheet of *tremulous*⑪ silver. The moon was bright and rose higher and higher. Though the tops of hills were swallowed up by mist and smoke, the *picturesque*⑫ surroundings were not invisible. Having enjoyed ourselves we started rowing back and arrived home at midnight.

---

① 以……著名
② 迷人的
③ 常去；常到
④ 闪耀的
⑤ （船）滑行；轻轻驶过
⑥ 平静的
⑦ 灼热的
⑧ 与……和谐、协调或一致
⑨ 小提琴
⑩ 疲劳
⑪ 微动的；颤动的
⑫ （风景）美如画的

(5) A Visit to Mount Lion

The other day I visited Mount Lion with three friends. We started very early in the morning and got back to the city towards evening. We spent about four hours on the hill.

We arrived at the foot of the hill at half past nine. Owing to the fog we had to wait some time before we *ascended*①. We took the chance to rest for a while, chatting all the time.

We spent only a quarter of an hour in climbing. We enjoyed doing it and did not feel tired at all. But when we had got to the top, we found ourselves sweating and *panting*②. We had to sit on some stones in the sunshine to rest ourselves.

We entered a temple, and several monks received us very kindly. They offered us tea. We drank it very eagerly, as if we had never tasted tea before. One of the young monks gave each of us a small cake, and we gave him some money *in return*③. He thanked us, saying that he hoped we would visit the temple every day.

There are many trees on the hill, mostly *pine trees*④ and *elm trees*⑤. According to the old monk, two of the trees are over five hundred years old.

A little south of the temple there is the tomb of a famous scholar of the *Yuan Dynasty*⑥. We could hardly read the characters on the *tombstone*⑦.

Before descending we said goodbye to the old monk and promised to come again next month.

---

① 登山
② 气喘吁吁
③ 作为回报
④ 松树
⑤ 榆树
⑥ 元朝
⑦ 墓碑

No.35 Tourism
旅行与旅游

（1）Tourism

*Tourism*① is now becoming a *boom*② industry in many countries.

It is obvious that it leads to the development of hotels and shopping facilities and creates jobs for local people — jobs which would not *otherwise*③ exist. Since visitors are especially fond of examples of local *crafts*④, a number of new industries tend to be developed to *meet this demand*⑤.

Still, the arrival of visitors always leads to improvements in *docks*⑥, airports and roads. Local people then benefit from these improvements themselves. Meanwhile, the amusement parks, zoos and other *amenities*⑦ gradually develop to attract more and more tourists.

With the frequent contact between people from different places and different nations, the exchange of culture and science is

---

① 旅游；旅游业
② 兴旺；繁荣
③ 否则；要不然
④ 工艺品
⑤ 满足这一需求
⑥ 船坞；码头
⑦ 令人愉快的环境；休闲去处

bound① to be promoted, possibly leading to the better understanding of peoples all over the world.

(2) Travelling

Travelling is a very good activity. When you *are fed up*② with your work and study, and when you can get a holiday, you can go to the beautiful spots to enjoy the beauty of nature and the special characters of other cities. You can breathe fresh air, meet different people and make friends with them. In so doing, you will forget your tiredness and troubles and build up your health. As a result, you will feel fully relaxed and you will have the energy to undertake the new tasks waiting for you.

But sometimes, travelling is not an enjoyable thing. For example, when the bus or car you ride in has an accident, you just sit in it and waste your precious time. Furthermore, the weather can be changeable. If you are climbing a mountain, it may rain suddenly. You may *be caught in*③ the rain and may catch a cold. The worst thing is that you may have your money stolen and you may have an injury. All these are terrible things which can happen to a tourist.

Therefore, when you are going on a trip, you must prepare yourself carefully. Firstly, you must have clear information about the weather. Secondly, you should choose a good companion so that you can help each other. Thirdly, you must be careful everywhere and try to avoid accidents. If you do this, you will surely enjoy your travels and avoid any unnecessary troubles.

---

① 一定的；必定的
② 对……极其厌倦
③ 被雨淋

(3) Travelling by Air

Air travel is very fast and enjoyable. A modern jet plane can take us to the other side of the world in a little more than ten hours. It seems the world is becoming a smaller place to live in and to *get around*①. In the future, air travel will become more common and convenient. We'll fly faster and *in greater comfort*②.

However, air traffic is *a mixed blessing*③. Though time-saving, it has created many challenging problems. Both the plane and the airport cost huge sums of money to build. Jet pollution is very harmful to health and property. *Sonic boom*④ is *driving us mad*⑤. How many people wish the *cursed*⑥ bird would disappear from the sky! Shouldn't air traffic be developed *under closer control*⑦?

I believe someday we'll have clean planes *run*⑧ on *solar energy*⑨ or a fuel that does not pollute. When this comes true, we will enjoy air travel even more.

(4) Which Mode of Travel Do You Like?

With the rising of the living standard and the working week becoming shorter, more and more people are able to make a

---

① 旅行
② 舒适地
③ 喜忧参半
④ 声震(以超音速飞行的飞机在降近地面时因机头冲击波受阻而发出的爆音)
⑤ 使……发疯
⑥ 可恶的;该咒的
⑦ 在更为严格的控制之下
⑧ 开动;驱动
⑨ 太阳能

holiday trip to places of interest. While many like to join *package tours*① for convenience, I prefer to travel on my own.

  I like travelling on my own not only because it costs much less but because it gives a great degree of freedom. Travelling on my own, I'm my own boss and can decide when to start on my way, where to *linger*② a little longer and which spot to skip over to save energy for another. I can always adjust my plan. On the contrary, in a package tour you are deprived of freedom. At the sound of the whistle, you have to jump up from sound sleep and hurry to the gathering place and sleepily board a coach. At the sight of the little flag, you must immediately tear yourself away from the scenes you are *marvelling at*③ and follow the guide whose sole interest is to cover all spots according to his strict schedule, regardless of the weather or your health condition.

  True, you may encounter inconveniences if you travel individually, for instance, getting accommodations for the night and finding a place for meals. But nothing can be compared with the freedom which is vital to a person who takes a holiday trip mainly to escape from constraints of the routine life.

---

① 组团旅游
② 逗留
③ 对……惊奇

No.36 Transportation
交通工具

(1) Automobiles

Automobiles have been playing a vital part in the daily activities of our society. In most cities, the majority of people get around either by car or by bus. Also, the automobile industry provides jobs for countless workers and strong support for other industries. In fact, automobiles have become indispensable.

But automobiles *have given rise to*① a series of problems. They are responsible for a very large *proportion*② of air pollution, causing a lot of diseases to man, animals, and plants. Traffic accidents kill hundreds or thousands each year and *disable*③ many more. Slow movement and jams on busy roads delay us painfully. Automobiles drink up precious gasoline and new roads eat up precious land. The consequences of all these are becoming even more serious.

Obviously, automobiles, like anything else, have more than one face. Engineers are working hard to *give fuller swing*④ to their merits and overcome their shortcomings. Improvements are being made. We believe future automobiles will be better.

---

① 引起了
② 部分
③ 使残废
④ 更好地发挥

(2) Private Cars in Large Cities

Today, people's living standard is improving rapidly. As a result, some people have bought cars of their own, and others are planning to buy cars.

There are some advantages in owning a private car in large cities. First, a car allows one to move freely. With a car, there is no need to wait for the bus in the cold or under the burning sun. Second, a car makes it easier and more comfortable to travel. One can set out whenever he likes.

There are, on the other hand, some disadvantages in owning a private car. First, it may cause more traffic jams if the road conditions cannot be improved. Second, more cars will result in more serious pollution. Finally, parking will be a problem since there is not much space left in large cities.

In a word, if conditions permit, owning a private car can make us work more efficiently and our life will become more enjoyable.

(3) Bicycles

Bicycles are the most popular vehicle in China today. Wherever you go, you may find many people riding on bicycles to go to works, to do shopping, to visit friends, or to go to school. During the rush hour, you can often see *a boiling sea of*[①] bicycles in all directions. In fact, China is sometimes called the Kingdom of Bicycles as it has the largest number of bicycle riders with millions of bicycles made every year. All these show that bicycles are the most important and popular transportation tool in China.

Compared with cars, bicycles have many advantages. First,

---

① 非常多的；大量的

they are not very expensive and almost every family can afford to buy and repair them. Secondly, though they run more slowly than cars, bicycles are very handy and convenient. With a bicycle, you can go wherever you like and needn't look for a large parking place in a crowded downtown area or get a garage at home. Thirdly, bicycles don't cause air pollution. On the contrary, they do good to your health. In addition, it is much easier to learn to ride a bicycle than to drive a car.

However, bicycles have also brought about many problems. For example, they make the streets more crowded and cause many traffic accidents every year. But as long as these problems can be properly solved, bicycles will still be widely used by people in China.

(4) Cars for Tomorrow

Small cars may some day take the place of today's big automobiles. With the increase of population and development of industry, we'll have not enough space to park our cars. If everyone drives such small cars in the future, it will be easier to find space for parking in the cities. Besides, the streets will be less crowded because three such cars only occupy the space now needed for one car of the usual size.

There are other advantages, too. The little car will cost much less to own and to drive. Driving will be safer, too, as these little cars can go only 65 kilometers per hour. Meanwhile, they cause less pollution in the air.

However, there are also disadvantages. These cars will not be useful for long trips. They will have to stop for gasoline after going for 450 kilometers. Moreover, two sets of roads will be needed: one for the big, fast automobiles, and the other for the slower, small automobiles if big cars are still used along with the small ones.

(5) Taxi

    I well remember the days when my mother sent me to kindergarten by bus every morning. We had to wait for hours until we finally got on board a bus. Being *squeezed*[①] out of breath in an overcrowded bus, we felt lucky when we saw women with children waiting helplessly at bus stops in heavy rain or bitter cold. Now we have taxi as an alternative, and people like its comfort, its convenience, and its reasonable price.

    Taxi is gaining popularity for several reasons. First, traveling in an air-conditioned taxi is comfortable. Wherever you go, the driver takes care of everything; what you do is just sitting in cozy seats, enjoying yourself in all kinds of weather at any time. Taking a taxi also saves you time and a world of trouble of driving. Second, taxi is convenient, especially in an emergency or on special occasions. For example, if you are suddenly very sick deep at night with nobody to turn to for help in an unfamiliar place, taxi is always availble to help you to a hospital. Finally, taxi is affordable. Even you have a car, you have to pay the bills of gas, insurance, and car maintenance. What is more, parking cars in big cities could be a headache.

    With the rapid improvement of living standard, taxi has become an important means of transportation in China because of its reasonable price, its availability, and the comfort it offers. In fact, many people depends on taxi to go to work and almost everyone has the experience of taking a taxi on special occasions. I am happy for not having buses as the only choice any more.

---

① 挤

No.37 Dwellings
民居

(1) My Home

My home is a newly-built house in the east of the village. With a tall roof and large windows, it is very comfortable. We have quite a lot of new furniture and electric things. But we still use firewood for cooking. And, of course, we raise pigs and *poultry*[①] in the yard. Behind the house there is a garden, where we grow vegetables and a few fruit trees. The old house, in which we lived for generations, is now a *barn*[②]. We also keep seldom used farm tools there. We have very kind neighbours. They belong to the farming community, too. I always believe that, east and west, home is the best.

(2) My Flat

Our flat is situated in the western district. People may think that it is a good one, because it looks quite nice from outside. But when friends and relatives come to visit us, they are surprised to find that our flat looks like a *tent*[③], for the *ceiling*[④] is completely

---

① 家禽
② 谷仓
③ 帐篷
④ 天花板

covered up with cloth.

At the beginning, when we first moved into this flat, it was painted like a new one, although it was built about twenty years ago. But in only a month's time, much *plaster*① had dropped off from the ceiling. So my mother covered it up with cloth, and our flat now looks like a tent.

It is the top flat that we live in. So when it rains, it leaks. This gives us a lot of trouble. I would say that this flat is no good at all.

Anyhow, although it is not a comfortable place to live in, we do not mind, for many other people's *abodes*② may even be worse than ours and there are people who do not even have a home.

(3) My New Home

Last year, I lived in an apartment building known as "Dormitory One". When the time came to move out, my joy was beyond description.

"Dorm One" exactly resembled the film "Neighbours". The long corridors serving as a kitchen were lined with gas stoves. The public toilets were often wrong with their *drainage*③. While I ate, the polluted air ruined my appetite. When I slept, a sudden noise would *startle*④ me like a nightmare.

Compared with the dorm, my new apartment seems like a paradise. It is so quiet that I can't hear any noise except the ticking of the clock. When I am tired, I step onto the balcony to

---

① （涂墙用的）灰泥
② 住所
③ 排水设备；下水道
④ 使受惊

enjoy fresh air and sunshine. The clean, quiet and *roomy*① *privacy*② makes me energetic and enables me to work late at night, for I always have a good sleep.

① 宽敞的
② 此处意指"不受干扰的住处"

No.38 | Money
金钱问题

(1) Money

　　Money is considered by some people to be the most powerful and important thing in life. In their opinion, everything in the world such as *luxurious cars*①, *magnificent mansions*②, etc. can be bought with money, if you can afford them. In some countries, even a post as a *senior official*③ could be bought with money.

　　But there are certain things that cannot be bought with money. A millionaire who suffered from serious cancer was willing to buy his health by selling all his expensive property. But he failed and soon died in despair. An old rich merchant was willing to buy the true love of a beautiful young girl *at any cost*④, but his wicked dream never came true. Many other things such as *devoted*⑤ friendship and real honour are invaluable and cannot be bought with money, either. So money is far from *omnipotent*⑥.

　　Money can bring us misery as well as happiness. Those who

---

① 豪华的汽车
② 豪华的住宅
③ 高级官员
④ 不惜任何代价
⑤ 忠诚的；忠实的
⑥ 万能的；无所不能的

make money through their own mental or physical labour usually lead a *frugal*① but happy life. But those who make "dirty money" through illegal means such as stealing, smuggling, corrupting, will never have true happiness. Every day and every hour they will be worrying about being arrested and imprisoned by the authorities. And in the end this may well happen. They are *doomed to*② a miserable future.

(2) Money and Greed

Few people in the world today can survive without a certain amount of money. In ancient times people were, for the most part, self-sufficient. Individuals farmed, bred animals and livestock, and supported themselves without having to depend on a market. With improvements in technology and transportation, the world's economies have changed to include a greater variety of goods, most of which come from distant sources. In order to exchange goods, money is needed. Today money has become the requirement of an improved life style.

Though the system of monetary exchange has helped to improve the life of modern man, it has also created new social problems. It is a fact that money is the major cause of crime and violence in the world today. Robbery, theft, burglary, and murder are most commonly committed for the sake of money. Money often *drives*③ powerful people such as officials and distinguished businessmen to corruption and dishonesty. In addition to crime, money has been the cause of class differences in many countries throughout the world. These class differences

---

① 节俭的
② 注定
③ 驱使

have, in turn, created much political *strife*① and *discontent*②.

Perhaps the problem at hand is not actually money itself but greed. If human beings could learn to be satisfied with living simply and *moderately*③, if they could learn to share, to think about the good of the public rather than the good of the self, money might not be such a source of trouble in the world.

(3) My View on Bank Loan

It becomes a common tendency these days for people to ask for bank loans to buy a house or a private car. Many people are opposed to this practice because they think to get bank loan is a trap to get into debt, and they will always feel burden on their back in the coming years. They also argue that they will not buy anything before they are capable of paying it in cash.

In my mind, however, I can't agree with these people on this occasion. It takes many years for common citizens to earn enough money to buy a house or a car, and asking for a bank loan certainly shortens the distances between dream and reality. At the same time, it is not too difficult for people to *pay by instalments*④ if they have normal jobs. In addition, applying for bank loans can be a form of investment, which makes it possible for people to earn more money

In conclusion, obtaining a bank loan will certainly do us good so long as we make it reasonable.

---

① 冲突;斗争
② 不满
③ 适度地;节制地
④ 分期付款

(4) Can Success Be Measured in Terms of Money?

There is a *deep-rooted*[①] concept in the minds of many people that money is the only yardstick of success. What they do not realize is that there are many types of success, and some are associated with wealth and some not. It is high time that such people opened their eyes and took a *sober*[②] look at the world around them.

While it is true that a successful businessman or inventor will usually become rich, many other people who are outstanding in their fields do not reap monetary rewards. One example is the rocket scientists who make great achievements in the field of astronautics gaining glory for their country, but draw a modest salary. Another example is Lei Feng, who has marked his name in history because his life was devoted to helping others, although he owned almost no personal possessions.

Measuring success by money alone leads people to strive to make money by fair means or foul. If one's only goal is to become rich, without serving others or making any worthwhile achievements, then one certainly cannot regard oneself as successful. Furthermore, those who spend their lives scrambling for money only, even though they gain it, are the biggest losers of all.

---

① 根深蒂固
② 清醒的,认真的

No.39 Generation Gap 代沟

(1) What Kind of Life to Live — Realistic or Romantic?

There has always been an argument between the young and the old about what kind of life to live — realistic or romantic. Young people tend to think that real life is as *dramatic*① and *fascinating*② as it is in the novels and movies, while more experienced adults think this naive daydream is certain to be broken by later experiences and everyone should learn to get used to the dull routine of his everyday life.

However, there are some inadequacies in the opinions on the part of both sides. Life will be unimaginable if everything we do is only for realistic purposes, and the same is true if what we do every day is just to enjoy ourselves. So it's not difficult for us to see that neither way can ensure a happy life.

In my opinion, a real happy life can never be separated from either of the two ways. On the one hand, let's enjoy life — enjoy the blue depth of a clear sky, enjoy the *harmony*③ on violin strings and enjoy the excitement of sports. On the other, let's not forget our work. Happy life can never go without hard work.

---

① 戏剧性的;充满激情的
② 迷人的;令人神往的
③ 和谐悦耳的声音

(2) Mutual Understanding Is Important

Parents and teenagers often disagree about the amount of freedom and responsibility that young people are to have.

Teenagers often want to be free to choose their own direction to spend leisure time. Some like to learn photography or painting, while others prefer to sit around and talk or sing. Still others wish to be free to select their own courses in school and plan for their own vocational goals. Young people, as a whole, are anxious to be understood by their parents.

On the other hand, most parents don't quite understand their children. They regard it as their responsibility to teach *offsprings*① traditional beliefs and they want the young people to be obedient and do well in school. There always exists a tendency for parents to interfere in children's daily activities, insisting that homework be completed, while teenagers' particular interests and hobbies are often neglected or even ignored.

Personally, I think most problems between teenagers and their parents *yield best to*② joint planning and decision making. Within any *given*③ family disagreements are avoided and problems are solved when all of the persons take interest in the situation and share in working it out. Hence parents and young people must realise the necessity to learn how to understand each other and develop skills in communication — speaking and listening. Thus, even the most difficult problems can be solved.

---

① 儿女；后代
② 最好被……代替；最好让位于……
③ 特定的；一定的

(3) Generation Gap Between Parents and Children

Nowadays, there are more and more misunderstanding between parents and children, which is caused by so-called generation gap. It is estimated that 75 percent of parents often complain their children's unreasonable behavior while children usually think their parents too old-fashioned.

Why have there been so much misunderstanding between parents and children? Maybe the reasons can be listed as follows.

The first one is that the two generations, having grown up at different times, have different likes and dislikes, thus the disagreement often rises between them. Besides, due to having little in common to talk about, they are not even willing to sit face to face. The third reason is that with the pace of modern life becoming faster and faster, both of them are so busy with their work or study that they don't spare enough time to exchange ideas. To sum up, the main cause of generation gap is due to lack of communication and understanding between each other.

It is high time that something be done about it. For one thing, children should respect their parents. On the other hand, parents also should show *solicitude*① for their children. All these measures will be helpful to bridge the generation gap though we still have a long way from providing sufficient solutions.

(4) The Generation Gap

The generation gap, a division between the young people and their elders, is one of the social problems in modern society. It appears when parents complain that their children do not show

---

① 关注,关怀

them proper respect and obedience, and the children complain that their parents do not understand them at all. But what brings along the generation gap?

One important cause of the generation gap is that young people tend to choose their own life styles. In more traditional ways, grown-up children are expected to live with their parents to carry on the family occupation. Furthermore, the parents often expect their children to do better than they did — to find better job, to make more money, and to do all the things that they were unable to do. In modern society, young people often travel great distances for their educations, move out of the home at an early age, marry or live with people whom their parents have never met, and choose occupations different from those of their parents. Finally, they discover they have very little in common with each other.

The generation gap will continue to be a feature of our life for some time. All things change rapidly in modern society and the knowledge of a lifetime may become out-dated overnight. The young and the old seem to live in two very different worlds, separated by different skills and abilities. It may be safely said that the generation gap is rooted in the very heart of our society and civilization, and in the rapid change as times progress and society advances.

No.40 | Women
妇女问题

(1) On Women's Problems

Women's problems exist all over the world mainly in two respects — in work and life.

It is rather difficult for women, even postgraduates with honours, to get well-paid jobs. Some enterprises positively reject their applications just to avoid the trouble of childbirth and childcare. Some bosses consider women inferior in professional skills and *initiative*①. They argue that before marriage, females' dependent nature largely *chains their attention to*② fashionable dresses and various high-grade cosmetics, and that after *matrimony*③, especially with a child, their minds *dwell on*④ nothing but the comforts of life, baby-care, and housework.

Even if some ambitious young ladies fight their way to get a position, promotion for them is *out of the question*⑤. The number of top women executives in science, government, business, education, etc. is so few as to be only tokens. Besides, a female's success may become a great obstacle to her family life, as most

---

① 主动性;积极性
② 此处指"将注意力集中在……"
③ 婚姻生活;婚姻
④ 此处指"考虑;关心"
⑤ 不可能的

males prefer a good wife and wise mother.

As for housework, these gentlemen usually think it is the women's task; the wives' sacrifices are sure to set the husbands up for great success. So work for females involves the responsibility for household, baby, and job as well.

In a word, as long as men's traditional ways of thinking dominate society, the above-mentioned problems of *sexual discrimination*① may *linger on*②.

(2) Women in Our Society

Women are playing an increasingly important role in our society. They are emerging in all fields. In some professions, they *constitute*③ the majority. And some of them are *holding key positions*④.

With their changing role in society, women's place in the family is improving as well. Marriage is much more *of their own choice*⑤. Many are *on an equal footing*⑥ with their husbands and have a lot of *say*⑦ in deciding family matters.

In spite of all this, the liberation of women has not yet been completely realized. There is still a long way to go. Compared with men, women have less education. Many work hard with low pay. There are still few women in key positions. And even today, many women have to stay at home to take care of the family. All in all, the trend is towards greater equality for both sexes.

---

① 性别歧视
② 继续存在
③ 构成;组成
④ 担任要职
⑤ 自主选择
⑥ 平等的;处于平等地位的
⑦ 发言权

(3) Women Are as Perfect as Men

Our present age is supposed to be an *enlightened*① one, but one will not be convinced until one sees men regard women as their equal. Women, in fact, are as perfect as men.

In addition to bearing and rearing children, women frequently succeed brilliantly in such fields as drivers, politicians, university professors, scientists, and presidents of countries. Take driving for an example. Though men *sneer at*② women for their driving, women really cause far fewer accidents than men. Women are too *conscientious*③ and responsible to drive like *maniacs*④. By extension from this *quibbling*⑤, women have succeeded in any job one cares to name.

Moreover, to recognize the fact that women are as perfect as men, it is necessary to correct the bias that there are many jobs women can't do. Not only are women denied some jobs reserved for men, but also men refuse to acknowledge women's abilities and to *give them their due*⑥ even if they have proved themselves.

In a word, women are as good as men.

(4) Women — Still as Second-class Citizen

Although there are great changes to women, the liberation of women has not been completely realized in some areas. A number of men still jealously guard their so-called rights and regard

---

① 开明的;有知识的
② 嗤笑;嘲笑;讥笑
③ 小心谨慎的;认真的
④ 狂人,疯子
⑤ 由此推而广之
⑥ 公平地对待某人(此处指妇女)

women as second-class citizens or incapable creatures. For instance, top-level political negotiations between countries, business, and banking are almost entirely controlled by men. Few women are allowed to attend important international conferences dominated by men. Some men still maintain that there are many jobs women can't do, so they don't receive women as their workers. Even when women do the same work, they are often paid less than men. When women prove their abilities, men refuse to acknowledge them and give them their due. This is really one women's problem which we should solve immediately.

(5) Women's Liberation: a Long Way to Go

People began to pay attention to the Women's Liberation Movement in the 1960s and 1970s. Women in the U.S.A. and elsewhere demanded equal rights and treatment. The story has usually been the same. When a woman looks for work, the first question is "Can you type?" No consideration is given to her schooling or qualifications. Women have been thought of only as office workers in government and business, but not as *executive*①; as nurses and teachers, but not as doctors and lawyers.

Nowadays, because of the struggle put up by the Women's Liberation Movement, the prejudice against women is weakening and the idea of emancipation is becoming stronger. Women are managing to get more and more important jobs in business, government and the scientific research. "Women's Lib" has in fact become one of the most important movements in the United States, Britain and, indeed, the world. Women get together in small groups to describe to one another their own experience as

---

① （公司）高级职员；行政官

second-class citizens.

Change may come slowly for equality between men and women, but those who believe in women's liberation continue to hope, and to work, for a change.

(6) Send Women Home and Double Men's Salary

With millions of graduates pouring into the already crowded job market each year, employment is getting more and more competitive. In this context, some people propose to send women home and double men's salary. They say it is right for the women to play the traditional role as a wife and mother, so that men can concentrate on their jobs and best serve the society.

Others hold that the proposal does not conform to the equality principle. Women who stay at home all the time may feel prejudiced and second-class. Besides, the absence of women from job market is a waste of human resource. Women are good at many jobs that men cannot do just as well. They conclude that it is absolutely unwise to keep women home; meanwhile, it is impossible to double men's salary.

In my opinion, the proposal of sending women home and doubling men's salary is not acceptable at all. On the one hand, sending women home is definitely not the answer to the question of employment. On the other hand, it is a domestic business to decide who from the family is to stay at home and take care of the family and who is to go out and work as the breadwinner. Why don't we consider doubling women's salary and keeping men at home, since men could do housework just as well and housework is just as important as work outside homes?

No.41 Population 人口问题

(1) Population Explosion

Population explosion, or overpopulation, has become a familiar issue for almost everybody in the world, and a serious problem as well. In fact, the rapid growth of population has brought about many other problems.

The most *pressing*① problem created is perhaps the increasing demand of food, while the area of the earth can never be expanded for more *cultivable land*②. Along with the shortage of food, there are also the problems of decreasing supply of water, less job opportunities, insufficient houses, schools, and health care. These problems are not limited to developing countries alone. Rather, as the rapid growth of world population continues, the whole world will face the problems of natural resources being used up at an increasing speed, which, in turn, can only bring about ever serious threat to mankind.

The best, perhaps the only, solution to solve the problem of overpopulation is to exercise birth control. Fortunately, many countries have started doing so. China, for example, has successfully carried out the one-couple-one-child policy and its

---

① 紧迫的
② 可耕土地

birth rate is much lower than before. Only by this means can population growth be *checked*① and related problems be solved.

(2) Population Control

Progress in science and the improvement of living conditions have led to the rapid growth of the world population. Modern medicine, for example, has made it possible for babies to grow up healthily and for people to live longer. With improved living conditions, particularly in the countryside, people tend to have larger families. As a result, the world population has increased so rapidly that it has now exceeded 6 billion.

But the overgrowth of population presents a threat to the existence of human society. A large population demands a great deal of food supply and shelter space. However, the limited *productivity*② and *scarce*③ world resources can hardly meet the needs of the everincreasing population. Thus, *in the long run*④, the overgrowth of the world population will only harm mankind.

To *guarantee*⑤ the steady development of human society, mankind must realize the consequences resulting from a fast population growth and carry out a family planning programme. Only by adopting effective measures can human society develop steadily and have a bright future.

(3) China's Population Problem in Rural Areas

The huge population of China is a very serious problem especially in rural areas. Although the government has made

---

① 得到控制
② 生产能力
③ 缺乏的
④ 从长远看；终究
⑤ 确保

every effort to control the birth rate in recent years, the work has met strong resistance in the country.

Many people think that the feudal tradition with its premise that it was good to have more children in order to have more working hands is *to blame*① for this. However, this only *constitutes*② half of the reason. In the country there are no pensions and no free medical care for the old. Many young couples are afraid that once they are old, there will be nobody to care for them. So they want a son who can take care of them all their lives.

In my opinion, although the feudal influence is strong, the younger generation in rural areas can understand the importance of family planning, and what worries them most is their own old age. So if we can *raise more funds*③ for the elderly and build more *old folks' homes*④ and other *welfare institutions*⑤ for them, the farmers can put their minds at rest.

(4) How to Solve the Problem of Employment and Population

The problem of employment and population is a world one. It is difficult to solve this problem. Perhaps you think we can build more factories so that more people can get jobs; or we can adopt strong measures of retirement. However, these cannot solve the problem thoroughly because of many factors. First, to build, maintain and improve factories needs great financial resources. Where do they come from? Secondly, to run factories, as we know, energy must be supplied from resources such as coal, water, electricity and oil, but these natural resources are limited.

---

① 该受责备的;(是)某种不良后果的原因
② 构成
③ 筹集更多的基金
④ 敬老院
⑤ 福利机构

人口问题
Population

No.41

Thirdly, we all know that the number of young people who have not got jobs is much greater than that of the retirement. So in my opinion, the best solution to this problem is to adopt strong measures of birth control because the greater the population, the less the opportunity for everyone to get a job.

No.42 Traffic Problem
交通问题

(1) Modern Transportation

It is known to us all that modern transportation plays an important role in our life. In the past, people used to suffer a great deal if they had to make a long journey or convey some heavy goods. The fact is that the transport means at that time was simple and rare. Today, various vehicles, ships and airplanes have enabled us to go wherever we like. Not only does modern transportation carry people with much convenience, but it also *frees people from the hard work of conveyance*①. More importantly, modern transportation has saved much of our time so that we can do more work and increase our knowledge.

In addition, the development of our society is impossible *in the absence of*② modern transportation. But for means of modern transportation, the exchange of friendly visits and trade contacts between countries would be very difficult and many badly needed products would keep piling up in factories and fields. People would have trouble going to work on time because transport had come to a standstill. Many cities would be in chaos for the lack of energy, daily necessities and other things to keep the cities going.

Despite its importance, modern transportation has brought about some problems. At present, traffic jams and accidents are

---

① 使人们不再从事运送货物的繁重工作
② 缺乏;没有

increasing rapidly because of modern transportation. In addition, *exhaust gas*① and dust by motor cars have added to air pollution, and the noise of various conveyances almost drives people mad. So it is urgent that governments and experts take measures to solve these problems in order that modern transport become a better service to people.

(2) Only Stricter Traffic Laws Can Prevent Accidents

Though the possibility of living a long and happy life is greater than ever before, every day there exists the incredible slaughter of men, women and children on the roads. It is a never-ending battle which man is losing. Thousands of people the world over are killed or horribly *mutilated*② each year and we are quietly sitting back and letting it happen.

It has been rightly said that when a man is sitting behind a steering wheel, his car becomes the extension of his personality. There is no doubt that the motor-car often brings out a man's very worst qualities. People who are normally quiet and pleasant may become unrecognizable when they are behind a steering-wheel. They are ill-mannered and aggressive, willful as two-year olds and utterly selfish.

The surprising thing is that society smiles so *benignly*③ on the motorist and seems to *condone*④ his behavior. Everything is done for his convenience. Cities are allowed to become almost uninhabitable because of heavy traffic; the countryside is *desecrated*⑤ by road networks; and the mass annual slaughter becomes nothing more than a statistic, to be conveniently forgotten.

---

① 废气
② 致残,使……残疾
③ 仁慈地
④ 宽恕,赦免
⑤ 被亵渎,被玷污

It is high time that a world code were created to reduce this senseless waste of human life. With regard to driving, laws of some countries are notoriously lax and even the strictest are not strict enough. A code which was universally accepted could only have dramatically beneficial effect on the accident rate. Therefore, stricter traffic laws must be strictly carried out to prevent accidents.

(3) Problems Brought About by Automobiles

Although the automobile has brought convenience to us, many people have begun to realise that it is the source of trouble as well. Because of too many automobiles, traffic accidents happen again and again all over the world. Worst of all, waste gases sent out by the automobiles *give rise to*① air pollution and do great harm to people.

In order to solve the problem of air pollution, some automobile manufacturers are trying to build cars that do not pollute and some inventors are working on cars powered by steam or electricity. But now this is only a dream.

The governments in some countries, for example, in the United States, are trying to reduce the number of privately-owned cars and ask their people to use public buses. But this causes other problems, too. It is, therefore, very difficult to make these changes *for the present*②.

(4) *Pile-up*③ Traffic Accidents

During the rush hour one evening, two cars collided and both drivers began to argue. The woman immediately behind the two

---

① 引起；导致
② 暂时；目前
③ 几辆车相撞；汽车追尾

cars happened to be a learner. She suddenly got into *a panic*① and stopped her car. This made the driver following her *brake hard*②. His wife was sitting beside him holding a large cake. As she was thrown forward, the cake went right through the *windscreen*③ and landed on the road. Seeing a cake flying through the air, a lorry driver who was drawing up alongside the car, *pulled up*④ all of a sudden. The lorry was loaded with empty beer bottles and hundreds of them slid off the back of the vehicle and on to the road. This led to yet another angry argument. Meanwhile, the traffic piled up behind. It took the police nearly an hour to get the traffic on the move again.

(5) A Road Accident

There was a road accident near our school gate this morning. I was just riding on my bike through the school gate when I heard a loud bang behind me. I turned round and saw a green Ford car *come into collision*⑤ with a blue Japanese-made car. The blue car was driving east. Judging by its position on the road, it had tried to overtake another car. Because of his carelessness, the driver didn't check before *pulling out*⑥. As a result, it crashed into a green Ford car which was travelling in the opposite direction. The driver of the green Ford was killed instantly while the driver of the blue car was badly injured. It was not long before an ambulance arrived and left with the injured and the dead drivers. Both cars were seriously damaged. So many people gathered to

---

① 惊慌；恐慌
② 猛踩刹车
③ 挡风玻璃窗
④ (使车辆)停下
⑤ 跟……相撞
⑥ 驶出

see what had happened that many cars, buses, etc. were caught in the traffic jam. A whole hour passed before the crowd slowly *dispersed*①. This accident would not have happened if the driver of the blue car had checked before pulling out. *Haste makes waste.*②

---

① 散去；散开
② 性急易错

No.43 Environmental Protection
环境保护

(1) Pollution

Pollution is becoming more and more serious all over the world. For example, the poisonous gas sent off by factories and automobiles has made the air unhealthy for people to breathe. For another example, waste water keeps *pouring*① into rivers and lakes; as a result, many water species are *dying out*②. Furthermore, everywhere we go today, we can find rubbish carelessly disposed. Pollution is, in fact, threatening our existence.

People are *showing* a real *concern over*③ the problem. There is an increasingly loud *voice*④ from the public calling for firm actions against pollution. Scientists have warned that unless effective solutions are worked out, the problem of pollution will eventually *get out of hand*⑤. Indeed, the earth is our home and we have the duty to take care of it for ourselves and for our later generations.

Fortunately, measures are being taken to cope with the situation. First, many new laws have been passed to place strict

---

① 倒入;注入
② 消失;灭绝
③ 对……表示关心
④ 呼声;意见
⑤ 无法控制;不可收拾

controls over industrial pollution. Secondly, a large-scale program *is now under way*① to educate people to be responsible citizens in fighting pollution. Finally, the government has started building various facilities like *sewage treatment*② plants and has encouraged scientists to work out more and better ways to reduce pollution. It is hoped that all these measures will be effective and bring back a healthful world.

(2) Cars and Air Pollution

Too many cars have created a lot of serious problems in our world. Besides *congestion*③, accidents, and fast *fuel consumption*④, cars are responsible for a good part of air pollution. All the time, they are *pumping*⑤ huge amounts of waste gases into the atmosphere. These gases are very harmful, causing diseases and even deaths. Car *fumes*⑥ form smog over large cities, making the sky gloomy. Air pollution from cars is unbearable in many places.

To *tackle*⑦ the problem of air pollution, engineers are working to design clean cars and clean fuels. There are several possibilities. Yet progress is slow. No practical *model*⑧ will be available in a few years.

If we are to *eliminate*⑨ air pollution together with other

---

① 正在进行中
② 污水处理
③ 交通拥塞
④ 燃料消耗
⑤ 把……灌入；倾注
⑥ 烟气
⑦ 对付；解决
⑧ （汽车等的）样式；这里指"新式样的汽车"
⑨ 消除

*plagues*① caused by cars, far more *drastic action*② must be taken. We will have to look for an overall solution. At present, the development of underground mass transit systems seems to be the best possible way out for large cities.

(3) Water Pollution

Everyone agrees that water pollution is a serious problem today. Rivers, lakes, and even oceans all over the world are becoming polluted with garbage and dangerous chemicals. Factories *contribute to*③ the problem because they rely on rivers for *disposing of*④ wastes. Oil and other chemicals can kill fishes and make water unsafe for drinking. Polluted water is *a hazard*⑤ to everyone.

Since people are dependent on water, they should be involved in finding a solution to this problem. Recently, certain *counter measures*⑥ have been taken. Above all, many governments, both in developed countries and in developing countries, have *laid down rules and regulations*⑦ in respect to pollution problem. Factories in towns and cities are forbidden to *drain*⑧ waste liquids into rivers, lakes, and seas before they are totally treated and purified. With the progress of science and technology, a series of advanced methods have been developed to treat *contaminated*⑨ water. And certain remarkable results have been achieved in this

---

① 灾害;祸患
② 严厉的措施
③ 此处指"导致、造成"
④ 消除;除掉
⑤ 公害
⑥ 对策
⑦ 制定规章制度
⑧ 排放
⑨ 受污染的

respect. Rivers which used to be polluted by industrial chemical wastes are now being cleaned and fishes which could not live there a few years ago can be caught again.

I believe that the problem will be solved to a great extent when everyone realizes the urgency to cope with it and seeks solutions for its control.

(4) Deserts

Over vast areas of every continent, rainfall and vegetation are disappearing. Already more than 40% of the earth's land is desert or desert-like. And deserts are spreading at a rate of 60,000 square kilometers a year. If things go on like this, sand will bury everything on land in 2,500 years!

Deserts are largely created by man himself. *Overgrazing*①, poor farming, tree-cutting, *strip-mining*②— all leave land unprotected. Rain water washes topsoil into rivers and seas, and in dry seasons wind blows away *loose soil*③.

To meet the need of an increasing world population, the expansion of deserts must be stopped. Experiments are being made and some measures have been taken. But deserts are still *edging*④ forward to bury a world that regards profit as a *supreme*⑤ value.

(5) Let's Plant More Trees

Trees are very useful and important to human beings. They

---

① 过度放牧
② 露天剥采矿石
③ 松土
④ 徐徐移动;逐渐移进
⑤ 最大的;最重要的

provide us with wood, which is not only important for us to build houses and boats, but also indispensable to us for making furniture, paper, matches and many other things. Trees can also protect the fertile surface of soil from being washed away by strong winds and heavy rains. With the loss of soil, the land will become a desert where nothing can grow.

Trees also do good to our environment. They can make our world greener and more beautiful. They also produce oxygen, making the air fresher and better for our health. What's more, trees help maintain *ecological*[①] balance, which is essential to our existence.

To protect the environment, it is necessary to plant more trees. Now the government has launched a National Tree Planting Campaign. It encourages us to plant trees wherever possible, such as in big mountains, on small hills, along both sides of streets, and around our houses. When we plant trees, we are helping make our world richer and more beautiful and our *descendants*[②] happier and richer.

(6) Man and the Environment

The world we live in is becoming more and more intolerable because of environmental destruction. For example, forest destruction results in unpleasant weather. In addition, man is faced with problems of water pollution and air pollution.

Many *remedial measures*[③] have been taken. Planting trees helps improve and beautify the environment. Also, laws concerning environmental protection have been *put into effect*[④]

---

① 生态的
② 子孙后代
③ 补救措施
④ 实施;实行

and achieved good results.

However, the problem of environmental protection remains far from being solved. On the one hand, environmental pollution and destruction are getting worse and worse in the modern world. On the other hand, the lack of knowledge about the importance of protecting the environment *hinders*① the solving of the problem. In a word, there is a long way to go before we enjoy a clean and comfortable world.

(7) Protecting Natural Environment

We are facing major environmental problems. *Vast stretches of*② productive lands are being turned into deserts. The reduction of wooded areas has already led to increased flooding and water shortages in dry seasons. It is reported that as many as 70% of the woods in Asia will be *gone*③ in 20 years unless actions are taken now to save them.

There are two basic causes for these problems. One is manmade. For example, someone does such a thing as cutting down trees to receive benefits or to get necessities, so that the natural environment is damaged. The other is natural *catastrophes*④. Perhaps the most serious threats are forest fires and the rapid *shrinking*⑤ of Asia's rainforests.

Then, how should we protect the natural environment? One method is by creating laws. Although this method has worked, laws *alone*⑥ in poor places, where people damage the environment

---

① 妨碍
② 大片大片的
③ 此处指"被用光了"
④ 大灾难
⑤ 缩小；减少
⑥ 只有；仅仅

环境保护 Environmental Protection No.43

out of necessity, are not enough. Or perhaps *imposing a fine*① is a better way to stop the man-made destruction. In addition, new *environmentally constructive*② means must be found through scientific and technical work.

(8) How to Save Wild Animals

Many wild animals are facing the danger of *extinction*③, because the environment that they are living in has changed greatly. For example, with the development of cities, the using of insecticide, and pollution, their living area becomes narrower and narrower. Many of the wild animals now are confronted with food crisis. At the same time, man is *killing off*④ species at the rate of one a year just for getting their fur, skin, horn, teeth, and meat.

In order to protect our ecology of resources and balancing factors, people should realize that the loss of any species is at least the loss of a source of knowledge and a source of natural beauty. Therefore, the following measures should be taken: pollution standards are made to *keep down*⑤ poisons; killing of certain rare species is prohibited; national parks should be set up as *reservation*⑥ for wild animals.

Only if we human beings take some more drastic measures can wild animals be preserved.

① 处以罚款
② 有利于环境建设的
③ 灭绝
④ 逐一杀死；消灭
⑤ 控制
⑥ 保留地；专用地

(9) Earth Day[①]

On April 22, people all over the world will take time out to celebrate and appreciate the Earth that we all share. It is a special day to learn about our planet and how to take care of it! It is Earth Day.

The idea for Earth Day came from a US *senator*[②] from *Wisconsin*[③] who was worried about pollution and the health of plants and animals. In 1969, Senator Gaylord Nelson decided that a special day to teach everyone about the things that needed changing in our environment could really help our planet.

Eventually, Earth Day became a global celebration marked by people all over the world. In 1990, 200 million people from 140 countries took part in marches, concerts, festivals, street fairs, clean-up, planting and other environmental events on Earth Day.

Today there are many forms of human-caused pollution that threaten the Earth. Among just a few are global warming and threats to endangered animals, clean water, healthy forests and clean sources of energy. There's a lot you can do on your own to make the Earth a safer, cleaner place.

(10) Limiting the Use of Disposable Plastic Bags

Flexible and easy to carry, disposable plastic bags are one of the greatest inventions of the 20th century. However the damage they bring is becoming even more obvious as they increase in

---

① 地球日
② 参议员
③ 威斯康辛州

popularity among people today.

Disposable plastic bags could cause *irreversible*[①] harm to the environment. As these bags are not *biodegradable*[②], they might block the drainage system and thus cause water pollution. Random disposal of plastic bags on streets is a disgrace to our cities. They are hard to track and get rid of because they travel easily in a blow of wind. It is certainly not pleasure to live in a city with plastic bags in the middle of the street and high up on tree branches or electric wire poles.

One of the best ways to reduce the harm caused by plastic bags is to limit them in number. There is already such a limit in supermarkets and shopping malls, which has achieved satisfactory effect. In fact, it is a win-win method as it not only lessens environmental harms but also helps to cut the costs of supermarkets and shopping malls.

(11) Noise Pollution

In the past, noise was rarely associated with pollution. Recently it is found that many mental diseases are closely related to noise. Therefore it is also labeled as a kind of pollution nowadays.

That there is too much noise afflicting our daily life is a manifest fact. Especially in big cities it is almost a dream to enjoy a short period of noiseless, tranquil leisure time except at dawn or in the depth of night. Whistling vehicles, bustling crowds of people, untiring loud-speakers of various stores and lots of others produce nerve-racking noise. Noise diverts our attention, disturbs our sleep, and destroys our ears. As a consequence, we are

---

① 不可逆转的
② 能进行生物降解的

becoming more and more *fidgety and upset*① because of the *intangible*② pollution.

It is high time that serious consideration was given to noise pollution. Moreover, measures should be taken to protect people against noise and secure us a quiet environment.

(12) Man Is to Survive

Let's take a look at the present world: the sky is no longer blue; the air is no longer fresh. The beautiful hills that used to be covered with trees are now bald; the crystal-clear rivers are now filthy ditches. Our precious energy reserves are consumed at a faster speed than ever. Many incurable diseases are emerging one after another. What a mess!

No wonder some people take pessimistic views towards the prospect for human beings. For instance, some movies produced in Hollywood describe the future of the world as completely dark and deserted. Men will have to wear masks to take in *filtered*③ air. Fresh water will be more valuable than gold. It seems the world will not be suitable for man to live in.

But great efforts have been taken to solve these problems. A good case in point is the air-cleaning project in Beijing. In the united effort of the government and the public, the previous grey sky has resumed its blue. So I think man has a bright future. He is and will still be the master of the world.

(13) Relationship Between Man and Nature

It is self-evident that man depends on nature for survival and

---

① 烦躁不安
② 无形的
③ 过滤

development. Nature provides man with food to eat, shelter to live in, clothes to wear, water to drink, even air to breathe. Without these basics of life, how could man exist?

With the development of human society, man has done much harm to nature. For example, pollution of various kinds has become very serious in many parts of the world. The air is no longer clean; the water in seas, rivers and lakes is dirty. A great deal of land is taken up by solid wastes, and acid rain sometimes pours down from the sky. As a result of man's pollution, many plants and animals disappear from the earth each year. Moreover, natural resources are becoming scarce in some parts of the world owing to man's *excessive exploitation*[①]. Besides, some rare animals are endangered because of man's greedy hunting. Man has, in fact, become the No. 1 enemy of nature.

All of these issues deserve our close attention. For the sake of man's continuing development, man must change his attitude toward nature. This planet is our only home. Instead of destroying it, we have to protect our environment. Without a harmonious relationship with nature, man will not only harm nature, but also destroy himself in the final analysis.

---

① 过度开发

No.44 Resources 资源

(1) Water

Water is indispensable to life. Every day people use water for drinking and washing. It is also needed in great quantity in industry and agriculture. Without water, there would be no life.

However, not all the people are aware of the importance of water. They think water is plentiful enough and they can use as much as they like. Hence, *cases*① of wasteful *consumption*② of water are very commom across the country. In fact, water shortage has become very serious in many cities, even in our capital, Beijing, because of the huge population and the rapid development of industry. If excessive consumption of water is allowed to continue, the problem will become worse and worse.

In order to cope with the water shortage problem, the government has taken some practical measures. *Fines*③ are *imposed on*④ those factories and units which *squander*⑤ water *lavishly*⑥; meanwhile, the government is carrying on education

---

① 事例;实例
② 消耗
③ 罚款
④ 把……强加于
⑤ 滥用;浪费
⑥ 浪费地;过度地

among the people. On our part, we should economize on water *conscientiously*①.

(2) Shortage of Fresh Water

We often take it for granted that fresh water is *inexhaustible*②. When talking of fresh water, we think of rain falling down from the sky and countless rivers running across the earth. We also have springs that flow down from mountains and we can pump water from under the earth. How come that we will be short of fresh water?

But we fail to realize that our population has been increasing, the countless factories are consuming large amount of fresh water everyday, and blocks of farmland are waiting for irrigation. And at the same time, fresh water in many places is being polluted with garbage and dangerous chemicals. Fresh water, therefore, is rather limited and the situation is getting worse and worse.

Fresh water is of vital importance to us. We should make all people aware of the fact that we are running short of fresh water and call on them to *economize*③ on fresh water. We must take measures to keep it from being polluted. We should also plant trees and grasses to better our environment.

(3) Rivers

Rivers are the birthplace of civilization. The Chinese nation orginated from the Yellow River. The Nile is still the lifeline for

---

① 认真地；诚心诚意地
② 取之不尽的
③ 节约，有效利用

the Egyptian people. To the Indians, the *Ganges*① is *sacred*②. A river is often used to represent a nation. Actually a river is considered as a part of the culture and the history of a nation.

Today large cities are usually located on or near rivers. For one reason, they are a source of water, which is necessary for a large population and big industries. For another, they serve as a route of transportation, which is important for city development. A third reason is that they offer opportunities for urban inhabitants to be close to nature and to have fun.

However, these large cities pollute rivers. As urban population grows and industry develops, the rivers are polluted with daily garbage and chemicals from factories. In some cases, they are no longer a source of water, but a source of bad smells and dead fish. So we should do a great deal more to keep our rivers clean if we want to continue to enjoy their benefits.

(4) Food

Nothing is as long to man as the struggle for food. But food is still a big problem today and in the years to come. Of the six billion people in the world now, about 800 million do not have enough to eat. Many die of hunger each year.

In *cultivatable*③ areas, a large proportion of land is used to build cities, towns, industries and roads. And more new uses are swallowing up land at an increasing speed. To make things much worse, deserts, which cover over one-third of land, are spreading very fast. There will be less and less land for crops.

On the other hand, population growth is always out of

---

① 恒河（亚洲）
② 神圣的
③ 可耕作的

control, especially in poor countries. By the year 2010, there will be eight billion people. Where can we find food to feed so many bottomless mouths?

Scientists are developing new ways of food production. Production under closely controlled conditions will greatly increase output and ensure crops from failure. Scientists are *breeding*① new types of crop plants which give high *yield*② and *thrive*③ in many different environments. They are also turning to the sea, which covers some 70% of the earth's surface, for *marine*④ plants and animals as food. However, developments are *easier said than done*⑤.

More important are population control and planning of land use, including saving land from deserts. If these problems are not solved, no science will save the world from hunger.

The struggle for food remains a hard one.

(5) Land Resources

We are now faced with a very important problem, that is, the rapid increasing pressure of population on land, *or rather*⑥, on land resources. Most people consider it a serious problem because land resources are limited. However, we need not to be *pessimistic*⑦ about it.

Although land has long been the main source for our food supply, it is not the only one. We have vast sea areas in the world

---

① 培育
② 产量
③ 茁壮成长
④ 海生的；海产的
⑤ (谚)说来容易做来难
⑥ 更确切地
⑦ 悲观的

waiting to be cultivated and developed. *Fish farming*① is playing a more and more important role in providing us with food. In the future we can grow fish and plants in the sea and harvest them.

Another thing we can do is to develop new *strains*②. Many scientists have achieved good results in this field. For example, a kind of new strain of corn invented by American scientists has already produced more grain and caused an enormous world increase in food production. It is certain that further research work should be done to produce higher yields.

(6) Land Use Today

Today land is reaching its limits. In river *valleys*③ and *coastal*④ areas, practically *every inch of land has been claimed and put to use*⑤, and more new uses are swallowing up land at an increasing speed.

But useable land is *diminishing*⑥. Deserts are spreading at a rate of 60,000 square kilometres a year. Already over 40% of land is desert or desert-like.

On the other hand, the population is exploding. There are now 6 billion people. And in ten years, this figure may become 7 billion. Where shall we find land to meet a *thousand and one*⑦ needs of the new-comers to our crowded world?

As land is limited, land-use problems often cause social conflicts.

---

① 养鱼
② (植物)种
③ 流域
④ 沿海岸的
⑤ 每一寸土地都已被占用
⑥ 减少
⑦ 无数;非常多(此语来自阿拉伯故事集《一千零一夜》)

资源 Resources No.44

A proposal for a new railway may *draw*① fierce debate and *opposition*②. Everybody wants the iron snake to crawl in somebody else's backyard. Yet if it is needed, it has to crawl somewhere. Anyway, disputes between interest groups have to be settled.

What use should we put to a certain piece of land? We must plan carefully, with possible consequences taken into consideration. Equally important are population control and saving land from deserts. In short, we should always keep in mind that our land is limited.

① 引起
② 反对；对抗

No.45 Energy Supply
能源

(1) Energy Resources

China *is rich in*① various energy resources. For example, coal, an abundant source of energy, can be found in many provinces. China also has a few large oil fields, and usually nat-ural gas accompanies oil production fields. In addition, large and small power plants have been built on vast rivers since liberation.

These energy resources are being used up rapidly. We use energy to run our factories, run our cars and trains, and heat our homes. In a word, we have a great need for energy for our economic growth and in our daily life.

To avoid an energy crisis in the future, the government must take some actions. For one thing, factories and individuals should be encouraged to save energy. For another, scientists should be encouraged to develop *alternatives*② to the present sources of energy.

(2) Solar Energy

A growing energy shortage in the world today makes it very necessary for scientists to do much research into the practical use

---

① 富有
② 替代品

of the sun. The advantages of solar energy are considerable. Unlike nuclear energy, it gives rise to no *catastrophic*① accidents. While solar-heated water provides not only the building of hot water requirements, but space-heating as well, we save large amounts of oil and coal, which can be used for many other purposes for which they are in urgent need.

There are, however, some disadvantages of solar energy. The energy is available only during the day and only when there is not a great deal of cloud cover. The storage of solar energy is now a big problem. Since the sun is such a large relatively *untapped*② source of *pollution-free*③ energy, that greater efforts should be made to bring the world out of energy shortage by *harnessing*④ the sun, I think, is *worthwhile*⑤.

(3) Electricity

Electricity plays *a vital role*⑥ in our society. First of all, electricity is used for lighting. Electric lamps illuminate millions of families, bringing people brightness, comfort and convenience. Secondly, in industry, as one source of energy, electricity is used to drive machines. It helps to raise productivity, which makes it possible for mankind to produce a great quantity of goods. Moreover, electrified trains, films, televisions and refrigerators are all based on electricity.

If the world were deprived of electricity⑦, the whole

---

① 灾难性的
② 未开发的
③ 没有污染的
④ 利用
⑤ 值得(花时间或精力)的
⑥ 极其重要的作用
⑦ 如果世界上没有电

society would be unable to function in its normal way. Cities would *be plunged into darkness*①, industrial production would *be reduced to standstill*②, and all electric apparatus would stop working. In short, people would feel totally helpless.

Therefore, people should realize the importance of electricity and do everything to guarantee a steady supply of power. On the one hand, we should *cultivate a sense of saving electricity*③. For example, we must make sure that the light is turned off when we leave a room. On the other hand, more power stations should be built and other energy resources must be found so as to provide sufficient power for the increasing demand.

(4) Save Every Drop of Water

As we all know, water *is indispensable to*④ life. Just imagine a thirsty man struggling in a *scorching*⑤ desert: a drop of water is more precious than anything else because only water can free him from his suffering and save his life.

In fact, water shortage has become a worldwide problem, which is more serious in China, large cities *in particular*⑥. The population explosion, rapid economic growth and industrial pollution have considerably reduced our limited water resources. Water shortage is threatening our lives. For example, in dry seasons, many factories are closed with heavy losses; people do not have enough water to drink, *to say nothing of*⑦ having a bath.

---

① 陷入黑暗
② 陷入停顿状态
③ 培养节电意识
④ 必不可少的
⑤ 灼热的
⑥ 尤其是
⑦ 更不用说

能源
Energy Supply "No.45"

We can *minimize*① damage caused by water shortage by saving water. We cannot afford the *reckless*② waste of water any more. In fact, there are many ways to save water. We could purify and reuse the industrially polluted water, develop water saving *schemes*③ to irrigate farmland, stop the *leakage*④ in our water taps, use bath water to wash cars. What is important is our awareness of water crisis.

To make our world a better place to live in, we must make the best use of every drop of water and work hand in hand to protect water resources.

(5) Different Forms of Energy

There are different forms of energy, such as heat energy, sound energy, light energy, electric energy and so on.

Energy can be changed from one into another in different ways. For example, electric energy becomes sound energy in the radio set or becomes light energy in the TV set. But energy can neither be *finished off*⑤ nor be produced. This is called *the law of conservation of energy*⑥.

It is important for us to make use of energy. *Expanding gases*⑦ can be used to run a machine or to make airplane fly in the air. Heat from the sun and water power can be controlled. And atomic energy can be used to do many things. We are now doing our best in making use of energy in our national construction.

---

① 减小到最低限度
② 不顾后果的
③ 方案
④ 漏水
⑤ 用完
⑥ 能量守恒定律
⑦ 膨胀气体

No.46 Economic Development
经济发展

(1) Management

Management is a practical science, which is especially important in our modern world. We depend on it for the smooth running of the social machine. Good management can always make wise use of human and material potentials to produce the best possible results.

Management involves investigation, evaluation, planning, and control. Very often, *readjustment*① is also indispensable. Before deciding on anything, all relevant factors have to be taken into consideration. When one thing conflicts with another, *priority is given to*② that which will help bring about greater success.

Few people are responsible for important management, but practically everybody is *in the position*③ of managing one thing or another. It is necessary for us all to learn something about the art of management. More essential, perhaps, is that persons in a common effort should work under *unified*④ management.

---

① 重新调整、组合
② 给……优先权;优先考虑……
③ 能够(做某事)
④ 统一的

(2) Advantages and Problems of Private Enterprises

Millions of private businesses have mushroomed all over China and their great impact on the rapid growth of China's economy has attracted extensive attention worldwide.

These energetic private businesses possess many advantages. Unlike large state enterprises under the central planning system, the private ones enjoy more freedom but fewer social responsibilities in the market economy. The state enterprises have to provide service to their employees from cradle to grave and are overloaded with many nonprofit subunits like apartments, schools, and hospitals. Situated in rural areas with easy access to raw materials, private factories can absorb cheap labor and reduce production cost. What's more, they often enjoy the *favorable policies*① because they can boost local economy.

These private companies, however, also have problems. First, there is still room for improvement in their management. Second, shortage of well-educated *professionals*② and skilled workers often adversely affect their future prospects. Third, *commercial scandals*③, *tax fraud*④, *briberies*⑤, and producing *fake products*⑥ have been found in many private companies. Finally, most private factories use *obsolete*⑦ equipment, which usually results in environmental pollution or waste of energy.

Nevertheless, these problems are being solved step by step.

① 优惠政策
② 专业人员
③ 商业丑行、丑闻
④ 税务诈骗
⑤ 行贿受贿；贿赂
⑥ 伪假产品
⑦ 过时的；被淘汰的

With the guidance of the government, the private businesses are growing healthily and playing an important role in China's economy.

(3) What Is Commerce

A shopkeeper selling things to the people is said to be doing business. In a society, there are all sorts of shops selling different kinds of goods to meet different needs of people. That is what commerce means.

Commerce is not confined to a society or a country. It also carries on between countries. As various countries in the world differ from one another in geographical position and climatic conditions, they differ in their products. And since their citizens possess different standards of ability and skill, they also differ in their manufactures. In many cases, the *surplus*① of one country is the wants of another, hence the necessity of international commerce. Native goods sent abroad are exports, and foreign goods brought into the country, imports.

By comparing the imports of one country with its own exports, we note two principal points of contrast. Rich is the nation whose exports exceed imports and poor is the one that she imports more than she exports. Again, a nation whose imports consist of more raw than manufactured products and exports, of more manufactured than raw products, will surely become wealthy; when the order is *reversed*②, her *financial decline*③ is certain.

---

① 剩余（物资）
② 颠倒
③ 金融衰退

(4) Tasks of Production Managers

Production managers are responsible for three major activities. First, they must make plans for *production inputs*①. This involves determining the inputs required for the firm's operation, including such decisions as product planning, plant location, and provision for adequate supplies of raw meaterials, labor, power, and machinery. These plans must be completed before the conversion process from raw materials to finished product or service can begin.

Second, production managers must make decisions about the *installation*② of the necessary inputs. These include the actual design of the plant, the best types of machines to be used, the arrangement of the production machinery, and the determination of the most efficient flow of work in the plant.

Third, production managers must *coordinate*③ the production processes: the routing of materials to the right places, the development of work schedules, and the assignment of work to specific employees. The objective is to promote efficiency.

(5) Preserve Every Inch of Farmland

As we all know, farmland constitutes the most important material basis for mankind's survival and prosperity. All over the world, almost every country works hard at *farmland preservation*④.

In spite of these efforts, shrinking farmland poses a serious

---

① 生产投入
② 安装
③ 协调
④ 农田保护

threat to our country. Originally, the amount of *arable*① land in China is far from sufficient. To produce enough grain to feed 1.3 billion people, we have cultivated almost all fields available, and there is not much *virgin*② land left. With the rapid economic growth, the construction of highways, factories, mines, apartments, golf courses, and graveyards, has *chewed up*③ large amounts of fertile fields. Moreover, industrial pollution, fertilizer abuse, sandstorms, floods, and droughts further erode our farmland. With a fast growing population to feed, how can we relax our efforts in farmland preservation?

From now on, we should try every means, fight any battle, and pay any price to preserve our farmland. There is only one Earth we can dwell on, and we can not afford to waste any good land. The *far-reaching*④ consequence of land preservation is the safeguarding of our life and the insurance of our nation.

(6) Made in China or Created in China

In present-day China, a controversial issue has been brought into *limelight*⑤: whether China's future economic development should depend on products labeled as "Made in China" or "Created in China". From my point of view, China should devote more efforts to the invention and manufacture of technology-intensive products.

It is a general assumption that with its large population, the future development of China's economy will have to depend on the manufacture of labor-intensive products which are labeled

① 可耕的
② 未开垦的
③ 此处指"吞噬、占用"
④ 意义深远的
⑤ 引人注目的中心

"Made in China". However, the negative outcome of mass production, such as industrial pollution and *exhaustion*① of natural resources, is emerging gradually. The old production model is barely sustainable. Therefore, concentration on technology innovation is the only way out because it can *boost*② Chinese enterprises' competitive advantages and bring about higher added value.

In a word, it is highly recommended that China give more priority to products created in China to ensure a *sustainable*③ economic development.

(7) The World Exposition④

It is reported that Shanghai will host the 2010 World Exposition.

Unlike a *trade fair*⑤ in the usual sense, participants in the World Exposition are mainly governments of various countries and international organizations. It is an *arena*⑥ for the participating countries to display the achievements and prospects in their social, economic, cultural and technological sectors and a grand event where people from various countries get together to exchange experiences, learn from one another and enter into cooperation. Known as the "*economic, technological, and cultural Olympic Games,*"⑦ the World Exposition is held every five years. Since its inception in London in 1851, it has been

---

① 枯竭
② 推进
③ 可持续的
④ 世博会
⑤ 贸易性博览会
⑥ 舞台,竞技场
⑦ 经济、科技、文化领域内的奥林匹克盛会

invariably held in developed countries. China is the first developing country to host the World Exposition.

Hosting the Exposition will have a positive impact on China. China will be able not only to draw useful experience of other countries to further its reform and opening-up process and, in particular, promote its economic development but also to strengthen its friendly relations with other countries.

(8) Peace and Development: The Themes of the Times

Peace and economic development are the themes of the times. People across the world should join hands in advancing the lofty cause of peace and development of mankind.

A peaceful environment is indispensable for national and global development. Without peace or political stability, there would be no economic progress to speak of. This has been fully proved by both the past and the present.

In today's world, the international situation is, on the whole, moving towards relaxation. However, conflicts and even local wars *triggered*[①] by various factors have kept *cropping up*[②], and tension still remains in some areas. All this has *impeded*[③] the economic development of the countries and regions concerned, and had adversely affected the world economy. This is against the will of the majority of the people and against the trend of the times. People around the world should live and work in peace and focus on economic development. Only when continued efforts are made to advance the cause of peace can the economic prosperity be promoted.

---

① 引发
② 突然发生
③ 妨碍

No.47 Science and Technology
科学技术

(1) Effect of Advanced Technology on Human Beings

Advanced technology has offered great convenience to human beings. Fast airplanes take us anywhere we wish at any time. Electric appliances like microwave ovens make our home life much easier. What's more important, with advanced technology, the doctors have saved lots of patients' lives.

Nevertheless, the use of advanced technology has resulted in some serious problems. The most serious one is pollution. Modern transportation means have also brought about air and noise pollution. The *abuse*① of computer *data banks*② has invaded the privacy of some individuals, which has caused considerable concern.

In spite of this, advanced technology has given us a lot more benefits than disadvantages. Therefore, while we enjoy the great convenience it has brought to us, we have to learn to use high-tech under careful planning and control.

---

① 滥用
② 数据库

(2) Space Travel

Ancient people wondered what the moon and stars were. They imagined how winged men and women flew to distant heavenly worlds. Beautiful fairy tales about space travel were created and told from generation to generation.

Today this old dream has become a near reality. Back in 1969, man set foot on the moon. This marked his first *gigantic*① step into space. So far, thousands of satellites have been *orbiting*② the earth, and *unmanned*③ spaceships have explored several planets in the *solar system*④.

Man's next visit may be to Mars. Plans under way are space stations or space islands orbiting the earth. But scientists say that the first space travel available to ordinary people would be to the moon because this would be cheaper and technically simpler. Perhaps some lucky ones would be welcomed there in this century. Space stations and bases on the moon will serve as *stepping-stones*⑤ to Mars and other heavenly bodies.

(3) Do We Need Space Exploration?

Man has been fascinated by outer space for thousands of years. It has been almost over forty years since man's first landing on the moon. Now, some people believe that space exploration is sheer waste of time and money. They point out the fact that it cost billions of dollars to carry on the space research,

---

① 巨大的
② 环绕(天体等)做轨道运行
③ 无人驾驶的
④ 太阳系
⑤ 达成目的的手段;此处指"(去往火星的)第一步"

but a little information was brought back.

However, the majority of people believe that space exploration has more advantages than disadvantages. Many new products, such as weather and communication satellites, are also products of space programs, and they have benefited people all over the world. And what's more, scientific knowledge about outer space has been acquired by mankind.

We believe that space exploration will bring more benefits in the future, which we can not even imagine now. Space exploration is a challenge to human beings. That's why several nations have tried hard to carry out space exploration continuously.

(4) Material Science in the 21st Country

The *advent*① of new material often lays the foundation for the development of advanced science and technology.

There are three ways in the *R & D*② of materials. One way is to select appropriate materials for the appropriate application which is a passive approach. The second is to improve *properties*③ of the existing materials. And the third is to create entirely now specialized materials. In developing new materials, a new compound is often formed; its properties are studied and its applications are explored.

Human civilization has been divided into Stone Age, the Bronze Age, and the Iron Age, according to the materials used in the respective eras. The 21st century is often referred to as the Plastic Age, the Semiconductor Age, or the New *Ceramic*④ Age.

---

① 出现,到来
② 研究与发展(research and development 的缩写)
③ 性能;特性
④ 陶器的,陶瓷的

None of these, however, has prevailed over all other specialized materials. In the 21st century, we will be in the age of diversity.

(5) Advantages and Disadvantages of Cell Phones

Cell phones have become increasingly popular in China these days. Wherever you go you can see people using cell phones. Many college students, even high school students, have cell phones.

As modern convenience, cell phones have brought people a lot of benefits. With cell phones in their hands, they can keep in touch with anybody they want. If they want to get some information from the Internet, they can easily have their dream realized via cell phone. Furthermore, if someone has a heart attack or a traffic accident, a call to emergency hospital or to the police can quickly bring him the help he needs urgently.

However, cell phones can also bring people problems. The most serious is the electric wave *radiation*① which is thought to be harmful to users' brains. Another problem is that when people are having a meeting or having a class or at a concert etc., the ring of the cell phone may interrupt others. So I think people should use cell phones as little as possible and turn them off when they are attending meetings or classes.

(6) The Digital Age

Nowadays with the rapid development of advanced digital technology, more and more digital products are commonly and widely used in everyday life, ranging from computers and MP4s to mobile phones and digital cameras. We are indeed coming into

---

① 辐射

the digital age.

The popularity of digital products will have great influence on our work, study, and everyday life. On the one hand, the digital products really *facilitate*① our life. With the help of computers, we may even deal with our work at home, enjoying music at the same time. With digital cameras, we may take photos to our hearts' content, keeping happy occasions as a *permanent*② memory. With digital TV programs, it is convenient for us to watch whatever programs at any time we like. But on the other hand, some people are becoming too dependent on digital products and almost becoming slaves of advanced technology. Nowadays some students even cannot calm down to their study without wearing their MP4s and mobile phones at hand. What a terrible scene.

To conclude, digital products are just like a double-edged sword. With them we may have less trouble dealing with problems in life and enjoy a better-off life. However, one point should be kept in mind that we should take sensible use of them, always being the master of them.

(7) Modern Technology and Human Intimacy

With the development of technology, some believe that people become more intimate. There are several reasons for this phenomenon. The popularity of cell phones and Internet makes it available to contact friends or relatives both at home and abroad. What's more, it is more convenient to pay a visit to someone due to the constant improvement in vehicles.

However, there are people with the opposite view. For their

---

① 使容易,使便利
② 永久的

viewpoint, modern technology has not narrowed the gap. An important reason is that calls, online chat, or *text messages*① lack emotional cue, and they can never replace face-to-face communication. However, with the popularity of modern technology, more and more people tend to ignore real communication, and become addicted to the isolated *virtual*② world.

In my opinion, technology does not play a decisive role. It is our attitudes that count. If we value friends and relatives, we should get close to them in person and build up intimate interpersonal relationship.

---

① 短信息
② 虚拟的

No.48 | Computer and Internet
计算机与网络

(1) Computers

Computers are playing a more and more important role in modern society. They are already widely used in industry and in universities to do extremely complicated work in all *branches*[①] of learning. They can solve the most complex mathematical problems or put thousands of unrelated facts in order. Because they work accurately and at high speeds, they save research workers years of hard work. They play a key role in automation. Besides, they have found applications in business, transportation, education and other fields. Computers have brought important *social consequences*[②].

Computers are also entering ordinary families. As computers are being made small, cheap, and at the same time easy to use, more people buy computers for their homes. We use computers to control the work of washing-machines, TV sets, electrical cookers and other *electrical appliances*[③]. We use computers to process and store all kinds of information. We also use computers to entertain ourselves by playing games on them. There is no limit to the application of computers in our lives.

Despite all the advantages, computers can never take the

---

① (学科)分支
② 社会后果;此处意为"社会效益"
③ (家用)电器

place of human brains. Although computers work much faster and much more accurately than human beings, they cannot "think". They need detailed instructions from human beings in order to be able to operate. They can never lead independent lives, or "rule the world" by making decisions of their own. No matter how capable they are, they are our servants, not our masters.

(2) Computer and Man

It is believed that the computer can do almost everything. At the time the computer was invented, scientists, *carried away*① by its calculating speed, felt that they had created a miracle. It was gradually used not only in mathematics, physics, chemistry and astronomy, but in places like the library, hospital and military army to replace the works of man. For this reason, the computer was entitled "Electronic Brain" *in terms of*② appreciation.

Can man be controlled by computers? The answer is negative. Although a computer works faster and more accurately than man, a fact is *undeniable*③: it is designed, manufactured and programmed by man, and therefore controlled by human beings. Of course, *science fictions*④ have made up many fascinating stories about a computer, or rather, a robot, who conquers man and the earth, even the whole universe; however, they are only unrealistic imaginations. A horse helps man a lot and runs much faster than we do, but it is only a slave.

The future for the computer is very *promising*⑤. With the

---

① 使激动；兴奋
② 以……的观点；以……的措词
③ 不能否认的
④ 科幻小说
⑤ 有希望的

help of it, we can do things that could not be done before. Conquering the universe, discovering new things, explaining mysterious *phenomena*① puzzling us at present — all are made possible by the computer.

(3) Internet—*a Two-edged Sword*②

Internet is playing an increasingly important role in people's lives. Surfing on the net, researchers can get a global look at the latest development in their fields. Besides, Internet serves as the most convenient means for communication. Through Internet, people can discuss various problems and make friends with each other. Internet is also a faithful aid in our daily life since people can go shopping and get medical services online. So Internet is indeed one of the most interesting and important inventions man has ever made.

But just as a coin has two sides, Internet has its own drawbacks, which should not be neglected. First, computer viruses may easily break into our computers and cause many troubles. Second, it is often difficult for people to ensure the safety of their personal data on the net. Finally, it is sometimes not efficient enough to find the right information they need since there is too much rubbish on the net.

But just as one proverb says, *"We should not give up eating for fear of choking."*③ I think we should further develop the net and also exert supervision over it so that it can benefit both the government and the ordinary people.

---

① 现象
② 双刃剑
③ 因噎废食

(4) Positive and Negative Effects of Computers

When the computer was first invented decades ago, no one ever imagined the situation we find ourselves in today. Nearly everything we do in the modern world is helped, or even controlled, by computers.

Computers are being used more and more extensively in the world today, for the simple reason that they are far more efficient than human beings in some aspects. They have much better memories and can store huge amounts of information, and they can do calculations in a fraction of time taken by a human mathematician. In fact computers can do many of the things we do, and do them much faster and better. They can pay wages, reserve seats on a plane, control machines in a factory, work out tomorrow's weather and even play chess, write poetry, and compose music.

However, as wider use is made of the intelligent machine, the negative aspects of a computer have also become obvious. Worst of all is the computer viruses developed by some *computer lunatics*① that can *paralyze*② millions of machines in a minute, causing loss of millions of dollars. And again, a completely new kind of crime has appeared. Some extremely intelligent computer "experts" who know how the computer works make huge amounts of money by cheating a computer, and it is very difficult to catch them.

---

① 黑客
② 使瘫痪

(5) Away from Net-bar Campaign

It has been reported that a middle school in Xuzhou City has recently launched a campaign named "*Away from Net-bar*[①]". More than a thousand students have signed for their solemn promise that they will not spend a single minute in the net-bars. As the summer vacation is drawing near, this campaign is especially meaningful for the healthy development of the *minors*[②].

The internet has brought people great convenience in getting information, entertainment and contact with others, and it has also benefited some businessmen, especially the owners of net-bars. While it is true that most net-bars are running legally, it is also true that some are offering unhealthy programs that involve violence and sex content. Since most middle-school students *are prone to*[③] be influenced and they can hardly tell which bars are doing well and which ones are not, it is only advisable that they stay away from all. Besides, staying away from net-bars also does good to students' physical health. By passively sitting too long in front of the computer screen, both their eyesight and physique suffer.

Obviously, the "Away from Net-bars Campaign" is an activity that is worth advocating and it merits other schools' reference.

(6) Shopping on the Internet

With the development of the Internet and the popularization of

---

① 远离网吧
② 未成年人
③ 易于,倾向于

computers, shopping on the Internet has become commonplace in our life. Here consumers can almost buy everything they need.

Shopping on the Internet has a lot of advantages, of which the most important one is perhaps its convenience. This is especially desirable to the old, the sick and the busy people who cannot go to the shops in person. The goods come in all shapes, sizes on the Internet. All the consumers need to do is to sit in front of their computers and click the mouse.

However, shopping on the Internet also has its disadvantages. The first one is that the consumers cannot see the goods or try them on personally. Sometimes, the real goods may not be the same as what they have seen on the computer. The second disadvantage is that some shops on the Internet are not registered. They will never deliver anything to you after they get the money from you. Their only interest is in your money becoming theirs. Once you are taken in, you will have nowhere to go to complain.

No.49　Television
　　　电视

(1) Television

　　Television presents a very vivid world to us. On television, we can watch exciting football matches or Olympic *marathons*①. We can "travel" to New York to have sightseeing or to London to attend the royal wedding. We can also "go" to a concert with a cup of coffee in our hand. From TV, we can learn many things happening in the world without having to go out of our houses.

　　Television also plays an educational role in our daily life. By providing various TV university courses, television offers various educational programs for different viewers. Children like "*Tangram*"②; young people like "the ABC of Computers"; and elderly people like "Life and Health". Of all the programs, "English on Sunday" is my favourite.

　　However, television can also be harmful. It hurts our eyes and can cause near-sightedness. Watching TV too much influences our sleep and work and cuts down children's study time. Furthermore, some TV programs are not *ideologically*③ sound and thus we should choose what is good to watch. In short, we should regard television as our assistant, not our

---

① 马拉松长跑
② 七巧板
③ 在思想内容方面

master.

(2) My Favourite TV Programme

China Central Television Station (CCTV) today offers a great variety of programmes to satisfy different needs and tastes. For example, the weather forecast is of special interest to farmers. For another example, the concert programme *appeals* greatly *to*① music lovers. The sports world attracts large numbers of sports fans. My most favorite programme, however, is news.

The news programme has several points that are worth mentioning as far as its contents and *features*② are concerned. For one thing, it covers news about important events both at home and abroad. Besides, the news it provides is *timely*③ and reliable. Finally, broadcast in the evening during the so-called "golden time", the news programme reaches a wide audience.

I like this programme chiefly for two reasons. One is that it keeps me informed of the state of the nation and the world *at large*④, which is essential to a college student. The other reason is that, since the news covers a *comprehensive*⑤ area and is fairly brief, it saves me much time reading through newspapers for current affairs. In short, watching the news on CCTV has become part of my daily life.

(3) The Harmful Effect of TV on Children

Many people are now worried about the harmful influence of

---

① 有感染力;有吸引力
② 特点
③ 及时的
④ 普遍的;整个的
⑤ 全面的;综合的

TV upon children who grow up watching it. Several arguments sound very reasonable.

Firstly, television has taken away the child's ability to form mental pictures in his mind, resulting in children who cannot understand a simple story without visual illustrations. Secondly, too much TV takes up too much children's time and causes them to *withdraw*① from real life. Thus they grow up to be passive viewers who can only respond to action, but not *initiate*② it. But the most serious result comes from the unhealthy and low-interest scenes on the TV screen. While watching TV, children are often exposed to the scenes of violence, murder and sex. They come to regard them as *a matter of course*③, and tolerate these behaviours in others. Worse still, children may *imitate*④ harmful acts that they witness on television.

(4) Television Is Doing *Irreparable*⑤ Harm

The young generation are growing up *addicted to*⑥ television. Food is left uneaten, homework undone and sleep is lost. The television is also a universal *pacifier*⑦. It is now standard practice for mother to keep the children quiet by turning on the set. It doesn't matter that the children will watch *rubbishy*⑧ programmes so long as they are quiet.

Television also prevents us from communicating with each

---

① 离开;退出
② 着手;开始
③ 理所当然的事
④ 模仿
⑤ 无法弥补的
⑥ 沉溺于;对……上瘾
⑦ 镇静剂
⑧ 像垃圾一样的;无聊的

other. Every day, we *gulp down*① our meals to *be in time for*② this or that programme and have even given up actually telling each other what is disturbing us. The monster demands and obtains *absolute*③ silence and attention. If any member of the family dares to open his mouth during a programme, he is quickly silenced. We become *utterly*④ dependent on the two most *primitive*⑤ media of communication: pictures and spoken word.

Furthermore, television encourages passive enjoyment. We *become content with*⑥ second-hand experiences. It is so easy to sit in our armchairs watching others working. Little by little, *glued to*⑦ our sets, we get so lazy, we choose to spend a fine day in semi-darkness, rather than go out into the world itself. We'd better quickly discover what irreparable harm television is doing.

---

① 狼吞虎咽地吃
② 赶上看（节目）
③ 绝对的
④ 完全地
⑤ 原始的
⑥ 满足于
⑦ 贴着于；此指"不愿离开"

No.50 Mass Media
传播媒介

(1) The Mass Media

The *mass media*① consist of radio, television, and newspapers. Newspapers are the oldest form of *communicating*② news. Today many people still begin their day by reading the morning newspaper while having breakfast. Newspapers continue to influence how we view the events around us.

The invention of radio has had a tremendous influence on the world. It is able to bring *up-to-the-minute*③ news to distant places *in a matter of seconds*④. The development of radio has made the world a smaller place.

Television, the most recently developed means of communication, allows us to see as well as hear the news. Being able to see *visual images*⑤ has greatly influenced humanity's *perceptions*⑥ of world events. We select our leaders as much by their acting ability as by their political views. Each day television changes our perceptions of life on the earth.

---

① 传播媒介;大众传播媒介
② 传达;传送
③ 最新的
④ 片刻
⑤ 看得见的图像
⑥ 认知力;洞察力

(2) Newspapers and Television

Newspapers and television are very important news media. Every day they provide people with information concerning politics, economy, and education. You can learn from them about what happened in the past, what is going on at the present, and what will be like in the future.

Both newspapers and television have their own advantages. Reading newspapers is convenient and cheap. And it is easy to note down important *coverage*① from newspapers. Television presents vivid pictures about the whole world. Turn on the switch and you can see what is happening "*on the spot*"②.

However, improvement is still needed for both. Some newspapers are often delivered late. Many people cannot watch news on TV because the broadcasting time is generally fixed.

(3) Newspapers

Many kinds of newspapers are available nowadays. There are serious papers, such as *People's Daily*, *Guangming Daily*, and many *provincial papers*③, for those who want to know about important happenings everywhere, both at home and abroad. There are popular newspapers, such as *municipal*④ evening news and various TV guides and *digests*⑤. There are also some specialized papers, such as *Football* and *Market News*. All these

---

① 新闻报道(范围)
② 在现场
③ 省报等;首都以外的报纸
④ 市的;地方(性)的
⑤ 文摘报

papers are easily available in the post offices and *newsstands*① all over the country.

Newspapers play an important part in our everyday life. Besides news and government policies, newspapers also provide many other kinds of information. They carry articles concerning our clothing, eating, lodging, and transportation. They provide all kinds of entertainment. They also teach us how to do many things, from fixing radio sets to playing bridge. In fact, everyone can find something he wants in newspapers, and everyone enjoys reading newspapers every day.

However, not all newspapers are worth reading. Some reports in newspapers are inaccurate and some articles are quite misleading or even harmful. Therefore, we should read newspapers critically.

(4) The News Media

The news media consists of newspapers, radio, and television. Newspapers are the oldest form of communicating news. The development of radio has made the world a smaller community. But in my opinion, television — the most recently developed means of communication — is the best source of news.

Firstly, television is the combination of sound, light, pictures, and colors, which enables us to watch as well as to hear the news. Being able to see visual images has greatly influenced humanity's perceptions of world events. We select our leaders as much by their acting ability as by their political views.

Secondly, television can save you a lot of time. Today, many people begin their day by watching news on TV instead of reading newspapers while having breakfast. They don't have time to read

---

① 报摊

the news carefully and sometimes they may be in such a hurry that they only glance at the headlines. If they want to learn the details about the news, they have to turn on the TV and hear the news with a cup of coffee in one hand.

In short, there is no denying that TV will become more and more popular in the world while human life is developing step by step. Naturally, TV should be selected the best medium of news, as more and more *couch-potatos*① emerge among us. Are you one of those?

---

① 此处指"长时间呆在沙发上的电视迷"

No.51 Advertisements
广告

(1) Advertisements

Advertisements are *getting their way into*① people's lives. As consumers, people depend much on advertising in their daily life. As for manufacturers and salesmen, they need advertisers to promote their *merchandise*②. As a result, nearly every product is advertised. Thus, to some extent, good advertising can mean success while bad advertising failure.

There are many ways to advertise and "ads" come in different forms. Newspapers carry advertisements. Some products are announced on TV and radio which have a wide audience. *Billboards*③ also carry advertising. Advertising is a big industry now and many *agencies*④ have been set up to meet a variety of growing needs.

However, advertisements are not always *truthful*⑤. A product is often *misrepresented*⑥. The advertiser tends to *exaggerate*⑦ the benefits/strengths of the merchandise he wants

---

① 进入；闯入
② （总称）商品
③ 广告板(牌、墙等)
④ 代理机构
⑤ 真确的；如实的
⑥ 歪曲；表述失实
⑦ 夸张

to sell. Thus, the consumers *become victims of*[1] such advertising. In fact, millions of people have bought advertised products only to find out that they are not as good as advertised.

(2) The Arguments on Advertising: For and Against

An argument for advertisements asserts that ads give up-to-date information about products. The contrary argument against ads is that they do not give information but rather try to persuade us to buy.

Pro-advertisement[2] people tell us that if there were no advertising, consumers would only know about goods in their local shops. Anti-advertisement people say that, in reality, ads create a demand for goods that are not really needed.

Advertisers claim that advertising helps to sell to a bigger market. Therefore, the more goods are sold, the cheaper they become. People who disagree with advertising argue that it actually adds to the cost of goods.

Finally, people in favour of advertising say ads provide income for newspapers, magazines, etc.. Those who dislike advertising say they do not enjoy seeing them everywhere, such as in newspapers and on buses. They say advertisements are generally ugly to look at and spoil the environment.

My opinion is that advertisements do not *portray*[3] reality, but give us unrealistic expectations for ourselves and *fuel greedy desires*[4]. They are everywhere and unavoidable even if we try to get rid of them. I wouldn't like to see advertisements any more.

---

① 成为……牺牲品
② 赞成做广告的
③ 描述
④ 此处指"助长了种种贪婪的欲望"

(3) Advertisement Paper

Nowadays, a lot of *advertisement papers*① are sent out in Beijing every day. In many streets or corners, you can see many people sending different sorts of advertisement papers to passing by pedestrians and bicycle riders. Sometimes, you may even not see those people, because they place the papers in the basket of your bicycle without telling you or even on the door nob when you're in your home or dorm.

Actually, told to do that, those people simply regard this work as a way of earning money. They finish the task when they send all the papers out. So they try their best to get the job done and care nothing about how people will accept the papers. But what are the results of sending so many advertisement papers?

I dare not say that none of us are interested in what the papers say, but I think only few of us are. Some people are just curious about the advertisement and want to know what is on the paper. Once they know, the papers may become useless. Other people, however, are forced to receive them, such as the papers in the bicycle basket or on the door nob, but they wouldn't accept them. These two kinds of people will probably throw away the papers as rubbish. That's why we can often see the dustbins are jammed with these papers.

As far as I am concerned, I don't think it is an efficient way to spread information. To begin with, a lot of people have prejudice against spreading ads. Even though the content of an ad is useful to him (or her), he (or she) dislikes to read it carefully. Second, it destroys our environment and makes a bad impression on foreigners. Third, it causes a huge waste of paper and labor power. In a word, advertisement papers do no good to people's life.

---

① 此处指"广告散页"

No.52 Daily Happenings
生活琐记

（1）Haste Comes Not Alone[①]

One day, going home from school, I came to understand for the first time how costly haste can be.

The sky was very dark, and people were walking quickly across the streets through the afternoon traffic. The air was heavy, and lightning *flickered*[②] here and there behind the *overcast*[③]. Suddenly, it began to rain, and everyone began to run in a hurry for shelter. At the street corner ahead of me, two girls, running from different directions, crashed together. A boy riding a bicycle *slammed on his brakes*[④] to avoid them, he went *skidding*[⑤], out of control, into the middle of the street and ran into a car.

Next day, still stunned, I read in the paper that he had died on the way to hospital. People should not lose their heads at the very time they need them most. Haste comes not alone.

---

① ［谚语］忙中出乱；匆忙必有患
② 闪烁
③ 阴暗的天空
④ 刹车
⑤ 刹着车滑行

(2) A Miserable Moment

The bell had just gone. We all *packed up*① and hastened down the street where there was a bus stop.

As we stood there waiting for the bus, it began to rain heavily. We were all soaked to the skin. At last, one bus came, and in order to get on, all of us crowded towards it. Thank heavens, I was the nearest one from the entrance. As I placed one of my feet upon the steps which led to the bus, my shoe fell from my foot. I cast my eyes round me but could not find it. People were looking at me, shouting. The *conductor*② was angry with me, and called the others to hurry up and get on the bus.

I went into the rain again, wandering, intending to find my shoe. Oh, there it was, just under the bus. I was completely wet through like one who had come out of a swimming pool. Oh! What a miserable moment!

(3) Catching Cold

Last night I did not feel very well, so I had to stay at home from school. My mother thought I had the flu. She called the doctor this morning. I hope I'll get well soon because I do not like missing school.

First my head started to ache. Then I had a fever, so my mother put a cold *compress*③ on my forehead. She also gave me some aspirin and cough medicine for my sore throat and took my temperature after she sent me to bed. I *tossed and turned*④ all

---

① 停止工作
② 售票员
③ 敷布
④ 翻来覆去

night long and did not get much sleep, so I don't have enough energy to go to school today. My nose is still running and my muscles and joints are stiff, so I will stay home today and watch TV and *blow my nose*① whenever I feel the need to do. I feel better than last night, though, and tomorrow I will go back to school.

Staying home is fun once in a while, but the flu is not. Next time I will be more careful to eat right and wear warm clothes when it is cold or raining outside. It is always easier to prevent the flu than to fight it.

(4) Seeing a Doctor

These days I don't feel quite well. I have lost my appetite for any food. During the day I often feel dizzy, and at night I suffer from *insomnia*② accompanied by headache. To make things still worse, I am easy to catch cold, which gives me a sore throat and *gets me constantly sneezing and coughing*③.

Yesterday I went to the hospital of our university to see a doctor. The doctor gave me a thorough examination after I told him all my symptoms. He listened to my chest with a *stethoscope*④. Then he asked me to lie down to feel and touch my stomach. After that he measured my blood pressure and asked me to *get my lungs X-rayed*⑤.

When all these finished, the doctor made a *diagnosis*⑥ about my case and told me about it:

---

① 擤鼻涕
② 失眠
③ 使我老是打喷嚏和咳嗽
④ 听诊器
⑤ 让我接受肺部 X 光检查
⑥ 诊断

"Well, there is nothing that matters with you. Your heart, lungs and lever are all right, but you are rather *run-down*①. You have been working too hard. You know you can't *burn the candle at both ends*②. I advise you to have a real rest and take some physical exercise."

With a *relief*③ I left the hospital, thinking how to follow the doctor's advice in order to have a quick recovery.

(5) *Fortune-telling*④

Nowadays, there is an unbelievable fortune-telling fashion among college students. Some college students now resort to fortune-telling to choose their future job after graduation. Walking on the street you may find some people squatting on their heels in the corner of a building. Well, they are fortune-tellers. Believe it or not, they earn quite a sum by *deceitfully*⑤ telling the students what is to come about in their future life. This phenomenon is perhaps the result of the growing employment pressure. With the prevalence of higher education, college graduates now have to face the job market directly and now the job market is getting smaller and smaller. The anxiety of finding a good job, the great gap between ideal and reality, and the fierce career competition have become graduates' new burden that kills their confidence. Thus these confused young people come to fortune-tellers to seek comfort in spirit.

In my opinion, this blind trust of fortune-telling shows their lack of confidence and scientific knowledge. The students should

---

① 衰弱的(尤指因劳累)
② 操劳过度;由于超负荷地工作而耗尽精力
③ 松了一口气;放心了
④ 算卦,占卜
⑤ 骗人地

take effective measures to adapt themselves to the society, to strengthen their confidence, and to solve the problems by themselves. We should remember the proverb: "*Fortune favors those who use their judgement.*"①

(6) *Sending Gifts*②

  Sending gifts is common in China. People give each other gifts out of different reasons. Some send gifts out of love, gratitude or respect; they think that their feeling can be best expressed by presenting gifts. Some do so because of the general practice in the society that they have to adapt to. There are still some others who do it out of personal purpose.

  It is sometimes necessary to send gifts to people to show our love, appreciation, gratitude or respect, but it is really unnecessary to send gifts because of the pressure of general practice in the society or out of personal purpose, for it corrupts people's minds.

  Those people who send gifts without sound reasons would do nothing good to both themselves and the receivers. They may feel the pressure if they are not rich enough, and this may be the cause of the gifts' recycling. As for the receivers, they may feel awkward if they dislike receiving them, or they may become greedier if they prefer accepting them. Accordingly, with the advance of the society, it is high time that we called on people to maintain our traditional virtue and did away with the *dross*③ in order to develop a healthy human relations.

---

  ① 命运眷顾能(自己)作出明智判断的人
  ② 送礼
  ③ 没有价值的东西,糟粕

(7) Daydreaming

Daydreaming is a dreamlike musing while fully awake to the fulfillment of wishes. Until quite recently most people hold a hostile attitude towards daydreaming. Some people view it as an escape from duties and responsibilities, while others consider it a sheer waste of time.

Recent research, however, shows that daydreaming is of great benefit in many respects. Daydreaming, scientists tell us, is a good means of active relaxation. Surprisingly enough, it also improves our ability of getting along with others. The most remarkable thing about daydreaming is that it is useful in shaping our future life as we dream to be. If you always hold an ideal self-image in your *mind's eye*[①], you will probably see it come true step by step.

Now that we can draw the conclusion that daydreaming is beneficial, why not make good use of it to make life rich and rewarding?

(8) A *Glimpse*[②] of the Market

Yesterday morning, my mother and I went to the market together. The market is located a couple of blocks away from my house, and every morning is the busiest time of that patch of area.

When we arrived there, the whole place was already full of people. Everywhere crowds of people were *jostling*[③] each other in front of the stalls.

---

① 心目(中),想象
② 瞥
③ 推挤

People were buying, selling and *bargaining*①, and some looked very pleased with themselves, having made a good bargain. I could hear all kinds of noises in the market. Hawkers shouted to attract customers while patient vegetable vendors stood bargaining and *haggling*② for prices with customers. The meat stall was doing a roaring business. The fat man in charge just kept on cutting amounts of meat specified by customers.

After almost an hour's selecting and bargaining work in the little *bustling*③ place, my mother and I came back satisfied, our basket laden with our fine purchase. The market is really an interesting place.

---

① 讨价还价
② 争价
③ 熙熙攘攘的,忙乱的

No.53 | Social Issues
时事话题

(1) Law and Order

  A man cannot live alone in this world. He must join other men to form groups, large or small. The simplest of these groups is a family. A village, a district, a club, and a society are all groups of men. They differ from each other by their size and aims. A nation is but a very large group of men within a fixed territory and under a common government.

  Since a nation consists of a great number of persons, every person should always think of the others. When he works for himself, he must first think whether his work is harmful to others. He must remember that if the nation suffers, he suffers, too. He must help the government to keep order, whenever he can. He must try to *confine*① his actions within certain limits in order to *avoid conflict*② with others.

  Every group of men requires some rules to keep its members in order. A nation requires laws to preserve peace. If there were no law, every man would become a thief, a robber, or a murderer. Life and property would be always in danger. When people fight, no one would stop them; and when they steal, no

---

① 限制在……
② 避免冲突或矛盾

one would punish them. A strong man could do what he likes, for weak men were not able to stand against him. Therefore, a nation without laws would be intolerable.

If a man steals other persons' property, he must be sent to prison. If he kills another person, he must be hanged, shot, or in any other way put to death. Every crime should be punished, and justice should be valued. The careful observance of the law is the best way of protecting the people.

(2) Fight Against Crime

Today the crime rate in some cities seems to *be on the rise*①. Many citizens complain about the robberies which take place in streets or around their blocks. Therefore, more and more people *are appealing to*② the authorities to take strong measures to reduce the crime rate.

Faced with criminals, different people take different attitudes towards them. Some become so frightened that they tend to give up fighting or to *turn a blind eye to*③ the criminals. Others, however, are brave enough to fight against the criminals even at the risk of their own lives. In their eyes, responsibility is the most important of all the values that hold honest people together. Without it, there can be no self-respect, no trust, no law, and, ultimately, no society. There is no doubt that they set a good example for all of us to follow.

My suggestions are as follows. In the first place, every one should receive law education. Secondly, criminals must be punished severely. Finally, it is urgent to set up a foundation to

---

① 正在增长
② 向……呼吁、求助
③ 装作没看见

reward those who fight against criminals. In this way we can *stand up to*① any criminal and *smash*② any crime.

(3) Cooperation and Competition

Staying cooperative, in my opinion, certainly brings people many benefits. Staying competitive, without doubt, pushes one to *strive ahead*③ for success or to beat others. Take a race for instance, only when you dash along can you win special honor. But the jealousy that comes with the honor is the last thing you want to see.

One's ability is, after all, limited. Whatever you do, as long as you are cooperative, the achievement will be far greater than that you have made with your own effort. If a construction project, for example, is totally left in the hands of a single person, some *irreparable*④ damage may come into being because his planning is inevitably short of perfection. Two heads are better than one. Team-work is forever the foundation of achieving success. It is, therefore, my philosophy of life to be cooperative in my *undertaking*⑤.

(4) Challenges

For thousands of years, people have accepted challenges in different fields. There are not only physical challenges, but also social and intellectual challenges. Some people risk their lives in playing sports to see how well they can do. Others try to make

---

① 对抗
② 消灭
③ 奋斗;努力向前
④ 无可挽救的
⑤ 事业;任务;工作

and invent something to make life easier. They all enjoy challenges.

Why do people enjoy these challenges? There are probably two reasons. One is curiosity. The other is the personal feeling of success, and of achievement. In fact, nowadays, to some people, challenge is a business.

Today we still have many challenges before us. Medical science faces the challenges of conquering many diseases which still attack human beings. Engineers and planners must build new cities and design and produce new kinds of transportation. Scientists must develop new forms of energy. In short, we live in an age full of challenges.

(5) Problems in Our Grain Production

With the rapid growth of our economy, we do not worry about food shortage. But can we grow much more grain to feed our growing population? Based on extensive research, agricultural experts warn that grain production will decrease considerably worldwide for the next ten years. The situaton is more serious in China.

There are at least three major problems in grain production. First, our farmland shrinks rapidly because of the construction of factories, apartments, golf courses, *shopping malls*[①], and graveyards. Moreover, peasants are eager to produce tobacco or flowers to get higher profits. Second, shortages of water often result in poor harvests because the rapid expansion of cities and towns uses up most of the water resources. In most dry provinces, a mild drought may cause poor or no harvest. Finally,

---

① 购物中心

since their *life in rural areas is a perpetual struggle against poverty*①, millions of young peasants rush to cities for easier jobs and leave fertile fields wasted.

In summry, lack of manpower, shortage of water and decrease of farmland are the major problems to be solved. With only 7% of the world farmland, we already produce enough food for 22% of the world population. If we focus our attention on the solution of these problems, we will ensure that everyone has enough to eat.

(6) The Gap Between the Rich and the Poor

Recently, there is a widespread concern over the large gap between the rich and the poor in China. We are surprised to learn that a singer *leisurely*② made 9 thousand dollars one night, which it will take 100 years for an *industrious*③ peasant to earn.

Many millionaires *have sprung up*④ in the last ten years. We do not envy with green eyes those millionaires who make money honestly. But we strongly resent those who get rich by dirty means. For example, some people *take advantage of the loopholes in the law to amass a great fortune*⑤. Various criminals like smugglers, drug dealers, and all sorts of *impostors*⑥ make big money illegally. What is worst is nationwide corruption. The multi-layered corrupted bureaucrats abuse the power at hand to accumulate large fortunes by stealing state property, by supporting organized crime, and by bullying honest people. In

---

① 生活在农村地区就意味着永不停止地与贫穷抗争
② 悠闲地；从容地
③ 勤劳的；勤奋的
④ 迅速或突然地出现
⑤ 钻法律条款的空子积累了大量财富
⑥ 此处指"骗子"

contrast, life is tough for millions of unemployed workers in cities and peasants in remote areas.

While there exist people who are illegally reaping big profits, we should never stop *waging a war against*① them. *Mild criticism will not work.*② Our government should take effective actions to help the poor and reduce the gap by strictly reinforcing the law to *eliminate corruption*③. Otherwise, China will be in big trouble.

(7) Certificates or a Sound Education

Nowadays, university professors are worried about the fact that all sorts of poorly organized workshops on campus are always crowded, *overflowing with*④ enthusiastic students. In contrast, many classrooms look like cheap movie theaters.

Some college students often stay away from classroom and work very hard to earn various certificates such as driving licenses, accounting certificates, licensing as computer programmers, or English translators. It is true that for the time being, these certificates may help them be competitive in getting *jobs with a fatter payroll*⑤. However, they neglect their main task and the fact that China badly needs a large number of well-trained young talents, who are potential scientists, engineers and scholars. A job with high salary is not necessarily a good job which deserves one's talent and *dedication*⑥. There are so many important things for them to learn in the classroom that they

---

① 打一场战争；此处指"开展一场反对……的运动"
② 和风细雨般的批评起不了作用。
③ 消除腐败
④ 此处指"挤满了……"
⑤ 薪水丰厚的工作
⑥ 奉献

cannot afford to waste their talents, their precious time, and golden opportunity now.

We should, first and foremost, focus our efforts on our main task before we can direct our attention to some practical training. Certificates are OK; we can pick some up easily in our spare time. It is not what certificate we earn but the sound higher education we receive that really *counts*①.

(8) What Should We Learn from Americans?

Nowadays, many Chinese youths are eager to imitate Americans. They try Coca-Cola, rock and roll and even dye their hair gold to look like Americans. However, they fail to realize what they should learn from Americans.

Then what should we learn from Americans? There are indeed many good things in American culture that we lack and deserve our serious attention. Apart from the advanced science and technology, we should learn that Americans love freedom and independence. They honor successful people such as pioneers, scientists, great athletes, and national heroes. American children are educated to be independent, creative and *ambitious*②. Later on, they are encouraged to *bear hardships*③. Even today, they still cherish the spirit of the pioneers' courage, hard work, and *love of adventure*④.

We have to realize that it is neither Coca-Cola drinking nor disco dancing, but the many good American *heritages*⑤, that have brought about the prosperity of the United States. That is just

---

① 重要
② 有雄心壮志的
③ 经受苦难
④ 酷爱冒险
⑤ 文化遗产

what we should learn from them.

It is easy to imitate Americans, but it is difficult to learn the secrets of their success. There is a long way to go to build China into a powerful country; we should learn anything valuable from all nations in the world, the United States in particular. Meanwhile, we should watch out for evil things such as violence, drug abuse, and *racial discrimination*①.

(9) Care for Our Community

Besides *littering*②, *spitting*③ and smoking in public places, *damaging telephone booths*, *smashing garden seats and ruining public toilets*④ have become serious problems in many cities. Such bad behavior *degrades*⑤ our communities and injure China's international prestige.

Effective measures should be taken to cure such social diseases. First, mass campaigns should be launched to *denounce*⑥ bad behavior and make everyone understand that it is their responsibility to love and care for our community. Next, those who intentionally break the regulations should be exposed publicly and punished in such a way that he will permanently learn his lessen. Lastly, education on good manners should be constantly emphasized in all our schools, colleges, and communities. The problem is not that people like bad manners; the problem is that the uneducated don't know the right things to do. So, we should make our first priority on education. Only

---

① 种族歧视
② 乱扔垃圾或废弃物
③ 随地吐痰
④ 破坏公用电话亭,砸碎公园坐椅,破坏公共厕所
⑤ 使……丢脸
⑥ 检举;谴责

when China becomes a better educated country can we realize modern civilization.

These social problems must be solved quickly not only because they degrade the quality of our life and damage China's international prestige, but also because they slow down China's economic growth. A great nation like China will surely get rid of all these evil things.

(10) Patriotism

Patriotism implies a love for one's country. It is the noblest of human sentiments. Every citizen should possess some spirit of patriotism. Patriotism, however, is not to *be testified*① by the *tongue*②; it should *be manifested*③ in action. With this definite object *in view*④, one must do his best for his country, and, at any moment, be ready to make sacrifices for her. The man who posesses such will is a patriot *at heart*⑤.

Patriotism may be shown in various ways: soldiers display it by fighting for or defending their counrty; businessmen by carrying on trade with foreign countries, and thus increasing her wealth; farmers and miners by bringing out her natural *produce*⑥ and supplying her trade and industrial production; scientists express it by doing constant research work so that more advanced technology can be introduced and utilized in the construction of their country; students can show it by studying hard, and with their knowledge thus gained, they may serve their country in the

---

① 证明；证实
② 语言
③ 表明；证实
④ 此处指"头脑中有……想法、概念等"
⑤ 在内心里；本质上
⑥ 产品

future. Who are all these but true patriots?

(11) Copyright Infringements[①]

In recent years, intellectual property rights violation has turned into a heated problem in China. Plagiarism grows rampantly and copyright infringement is a typical case in point. There are many reasons for the situation. The chief one is that Chinese people has little awareness of intellectual property rights protection, which is a terrible heritage of traditional culture. People lack legal consciousness to protect the original author, being unaware of the fact that copyright violation is a crime that should be severely punished. Another reason lies in the incompleteness of legal system. The state has not yet developed sufficient powerful laws to protect intellectual property rights. And the ill-behaved people have chances to take risks and copyright infringement appears.

Since intellectual property rights are everywhere, home and abroad, intellectual property rights protection is of great significance. Therefore, the government should take serious and feasible measures to protect author's rights and set up complete legal system to punish those violating deeds and eliminate copyright infringement completely.

(12) The Effect of the Global Financial Crisis

The international financial crisis is getting *from bad to worse*[②], whose impact on Chinese economy is in further expansion. It has extended into every aspect of our society, for

---

① 侵犯版权
② 每况愈下

example, manufacturing, energy, food, IT and so on.

Many international companies went bankrupt, and more companies began to lay off employees, or cancell the original *recruitment plan*①. Around us, many people are unable to find a job.

This is a global economic crisis, which no one can disregard. However, everything has two sides and the financial crisis is no exception. It has let the investors consider about the long-term growth prospects field such as the field of new energy. It also provides China with opportunities of increasing the input of new energy.

We ought to face this crisis optimistically and try to *tide it over*② by bringing all our potentialities into full play.

(13) The Growth in the Number of Foreign Visitors to China

Recent report shows that there was an obvious growth in the number of foreigners entering China between 2006 and 2007. Take Japanese visitors for example. Their number went up steadily from 2.548 million in 2006 to 2.582 million in 2007. People from geographically remote countries like America also increased within these two years. Compared with the visitors from America in 2006, the number of Americans grew dramatically by 40,000 by the end of 2007.

Foreigners have a variety of purposes for coming to China. Since the opening-up drive in the late 1970s, China has grown into a land of opportunities. To meet China's booming trade, many business people from abroad waste no time in doing business with Chinese partners. Another major reason is that amazed by

---

① 招人计划
② 渡过,克服

Chinese ancient civilization, more and more travelers go on a tour to China's many tourist attractions.

In order to make China more appealing to foreigners, we still have big tasks to accomplish. To further *expand Sinoforeign economic cooperation*[①], China should continue to improve its investment climate by speeding up the construction of basic facilities such as highways and telecommunications, adopting flexible policies and providing better services for foreign investors. Besides, major cities in China should improve credit card systems so that overseas visitors will find it much safer to move about in China. Finally, open more scenic spots and build China into one of the biggest tourist countries in the world so as to attract still more foreign visitors.

(14) Unemployment

Unemployment is viewed as the number one problem in China now and the government has launched a major attack on the problem.

The steps the government has taken to deal with unemployment are as follows. Firstly, unemployment fund has been established to help the unemployed workers to support themselves. Secondly, the unemployed receive *vocational training*[②], which is expected to *pay off*[③] in the short term and give the unemployed an advantage in the job market. It is due to the lack of professional skills that these workers have lagged behind in the society. These training programs aim to equip the workers with some special skills, such as typing, sewing, and

---

① 扩大中外经济合作
② 技能培训
③ 收到效益,取得成功

cooking. Finally, psychological advice is also available, since unemployment, apart from exerting financial pressures, brings enormous psychological discomfort. With the advice, the unemployed will learn how to adapt to the fierce competition in the technological age.

With the joint efforts of the government and the society, we are optimistic that we will gradually solve the problem of unemployment.

(15) On Food Safety Issues

While it is true that there is a decline in the number of cases related to fake foods and foods of poor quality, the safety of food remains a serious problem in this society. Food-born diseases are largely responsible for high levels of sickness and *mortality*[①] in the general public, particularly for infants, young children, and the elderly.

There are various reasons for this heartbreaking fact. In my opinion, the responsibility goes for the most part to the food producers especially those who fail to meet safety standards. In order to make the most profit, some food producers may even intentionally use chemicals just to make food look or taste good. At the same time, the government departments responsible for quality control failed to fulfill their duties, which makes the danger turn into a reality. Besides, the media actually cheated the customers in their deliberate efforts to advertise the problematic food.

To make sure the food we eat is safe, the *supervision*[②] of food production should be highly responsible. What's more, it is

---

① 死亡率
② 管理,监督

important for the government to drastically increase legal *penalties*① on those who neglect food safety regulations. Nevertheless, the general public should be more aware that a healthy life relies on the safety of food stuff.

(16) The Aging Problem

Around the world, many countries have entered the so-called old-aged society. The *proportion*② of the people over 60 is quite big in the total population, and it is still rising. This is the result of the people's prolonged *life span*③ and the falling birth rate.

In China, the aging problem is becoming even more critical. In many big cities, the proportion of old people has been over 40 percent. As a result of family planning, every one-child family will have 4 to 8 senior family members to be looked after. That is obviously beyond an individual's ability. Then how to provide the old people with a happy and comfortable life is an urgent problem to solve.

To solve the aging problem, the government and society should make joint effort. The government may issue some favorable policies aiming at helping the old. Through education and the guidance of mass media, it can also try to change people's traditional ideas of nursing the old in family only. The society, on the other hand, should shoulder the responsibility of supporting the old. Every community should build recreational center for the old and provide all the facilities they need. In a word, as a nation of traditional virtues, we should try our best to help the old in their later years.

---

① 处罚,罚款
② 比例
③ 寿命

No.54 | Aspects of Life
生活面面观

(1) Finding Meaning in Life

To find meaning in our lives has been *an unending quest*① since the beginning of man's recorded history. Every action we perform has a reason or purpose, and thus we are led on in our search for this meaning.

Some find meaning or motivation by helping others. An example is the hospital nurse who finds *fulfilment*② in contributing to the recovery of her patients. For when a nurse helps a poor, aged *invalid*③, she knows that she is giving him the assurance that his well-being and comfort are important.

Others find meaning in life through God, that is, in the goodness and kindness of a Supreme Being. In believing that one day they will be blessed with *an eternal life*④, they have found something to love for and to anticipate.

But actually the best example of meaning in our lives is love. Love is one of the strongest of all emotions. The love of a man for a woman serves as the basis of happiness and success. The love of a parent for a child may provide the basis for a whole life of achievement. The love of a youth for his mother may be the

---

① 永无止境的追求、探寻
② 满足
③ 病弱者；伤残者
④ 永生

means of shaping his life as a man.

The question of meaning in life is still unanswered—and it will remain so for generation to come. What gives meaning and purpose to the life of one person would not answer the needs of another. It is an individual affair, and unless we turn into a world of mass *conformists*①, the quest for personal meaning and identity will continue indefinitely.

(2) What Is the Best Preparation for Life

In life we face with many types of situations. Each situation requires us to behave in different ways. In school or at work, we may be faced with a large project which demands the cooperation of many individuals. In this instance, each person must be flexible, supportive, and be willing to *compromise*②, because he is only a small part of a much larger machine.

Being competitive also has a place in life. The desire to succeed and do better than others will motivate us to work hard on the job and study diligently at school. But competition has its limits. Sometimes it may become selfish and destructive.

Some people say that the best preparation for life is learning to work with others and be cooperative. Others take the opposite view and say that learning to be competitive is the best preparation.

But in my opinion, in order to succeed in life, we must learn to be both cooperative and competitive. The most important thing to learn in life is to know when to be cooperative and when to be competitive.

---

① 循规蹈矩的人；此处指"人人变得一模一样"
② 妥协

(3) Is *Social Skill*① Important?

Many smart people with the best education may fail as ordinary people. They do not fail for lack of knowledge, but rather, more often than not, for only one simple reason — the lack of social skills.

In Chinese schools, we overemphasize academic achievements and neglect the development of social skills. After graduation, you may *get along on brilliance*② for a while, but most careers involve other people. You may have great academic intelligence and still lack social intelligence — the ability to make friends, to be sensitive to the feelings of others, to give and take criticism as well. People with high social intelligence take their share of blame and move on. They know how to build team-work and take leadership. If people don't like you, they may help you fail easily. If you are likable, things will be different. For example, you can get away with serious mistakes. Your supporters usually help you recover. A mistake may actually further your career, if your boss thinks you can handle the situation in a mature and responsible way. Many without much education have succeeded that way.

Social intelligence is so important that we should develop such skills *conscientiously*③. Like good manners, they can, after all, be learned. If we have academic and social intelligence, we may come back stronger than ever after our failure.

---

① 社交技能
② 进展顺利;很成功;很出色
③ 认真地

(4) Are Pets Good for People?

Are pets good for people? The answers to this question vary from person to person.

Some people say that the good thing of pets is that they keep us company, as we all need companions to feel happy. Often, a cat or a dog can comfort us at times when human words do not work. A pet in a family makes people feel closer to the natural world.

Others think that keeping pets is just a waste of time and resources. Besides, some pets can cause serious diseases. There is still another problem. Some people are so crazy about pets that they even neglect others' health and *public hygiene*①.

Personally, I am for the latter argument. Though pets can keep some people happy, it is necessary to think of others' happiness and health. In fact, pets are not good for all people.

(5) Some *Fire Hazards*② Around Us

Fires can be disastrous in our lives. In the shocking fire in Kelamayi, hundreds of people were killed or injured; most of them were children. The big fires occurring recently have revealed that there still exist too many fire hazards around us.

Carelessness is a leading cause of fires. One kind of carelessness is simply the *mishandling*③ of small flames. Throwing a burning match or *cigarette butts*④ into a wastebasket,

---

① 公共卫生
② 火灾隐患
③ 处理不当
④ 烟蒂

placing a lighted candle near curtains, playing with *fireworks*①, or failing to extinguish(or put out) a flaming fire is a foolish thing to do. Another type of carelessness is the misuse of *flammable*② liquids. Using gasoline to clean clothes in the house may lead to a bad fire.

Another fire hazard is the use of equipment with unsafe electrical parts. A worn or broken *power cord*③, a damaged socket, or wires which become overheated when used to supply enough power for too many appliances should be replaced.

Therefore, the *abuse*④ of electrical devices and personal negligence are the main hazards. Prevention is better than cure. If all these hidden fire hazards are completely removed and all possible precautions are taken against fire, no fires may occur any more.

(6) *Euthanasia*⑤

In modern times when new medicines and medical equipment are being developed constantly to extend human life, "euthanasia" has brought about a long and heated debate.

Some people are in favour of "euthanasia" when it is used on a patient whose condition is beyond hope and who, *of his own accord*⑥, wishes to end his life. They say that a person should have the right to choose death when the conditions of his health become unbearable and hopeless. Euthanasia stops his pain and lets him die peacefully. What is more, it can reduce the

---

① 烟火
② 易燃烧的
③ 电线
④ 滥用
⑤ 安乐死(亦称 mercy killing, painless death)
⑥ 自愿地

unnecessary expenses in sustaining his life.

Others argue that the duty of doctors is always to save patients and extend their life as long as possible. It is often the hope and effort of doctors to save a life at the last minute. If doctors often *resort to*[①] euthanasia, it will hinder the development of medical technology.

(7) Dining Out in a Fast Food Restaurant

Nowadays, fast food is popular in Beijing. Fast food restaurants have mushroomed everywhere and many woking couples and school children enjoy having their breakfast and lunch there.

Fast food restaurant is rapidly gaining popularity in China for quite a few reasons. Firstly, there are a variety of fast foods available. If you are busy or tired of cooking, you, may for a change, have American hamburgers, French fries, an Italian pizza, or numerous traditional Chinese foods cooked quickly by modern technqiue. The food often looks so nice and smells so good that you cannot help trying it yourself. Secondly, fast food satisfies peoples' needs. It is convenient, nutritious and delicious; the price is also reasonable so that everybody can afford it. Finally, with fast food, you can save time and a world of trouble, such as shopping, cooking, cleaning up tables and washing *greasy*[②] dishes. Consequently, it benefits people a lot. You may taste all kinds of food, listen to soft music, relax, and have time to do more important things. Fast food has already changed our ways of living. With the rapid development of science and technology, fast food will give us better service and possibly

---

① 凭借；依赖
② 油腻的

become indispensable to our modern life.

(8) Fate

Do you believe in fate? Do you think that a man is born with certain *destiny*① which is beyond his control? Maybe you share the same point of view with me: one's fate is in his own hand.

It is believed that a man is controlled by his fate or is doomed to live a certain life that is unchangeable by his power. Suppose a person is very poor or unhealthy, he then will be considered to have been born poor or unhealthy, and he will never be able to change such a situation. In my opinion, this is a wrong idea. One should take his destiny into his own hand. He is poor because he may not have worked hard enough to create wealth; he is unhealthy because he may not have paid sufficient attention to his health. It is no good *putting all blame on*② his fate, with his own fault escaping away.

It is very important that one should be the master of his own future. If *discontented with*③ the present life, he should try to improve it instead of *shirking his responsibility*④ and shift the blame onto his fate. Having made up his mind to change the current situation, he should find his goal first and then go ahead towards it rather than wait for the fate to bring him success, which in reality will never come. If one can take his fate in hand, he will be happy, rich and healthy, or he may remain poor and unhappy.

It seems that many people are unwary of their potential abilities. They don't think they are capable of changing their life.

---

① 命运；天命
② 全部归咎于……
③ 不满足于……
④ 推卸责任

However, if they have the desire and ambition, will there be nothing impossible?

(9) Do "Lucky Numbers" Really Bring Good Luck?

People in some part of China are very crazy about some "lucky numbers". They connect their good fortune with numbers which sound like Chinese characters meaning good fortune. For instance, they connect 6 with smoothness and success, 8 with wealth and 9 with a long life. They would like to pay twice the usual price for a "lucky" telephone number, try to do things such as wedding and business – opening on a day with one of these numbers and wish their "lucky" numbers would bring them good luck and wealth.

Do "lucky numbers" really bring good luck? I doubt it, for some people's belief in "lucky numbers" lacks a scientific foundation and thus is *superstitious*[①]. There are too many examples telling us that good luck has hardly anything to do with "lucky numbers". I myself have a telephone number with three 6s and ending in 8, but so far it has brought neither luck nor fortunes. On the contrary, only through hard work, determination, and persistence can one achieve success and then maybe fortunes. All the world famous scientists and businessmen have worked very hard throughout their life!

(10) My View on Fake Commodities

Nowadays, it is not infrequent that you will encounter in the market fake commodities such as foodstuff, clothing, and even medicine.

---

① 迷信的

Fake commodities have done great harms to consumers and the society as well. Take for example the 2008 *Sanlu milk powder case*① in Hebei province. The incident was a disaster to the consumers: many children who had taken Sanlu milk powder suffered from *renal calculus*②. At the same time, it caused much damage to the society. What's more, the *carry-over*③ of the fear left people throughout the country in panic and confusion; they no longer have a trust in the daily producing industry.

Considering the great dangers inflicted by fake commodities, it is high time that measures were taken to fight against producing fake commodities. For the consumers, when shopping, they should go to reputable stores, and check carefully the packages before any purchase. For the sellers, they should get the goods from the factories with a good fame. For the manufactures, they should cultivate public health consciousness and abide by the corresponding laws. And for the government, it should punish more severely such unlawful acts as selling or producing fake commodities. With the joint efforts of this kind, it is hoped that fake commodities will be eliminated from the market and consumers' legitimate rights will be protected subsequently.

(11) The Problem of Workplace Safety

Rencently, accidents in workplace have become the focus of the society. People want to find the reasons and measures for those tragedies.

There are mainly two reasons for this problem. First, some businesses pay no or little attention to creating a safe working

---

① 三鹿奶粉事件
② 肾结石
③ 遗留

environment for employees. Second, workers' lack of training and unawareness of safety also bring more dangers.

Thus, the following three steps are highly recommended so as to prevent the tragic accidents from happening again. First of all, the goverment should enforce strict regulations and standards on work-place conditions. Second, the businesses should meet the required standards and thus provide safe workplace for employees. Finally, workers should learn how to operate dangerous machines; meanwhile, they should always closely follow safety rules.

(12) Youth More Liberal

Many old traditional values of China are not cherished by youth any more, and the young people living in the modern urban centers are the first to change.

With the influx of foreign movies and the *proliferation*[①] of popular fashion magazines from around the world, a survey found that the younger generation are more inclined to accept *extra-marital affair*[②] and sex before marriage.

Extra-marital affair is one of by-products of *affluence*[③]. Around 34% of those surveyed were both for and against. Some people condemned it and others said it was acceptable if the couple were getting divorced or in an unhappy relationship.

Sex before marriage, the dilemma of the teenagers, showed a little difference between the approval and the disapproval sides. Just over 35% were definitely against it, while only 3% less said that such relationship is the natural outcome of love, but 20%

---

① 扩散
② 婚外情
③ 富裕

agreed that it is acceptable only if the two people involved have no objections.

A few of the unusual results from the survey included: around 63% believed that couples should keep their activities private, 52% agreed with *a prenuptial property agreement*① and about 12% of those surveyed preferred to remain *celibate*②.

(13) Say No to Pirated Products

Nowadays, the problem of *piracy*③ has become more and more serious. Books, tapes, VCDs, and other high-tech products have been pirated. For instance, when a new product comes into market, most probably, its pirated counterpart will soon put on its appearance in the market too.

Piracy has caused a great loss to the legitimate products, inventors and writers in many ways. To start with, the pirated products often cost much less than the genuine ones so that they enjoy a better trading position in spite of their relatively poor quality. The genuine products, on the contrary, sell poorly. What's worse, pirated books sometimes do great harm to the authors' reputation due to some misprints. In the long run, pirated products may have a negative impact on customers. Those legitimate producers' creativity and enthusiasm may be deeply hurt by the fact that some customers are more interested in pirated products for the sake of small gains.

Now, it is high time that everyone started the battle against piracy. First, customers should develop their consciousness to resist the pirated products. Second, the government should take

---

① 婚前财产公证
② 独身
③ 盗版

effective measures to put an end to piracy. Finally, laws must be strictly enforced to completely ban piracy. Only in this way can the pirated products completely be wiped out of our life.

(14) My View on the Income Disparity

People's opinions on *the income disparity*① vary from person to person. Some people think that it is a necessary result with the development of our social economy. They hold the idea because they always look forward to making more money through hard work. Although the above view sounds reasonable, others think that income disparity will lead to *polarization*② and that is a serious social problem. In their opinion, the gap between the rich and the poor is contrary to the country's principle.

As for me, I am in favor of the first view because of the following reasons. First, the income disparity can stimulate people to create more products and meet the needs of society. Besides, while it is true that people with low income feel unfair to be compelled to take more pains, it doesn't mean that the division of social wealth is totally unreasonable. There are numerous examples around us to illustrate that condition.

Therefore, the most important thing is to set up a fair and reasonable criterion to divide the social wealth and give all people more opportunities to develop themselves. It is hoped that the income disparity will be eliminated in the future.

(15) My View on *Lottery*③

Some people say that lottery should be made illegal because

---

① 收入差别
② 两极分化
③ 彩票

Aspects of Life No.54

many people do not understand that the odds of winning are very small. It is gambling, cheating, even robbing. People buy lotteries because they want to make a fortune without working hard. Why should this unhealthy tendency be encouraged?

Other people say that lotteries are good because they generate funds for the government and fortune for the people. The money collected can be used in relieving disasters, construction, welfare and financing education. It is a quick and harmless way to collect money for public service. Even the Asian Sports Meeting and 2008 Beijing Olympiad were financed by lottery. As for the individuals, few people will lose enormous amount of money on lottery or *become addicted*[①] to it. Instead, it is a hope for better life and a helping hand to people in need, say, the children in "Hope Project".

Therefore, there is no need to make lottery illegal. People should be informed, however, that it is unrealistic to buy lottery as a chief means to make a fortune because it is only a chance in a million to win.

(16) Making Decisions

Parents in China tend to make all decisions for their children. It is not unusual that Chinese parents will choose schools for their children. Children's clothing and even timetable are often decided by their parents. Upon their children's graduation, Chinese parents tend to pick up a profession for their children.

Deciding everything for your children does not help them to make way and *establish themselves*[②] in the world. It is obvious that parents cannot accompany their children and make decision

---

① 上瘾,着迷
② 立足

on everything all the time. Deciding everything for your children will make them form a passive and dependent habit, which will do more harm than good in the long run.

Growing to be independent is the natural way for everybody. As a child grows up, he will graduate from a school or a college. After graduation he will work and then build up a family of his own. This is the way every parent has experienced. Therefore, giving advice rather than making decisions is more helpful and beneficial.

(17) Changing Fashions

In my opinion, changing fashions are nothing more than the deliberate creation of waste. Women are mercilessly exploited year after year because they spend large sums of money each year to replace clothes that have hardly been worn. Women who cannot afford to discard clothing in this way, waste hours of their precious time altering the dresses they have.

Fashion designers are rarely concerned with vital things like warmth, comfort and durability. They are only interested in outward appearance and take advantages of the fact that many women will put up with any amount of discomfort, providing they look sexy and attractive.

When comparing men and women in the matter of fashion, the conclusion to be drawn is obvious. Do the constantly changing fashions of women's clothes reflect basic qualities of *fickleness*[①] and instability? Do men's unchanging styles of dress reflect basic qualities of stability and reliability? This is for you to decide, but you had better not *make irresponsible remarks or comments*[②].

---

① 易变,无常
② 妄下雌黄

(18) On Clothes

Clothes are indispensable in our daily lives. They protect us from the strong wind in cold winter and prevent us from the unbearable heat in hot summer. They can even make men handsome and women attractive, though *a naturally endowed woman does not depend on fine clothes for beauty*[①]. They also distinguish people in different fields. For instance, we can tell a soldier from a policeman simply by the uniforms they wear.

Clothes can reflect many things about people. They can represent a person's social status, his likes and dislikes, his hopes, and so on. A quiet person, for example, might like to wear dark-colored clothes. An out-going person, on the other hand, might prefer to wear bright-colored ones. Old people tend to wear traditional clothes, whereas young people might tend to choose fashionable ones.

Clothes will continue to develop to satisfy our individual tastes. They will become more comfortable, colorful, fashionable and varied. People will find in the market more clothes they like to reflect their personalities or make them more *presentable*[②].

(19) On Personal Privacy

In recent years, many newspapers have exposed the privacy of actors, singers and some other famous men and women. We common people have already become used to it. However, this is against the law. If your privacy is exposed to the public, what should you do? Yes, take the law as arms and fight for your

---

① 天生丽质无需金装
② 中看的,体面的

rights.

Many reporters like to try to find out other people's privacy and make it public in order to sell the newspaper or magazine. But this *malpractice*① violates the law, which protects personal privacy. If your privacy is exposed without your permission, you have the rights to protect yourself. So far, however, there are lots of people who don't know their own rights or the relative law. They fail to take up arms of law to fight. So we should teach and help them protect their rights. We should make everybody depend on his own right consciously.

In a word, personal privacy should not be exposed; on the contrary, it should be protected. If everybody were conscious of it, our society would be more legal and harmonious.

(20) *Starbucks*② Should Leave the Forbidden City

As globalization *gears up*③, cultural conflicts arise. One example could be the issue whether Starbucks should withdraw its outlet from the Forbidden City. Heated debates recently emerged, unfortunately causing *a tempest in a "coffee cup"*④. Many people, especially the younger generation, oppose the suggestion, because people love Starbucks for a coffee, a snack and a place to rest.

However, it may not be appropriate to have a Starbucks outlet inside the Forbidden City. For one thing, the style of Starbucks does not match that of the Palace Museum. The American chain coffee store is a *tycoon*⑤ in the fast food industry,

① 不法行为
② 星巴克(美国咖啡连锁店)
③ 加快,增强
④ 小题大做
⑤ 业界巨头,大亨

and seems *out of place*① in a solemn royal palace. For another, the Forbidden City symbolizes China's culture, and so justifiably it should be free from solely commercial operations like Starbucks.

Of course, there is nothing wrong with a preference for Starbucks. However, one does not have to appreciate it inside the Forbidden City. An outlet nearby may be a better choice. It is still convenient for people to have a comfortable place to sit, drink, or chat, because it avoids controversy.

(21) Wenchuan Earthquake

On May 12, 2008, an 8.0-magnitude earthquake struck Wenchuan, Sichuan Province. Thousands of people lost their lives and even more people were left homeless. But, hand in hand, the Chinese people faced this disaster with compassion and courage.

People across China offered to make donations energetically. *Relief materials and funds*② were continuously pouring into quake hit areas. What's more, several rescue teams and medical professionals, at home and abroad, were sent to the stricken areas to search and rescue the survivals.

We students also provided our helping hands for the earthquake stricken *compatriots*③. We donated our spare money to the suffering people who were in urgent need of food and medicine. Blood donation was also of vital significance for those injured people. Students who were equipped with professional skills volunteered to the earthquake stricken areas to rescue more

---

① 不合时宜
② 救援物资
③ 同胞

lives. Besides, our support in spirit and sincere prayers worked in helping the broken hearts overcome the temporary disaster. What we young students did demonstrated that we have come up not only in intellectual attainments but also in political consciousness and in moral qualities.

(22) Should Free Music Downloads Be Banned?

With the development of the technology, more and more people are making use of the internet and they are enjoying downloading all types of materials. Some are especially fond of downloading free music. They argue that free music downloads not only enrich our life but also are good for the musician industry, because they help increase the popularity of music.

However, from my point of view, it is not advisable to allow free music downloads. For one thing, it varies from the international property's rights of musicians. For another, it causes *irreparable losses*[①] on the sales of musical products such as CDs, which may do harm to the whole musician industry. Without good returns, who would like to invest in the musician industry? In the order that musician industry can develop healthily, we'd better ban free music downloads. Let's all start to do so with ourselves.

---

① 无可弥补的损失

No.55 Perception in life
人生感悟

(1) The Best Age to Be

Each age has its joys and pains, and the happiest person is the one who enjoys what each age gives him without wasting his time in useless regrets.

Childhood is a time when there are few responsibilities to make life difficult. A child takes pleasure in playing in the rain, or in the snow. His first visit to the seaside is a *marvellous*① adventure. But a child has his pains: he is not so free to do what he wishes and he is continually being punished for the mistakes he has made.

When the young man starts to earn his own living, he becomes free from the discipline of school and parents. If he works hard, he may have the happiness of seeing his own success. But at the same time he is forced to accept responsibilities. He has to work hard if he wants to live comfortably. After 40, one's responsibility may be heavier, but he should be valued for his experience, *know-how*② and judgment. Most of the major rewards of success in life tend to accumulate at this age.

---

① 奇妙的
② 实际知识;技能,诀窍。

Old age has always been thought of as the worst age to be, but the old men have the joy of seeing their children making progress in life. And perhaps best of all, they can feel the happiness of having come through the battle of life safely and of having reached a time when they can lie back and rest, leaving others to continue the fight. It is true that *to be interested in the changing seasons is a happier state of mind than to be hopelessly in love with spring*①.

(2) Satisfied or Dissatisfied

According to a Chinese saying, those who are contented with their lot will always be happy. I am not with the view, though. In my opinion, people should not be satisfied with what they have got for the following reasons.

Firstly, it goes against human nature to be satisfied with what one has. The desire to possess what people do not have is inherent in human nature. There is an English saying, "*Every body wants to keep up with the Joneses.*②" So it is natural for people to have admiration and jealousy. To prohibit such feeling is cruel because it is against human nature.

Secondly, being dissatisfied promotes people to reform the world. The world is getting more and more progressive and advanced because people always desire for new things and create new things that they do not have yet. If our forefathers had been satisfied with what they had, the world would still be primitive.

Thirdly, ambition is a good thing. Only with ambition can people make continuous progress and can the world become better and better.

---

① 充满兴味地置身于季节的变化比无望地苦恋春天更让人心情惬意。
② 人人都想与富裕的左邻右舍并驾齐驱

(3) *A Fall into the Pit, a Gain in Your Wit* ①

Since making mistakes is quite unavoidable for human, no one could claim that he has not ever made a mistake. However, *dwelling on* ② mistakes instead of drawing lessons from them is a pure waste of time and is totally senseless.

Looking back on history, we can find that the truth in the Chinese proverb — A fall into the pit, a gain in your wit — has helped in many cases. Take the China's development as an example. To feed a large population, China once put too much stress on its economic development without paying sufficient attention to the conservation. As a result, serious issues on environmental *deterioration* ③ emerged in succession. To our relief, China took immediate remedial measures to achieve sustainable development.

Now that gains from the falls mean so much for human beings, we should develop a positive attitude toward failures. Most important of all, we ought to bear in mind that it is not errors or failures but rather the loss of confidence and courage that can defeat people.

(4) Don't Be Complaining All the Time

Complaint is common in life. As there are always *deficiencies or inadequacies* ④, some people are prone to criticize or find fault with others. They complain about their leaders, their

---

① 吃一堑长一智
② 老是惦记着（担心着）
③ 恶化
④ 缺陷和不足之处

colleagues, their schools and even their families. Their *grievance*① and *grumble*② make both themselves and others unhappy. Complaint *mends no hole*③. Instead it results in hostility between the giver and the receiver of the complaint.

Those who complain only see the weak points of others and they think that they themselves are perfect. So they learn little or nothing from others, and, by and by, they will become one-sided or stubborn.

What we should do is the opposite of complaint — praise. *An ounce of praise is worth a pound of criticism*④. A man of good wishes always respects others and appreciates their work and efforts. In return, he himself is respected and appreciated.

So, let us complain less and praise more so as to make our society more harmonious.

(5) On Learning about Life

There is much discussion about which is the best way of learning about life. Some people believe that listening to the advice of family and friends is the best way. But those who oppose this opinion believe that the best way is through personal experience. As far as I am concerned, I cannot say that the first opinion is a wrong approach but that the second opinion is preferable.

It cannot be denied that listening to the advice of family and friends is a speedy and easy way for us to get more experience in a short term. But, we cannot neglect its unfavorable aspects. For example, you can get the advice from your family and friends, but

---

① 牢骚,不满
② 怨言,牢骚
③ 于事无补
④ 一份赞扬抵得上十份批评

no one exactly meets the same situation as you do. It is quite possible that your family's and friends' experience cannot suit you completely.

However, we can find lots of advantages in the second opinion. For instance, maybe you have heard a Chinese saying, "*A man does not know the difficulty of anything unless he does it personally*①." Besides, from your personal experience, you can learn something that really belongs to you. Most important of all, you can accumulate your own experience that no one can teach you.

On the whole, I believe that getting experience from your own life is the best way to learning about life and learning how to live.

(6) Don't Hesitate to Say "No"

In our daily life, there are many occasions on which we should not hesitate to refuse when asked for help. For one thing, when it is beyond our ability, we should give a direct reply "no". For another, when the thing we are asked for is unreasonable or even illegal, we should say "no" without hesitation.

However, it is not the case in our real life. Many people prefer to say "yes" when they should say "no". Some are afraid to lose their face, since they think refusal means their inability. Some people are afraid to offend their acquaintance, their friends, relatives and so on.

In fact, *to save face at all costs*② is quite harmful. If you agree to do the things beyond your ability, the result will only be worse. The other might as well have asked another person who

---

① 事非经过不知难
② 死要面子

can help. And if you agree to do the unreasonable or even the illegal favors, such as cheating in the exam, you are in fact not helping the other but hurting him. You yourself will get into trouble too.

(7) Reactions to Disappointment

It can be said that no one gets through life without experiencing many disappointments. Most people seem unprepared for disappointment and react to it in negative ways. They feel depressed or try to escape their troubles instead of using disappointment as an opportunity for growth.

One negative reaction to disappointment is depression. A lady trying to win a promotion, for example, has worked hard for over five years in her department. But the boss promoted one of her colleagues. Deeply depressed, the lady decided that all her efforts were doomed to defeat. She then told herself that doing a good job just wasn't worth the work. Another negative reaction to disappointment is the desire to escape. Wang Ming, for instance, failed to get into the college his brother was attending, and he thought he was a loser and decided to escape his disappointment by giving up his studies and getting completely involved in pleasures, parties and making amusement.

The positive way to react to disappointment, however, is to use it as a chance for growth. This isn't easy, but it is the only useful way to deal with an inevitable part of life. The lady, who wasn't promoted, could have handled her disappointment by looking at other options. And Wang Ming, who failed to get into the desired college, should look into other schools. And both the lady and Wang Ming could have worked out better ways to deal with disappointments. So it can be safely said that the best thing is to accept a disappointment and try to make use of it somehow.

(8) Enthusiasm

Years ago, when I started looking for my first job, my teacher, a scholar of great learning, urged, "Be enthusiastic. Enthusiasm will take you further than any amount of experience and knowledge." How right he was! From my own experience I have learned the enthusiastic people can turn a boring journey into an adventure, extra work into opportunity and strangers into friends.

Enthusiastic people love what they do, regardless of money or title or power, because they know that years wrinkle the skin, but to give up enthusiasm wrinkles the soul.

We need to live each moment wholeheartedly, with all our senses — finding pleasure in the fragrance of a back-yard garden, the crayoned picture of a six-year-old, the enchanting beauty of a rainbow. It is such enthusiastic love of life that puts a sparkle in our eyes, a *lilt*[①] in our steps and smoothes the wrinkles from our souls.

(9) You Are What You Think

Do you see the glass as half-full rather than half-empty? Do you keep your eye upon the *doughnut*[②], not upon the hollow? Suddenly these *clichés*[③] are scientific questions, as researchers *scrutinize*[④] the power of positive thinking.

If people are pessimistic and feel hopeless, they don't bother to acquire the skills they need to succeed. The secret to an

---

① 轻快而有节奏(的步伐)
② 面包圈
③ 老生常谈
④ 仔细考察

optimist's success is in his positive thinking. When things go wrong the pessimist tends to blame himself. "I'm no good at this. I always fail." The optimist looks for *loopholes*① and tries to remedy an unfavorable situation.

The optimist feels in control of his own fate. If things are going badly, he acts quickly, looking for solutions, forming a new plan of action, and reaching out for advice. The pessimist feels like fate's plaything and moves slowly. He doesn't seek advice, since he assumes nothing can be done, and in the end he becomes hopeless.

As a matter of fact, we are what we think and *life is what we make it*②. So try to be optimistic and make your life beautiful.

(10) The Gap Between the Rich and the Poor

In recent years there has been much discussion about the gap between the rich and the poor. Though it is an inevitable phenomenon in the process of reform, the ever-growing contrast between the rich and the poor in China may give rise to lots of problems.

First of all, dissatisfied with their poor life, lots of people from poor regions flock to the big cities for better life and more enjoyment. Since not all of them have the necessary means or skills to earn their own living, some of those people resort to violence and commit various crimes.

Furthermore, the *disparity*③ in income may lead to inequality in education. In poor areas, some bright kids have to drop out of school because of the poverty, while those from

---

① 漏洞
② 人生皆由自己缔造
③ 悬殊,不等

wealthy families can study in schools with good teachers and adequate facilities in spite of their reluctance to study. Equal educational opportunities should be available to all, urban, suburban and rural, rich or poor.

Considering all mentioned above, it is high time that our government took effective measures to improve the situation. It should create more work opportunities for urban residents and increase investments in poor regions so that people there can also enjoy the benefits of our economic reform. This is not a problem that can be solved overnight but should not be ignored.

(11) Change Is Opportunity

Nothing bears but change[①], and in that change there is always opportunity. So watch the change and see how you can make the best of it.

Change will surely come. It will bring with it new challenges, to be sure. It will also bring new positive possibilities. Always keep in mind that change equals opportunity. The bigger the change is, the bigger the opportunity will be.

If you fail to see and make the most of that opportunity, the day will come when you will regret it. The world is changing faster than ever, so what does that mean? It means more opportunities than ever before. Rather than worrying too much about the change, seize the opportunities that are embedded in it. Find a way to make change your friend, and you will certainly succeed in whatever you do.

---

① 变化是永恒的

(12) Being Thankful

One of the first steps in turning a negative factor into a positive one is finding something for which you can be thankful.

A case in point is when someone criticizes you, your natural reaction is to get a little angry, resentful, defensive and even irritated. But consider what would happen if you could, instead, genuinely say "thank you." When you find a way to say "thank you" for criticism, you can find something positive to learn from it. Indeed, it is difficult to be thankful when you are in pain, but gratitude can begin to truly ease and extinguish that pain. The time when things are at their worst is when you need most the strength of your *blessing*s[①].

In short, if you practice gratitude even in the midst of despair, it will open your eyes to the positive possibilities all around you.

(13) A Day without Hope Is a Day without Sunshine

Little children look forward to the arrival of lunar New Year, and adults to that of spring. When I was a child I couldn't understand what the adults hope for. But New Years Day was always the greatest red-letter day of all the year.

Days with hope come and go very fast. Very soon I finished primary school, went to junior and senior middle school, and finally to college with ever greater hope for more things: for graduation with honors, for an ideal job, for a successful career, for a satisfactory wife... Climbing the upward steps of hope I had become a fully grown man before I was aware of it.

---

① 赐福

人生感悟
Perception in life
No.55

From my own experience I have learnt that a day without hope is a day without sunshine. There must be something to look forward to each day to brighten one's life. To a person cherishing hopes every morning rises a new sun, and everyday is a new life. Even if it is a *fantasy or an illusion*①, so long as it shows a ray of hope it still urges you on in pursuit of what is good and what is beautiful.

You've got to have hope; without hope you can not go.

(14) Smile

Smile is the universal language of kindness. What is meant by a smile can be understood with the following sayings: *smile somebody into good humor*②, *smile* somebody *out of his misgivings*③, and *smile away somebody's embarrassment*④.

What we refer to here is a sincere and good-natured smile that comes from the bottom of one's heart. We do not mean a smile specially put on to please others, or a false one to fool people. That is to say, a smile should be mentally sound, optimistic and firm in faith. Only when a person has a strong love of life, for work and people can he or she always wear a smile.

Smile is inseparable from its owner, for it can neither be rented nor bought, neither borrowed nor stolen. It symbolizes the person's mind and serves many purposes: bringing strangers closer to each other, giving hope to the disappointed and replacing vexation with joy. It opens channels from heart to heart so that feelings can flow *reciprocally*⑤.

---

① 奇思或幻想
② 笑得某人高兴起来
③ 笑得使某人不再疑惧
④ 以微笑解除某人的窘态
⑤ 相互地

Where there is a smile, there is a light. A smiling world is a civilized one. Let there be more smiles and less worries.

(15) Packaging

A person, like a commodity, needs packaging, but going too far is absolutely undesirable. A little *exaggeration*①, however, does no harm when it shows the person's unique qualities to his or her advantage. To display personal charm in a casual and natural way, it is important for one to have *a clear knowledge of oneself* ②. *A master packager* ③ knows how to integrate art and nature without any traces of embellishment, so that the person thus packaged is no commodity but a human being, lively and lovely.

A young person, especially a female, radiant with beauty and full of life, has all the favor granted by Nature. *Any attempt to make up would be self-defeating*④. Youth comes and goes like rainbow, which can never last very long.

Packaging for the middle-aged is primarily to *conceal the furrows ploughed by time*⑤. If you still enjoy enough life's exuberance to retain self-confidence and pursue pioneering work, you are unique in your natural qualities, and your charm and grace will remain.

As long as one finds where one stands, one knows how to package oneself and enjoy the beauties of life.

---

① 夸张(的包装)
② 清楚地认识自己
③ 包装的高手
④ 任何涂抹都是败笔
⑤ 遮掩岁月的痕迹

No.56 Suicide
自杀问题

(1) Suicide

Suicide is quite prevalent at present. When we read the newspaper, the word "suicide" frequently meets our eyes. It is often the case that one commits suicide because of a disappointment in love, or some financial embarrassment.

But we should know that as self-preservation is an instinct of man, suicide is foolish thing. No one in the world likes to lose his life, though all men are mortal. Therefore, to kill oneself is sheer folly.

What is more, we all should regard our life as precious and noble as possible, for everyone has his own great responsibilities to perform. Yet, in today's highly competitive society, everyone is bound to suffer from stress and *adversity*①, *which, as it were, can be taken as a great schoolmaster*②. It is advisable for young men to know that where there is life, there is hope, and where there is hope, there is everything.

(2) Young People's Suicide

It is reported that the number of youngster's suicidal cases

---

① 不幸，厄运
② 但人们可以从逆境中得到教育

has constantly grown from 1990 to 2008 in a coastal city. The number almost climbs 3 times in the 15 years, with 6 young people among 100,000 committing suicide in 2008.

The reasons for the frustrating increase are as follows. For one thing, the blame should be laid on the tension and stress caused by the fierce academic competition. For another, youngsters of present days tend to be more isolated from their peers and relations. They pay less attention to communicating with others and even always keep their secrets and troubles to themselves.

The tragedy could be avoided if we keep in mind the following ways or *outlet*① of frustration and stresses. Firstly, try physical activity and release the pressure through exercises such as running, walking, and dancing. Secondly, share your stress. It helps to talk to someone about your anxiety and worries. Only when your frustration and tension is poured out will you feel relieved and your tension be eased.

(3) Suicide Among Students

A girl student was found dead in front of a high building. She jumped off its roof and left a note, explaining that stress and depression caused by the fierce academic competition were "driving her mad." What a tragedy! There were hundreds of students who committed suicide for this reason in the past several years across the land. An expression has been coined to reflect this *lamentable*② phenomenon: *death over study pressure*③. I suppose that such a tragedy wouldn't happen if the victims knew

---

① 发泄途径
② 可悲的
③ 过学死。这是近年来新出现的所谓"时尚用语"之一。多指高三学生因心理压力太大而导致的自杀行为,或因过分用功导致身体虚弱而猝死的现象。

the following ways to handle stress.

First, see your problem in different light. Instead of being depressed and worried about your exam, for example, you may say to yourself: "Two months from now I shall not be worrying about it, so why worry about it now?" Changing the way of looking at things will help you to free from the impasse you have reached. Second, share your stress. It really helps to talk to someone who knows you well about your anxiety and worries. Like the bursting of a *pent-up*① river, to cry your heart out is to unburden yourself.

As the competition is getting tougher and tougher in every field, nobody can live completely free of stress and tension. But you can *minimize*② their impact if you follow the suggestions above.

(4) On Opening Psychological Courses

Many universities and colleges have now decided to offer more psychological courses to their students. This is totally advisable and has been warmly welcomed.

In the first place, psychological courses are in urgent need in colleges and universities. Today's students are under tremendous pressures. They have economical and academic pressures, and pressures coming from interpersonal relations as well. These pressures may bring them anxiety, depression and despair. Some students even committed suicide for these pressures. The psychological courses may teach them how to deal with pressures, and thus can be very good for the students' mental health, and

---

① 被禁锢的;被压抑的
② 使减少到最低限度

sometimes can *rescue* a student *from the jaws of death*①.

In the second place, such courses may help students deal with problems in the future and are therefore beneficial to the whole society. The courses teach students how to regulate feelings and emotions in different situations, which can be of great use when they graduate and go to work.

As for me, I think it's a wise idea to offer more psychological courses to the students.

(5) How to Improve Students' Mental Health?

As is known to all, our human body health consists of two aspects — physical and mental health, and mental health is as important as physical health for a student during his growth. However, it's quite worrying that nowadays some students are not quite mentally healthy. The cases of suicide on campus reveal the importance of mental health.

It has been reported that in recent years quite a few teenagers who suffered serious mental problems committed suicide. Many suicides occurred without warning, leaving family and friends shocked and grieving. Psychologists may have discovered the most common cause of death among the students, but there is still a long way from providing solutions.

Therefore, colleges and universities should be responsible for caring students' mental health in their school life. Firstly, the authorities concerned should *enhance*② the awareness that mental fitness is very important to college students. Secondly, relevant courses and activities should be introduced to students so that they would learn to maintain and improve their mental health.

---

① 把……从死亡的边缘上救过来
② 提高,增强

自杀问题
Suicide
No.56

Thirdly, there should be a psychological *counseling*① hotline or office, even an on-line service for students to turn to when they need some psychological aid.

But school alone can not ensure the final success in improving students' mental health. Students should also take an active part in helping themselves. They should learn to be patient, understanding, and cooperative with others, and spend more of their efforts doing more meaningful things, such as study and sports.

---

① 咨询服务

No.57 Natural Phenomena 自然现象

(1) Earthquakes

*Earthquakes*① may take place anywhere on the earth. During an earthquake, the *vibrations*② make the earth's surface tremble, and even crack open. Houses fall, people are killed or injured, and sometimes whole cities are destroyed.

Can we do something to protect ourselves against earthquakes? Can we take *precautionary measures*③? We can. Scientists have made investigation into earthquakes. They have made maps showing the "*earthquake belts*"④. In areas along these belts, earthquakes are likely to occur. We should, therefore, build special houses to resist earthquake shocks and protect ourselves.

In the future, scientists will be able to predict exactly when and where earthquakes will take place. Then they will be able to tell people to take precautionary measures. Thus, lives can be saved and damage can be lessened.

---

① 地震
② 振动;颤动
③ 预防措施;防备措施
④ 地震带

(2) Gravity

"*Whatever goes up must come down*"① is a well-known proverb. Most people also know why the proverb is true: *gravity*②. Gravity is the attraction between objects in the universe, which keeps our moon going around the earth, which keeps the earth and the other planets going around the sun, and which brings down to earth any object tossed into the air. So if a rocket is launched into space, should it eventually come back down to its launching point? No. The distance between two objects, as well as their size and *mass*③, determines the strength of the *gravitation force*④ between them. Once a rocket gets a certain distance away from the earth, the gravitational attraction of other planets becomes stronger than that of the earth. A sufficiently powered engine can *propel*⑤ a rocket beyond the gravitational pull of all of the planets in our solar system. When the power finally runs out, the rocket will wander in deep space until the gravitational attraction of some distant star or planet pulls it in to *crash*⑥.

(3) *Typhoons*⑦ and Earthquakes

Typhoons and earthquakes are relatively common in coastal areas. Typhoons usually occur during one part of the year, the

---

① 有起必有落
② 万有引力;地心引力;重力
③ (物体的)质量
④ 吸引力
⑤ 推动;驱动
⑥ 坠落
⑦ 台风

summer and the fall. Earthquakes can happen at any time. Both can be very destructive and frightening.

When a typhoon hits, there is usually enough time to issue a warning. People in these areas are told to go inside. They should close the windows and lock the doors. Anything left loose may be blown away. A typhoon is a very powerful storm with strong winds and lots of rainfall. It blows down signs, trees, telephone poles, and anything else it can. A very strong typhoon is often followed by floods that can destroy houses. After a typhoon there is often a lot of damage for repair.

Earthquakes are less predictable than typhoons. They can occur any time of the day or night, any time of the year. Suddenly the ground begins to shake, windows rattle, *chandeliers*① and furniture move. A very strong earthquake may cause buildings to *collapse*②, killing people. Or it can start a *landslide*③ or an *avalanche*④.

As we know, typhoons and earthquakes are the two things that cause great damages and also make people nervous and scared. Then, how are they prevented from happening? Do you have any suggestions to make?

(4) UFO⑤

Now and then we hear about people seeing UFOs. But are there visitors from other worlds?

Scientists believe our earth is not the only home of life. Very probably highly intelligent beings are living elsewhere in the

---

① 枝形吊灯
② 倒塌；坍塌
③ 滑坡
④ 雪崩；山崩
⑤ UFO 为 Unidentified Flying Object 之缩写，意思是"不明飞行物"。

自然现象 Natural Phenomena No.57

universe. Their science and technology may be well ahead of ours.

In fact, our science is only 400 years old, beginning from the time when Galileo looked at the moon through his telescope. But today we can make a trip there in 75 hours, the rocket being thousands of times faster than a horse-drawn cart. If some space beings have a science 4000 years old, can't they do something *beyond our imagination*[①]?

Then, why don't space visitors get in touch with us? Perhaps they look down on us as *savages*[②] armed with *nuclear missiles*[③]. They just cannot afford to risk their lives.

However, most reports on close-up observations of UFOs have proved untrue. The observers were mistaken. What they saw might be an illusion or some natural phenomena which we do not understand yet. Still, the possibility of UFOs exists.

① 我们想像不到的
② 野蛮人；未开化的人
③ 核导弹

No.58 Climate
气候

(1) Climate

For the last hundred years the climate has been growing warmer. This has had a number of different effects. Since the beginning of the 20th century, *glaciers*① have been melting very rapidly. For example, the Muir Glacier in *Alaska*② has retreated 2 miles in 10 years. Secondly, because of rising temperatures the snowline has been retreating on mountains all over the world.

As a result of this, vegetation has also been changing. In Canada, the agricultural cropline has shifted 50 to 100 miles northward. In the same way cool-climate trees like *birches*③ and *spruce*④ have been dying over large areas of Eastern Canada.

The distribution of wildlife has also been affected. Many European animals, for example, have been moving northwards into *Scandinavia*⑤. Since 1918, 25 new species of birds have been seen in *Greenland*⑥, and in the United States birds have moved their nests to the north.

---

① 冰河；冰川
② 阿拉斯加（美国一州名）
③ 白桦
④ 云杉
⑤ 斯堪的纳维亚（半岛）
⑥ 格陵兰（岛）

Finally, the sea has been rising at a rapidly increasing rate, also *due to*① the melting of glaciers. In the last 18 years it has risen by about 6 inches, which is about four times the average rate of rise over the last 9,000 years.

(2) Weather

Weather affects all of us in one way or another, directly or indirectly. For example, good weather makes people happy and gay, while bad weather makes people sick and depressed. Besides, on a fine day, one can go out for a walk or play a game in the open. On a rainy day, however, he can only stay indoors. In a word, weather is part of life for all of us.

The first thing that many people do after getting up is to see what the weather is like. With a knowledge of the weather, people can arrange work and life of the day. If it is fine, one may decide to go on a picnic. If it is cloudy, one will have to take a raincoat or an umbrella with him when he is leaving the house. Whatever the weather may be, one tends to adjust his activities to it accordingly.

In order to know what the weather will be, special people are hired to provide this information. They collect data, analyse them and predict the weather of the coming day. This information, which is announced on the radio or on TV, is usually very accurate. Thanks to the efforts of those professionals, we can always know the weather in advance and prepare for it.

(3) Weather Forecasts

Weather forecasting is very important in modern life. For

---

① 由于

example, it helps farmers to plan their work well. In addition, planes fly safely only when the weather has been forecast accurately. We will surely meet many inconveniences in daily life without weather forecasting.

However, even a slight mistake will sometimes lead to serious destruction. Because many plans are based on weather, a wrong prediction on weather may make them *come to nothing*①. Even worse, great losses may occur. For example, an unexpected storm may cause great floods, ruining an area thoroughly.

Therefore, we should forecast as accurately as possible. In some areas, however, the weather is very changeable and facilities for predicting weather are simple. In spite of these difficulties, we should try our best to avoid any possible losses.

---

① 得不到结果；落空

No.59 Tree planting
植树造林

(1) Preservation of Forests

China's loss of forests has been enormous, perhaps greater than anywhere else in the world. Probably the forests were first *burned off*① because they gave protection to enemies and to dangerous wild animals. Then the constant cutting for fuel and *timber*② kept them from growing up again and further reduced the large forests which remained. As a consequence, bare hills are *cut into*③ by the water that runs down them, especially where very heavy rains come after a long dry season. Trees have difficulty in getting started, even when people plant and protect them. The barer the hills become, the drier the seasons are. The drier the seasons are, the more the water cuts away the topsoil of hills when rain comes. Then people suffer increasingly from droughts, as the soil is washed away or covered up with sand. Therefore, the preservation of forests means the preservation of plains and of *well distributed*④ rainfall. *Reforestation*⑤ (or the planting again of lost forests) will improve China's climate and soil, and will increase her streams and wood supply.

---

① 烧掉
② 木材
③ 侵蚀
④ 分布均匀的
⑤ 重新植林

(2) Trees and Man

Trees help man in some important ways. They provide us with wood and other products; they give us shade; and they help to prevent droughts and floods and to protect our *ecological distribution*①.

In many parts of the world, however, people have not realized that trees are so useful. In their eagerness to make quick profit from trees, they have cut them down in large numbers but they are too careless to plant or look after new trees. As a result, the rain easily carries away the rich topsoil and turns the farming land into desert.

In order to protect out limited farming land and improve our environment, we should plant more trees. Trees not only make the earth a more pleasant place to live in but also help man to produce more food to feed the increasing population. So, we need more trees and should plant more trees.

(3) Forest

Forests are valuable wealth of mankind. Ever since human society began to *evolve*②, forests have been making contribution to the building of the *edifice*③ of civilization. Forests provide timber that can be put to various usages. In addition, as nature's organic part, forests are essential to keep ecologic balance.

However, the coverage of the world's forests is rapidly diminishing. On the one hand, this is attributed to the

---

① 生态分布
② 发展
③ 大厦

*denudation*① and disastrous forest fires. On the other, industrial pollution, poverty and population explosion also account for it.

Mankind is paying dear for the damage done to forests. The loss of forests has upset the balance of nature. Weather has become *erratic*②. Some places are subject to floods, while others are frequented by droughts. There is soil erosion. Masses of land are reduced to sands. Many animal species are *on the verge of*③ extinction.

It is time for mankind to take steps to remedy the damage. For a better environment, for a continuous supply of timber, also for our offspring, we should spare no effort to protect forest resources, to plant more trees, and to *afforest*④ every mountain and hill. Let greenness reign over the world.

(4) Make Our Cities Greener

With the rapid growth of modern cities, urban *vegetation*⑤ has been greatly reduced. For example, trees have been cut down to *make room*⑥ for *new apartment blocks*⑦. For another example, public gardens and grass land have been replaced by *parking lots*⑧. As a result, cities are no longer as green as before.

But vegetation is essential to people's living in the city. Green plants provide fresh air and can reduce air pollution. Besides, trees and flowers can add beauty and charm to the outlook of a city. Finally, by growing plants in the city, we can

---

① 滥伐
② 反复无常的
③ 濒于
④ 造林于
⑤ (总称)植物;草木
⑥ 腾地方
⑦ 新住宅区
⑧ 停车场

improve the local climate. In short, without enough vegetation, life in the city will be unbearable.

　　Therefore, special care must be taken to ensure a sufficient amount of vegetation in the city. For example, in the planning of urban development, the *municipal authorities*① should *give full consideration to*② the planting of trees, and the *cultivation of lawns*③. The citizens, too, should be encouraged to grow flowers and other plants in gardens, on balconies, or even on roofs. Surely, if people in *all walks of life*④ pay enough attention to the problem of vegetation, our life in the city will be more enjoyable.

① 市政当局
② 充分考虑
③ 栽培草坪
④ 各行各业

No.60 Animals
动物

(1) Pets

A pet is an animal kept by a person as a companion. Many people, lonely old ladies in particular, like to keep a cat, a dog or other animals. They treat these animals as old friends and even as members of the family.

Pets are *affectionate*①. They are obedient to their masters. They *appreciate*② the care given them and seem to know how to express their thanks. Whatever happens, they always remain loyal to their masters. Although they sometimes *play mischief*③, they are innocent and even childish. This makes them all the more lovely. In addition, trained pets are very helpful.

As urban buildings keep us away from nature, more and more people like to enjoy the company of *tame*④ animals. In our neighbourhood, birds have recently become a favourite. We can often hear them singing. Their songs remind us that we should take more *tender*⑤ care of nature.

---

① 充满深情的;富有情感的
② (充分)领会;体会
③ 淘气;捣蛋
④ 驯服的
⑤ 温柔的;体贴的

(2) The Sheep

The sheep with its long *fleecy*① coat, its short, graceful legs, its pitiful and tender expression, is a much-admired animal. A flock of sheep grazing on a hillside makes a pretty picture. They are very fond of short, sweet *herbage*②, and the hilly slopes are generally well suited to their wants. Sheep are not strong animals. They cannot endure much exposure to the weather. If compelled to walk long distances, they become *fatigued*③; if much pressed, they will fall down exhausted. They are timid creatures.

The sheep is a very valuable animal, for, alive or dead, it is profitable. It *furnishes*④ us with both food and clothing. Its wool is manufactured into *garments*⑤ of various kinds. The value of woollen clothing, especially during the winter months, is known to all.

(3) The Dog

Of all tame animals, the dog holds the first place in our affections. He is noted for its faithfulness. This quality shows itself best under the most *trying*⑥ circumstances. Whether his master is poor or rich, in good health or sickness, young or old, beautiful or ugly, the dog is the same true, faithful, and loving friend.

---

① 羊毛的
② 草本植物
③ 疲劳的
④ 提供
⑤ 衣服
⑥ 难处的;艰难的

Sometimes it does its duty in tending sheep, sometimes in watching our property, and sometimes in carefully keeping guard over young children and aged persons. In some places, dogs are to be seen drawing *sledges*① on the snow. In *Switzerland*②, dogs are trained to *roam*③ over mountains in search of travellers who have been lost in the snow.

Whether in the finest *mansion*④ or the poorest cottage, receiving the greatest consideration or being treated harshly, this animal is to be found always anxious to please his master, and to prove his faithfulness.

(4) The Tiger

The tiger is very much like the wild-cat in appearance; in fact, our domestic pet is sometimes called a *miniature*⑤ tiger. Its length, from the tip of the tail to the nose, is about twelve feet. Its fur is of an orange colour *stripped with black*⑥, and thus it is not easily distinguished from the trunks of the trees among which it has its *haunts*⑦. Its paws are soft and *padded*⑧, so that it can move about with little noise. The tiger is chiefly found in India and other countries in the south of Asia. It *frequents*⑨ the neighbourhood of springs where other animals come to drink. It *prowls*⑩ about in the night-time, and for this its eyes are

---

① 雪橇
② 瑞士
③ 漫游
④ 大厦；宅第
⑤ 小型的
⑥ 此处意为"带有黑色条纹"
⑦ （动物的）生息地
⑧ 此处意为"长着爪垫"
⑨ 常去
⑩ （野兽等）四处觅食

extremely well adapted. Its claws are strong and sharp, and its strength is very great. It has been known to drag a buffalo from a *quagmire*①, which several men are unable to do.

(5) The King of Beasts

Far away on the great plains of Africa and Asia lives the lion, the king of beasts. He is not called king because he is wise, but because he is strong. With one stroke of his paw he can kill a deer, and he can carry off a young zebra almost as easily as a cat carries mouse.

Lions belong to the cat family. In many ways they are like the cats we see everyday. They have sharp claws hidden under soft *cushions*②. They make no noise when they walk. They have sharp teeth with which they tear their food to pieces. They like to sleep through the day and to hunt at night. A lion will lie for hours by a spring or river, waiting for the deer to come to drink in the same way that a cat watches over a hole of the mouse till the mouse comes out.

Although they seldom leave their *dens*③ before evening, yet when they are hungry, they may even be found in the day time roaring over the plains. There, large *herds of*④ *wild asses*⑤ and *antelopes*⑥ *go trooping*⑦ along. They *scent*⑧ a lion at a great distance; and when they hear his voice, they *scour*⑨ away over the

---

① 泥潭
② 垫子;此处指"爪垫"
③ 兽穴
④ 成群的
⑤ 野驴
⑥ 羚羊
⑦ 成群结队地走
⑧ 嗅出
⑨ 急速穿过

desert like the wind.

(6) Camels in the Desert

Camels are still ridden by the people of the desert today. They are well suited for carrying people and heavy burdens for long distances in hot, dry places because they can go for a long time without water. As a result of their thick hooves, camels can easily walk on the hot sand. Finally, camels can live in the desert because they are able to find even the smallest plant to eat hidden in the desert soil.

(7) Birds

Early in the morning in spring, when the sun has just risen and the dew is yet on the grass and leaves, the sweet *melodies*① of birds may be heard in the forest. After they have had enough of singing and chattering, they go out in different directions in search of food, and, having got some they return to their nest to feed their *fledglings*②. All day long they *dart*③ here and there like arrows from the bow. Towards evening, when the sun is gradually sinking in the west, they return to the forest in flocks. Then they start their noisy chattering again. But very soon they enter their nests to *roost*④ for the night, and then silence *reigns*⑤ in the forest. Such is the way birds work and rest everyday.

---

① 悦耳的声音
② 刚会飞的小鸟
③ 急速地飞
④ 憩息,过夜
⑤ 支配;占优势

(8) Animal Protection

The media have exposed several cases of animal *abuse*[①] recently. A youngster attempted to relieve his tension by mistreating adopted dogs. A lady was videoed in the Internet *trampling*[②] on a cat to death with a high heel. From my viewpoint, animal protection is of vital importance at present.

First of all, humans could go no further without co-existing with various kinds of animals. The harmonious co-existence makes a balanced eco-system possible. Were there no protection of animals, insects would devour farmers' crops and harvests. Moreover, it is animals that *render*[③] more colors to humans' life. Our daily life is delighted by birds' melodious songs and pets' lovely behavior. Children are amused and entertained by various species *conserved*[④] in zoos.

All in all, it is the duty of the general public to protect animals. Only in this way can we create a sustainable world and lead a colorful life.

① 虐待
② 踩,踏
③ 着色
④ 保存,保护

No.61 | Flowers
  花卉

（1）Flowers（Ⅰ）

There are so many varieties of flowers—both wild and cultivated—that it would be difficult to *enumerate*① them. Many flowers are the same in structure, but they differ in shape, size, and *hue*②. Some grow singly; others, *in clusters*③.

Flowers are to be found everywhere, even in hot deserts and the *arctic region*④, where they bloom according to season. The *tropical regions*⑤ are rich in flowers and so are the *temperate regions*⑥.

Flowers beautify the earth by adding colour to landscapes; they *adorn*⑦ our parks and gardens; they brighten our homes, and, in many ways, contribute to our happiness and pleasure.

No city is beautiful without parks and flower gardens; no home can look cheerful without flowers. A garden *in full bloom*⑧ is one of the precious sights in the world. In a single flower is to be found more beauty and *delicacy*⑨ than in the most beautiful

① 计数
② 颜色；色彩
③ 一簇簇；一群群
④ 北极地区
⑤ 热带地区
⑥ 温带地区
⑦ 装饰
⑧ （盛）开着花
⑨ 精美；雅致

and delicate works of man.

Flowers provide food for butterflies, bees, and other insects. They also supply us with *fragrant*① and *seductive perfumes*②. Almost everyone, young or old, rich or poor, civilized or savage, loves flowers. The love of flowers is inborn in all human beings. We decorate our *shrines*③ with flowers. We use flowers at weddings and at funerals. A gift of flowers is always acceptable.

(2) Flowers(Ⅱ)

When spring comes, the earth is bright with flowers. The small yellow flowers are *peeping*④ through the fence and sometimes nodding their heads to welcome the passers-by. The clustering *plum blossoms*⑤ are smiling on the green branches as if a group of innocent girls were smiling at their guests. The willow flowers are dancing confusedly with their long soft branches. The roses are blushing *in the presence of*⑥ the strangers. And at the same time the butterflies and bees are wishing to spend all their time *in the flowers' company*⑦.

When the north wind begins to blow, flowers *wither*⑧. Later on, only bare branches remain standing lonely against the north wind. Their smiles disappear; their blushing faces disappear; and their *nimble*⑨ bodies disappear. What remains is only ugliness. The butterflies and the bees make no appearance.

---

① 芳香的
② 诱人的香料
③ 圣祠
④ 窥视
⑤ 梅花
⑥ 在……面前
⑦ 在花的陪伴下
⑧ 凋谢
⑨ 灵活的

(3) Flowers(Ⅲ)

Flowers are of countless forms and colours. They grow most *abundantly*① in warm and tropical climates, for *on account of*② their delicate structure, they cannot endure severe cold. Nearly all kinds of flowers possess a fragrance which is different in each kind, and *serves*③ in one way to *distinguish*④ them.

In our country, each of the seasons has its own particular flowers, some being well-known to everyone. Thus, in spring we have the *violet*⑤, the *primrose*⑥, and the *lily*⑦, while a few roses appear in the hot-houses. In summer, our fields and gardens are gay with all kinds.

Flowers are of great significance to us. They fill the air with their agreeable *odours*⑧, they adorn the earth and delight us by their beauty; they possess in a remarkable degree the power of *gladdening*⑨ our hearts, and brightening our spirits.

How often do we see the sick cheered and *enlivened*⑩ by the sight of a few simple flowers, and by the sweet fragrance which they give forth!

A little flower garden in front of a cottage, or before a *parlour*⑪ window, adds a beauty and a pleasure to the home.

---

① 丰富地
② 由于……的(原因)
③ 适用;有用
④ 区别;辨别
⑤ 紫罗兰
⑥ 报春花
⑦ 百合花
⑧ 气味;香气
⑨ 使高兴;使快乐
⑩ 使有生气的;使快活
⑪ 起居室

No.62 Natural Produce
物产

(1) Coal

Coal is one of the commonest things that people see and use daily. But comparatively few know what it is composed of, where it is obtained, and how it is mined.

Though coal looks like stone or metal, it is really a kind of *non-metallic*① substance composed of vast forests that have remained underground for thousands of years. *On account of*② the pressure of the layers of earth and stone, these *blocks*③ of wood became more and more solid and decreased in size little by little, until they turned into a blackish hard substance which we call coal.

There are two kinds of coal, *anthracite*④ and *bitumen*⑤. The former, being hard and capable of lasting for a long time, is chiefly used for cooking and household purposes. The latter is required in trains, steamers, steam-engines, and other machines, as it can give a very strong fire.

On the whole, coal is good and cheap fuel, and industry depends largely upon it. If there were no coal people would

---

① 非金属的
② 因为;由于
③ 接连在一起的一片一片
④ 无烟煤
⑤ 沥青煤;烟煤

experience a very great difficulty.

(2) Paper and Its Uses

Paper is one of the most important products ever invented by man. The invention of paper meant that more people could be educated because more books could be printed and distributed. Together with the printing press, paper provided an extremely important way to communicate knowledge.

Paper, like many other things that we use today, was first made in China. In Egypt and the West, paper was not very commonly used before the year 1400. The Egyptians wrote on *papyrus*①. Europeans used *parchment*② for many hundreds of years.

When we mention paper, we think of newspapers, books, letters, envelopes, and writing paper. But it has many other uses. Only half of the paper that is made is used for books and newspapers, etc. People have made paper boats, but they have not yet made paper airplanes or cars. Just wait, they probably will.

(3) Cotton

Cotton is the soft *down*③ fibre contained in the *pod*④ of the cotton plant. Of this plant there are three principal kinds, the smallest of which is the most important. It is a shrub about two feet in height, with dark green leaves and a *pale*⑤ yellow flower.

---

① （古埃及人用的）莎草纸
② 羊皮纸
③ 绒毛；柔毛（名词）
④ 荚
⑤ 淡的

The flower is followed by a pod about the size of a walnut, filled with the cotton, mixed with small seeds. It is grown chiefly in India, China, some parts of Africa, and the United States. While the plant is growing, it is carefully *weeded*① and hoed.

A cotton field presents a very beautiful appearance, especially after the pods have become ripe and burst, showing the white soft *mass*② inside. This is gathered by farmers, and placed in bags hanging from their necks. It is then dried, and the seeds are taken out with great care.

The raw cotton comes over to cotton mills packed in *bales*③. After going through the different processes of *carding*④ and *spinning*①, it is woven into *calico*②, *muslin*③, *velvet*④ etc.

(4) Sugar

Sugar is very extensively used. Every *grocer*⑤ sells large quantities, and there is scarcely a home in which it does not find a place, for sweetening *beverages*⑥, and for other food purposes.

But do you know how sugar is made? Now let me tell you how it is made.

Most sugar is obtained from the sugar-cane. When ripe, the sugar-canes are cut and tied in bundles. They are carried to the

---

① 除草
② 棉团
③ 大包；大捆
④ （用梳棉机等）梳理
① 纺
② 白布
③ 平纹细布
④ 天鹅绒；丝绒
⑤ 食品商
⑥ 饮料

mill to be *crushed*① by means of heavy *rollers*②, which cause the juice to *run-out*③. A *cistern*④ is placed below to receive the juice. When this process is completed, the liquid is boiled, and all the impurities are *skimmed off*⑤ as they rise to the top. The remaining liquid is then poured into pans and allowed to cool. When cool, it *assumes*⑥ the form of *grains*⑦, and is known as raw sugar. It is next placed in *hogsheads*⑧, which have a number of holes in them through which a quantity of juice again *oozes*⑨. This juice is what we call *molasses*⑩. Raw sugar has to be purified still further before it becomes white sugar. The purification is done by means of lime and charcoal.

(5) Tea

Tea drinking *dates back to*⑪ ancient China and has spread over the world. Tea has greatly influenced the world culture. In Japan, for example, people have developed a special tea drinking *ritual*⑫, which is thought of as *a necessary means of cultivating character*⑬.

China grows several kinds of world-famous tea on account of its unique climate. The Chinese use different ways to treat and

---

① 压碎
② 滚轧机
③ 流出
④ (本文指接汁用的)槽,池
⑤ 撇去(浮渣等)
⑥ 呈(某种形式)
⑦ 晶粒;细粒
⑧ (容量为63—140美制加仑的)大桶
⑨ 渗出;分泌出
⑩ 糖蜜;糖浆
⑪ 起始于
⑫ 仪式
⑬ 修身养性的必要手段

process tea, making it into black tea, green tea, *scented tea*① and the like.

　　While the way of making or drinking tea differs from people to people, tea drinking has become part of their life. In China there are teahouses where people talk or play chess over a cup of tea. To receive a guest at home, the host brings him a cup of tea. People drink tea to refresh the mind and get rid of fatigue. Tea consists of *nutritious*② elements. Those who often drink tea are less *vulnerable*③ to heart and blood diseases.

(6) Silk

　　Do you ever think, when you put on your coats and *gowns*④, that the *gown material*⑤, beautiful silk, is made by a *worm*⑥? The worms are *hatched*⑦ in well-warmed rooms from the tiny eggs that looked like little grey seeds or *beads*⑧, laid by the female *silk-moth*⑨. In central and southern China they are fed on the *mulberry leaf*⑩ but in northern China on a kind of *oak*⑪.

　　When the worms are hatched they are *ravenous*⑫ little creatures, and immediately begin to *devour*⑬ the food provided for

---

① 花茶
② 有营养的
③ 易受伤的;脆弱的
④ 长服;宽松的长外衣
⑤ 外衣衣料
⑥ 虫;蠕虫(本文指"蚕",意同 silk worm)
⑦ 孵
⑧ 小珠子;有孔小珠
⑨ 蚕蛾
⑩ 桑叶
⑪ 栎树
⑫ 贪婪的
⑬ 狼吞虎咽地吃

物产
Natural Produce No.62

them. They grow very rapidly, and constantly *cast*① their coats. But after thirty-two days, when they are about two inches long and as thick as a man's little finger, they grow *drowsy*② and begin to spin the most beautiful cradles for themselves. The whole body is covered with a thick web of silk, called a *cocoon*③. Inside this, if left alone, the worm would change into a beautiful moth, and then bite its way out. The silkworm raisers, however, destroy the worms by heating the cocoons over a slow fire.

  Then the cocoons are thrown into boiling water, and women and girls unwind the delicate threads from which silk is made.

① 脱落
② 昏昏欲睡的
③ 茧

No.63 | Beautiful Sights 日月星辰

(1) Sunrise on the Western Hills

One early summer morning, there was a sunrise of wonderful sight. At first, the sun was wrapped by the clouds which soon gave way, so that the sun was visible just above the hills and showed warmly upon the earth. It looked like a golden wheel and gradually became smaller and smaller like a fiery ball when it rose higher and higher. The narrow streams on the hills were turned by the reflection of the sunlight into a beaming, yellow colour. Groups of birds flew out of their nests and made a confused, *shrill*[①] noise. The insects such as bees and butterflies came out and *darted*[②] among the beautiful, fragrant flowers. The *cicadas*[③] began to sing on the trees. The crows of farmers' cocks were heard. Oh, what a nice sight it is!

(2) The Sun

The sun seems as round as the earth on which we live. It rises in the morning and shines in the day. It gives vital power to every living thing that grows on the earth. Men, too, could not be happy unless it should appear and shine brightly. At twilight

---

① 尖声的
② 飞奔;此处意为"飞舞,上下翻飞"
③ 蝉

in the morning when grass chills on the ground, leaves thrill on their branches, and birds impatiently *cuddle*① in their nests, the sun mysteriously makes its appearance in the east, tapping them gently with its warm fingers of light. Then birds, apparently in a happy *frame*② of mind, *hop*③ out of their *dwelling places*④, and sing beautiful songs as if to offer heartfelt thanks to the sun for the tender love it has shown to them. Grass and leaves stand in high spirits and look their best as if they were joyful to see their heavenly guardian once more after a lengthy gloomy night. Boys and girls willingly get up to go outdoors to play where birds are singing and the sun is shining.

Although the sun often *renders*⑤ our life delightful, yet it is less welcome in hot season. It puts forth so much heat that the skin of those who work outdoors is often *scorched*⑥. Some people, it is said, even have been *parched*⑦ to death. But, as a whole, the sun does us more good than harm.

(3) Sunset

When the sun begins to set behind the mountains, its long rays light up the green fields of wheat or rice with a golden glow. The clouds above the sky become golden and the mountains turn to a lovely purple colour.

As the sun sinks lower and lower, it looks like a great fiery ball. Its light fills the sky and changes the colour of the over-

---

① 紧贴着身子睡;蜷缩着身子睡
② 心情;精神状态
③ （鸟等）跳跃
④ 住处;此处指"鸟的栖息地"
⑤ 使得
⑥ 烤
⑦ 烘;烤

hanging clouds from golden to red, glowing like a sea of red fire.

Then, as the fiery ball of the sun is gone altogether, the red colour of the clouds begins to fade until all the clouds are grey. The mountains show their black silhouettes① clearly cut against the pale sky, where the evening stars take the place of the sun and shine brightly.

(4) The Rising of the Moon

The full moon, which is bright without compare, is seen rising gradually in the east. Nothing is heard except the feeble sound of the long cry of cicadas and the murmur of streams. The moon, the size of a silver dish, hangs quietly in the evening sky, which is *sparsely*② dotted with some stars and looks like the evening gown on the back of a beautiful woman and irregularly *studded*③ with some gems.

The newly-risen moon is as white as *quick-silver*④, and sheds its light on all, so that the big black shadows of pillars and persons are thrown on the ground in the western direction. The hills, the fields, the trees, and the houses are all seen but dimly, as if they were seen by one who has just awaked from a sound sleep and sees all things as in a dream.

(5) The Moon

I love the moon. I love her round cheeks, her clean face, and her graceful manners. In the cloudless blue sky, how beautiful, mysterious, and charming the moon seems in the world it reigns

---

① 侧影；形状
② 稀疏地
③ 散布；点缀
④ 水银

over.

In the world flooded with moonlight, the dazzling sunrays are no more, so a poetic feeling arises and a softness pervades the atmosphere. At this time, a breeze often accompanies the silvery light of the moon and gives the world a peculiar appearance and the people a peculiar feeling. The air is *suffused*① with a sweet scent, and the ugliness and *squalor*② of the daytime have disappeared. With her soft silvery light, the moon covers all ugly and hideous things and comforts the distressed and wretched humanity. Any man who climbs to the top of a high hill will find the *rugged*③ *crags*④ transformed into pieces of pale stone, and the earth itself an *enchanted*⑤ land. Being *shrouded*⑥ in a misty gray, the large deep blue patches of the wood look like mysterious and soft young grass, large vegetable gardens look like boundless and flat roads, the houses of various sizes and heights look like lovely toys for children. If you sing a song, your voice will reach the clouds. If you give a low sigh, your tone of sadness will arouse men in their sleep. If you sing a *lullaby*⑦, its charms will put the whole nightless city to sleep.

(6) Stars

I love a moonlit night. But I also love a starlit night. When I was at my native place, I loved to see the numerous stars in the sky as I enjoyed the cool evenings in June and July. Now when I

---

① 充满;弥漫于
② 肮脏
③ 不平的;多岩的
④ 岩
⑤ 使心醉;迷人
⑥ 覆盖;掩蔽
⑦ 摇篮曲

look at the starlit night, I forget all and feel as if I were in my mother's arms again:

In my native place, my house had a backdoor. As soon as it was opened in the evening a peculiar feeling rose in me. It was a silent night, with a vegetable garden below and a star-covered sky above. To the naked eye, the stars looked tiny, but they made me feel their light to be *omnipresent*①. As I was then reading some books on astronomy, I could *identify*② some stars so that they became my friends and seemed to be talking to me.

(7) Sunrise

On a chilling autumn morning, my friends and I drove to the seaside to enjoy the amazing sunrise. When we reached there, the dark heavenly curtain had rolled up and it was bright enough for us to see distant islands *dotting*③ here and there on the sea. Yet, the eastern horizon was still completely *veiled*④ with a thick blanket of impenetrable mist.

Suddenly *streaks*⑤ of faint red hue were radiating across the sky. We were very much excited in spite of the bitter coldness attacking us. We stood motionlessly, with our eyes fixing at the far, far end of the sea.

The redness of the streaks intensified. All of a sudden, some mysterious clouds *wriggled*⑥ across the horizon, dividing heaven from sea. The mist, the clouds, the sea and the sky were *tinged*⑦

---

① 无所不在的
② 识别
③ 点缀,星罗棋布于
④ 以面纱遮掩、隐蔽
⑤ 条文
⑥ 蜿蜒起伏于
⑦ 着色

to bright red as if they were in a sea of flames.

Just at this moment, out from the misty sea and up from the brightening far east rose the sun. It was so red and yet so tender that we could gaze at it with naked eyes, and we were amazed by the fantastic wonder nature presented.

(8) A Moonlit Night

Night came. The lovely *crescent*① moon hung high up in the sky, throwing its silvery light on the earth. Long shadows of trees lay on the ground. The birds had gone back into their nests. A gentle breeze was *rustling*② the leaves.

The moonlight shone through the *clusters*③ of tiny leaves and dotted the ground in the woods with small faint spots. On the winding path were walking a couple of lovers. He looked back repeatedly at her. She held up her eyes and glanced at him, *smiling a graceful and bashful smile*④. They exchanged remarks in a tone full of tender feelings. When they came to the end of the woods, they began to walk shoulder to shoulder; Soon their hands met and clasped each other. Slowly they disappeared in the thin night mist.

What a silent and pleasant night! What sweet lovers!

---

① 弦月状之物
② 使沙沙作响
③ 簇
④ 脸上露出优雅的羞答答的微笑

No.64 | Changes of the Weather
风云雨雪

(1) Listening to the Wind

The force of circumstance has recently given me a liking for listening to the wind. During the recent years I have lived in the country near the sea. As there are no hills in the fields, the sea wind is free to sing round my house. The song continues day and night. Therefore I have got a liking for listening to the wind—as a matter of fact, I simply have to listen.

I feel that the music of the wind is grand, even as grand as the *war-cry*① on the battle-field. Sometimes when I am tired, I light a cigarette, *loll*② on the window, enjoying myself by listening to the wind; all my sad and troublesome thoughts are thus *banished*③: such is the *consolation*④ rendered by the wind.

Having got this liking, I wish that the music of wind would never cease; I need the wind as much as I need food.

(2) Clouds

As we look up into the sky, we see what we call clouds. Clouds, which are the condensation of water-vapour, are grey in

---

① 作战时的呐喊
② 懒洋洋地倚靠
③ 消除(顾虑,恐惧等)
④ 安慰

colour. Nothing in nature is so variable as clouds, especially in autumn, when they are not only changing in colour and shape, but also are moving and flowing all the time like the *ripples*① of the stream.

Sometimes clouds are *tinged with*② different colours and will reflect a beautiful rainbow due to the bright light of the sun which strikes on the raindrops in front of them.

Sometimes clouds will gather together in the shape of a fish's *scales*③ to form a picture of a *mackerel sky*④. Before rain comes we can see the threatening clouds that cover the whole sky and then the raindrops come.

Very often at the end of a rainstorm, the *banked-up*⑤ *remnants*⑥ of the retreating rain clouds are sights to see. Clouds are a wonderful scene especially when the sun comes out immediately after a rainfall.

Clouds will also do good to the people who have sunshine nearly all the time. To sum up, clouds afford us beautiful scenery as well as a kind of shelter.

(3) Summer Clouds

Summer clouds are beautiful in the morning, in the afternoon, in the evening, and in the moonlight.

Every morning, as soon as I open the window, light clouds, which have just taken off their sleeping clothes, greet the eyes.

---

① 涟漪;细浪
② 着色于;染……色
③ 鱼鳞
④ (气象)鱼鳞天
⑤ 堆积
⑥ 残余

The sun lies in their bosom, and they change colours and *chase*① one another. Gradually they move towards the middle of the sky and stay there.

In the afternoon, all the white clouds become like dogs and other animals chasing and fighting and *evading*② each other, as if a whole *menagerie*③ in the sky had been *let loose*④.

But in a moment all the animals change to waves. They are no longer lions, tigers, and *leopards*⑤ but *white-crested waves*⑥, of which one rises as another falls.

Now a flower show is held in the sky; various flowers of fantastic forms are exhibited, and, as they are divine flowers, they keep changing.

(4) A Thunder Storm

Grey clouds gathered fast in the sky. The sky became black. The gathering clouds became thicker and blacker as they spread over our heads. It was *stuffy*⑦.

There came a breeze, then a *gust*⑧ of wind. The wind became stronger and stronger. It *rattled*⑨ the windows, *turned up*⑩ the fallen leaves, bent down the trees. Distant rumbling thunder was heard and came nearer and nearer. Large drops of rain began to fall. Flashes of lightening lit up the sky. Thunder

---

① 追逐
② 躲避
③ (马戏团中)囚在笼中的兽群
④ 释放;放出
⑤ 豹
⑥ 白色的浪花
⑦ 闷热的
⑧ 突然一阵
⑨ 使格格作响
⑩ 吹起

roared overhead. Then the rain poured down.

The violence of the rain quickly increased. The darkness and the storm increased. *Thunder burst with a terrific crash.* [1] Rain poured down like sheets of water. Strong wind broke the trees. It *blew and rained*[2], blew and rained and blew and rained.

(5) A Shower

The sun moving a little to the west was beating down mercilessly on everything. The ground felt *scorching*[3] and the still air breathed stuffy. After lunch, dozens of people gathered in the shade of the huge tree, some chatting, some *dozing off*[4]. Even ducks seemed lazy in this hot weather. Instead of swimming in the pool, they *nestled*[5] here, their mouths wide open.

Suddenly a wind came from the southwest. And we noticed dark clouds gathering over the hills in the distance. As soon as we saw a sheet of rain there, the sun disappeared in the gloomy sky, lightning flashed and thunder exploded. Before we could run to our homes nearby, *torrents of rain*[6] were pouring down on us, on everything. A world of sunshine had become a world of *splashing*[7] water. Now the air felt cool.

The shower stopped just as suddenly as it had started. The sun shone burning hot again. Would another shower come later in the afternoon? Everybody was looking forward to it.

---

① 炸雷发出撕裂声。
② 风雨交加
③ 灼热的
④ 打瞌睡
⑤ 舒适地安卧
⑥ 倾盆大雨;骤雨
⑦ 溅泼着落下

(6) Snow

Snow falls at the level of the sea in all *temperate*① regions, and on the tops of high mountains it never melts. In the *northern hemisphere*② it falls most abundantly in the months of December and January.

The atmosphere always contains moisture, and if the temperature falls suddenly below the freezing-point, this moisture is condensed and falls in the form of snow. Its approach is generally known by the dull gray colour of the skies and the darkening of the air. When the moisture of the air is thus frozen, it always assumes a sexangular shape; most frequently there are six little arms reaching out from the same centre. These little arms are often broken off, or several flakes falling together become irregular in their shape; but when one of them which has fallen is examined under a microscope, it has a beautiful appearance, and no two are exactly alike.

After the snow has fallen, it lies like a great white sheet *strewn*③ over everything; and it thus protects vegetation from the severe cold, for snow is an insulator. On the tops of mountains it collects to such an extent as to push itself down by its own weight into the valleys below. In some places it comes down with such terrible and fast force as to sweep everything before it and cause great damage. This is called *avalanche*④. But elsewhere, it is pushed down very slowly, and winds along like a great river of snow and ice. This is called a glacier.

---

① (气候等)温和的
② 北半球
③ 铺盖,点缀;动词 strew 的过去分词
④ 雪崩

(7) A Snowfall

It was bitterly cold and a *cutting northeast wind*① had whistled for some time before *a few straggling snowflakes slanted across the wind*②. Then, with the wind *dying out*③, they *whirled down*④ noiselessly, shutting out distant objects from sight. The snow fell on trees, on hills, on roofs and by the river and the pond. The flakes crept into the *lintels*⑤ of the doors, into the corners of the windows and into every chink of the walls. Swiftly, silently, they covered the earth and infolded the dirt in the bosom of nature.

In the white stillness, through the hurrying snowflakes appeared a dustman, pulling an empty handcart. But promptly he was swallowed up by the whirling snow. After a while everything became white. It was a silvery world.

How beautiful the world was when it was snow-covered!

---

① 刺骨的东北风
② 几片雪花被风吹着歪歪斜斜地落下来
③ 渐渐变弱；减弱
④ 急旋着落下
⑤ （门窗的）过梁

No.65 Scenery of the Four Seasons
绚烂四季

(1) The Four Seasons

In a year there are four seasons: spring, summer, autumn, and winter.

In spring, the sun shines brightly in the blue sky. The warm winds blow gently. The snow and ice can no longer remain. The little streams again flow merrily on. The flowers show their pretty shapes by the wayside and in the gardens. The trees send out little buds and new leaves. Farmers begin to *till*[①] the soil and sow the seed. All nature is clothed in green colour and seems very attractive and lovely.

In summer, the sun shines blazingly and the heat is unbearable. But the days are very long and we can do much work. The thunder-storm will come often in *stuffy*[②] weather. All the sights are still fine. We have a long vacation in summer. We can go to many places to enjoy this pleasant season.

In autumn, the days gradually become shorter, and the nights longer. The mornings begin to be cold and the evenings are no longer warm. Farmers are reaping rice with scythes. It is the season for harvest. The leaves of the trees fall down. Most birds no longer sing, but *migrate*[③] to warmer regions. In the midautumn the silvery

---

① 耕种；耕作
② 闷热的
③ (候鸟等)定期移栖

moonlight becomes more delightful than ever.

In the last season of the year, the weather is extremely cold. The roofs are usually covered with frost in the early morning. Snow will come very often. Brooks and rivers will be frozen and the ground will be frozen hard too during the coldest period. All the insects sleep under the ground without eating. Nothing looks as fine as in the spring time.

(2) Spring

Spring begins on the new-year's day and lasts three months. It is a season of freshness and greenness. After the cold dreary winter months we are glad to see the leaves and to hear the merry birds. In the earlier part of spring east winds generally blow and are not at all pleasant. But when the gentle rains and the warm sunshine have caused the earth to become clothed with *verdure*[①], all is joy and gladness. The *hedgerows*[②] are then thickly covered with fresh green leaves. The grass of the fields becomes bright, and the common field flowers spring on every hand *in profusion*[③]. The birds fly about and sing cheerily. The sky is bright and is *in harmony with*[④] the earth. The days become longer and children play in the open air until they are quite tired out. Some children go into the fields and gather flowers which they make into *nosegays*[⑤] and *garlands*[⑥]. This is a very enjoyable way of spending spare time. If we wish to be happy, we must seek the beauties which abound on all sides, and in doing so

① 青绿；青葱的草木
② 栽成树篱的灌木
③ （鲜花）盛开
④ 与……协调一致的
⑤ 花束
⑥ 花环；花冠

we shall be made wiser, better, and happier.

(3) Spring Falls on Us

The globe never stops in its rotation. The time passes like the flowing of water. The bitterly cold winter, which we feared and endured, has gradually given way to spring.

The trees which were laid bare in winter have restored their flourishing branches. Instead of the cold wind, we feel the warm breeze blowing on our faces. The *angel*[①] of spring has brought with her glory and cheerfulness.

Spring makes its appearance in the little grass. We see that the little grass exposes its green colour — a sure sign that the weather will be warm soon. At the same time, the plants grow tall, the pretty flowers present their blossoms; the birds, like musicians, sing their melodious songs, and the butterflies, like colourful dancers, fly here and there. They are all happy. Spring is a time for us to be happy and to play.

(4) Summer

Summer begins with May and ends with July. The days gradually lengthen until near the end of June, when it is midsummer. The nights are very short, and sometimes very hot. The fields are now bright and green. The trees and *hedges*[②] are covered with *foliage*[③]. The corn and rice are of a considerable height, though not quite ripe. The fruit trees are laden with their yearly burden. Towards the close of the season the grass becomes so high that it is cut down, dried in the sun,

---

① 天使
② (矮树)树篱
③ (总称)叶子

and stored away for winter use. This is called "haymaking" and it is a very common sight in the country during the month of July. On a hot summer day, one is glad to leave the dry, dusty road, and to wander through the fields or woods which are enlivened by the songs of birds. To them no part of the year is so gladsome as this, and they show their happiness by their continual song. Now we *indulge in*① outdoor amusements of all kinds, and wherever there is a convenient place for the game, a group of boys is always to be found, in favourable weather, engaged in *cricket*②.

(5) A Pleasant Summer

In a pleasant summer the sunshine is very bright. The wind is very soft. The blue sky and the white clouds of various colours are very beautiful. The fresh air and transparent atmosphere are all but excellent. In such weather, our spirit is stirred up. We may either work or play.

Then the beautiful scenes present themselves to our eyes. The high mountains in the distance, the pure water in the nearby river, the green grass and the sweet flowers, the birds flying in the air, are all pleasing sights to the mind and the eye. A walk along a pond covered with fragrant *lily-flowers*③ or shadowed with various plants is also a very good pastime.

In spite of the hot climate in the day, a cool summer night is much to be enjoyed. The dazzling stars twinkle in the sky. The brilliant moon hangs herself among the trees. The delightful breeze blows lightly against our faces. The musical *cicada*④ sings merrily on the tree. What fun we may have!

---

① 沉溺于；纵情于
② 蟋蟀
③ 百合花
④ 蝉

(6) Autumn

Autumn is the third season of the year. The days in autumn are getting shorter and shorter, and the weather is getting cooler and cooler.

Only second to spring, autumn is a very pretty season. There is a touch of romance in the glorious *hues*① of falling leaves and the ripened colour of Nature! The fields are waving with yellow corn, and the trees and *hedges*② change their colour from a bright green to a *muddy*③ brown. The country is full of red and gold in the autumn. Even the sun seems to veil Nature with more glorious *lustre*④ in the autumn days.

There is a touch of sadness in autumn too. Towards the end of the season, the trees begin to lose their foliage, and the branches gradually become bare; all around, the ground is *strewed with*⑤ withered leaves. So autumn may be compared to old age. Autumn is the time for us to gather the fruits of our labour. It reminds us of the saying "*As a man sows, so he shall reap!*"⑥

(7) Winter

This season may be said to begin with November and to last for three months. The month of November is *notorious*⑦ for its

---

① 颜色；色彩
② （矮树）树篱
③ 土色的；泥土般的
④ 光泽；光辉
⑤ 点缀；铺盖
⑥ 种瓜得瓜，种豆得豆
⑦ 众所周知的

gloom and frequent fogs. The weather becomes colder and colder as the season advances until the end of the year; the days are very short, and in our country the sun is low down in the sky, while the nights are long and dark. East winds with their cutting cold *prevail*[①]; the temperature of the air is often below freezing point, and when this lasts for a few days, we have a hard *frost*[②], turning the lakes and ponds into great sheets of ice. Then, instead of rain, we have heavy snowfalls, covering the earth like a great white *mantle*[③]. Out in the country, the snow lies pure and white over the fields and hedges. The trees are now completely *stripped*[④] of their leaves, and they stand waving their great naked branches in the wind.

Though winter gives such a cold and cheerless appearance to everything, yet it is a season of great enjoyment, and all young people look forward to the New Year with eager expectation, especially if the weather is of such a nature as to permit them to indulge in skating, or in some amusement in the snow.

(8) My Favourite Month

June is the month that I like best. The weather in June is neither too hot nor too cold. The trees are green and there are flowers everywhere. The buds of May are in full blossom now and their fragrance fills the air. The birds are back from the south and sing happily all day. The colors of June are bright and gay. Everyone feels a sense of *renewal*[⑤]. Girls with their light summer clothes appear cheerful and graceful. Children are playing

---

① 流行;盛行
② 霜
③ 覆盖物
④ 剥去;剥光
⑤ 复活;梦醒;恢复

outdoors now and *anticipating*① the end of the school term. There is a general *feeling of release from*② care, and everyone is looking forward to the future with hope. Is it any wonder that June is my favourite month?

---

① 期待;盼望
② 从……中解脱的感觉

No.66 Sketches of Natural Scenes
山水的描写

(1) A Bay in the Moonlight

Seen from the inner part of the bay, the high lighted lamps on the ships look like stars; their shadows cast below look like snakes. The quiet hills in the moonlight look like a picture.

(2) A Bay

At the end of the narrow and fantastic gulf, all is fresh and green and lovely. The strong sea wind now suddenly stops, and the surface of the sea begins to assume a calm aspect. The warm air is filled with the fragrance of flowers. Cries of cicadas come ceaselessly from both banks, respond to each other, and cause the mountain to send back numberless echoes.

(3) A Calm Sea

The ever-changing views of the hills gradually disappear before our eyes. The green of the hills fades, and the rushes on the seashore assume a grey colour and look as if some *bluish*[①] plants grew among them. The wide *expanse*[②] of water is blue and

---

① 带蓝色的
② 浩瀚

extends to the distant horizon. In the sunshine there is a narrow red light. A long white series of foams runs along the seashore.

(4) A Pond

The water of the pond *trickles*[①] out of a hole, gathers on a *marsh*[②] in front of the hole, and then separates into several streams and flows into the heaps of fallen leaves. This is a natural pond, shaded by the surrounding trees and reflecting the sky in the middle. In the pond there grow rushes, and on its surface float round leaves of water chestnuts. Nothing is heard in the woods except the sweet, soft, and ceaseless sound of the spring. Sometimes some water insects stir about on the shore of the pond. Sometimes a *gold finch*[③] comes to drink water, being careful not to wet itself. Whenever a sound is made by the leaves, there is a small breeze ruffling the water.

(5) A Brook

In a valley surrounded by sparsely scattered hills, there flows a brook eastward, westward, and southward, thus forming many bays and sand banks, ponds and streams. Beside the brook there grow *entangled*[④] water weeds, fine and tall rushes, and groves of willow trees. The quiet water under the large lotus leaves and coarse water weeds shows many greenish and irregular patches.

---

① 淌,流出
② 洼地;沼泽
③ 金翅雀
④ 交缠的

(6) Lakes

The rising moon adds a silvery *tint*① to the purple sunset, and shows before them a trembling road, on both sides of which there lie dark and silent lakes. A blue forest appears in the distance as if in a fog. When we go up the mountain, thousands of similar glittering lakes and ponds shine from the other side of the forest, with a play of the bloody colour got from the sunset and silvery colour from the moon.

(7) A Moonlit Valley

Over their heads hangs a *precipice*②, which has been washed by the spring streams. At its top there is a group of rambling trees which are made bright by the moonlight and overhang the *chasm*③. The gentle slope on the side of the valley is covered with bushes. The valley itself is bright with moonlight, and looks like a vision seen by one half asleep or a dream dreamt by a tired man, being entirely *destitute of*④ signs of life. The steady *gurgle*⑤ of the streams enhances the lifelessness of the valley and conceals its melancholy silence.

(8) A Beautiful Precipice

The stone hill is naturally formed by the heaping of many rocks which keep down one another so heavily. The black and

---

① 色彩
② 悬崖；峭壁
③ 峡谷
④ 没有的
⑤ 汩汩地流

beautiful mountain tops join in the misty gorge and the path. Peeping through the gorge, we see precipices bathing in the soft sunshine, pink, purplish-white, and misty. When we pass through the gorge we see streams running down from high and striking the rocks.

(9) A Village in the Evening

The tiny village had an irregular road lined by small houses on either side. At the moment we arrived at it, the sun had set behind the bluish purple cliff, but a yellowish light *lingered*① in the cloudless sky. The village then was enveloped in the night. The rays of silvery light reflected as if to say good-bye. We simply *couldn't but be lost*② in this natural beauty, not knowing that we were being watched by a group of silent children. Though not a sound could be heard as we stepped down the stone-paved road towards the heart of the village, there were faces at every window, men in short sleeves standing outside their houses and old women peering from door-ways. Obviously, this small mountain village seldom had visitors at this hour.

(10) The Great Wall

The Great Wall is a rare construction and one of the wonders of the world. Besides, it is the only man-made structure that can be seen from the moon.

The Great Wall was originally constructed as a gigantic defensive project. Its beginning can be traced back to the 7th century B. C. In 221 B. C. the first emperor of a united China,

---

① 继续留存；留恋
② 完全沉浸

Qin Shi Huang, repaired it, making it stretch for about 10,000 Li.

The following dynasties from Han to Sui continued to strengthen and extend the Wall. And it was in the Ming Dynasty that the emperors ordered people to reconstruct and extend the Wall on a large scale. Between 1368 and 1600, the Wall underwent major repairs on 18 occasions.

By the Ming Dynasty period the Wall was 12,700 li long and stretched from the Yalu River in the east to *Jiayuguan*① in the west. More than 50 kilometers northwest of Beijing is a stretch of the Great Wall, typical of the Ming construction. This place is called *Badaling*②. The Wall there is high and solid, about 8.5 meters high and 5.7 meters broad at the base. The way along the top is wide enough to accomodate five or six horses walking abreast.

To fully appreciate its greatness, you must go and see it yourself. In China there is the saying, "*He who fails to reach the Great Wall is not a true man.*"③

(11) Mount Tai

Listed at the top of *the Five Sacred Mountains of China*④, Mount Tai, the Eastern Sacred Mountain in Shandong Province, has long been enjoying the reputation of "the first mountain under the heaven." Combining majesty, beauty, wonder, mystery and grandeur in one scene, and putting human, cultural legacy, mountain, water and wood in one picture, it seems to be an enormous natural museum of history and art.

---

① 嘉峪关
② 八达岭
③ 不到长城非好汉。
④ 五岳

For thousands of years, it has been the wish of most Chinese to climb this mount. Emperors came here *to offer sacrifices to heaven and earth*[①]; scholars came here to chant poems; men of letters came here to make inscriptions; religious believers came here to seek Gods' blessing. Nowadays, ordinary people come here to experience the pleasure of travel and they feel as if they were making a tour of fairyland.

---

① 封禅

No.67 | Sketches of Animals and Birds
飞禽走兽的描写

(1) Swallows

The swallows, with their steel-blue wings flooded with sunshine, fly round and round like *streaks of*① light, and bathe in the air of the sunlight.

(2) Ducks

Some of the ducks look to the left, some to the right, some up, and some down. All *quack*② in fear, as if some very strange phenomenon had occurred. They wag their tails and quack, and look this way and that in an inquiring manner, till they believe they have found what they were looking for. Then they crowd together quietly and clumsily.

(3) The Hens of a Farmyard

In the yard of the farmer's home the hens were roused from

---

① 一道道
② 嘎嘎地叫

sleep by the crow of the cocks and then peck about on the *dunghill*①. By a mud pit, the ducks trim their feathers. The cows come out of their pen and walk towards the sand slowly and awkwardly.

(4) Horses

The horse gallops along. There rise from under his feet clouds of dust mixed with snow. His feet glitter with the red light of the stars.

(5) A Lean Ox

We give the ox a great deal of fodder. He eats and *ruminates*① all day long. In spite of this, he is terribly lean. His *abdomen*② has a deep depression. His ribs are clearly visible. His shoulder-blades, his spine, his whole skeleton are brought into *relief*③ and look like a range of mountains.

(6) Dogs

The dog gets up, licks its belly and feet, gives some lazy snorts, and does some scratching and crawling. He walks towards the door of the house in a piteous manner, with his tail between his hind legs and his nose near the ground.

---

① 垃圾堆
① 反刍
② 腹部
③ 轮廓鲜明

(7) Sheep

Ten yards away from us, the grass land appears to be covered with something grey in colour and moving about, like the melting snow in spring. On coming nearer, however, we found it to be hundreds of sheep, which are sleeping in a confused crowd, so as to present a sheet of white in the night. Sometimes they *bleat*[①] piteously and bashfully.

(8) Cat

There is no human being in the room. There is only a cat *blinking*[②] and *purring*[③], and grinding her claws on a wicker chair near the window. On the floor, beside an overturned sculptured wooden frame, there lies a large ball of red *worsted*[④], which presents a sheet of bright colour because of the light of the setting sun.

(9) *Stork*[⑤]

That is a living and moving stork. Its little head is red. It is the same as the storks in pictures, with its long head, high back, and slender and long feet. Its body is entirely white except for a

---

① （羊）叫
② 眨眼睛
③ （猫）满足时呜呜地叫
④ 毛线
⑤ 鹤

black dot on the neck and the tail. Its back is so high that I have to stand on tiptoe and lift my hands to reach the same height.

(10) Sea-gull

A gull flies about hither and thither, with its two wings folded like an arrow, gives a sad cry, and drops behind a ship in the dark.

(11) Crows

As soon as it strikes four, the black crows which fly about in groups come to perch in a tree at the left of the villa, giving out a deafening noise. They move from one house-top to another as if they were *vying*[①] with each other. They cry very loudly and give rise to a black confusion among the grey and yellowish branches. This continues for a full hour.

(12) Eagle

An eagle flies over the fields gracefully, now and then coming to the ground, shaking its wings rapidly, and flapping its tail with them. It gives its body in a cylindrical form and *shoots up*[②] energetically, glittering in the great expanse of the sky.

---

① 争；竞争
② 迅速上升；此处指"迅速向上飞"

No.68　Sketches of Fish and Insects
鱼虫的描写

（1）Fish（Ⅰ）

On the surface of the water, there are wavelets about. A large *shoal*① of fish are swimming briskly against the current, close to the rocks, across the dark bottom, and across groups of seaweeds. They look like an endless lace meandering and fluttering freely.

（2）Fish（Ⅱ）

A number of fish move to and fro gayly in the shallow stream, now and then coming up to catch at the insects flying about over the water. A large fish swims under a tree near the shore, sending out white bubbles. Lightly going down, it gives rise to a faint circle on the surface of the water. The circle gradually enlarges itself till it disappears.

（3）A Butterfly

At this time there is a butterfly sitting on a *railing*② near us, spreading and fluttering its wings all the time. After sitting for sometime, it flies suddenly. It flies over the shaking ears of rice

---

① 鱼群
② 栏杆

and does not return till it has found its friends.

(4) Butterflies

Blue butterflies fly over and sit on the grass. Sometimes five or six sit on a single stalk, and fold their wings and go to sleep; the stalk bends a little under their weight.

(5) The Croak of Frogs

All the tiny insects in the water have wakened. The frogs *croak*[①] in a manner suggestive of anger. The toads send out, *intermittently*[②] and in different directions, their *metallic*[③] sounds, which I find short, monotonous, and melancholy.

---

① (蛙等的)呱呱地叫
② 断断续续地
③ 刺耳的

No.69 Sketches of Human Figures 各色人物的描写

（1）Myself

If you look at the picture of my class, you can easily *spot*① me from the group. In the middle stands a thin boy. He is half a head taller than the boys beside him. His pole-like figure makes a sharp contrast with the two *robust*② boys standing on his sides. That's no other than me.

Although I am not very athletic looking, it doesn't prevent me from being a sports fan. I like table tennis and basketball. It's taken for granted that for a boy of my stature I should be a born basketball player. For that matter, I'm envied by many of my playmates. Unfortunately, tall as I am, I'm no match for those short but *bulky*③ guys in body contact. Being aware of this vital drawback of mine I have to look for amusement in other fields, especially pop music. A collector of CDs, I find light music more appealing than those noisy raps. I enjoy listening to lyrical *soothing*④ songs in *solitude*⑤. That doesn't suggest that I don't like songs of quick tempo. Sometimes, after a day's hard

---

① 找出，辨认出
② 强健的
③ 粗壮的
④ 令人舒畅的
⑤ 独自一人

studying, I love to listen to some Disco music with the radio turned *at full blast*①.

By and large, I'm a person of many contrasts and one of few words, yet, behind this quiet and mediocre appearance, there is a heart of warmness.

(2) Grandma and Mother

I've never seen a better-looking woman than Grandma. I used to sit on the other side of the table watching her dress up in the mornings, admiring her graceful pose with wide-open eyes. She had long hair done in a knot, and her clothes were so well tailored that they shaped her figure perfectly. Her hair was dyed in black, so naturally done that no one noticed anything *artificial*② about it. Grandma told me that she dyed her hair with ashes from burned gourd before modern cosmetics were introduced into China. Grandma seemed to have lots of simple, inexpensive yet effective ways of staying young in appearance. I was amazed at her *resourcefulness*③ as well as her desire for beauty.

Whenever I saw grandma standing before a mirror, I couldn't help thinking of my poor *sloppy*④ mother. To tell the truth, mom is good-looking too though not as beautiful as grandma. Unmindful of her dress and appearance, she had her hair cut short, wore a *Lenin suit*⑤ that was popular in the 70's. I had never seen Mother standing before a mirror. People said jokingly that Mother looked even older than Grandma.

---

① 以最大的声量
② 人工的
③ 机敏
④ 衣着邋遢的
⑤ 列宁服(旧式女装)

Grandma and Mother are different in their appearance, but I love them both.

(3) My Father

When I was a little child, I always heard a ballad, "A child without mother is like a blade of grass." As a motherless child, I have never felt that way, because I have an extraordinary father who brings me a happy life with his abundant love.

For me, he is a mother-like father. He undertakes independently all the housework and the obligations of bringing me up. When I was in my primary school, because the school was very far from my home, everyday he sent me to school and fetched me back after the classes. For six years, he never failed! I'm not a spoiled child, and when I make mistakes father always has a serious and instructive talk with me; after that I will try all means to mend my way.

Although father is burdened with the heavy housework, he remains a *conscientious*① man at work. He is an outstanding professor in his university and enjoys a very good reputation. As the family has taken up a large part of his time, he has to *squeeze*② some other time for his job. Every time I wake up in *the small hours*③, I find the light in my father's study is still on!

Undoubtedly, I am the happiest child for I am blessed with the best father in the world.

(4) My Grandmother

My grandmother has always been my favourite person. She is

---

① 认真的, 尽责的
② 挤
③ 半夜一、二、三点钟

an elderly woman in her mid-seventies, with grey hair, who always wears clothes that she makes herself. You can tell that she has smiled a lot in her life from the wrinkles around her eyes.

She has a gentle, kind face, but when you first meet her you are immediately struck by the *shrewdness*① of her grey eyes behind her spectacles. If ever I had a problem when I was little, I used to go to her. I knew she would understand and be sympathetic.

She has always loved cooking and housework and still helps my mother in the house. Her hands are *gnarled*② now, and she walks with a stick, but I think she must have been very attractive when she was young.

(5) A Young Man

He is a young man about 18 and 1.75 meters in height. Being well-built, he looks like a sportsman with a tanned face. His hair is short, dark and thick with a part on his left covering most of his forehead. His two large shining eyes are accompanied by double upper eyelids and *bushy eyebrows*③. A small *mole*④ lies between his nose and right eye. Two nostrils look large for they grow a bit upward. When he laughs, his from-ear-to-ear smiling mouth is quite charming with his white teeth so well arranged. He speaks quite fast in a strong Beijing *dialect*⑤, but while speaking, he has a habit of *plucking up*⑥ his lips. Without this

---

① 敏锐;机灵
② 粗糙的;多皱纹的
③ 浓眉
④ 痣
⑤ 地方话;方言
⑥ 向上拽;此处意为"向上翘"

weak-point, I think, his good-looking face and *properly apportioned*① figure would *qualify*② him to be a film star.

(6) The Lady

Her hands were crossed one over the other, her charming face held slightly to one side. There was warmth but little colour in her cheeks; her large dark eyes were soft. But it was her lips—asking a question or giving an answer with that little smile—that people looked at. They were sensitive lips, *shapely*③ and sweet, and from them seemed to come warmth and *perfume*④ like the warmth and perfume of a flower.

(7) An Old Lady

She was ninety-two years old when I met her, a gentle, *diminutive*⑤ lady in European dress. Her face was deeply lined, and her coarse grey hair had yellowed with the years. She spoke softly in a *quivering*⑥ voice that was half-American, half-English. Her *gnarled*⑦ hand testified to the years of hard work on the farm in her homeland. Yet, in her dark eyes and in her gentle manner there was childlike simplicity as she told me her tale. I thought "She has the wisdom that comes with years of experience, and the gentle purity of a child—a wonderful but strange combination of *traits*⑧." I knew that I would never forget her.

① 比例恰当的;此处意为"匀称的"
② 使具有资格
③ 匀称的;美观的
④ 香味;芳香
⑤ 身材小的
⑥ 颤抖的
⑦ 多皱纹的;粗糙的
⑧ 特征;特点

(8) A Kind Person

Mr. Thomson is a very kind person. He is sixty years old. His children left home many years ago, and he misses them very much. Yesterday he posted a birthday card to his youngest son. He does this every year. To pass time, Mr. Thomson likes to go walking along the street. Sometimes he sees a baby in its mother's arms and smiles at it. Sometimes he helps boys and girls cross the street. Sometimes, when children have come home from school, he's very happy to play with them. A boy named John is ill today. He has to stay at home instead of going to school, but he doesn't feel lonely because Mr. Thomson will come to see him and he will bring him some interesting story books. John and his classmates always say, "Mr. Thomson is the kindest person in the world."

(9) An Outstanding Worker

Mr. Song is an outstanding worker. He has been working in the factory for 25 years. He is a party member and he was elected a model worker for his excellent results last year.

He has many good qualities. He does everything seriously and carefully, therefore the quality of his product is always good. In production, he often tries to save as much raw materials and electricity as he can. Besides, he is always ready to help others.

He is also a man who is creative and *innovative*[①]. Though he is busy, he attends classes in spare-time school three evenings every week. As a result of his hard-work, he has put forward many innovative proposals in production. With the help of some

---

① 富有革新精神的

engineers, he recently succeeded in manufacturing a new kind of *cutting instrument*①.

He has set a good example for us to follow. We all respect him.

(10) My Friend

One of my friends is a beautiful and clever girl whose name is Pan Lei.

With rosy cheeks, she has a pair of bright eyes, which shine below her new-moon-like eyebrows. Within her small mouth there are two lines of white teeth. Her hair is curled and long, hanging down to her shoulders. She is healthy and attractive.

She is very diligent in her lessons. She can also play the piano and sing sweet songs. Moreover, she is very skillful in playing basketball, volleyball, and other games. She is loved by all her classmates.

---

① 切割工具

No.70 Comparing and Contrasting 对照比较

(1) Different Ways of Living

For Americans, nineteen is not considered too young to leave home. Many American families do support their children through college, but quite often the students do not live at home. They live in a dormitory or an apartment. After graduation, even if they have been living at home, they are usually expected to move out and begin making their own living. They must go to work to support themselves. Some American parents expect their children to be financially independent immediately after high school.

However, Chinese families are different from American families. Chinese children are expected to live with their parents until a much later age. If we go to college, we usually live at home unless the school is in another town. Independence from parents is not encouraged in our country as it is in America. When we are young, parents take care of us. In fact, Chinese people would like their sons and daughters to stay with them forever.

(2) Two Friends

People different in character can become good friends. Mary and Alice are dissimilar in many respects. Mary is gentle. She speaks slowly and in a low voice. She does everything in order. Her schoolbag is always neat. She never bothers people with her own affairs, instead she often helps others in trouble. When she comes up to you, you'll believe her at first sight. Unlike Mary, Alice is *outgoing*① but careless. She often sings in such a loud voice that other children can't bear it and have to stop her singing. When you find a pencil or a piece of rubber left on the desk or on the ground, you needn't look for the owner, just pick it up and give it to Alice. But Alice is as kind as Mary. Once when Helen was ill, the two girls looked after her day and night. Helen and the other children have never been able to understand how two girls as different in character as Mary and Alice could become good friends. In fact, so long as people are kind to each other, they will make friends very easily.

(3) Two Girl Classmates

  I am amazed myself at how well I am getting along with two such different classmates: Miss Li and Miss Wang. First, their physical appearances differ greatly. With small eyes and long black hair, Wang is tall and lean while Li is tiny and, no more than five feet tall, she keeps her hair short. Looking out over a nose, her large eyes are "funny-looking".

  In other aspects, Wang likes reading or relaxing quietly in front of the television set. But for Li, the outdoor life holds more interest than books or screens. Every morning, in a bright orange sweat suit, she is jogging merrily down the road. She also swims and plays tennis.

  However, the most interesting difference between them is their approach to schoolwork. Wang often grows tense before an

---

  ① 开朗的

exam, because only grade "A" satisfies her, and she works tirelessly for it, whereas Li takes everything easy and exams are no exception. Without much effort or anxiety, she gets enough data into her head to earn grades that keep her happy.

Despite all that, they remain good friends.

(4) My Parents

There is an old saying that husbands and wives start to look and behave like each other after a while. I don't know if this was true of my mother and father. Both of my parents had brown hair and brown eyes and both had low voices and gentle *personalities*①. My father, however, was eight years older than my mother and taller and thinner. He was built as straight as an arrow and his face was longer and more *angular*② than my mother's. My mother was shorter than my father and had a rounder and fuller face and she looked as soft as a pillow. My mother was quieter than my father and talked much less than he did. She was also a much neater and more patient person than my father. My father was more intelligent and more experienced in life than my mother. He was *accustomed to*③ doing everything quickly, from working to talking. My mother, on the other hand, worked and spoke much more slowly. My father was always early for an appointment, while my mother was usually late.

(5) Two Sisters

The two sisters Mary and Ann are similar in many ways. In

---

① 个性
② 有棱角的
③ 习惯于……

fact, some people think the two girls are twins rather than sisters because they are close in age, and because they look and act a good deal alike. They are both tall and *slender*①, and they both wear their dark-brown hair long and straight. They even dress alike. What is most noticeable about the two girls is that they are both *talented*② and active in school. Mary is the vice monitor of her class and active in dance and drama. Ann, who is also a good student, is a star member of the tennis team. As might be guessed, my two sisters are both very popular.

(6) College and High School

Most people like college better than high school. While students have quite a lot homework in high school, they have very little in college. This means that in college students learn more freely than in high school. Besides, college is different from high school in that nobody watches students; in college, no one calls the parents if students do not attend class; in contrast, in high school if students do not attend class, the principal will call their parents to check on them. Basically, in college students are treated as adults, whereas in high school they are treated as children.

Some college students, however, think college is not different from high school. Just as in high school, they have to study hard. College students enjoy going to football and basketball games just as high school students do. High school students enjoy talking with their classmates, and college students do, too.

---

① 苗条的;细长的
② 天资高的;有才能的

(7) Spoken English and Written English

One of the differences between spoken English and written language is the degree of formality of informality appropriate for different situations.

When you are speaking, things such as your tone of voice and the expression on your face can help convey your meaning as well as the words you use. When you are writing you have to be more careful about your choice of words and phrases.

Writing a note of complaint to a neighbour you don't know very well is not easy. If the language is too formal, the complaint may sound *stern*① and selfish. If the language is too informal, it may sound *rude*②.

(8) The Sun and the Moon

The sun and the moon are immensely different heavenly bodies. It is quite interesting to compare them.

The sun is a huge mass of intensely hot gases giving off powerful heat and light all the time. Though only a *meagre*③ proportion of this energy reaches us, it is the source of all energy on our earth. But for the sun, our earth would be lifeless. Unlike the sun, the moon has no heat or light of its own. The side which looks bright is reflecting the sunlight and is *blazing hot*④, while the other side is near absolute zero.

The moon is 384,400 km from us and the sun is 400 times as

---

① 严厉的
② 没礼貌的
③ 少量的
④ 灼热的

far. But the sun is many times bigger in *diameter*①. Therefore, they look about the same size in the sky.

The sun has a mass of 330,000 earths, but the moon is only 1/80 of our earth in mass. Owing to much shorter distance from us, the moon exerts greater attraction on sea water, causing the tide.

The two heavenly bodies have many other different features, and scientists are trying to make more use of them in different ways.

(9) Differences Between the Two Models

Buying a car can be fun, but since there are so many models on the market to choose from, the final decision can be a very difficult one to make. Take the *Queen*② and the *Beauty*③ for example. The Queen and the Beauty have some very important differences. The first major difference is in their *dimensions*④. The Queen measures 199 inches in length, whereas the Beauty measures only 156 inches. The difference in size between the two cars is more than three feet. This means that the Queen is more *spacious*⑤ than the Beauty. On the other hand, the Queen requires a larger parking space, while the smaller Beauty is easier to *maneuver*⑥ in crowded city streets. Secondly, they differ in cost of *maintenance*⑦. The Queen gets rather poor *mileage*⑧, with 23 miles per gallon on the highway. Moreover, it requires

---

① 直径
② 汽车牌子
③ 汽车牌子
④ 尺寸；大小
⑤ 宽敞的
⑥ （敏捷地）操纵
⑦ 维修；保养
⑧ 汽车消耗一加仑汽油所行的平均里程

the more expensive gasoline. The Beauty, on the other hand, gets an impressive 40 miles per gallon on the highway, and unlike the Queen, it takes less costly gasoline. Thirdly, the two cars have very different equipment. The Queen has more *luxury*① features than the Beauty. For example, the Queen has an excellent airconditioning system, but in the Beauty the air conditioner does not cool the back seat area. Before making your final decision, you should consider these differences.

(10) Similarities and Differences Between My High School and College Lives

As I gradually get used to my college life, I sometimes like to compare it with my high school life, and found quite a few similarities and differences.

The similarities may exist in all school life. We mainly study in a classroom with kids of my age. Like myself, everyone is ambitious. In high school, I dreamed to go to a *prestigious*② university to *become somebody*③ in life. In college, I am taking solid step to realize my goal in life. My daily life changed but only a little, I shuttle from the dormitory, instead of home, to the classrooms. Lectures, text books and references are dearer than anything else to me. I still feel the joy of victory and the agony of defeat in exams. I am happy as before when I foresee a bright new world in front of me.

I gradually realized the many differences between the two lives. In high school, I was treated as a helpless kid and was pushed around by my parents and teachers. In college, I am treated like a grown-up man. I have to take care of myself, and I

---

① 豪华的
② 著名的
③ 成为有作为之人

can do what I want in my spare time. Besides, obedience and discipline are less important than independence. Passive acceptance of the teachers' wisdom was replaced by *disinterested*① search of truth. Things have changed so much. My college is very nice, but there is no place like home. I miss my parents and my former high school friends, who are so far away.

  I miss my high school life and cherish my happy college life too. All these school years, I have been working hard. My college life is dear to me, especially when I think of so many youths of my age with no college to go.

(11) Different Social Customs Between Americans and Chinese

  Social customs differ in different parts of the world. If we don't realize this, misunderstanding may arise between people who behave differently. In the United States, people are very informal in social situations. For example, they call each other by their given names when two people first meet. So does the young to the old. In China, it will be regarded quite impolite to do so.

  Another difference is about what can be talked about in conversation. A Chinese thinks nothing of being asked how much his coat cost while Americans think it impolite to ask such a question. A Chinese woman doesn't care much if she is asked about her age. Politics, religions, as well as incomes are often talked among the Chinese. But in the United States these kinds of subjects are usually avoided in conversation.

  Since there are many other different social customs between Americans and Chinese, the way we behave and the content we talk about require our attention. If we keep these in mind, we

---

  ① 无偏向的;公正的

will do it better and understand each other better.

(12) A Comparison Between Two Kinds of Clothes

Clothes made from plastic fibres have big advantages over those made of natural materials such as cotton, wool and silk. First of all, they are more durable. That is to say, they don't wear out so quickly. Second, they are easier to wash and dry. So the wearer can spare time while washing and drying them. Besides these two advantages, clothes made from plastic fibres are lighter, and they keep their shape longer.

In spite of this, clothes made from plastic fibres cannot match those made of natural materials in several respects. They are not quite as beautiful as silk, as soft as wool, and as cheap as cotton. They make the wearer feel hot and *sticky*[①], therefore, less comfortable than clothes made of natural materials.

As each kind has its advantages, it is hard to say which I prefer. There are clothes made by mixing cotton or wool with plastic fibres. They make up the *deficiencies*[②] of the former by acquiring the strong points of the latter. I prefer this kind of clothes.

---

① 黏糊糊的
② 缺点

No.71 Procedure
操作程序

(1) Making Bread

There are four separate stages in making bread. The first stage begins by mixing *yeast*① with warm water. This mixture is then added to half the amount of flour. The resultant *batter*② mixture is then left for an hour. At the next stage the rest of flour is added to the *risen*③ batter mixture, along with salt and oil. The main step in the second stage is a thorough kneading of the dough, after which it is left to rise. The third stage involves shaping the dough into *loaves*④; the shaped loaves are then put into bread tins and left to "prove"(rise). In the final stage the bread is cooked in a hot *oven*⑤. The whole process of bread making finishes when the bread is taken from the oven and left to cool on wire *racks*⑥.

---

① 酵母
② 糊状物
③ (面)发起了的
④ (面包的)条
⑤ 烘箱
⑥ 架

(2) How to Make Hamburgers

Making *hamburgers*① is really very simple. All you need is a pound of *minced*② beef which you mix with the other things—salt and pepper, a teaspoon of *mustard*③, and an egg as well. You break the egg in a bowl, and mix all the things together with a fork. When it is smooth and well-mixed, make round hamburgers from the mixture, and roll them in some flour. Then you need a *frying pan*④ and some oil. Fry the hamburgers on both sides for about 15 minutes until they are brown. When they are ready, get some soft bread rolls and cut them in half. Put the hamburgers inside them and eat them as soon as possible.

(3) How to Take Photographs

In order to take photographs with your new camera, you must follow these simple instructions. First, take the film cassette out of its packet, and *insert*⑤ it into the back of the camera. Wind the film on until a number 1 appears in the film window at the back of the camera.

Now *set*⑥ the *aperture*⑦ to one of the five positions, marked by the sun or cloud signs, according to the lighting conditions. (Don't forget to take off the *lens cover*⑧!)

---

① 汉堡包
② 剁(或绞)碎的
③ 芥末
④ 煎锅
⑤ 插入
⑥ 调整
⑦ （照相机的）光圈孔径(大小)
⑧ 镜头盖

操作程序 "No.71"
Procedure

Look through the *view finder*① and move the camera until what you want to photograph appears between the white lens. Hold the camera steady and press the *shutter*② release button slowly. That's all you have to do to get perfect pictures!

(4) **Change a Wheel**

Mr. Kelly stopped his car at the side of the road and got out of the car. He looked at one of the front wheels and found out that the *tyre*③ was flat. He decided to change the tyre himself, so he went round to the *car-boot*④ where the *spare*⑤ wheel was kept. He lifted it out and then got out the *jack*⑥. He had to get down on his knees to put the jack under the car. When it was in position, he started to move the handle up and down. It was hard work. Slowly the *chassis*⑦ was lifted away from the ground. Mr. Kelly then took a *spanner*⑧ and removed the *wheel nuts*⑨. Now he could take the wheel with the *punctured*⑩ tyre off the *axle*⑪. He put this wheel in the boot and fitted the spare wheel back on the axle. He replaced the wheel nuts. The new wheel was firmly in place.

① 取景器
② 快门
③ 轮胎
④ (汽车的)行李箱
⑤ 备用的
⑥ 千斤顶
⑦ (汽车等)底盘
⑧ 扳手
⑨ 固定车轮的螺母
⑩ 被刺破的
⑪ 车轴;(轮)轴

No.72 Writing Based on Pictures
图表及图画说明

(1) Area and Population of the Continents

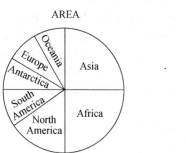

The charts indicate that the continent which occupies the largest land area in the world is Asia. Asia is also the most populated continent—over half of the world's population lives here. Asia is obviously much more densely populated than Africa. Even though the two continents are about the same in physical size, the population of Asia is five times greater than that of Africa. However, Asia is not yet the most densely populated continent. Europe, with the second highest population and the second smallest land area, is the most densely populated continent. The least populated continent is *Antarctica*①. While it

---

① 南极洲

has a land mass larger than Europe or *Oceania*①, virtually no one lives there.

North America is more than twice as large as Europe, but has only more than half of the population of Europe. With the exception of Antarctica, Oceania has the smallest population. South America has twice the physical area of Oceania and five times more people.

Even though the physical area of North and South America combined is nearly the same as that of Asia, Asia has more than three times their combined population.

(2) Cooperation

As can be seen from the cartoon, two handicapped men are bound together. They are walking at a high speed and with great confidence. Obviously, their physical disadvantages do not disable them.

This cartoon is thought provoking and reveals to us a solid truth: solidarity makes us strong. On the one hand, no one is lucky enough to be advantageous in all aspects. We do need the help of others to achieve higher goals. On the other hand, the challenges and difficulties we may face are always so tough that we have to work together to get out of a tight spot. Therefore, it is no exaggeration to say that united we stand, divided we fall.

As far as I am concerned, I often attach great importance to cooperation. Living in the one-child age, I find teamwork not only brings me more opportunities, but also makes me more powerful. I firmly believe success relies on many factors, among which cooperation undoubtedly accounts for much.

---

① 大洋洲

你一条腿，我一条腿；
你我一起，走南闯北。

(3) Touch Online or Contact Directly

This picture features two things, the spiders web and the "*cubicle farm*①". The spiders web is of course our modern metaphor for the internet, which connects one point to every other point, and thus allows a web user to access a great deal of information. Being interconnected like this is what makes the internet so popular, as people can communicate with anyone in a variety of ways from all over the world. The second thing about this picture is the common office cubicle farm, people at their desks using the computers, but without a lot of face to face contact with real people. Some people might argue that while the internet allows people to stay in touch more, make more friends and even find romance online, a *down*② side is that sometimes it makes people more isolated. Some people stay in their homes and only make online friends, chat online and never experience direct human contact. If their average day at work is like this too, the internet may be *a curse rather than a blessing*③.

---

① 格子式的办公室
② 令人沮丧的
③ 是祸而不是福

图表及图画说明
Writing Based on Pictures
No.72

(4) College Students' Booklist

	1985	1995	2005
Philosophy and Society	45%	23%	13%
Novels	33%	17%	5%
Foreign Languages	11%	31%	39%
Computer Science	2%	19%	30%
Others	9%	10%	13%

  The table shows the changes of students' choices of various kinds of books from 1985 to 2005. Obviously enough, the number of novels and books of philosophy and society has *declined*① gradually, with that of foreign languages books and computer science ones enjoying much more popularity.

  Though different readers have their own particular tastes, this phenomenon involves several complicated factors. Firstly, nowadays, most of the college students tend to buy more books concerning foreign languages learning and computer science,

---

① 下降

mainly because there is a *pressing*① need of foreign languages and computer skills for their future employment. Secondly, novels are still popular though the selling number decreased *thanks to*② the availability of the Internet. Most of popular books could be read online.

I always buy books of computer science, firstly because it is my major. Secondly, it is well known that computer science often witnesses the fastest changes, thus in order to keep up with the pace, I have to constantly arm myself with new information.

(5) Average Monthly Rainfall in Country A and Country B

Average Monthly Rainfall (in millimeters)

Month	Country A	Country B
January	0	39
February	0	41
March	1	47
April	3	47
May	7	61
June	8	60
July	11	68
August	18	69
September	14	67
October	2	53
November	0	40
December	0	42

As can be learned from the table, average monthly rainfall in Country B is by far greater than that in Country A. Country B has

---

① 迫切的,紧迫的
② 由于

plenty of rain every month while Country A has almost no rain except from July to September. The two countries may differently suffer from the bad effects of rainfall.

On the one hand, water shortage in Country A may slow down its development of industry and agriculture, and the dry climate there may lead to a scarcity of plants and animals. Whereas too much rain in Country B may not only affect its agriculture but also cause severe floods.

It can be seen from the above-mentioned that both countries should take effective steps to solve the problems concerning rainfall. In Country A, people should make good use of water and try to find new ways of getting water. In Country B, people should make proper use of water and try to prevent rainfall from doing harm to them.

(6) How to Use Water Properly

Washing clothes ·· 10%
Washing hands, brushing teeth, shaving ················ 18%
Showering ··· 18%
Washing dishes ··· 20%
Flushing toilet ··· 30%
Other ·· 4%

Daily Water Used in the U. S.
(90 gallons/ person)

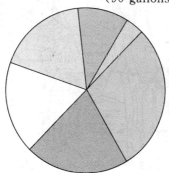

It is reported that an average American consumes as much as ninety gallons of water every day. Of all the water used, 30% goes for flushing toilet, while 20% is used for washing dishes. Up to 18% of water is used for showering and an equal amount goes for washing hands, brushing teeth and shaving. On the other hand, the water used for washing clothes accounts for no more than 10%, and other uses including cooking take up only 4% of daily water use.

As compared with Americans, we Chinese use far less water daily. We use most of the water for washing clothes as well as flushing toilet. Besides, the water used for cooking also takes a great percentage in our daily use.

Of course, the difference between the American and the Chinese in using water mainly lies in the different living conditions and customs of these two countries. Nevertheless, it is worth pointing out that if people all over the world used as much water as the Americans, there would be soon a global water shortage, and the world would fall into great trouble. Therefore, we must save on water, using it to the best advantage.

(7) An Incident

The picture is about a routine incident in our life.

A woman is about to go upstairs, with a parcel and a bag of apples in her arms. A middle-aged man is just coming down the stairs, with a suitcase in his right hand. They run into each other on the landing so that some of the apples slid out of the bag, rolling onto the floor. The man feels *compunctious*①. *Promptly*② he takes off his hat, bows to the woman and says, "I'm sorry, I'm very sorry." The woman replies, "That's all right."

Some people are always polite while others are not. Whether a person is polite or not depends on how well he or she is educated. A well-educated person can never be impolite to others. The more the education is developed, the better the relationship between people will be.

(8) Sex Discrimination

Jiang Li is an excellent student graduating from a famous university. She is generally acknowledged as very good in her grade. But she comes across an unpleasant thing when she applys

---

① 抱歉的；后悔的
② 立刻；马上

for a post in an institution.

   She is plainly dressed—a short-sleeved checked shirt and a white skirt. The diploma is under her arm. The certificate is in her left hand. She looks timid and fresh from the university. The boss in a Chinese *tunic suit*① sits back and holds his head up. When he sees her, he says casually, "Woman again!" Obviously he is so contemptuous towards the girl. Jiang Li is very upset and puzzles why one's sex is more important than one's other qualities.

   Equality of the sexes is certainly a very complicated problem. Just having equal right to vote and equal pay for equal work has not solved the problem completely.

(9) The Swallow

   When spring comes, people will see a little bird coming back with it. This is the swallow. This lovely bird has a black bill and a black back, but the under part of its body is white. People often compare the shape of the feathers at the end of its body to a pair of scissors.

   Some swallows like to build their nests in the inside of the

---

① 长外衣

chimneys or under the caves of roofs. They make their nests of mud, straw and grass. After the construction of their nests is completed, the mother bird will lay eggs and sit upon them. The father swallow watches by her side and feeds her. When their children come out of the shells, the parents work much to feed them. Swallows fly quickly and gracefully. They are good friends of man.

  When cold weather draws near, they will begin a long journey to the warmer parts of the world.

No.73 Letters 书信

A. Private Letter（私人书信）

(1) A Letter from a College Volunteer Teaching in the Rural Area of Gansu Province

June 1, 2006

Dear Sir or Madam,

  I am a college volunteer teaching in a rural middle school of Gansu province during this summer. I feel obliged to write you this letter to report the real situation there.

  The facilities in that middle school are rather poor, and more than 100 students of different grades crowd in one classroom with broken desks and chairs. Most of them cannot afford the tuition and fees and other expenses related to study. They have never seen a computer, let alone experiencing the modernity brought by the Internet. However, they are very intelligent kids and all are keen to study but lack minimum financial resources from their family. For the healthy growth of these kids, the school situation should be improved as soon as possible.

  I hereby sincerely appeal to you in the name of those kids in a rural middle school for more attention from the outside world.

  With best regards!

Yours respectfully,
Li Ming

(2) A Letter to My Teacher on Teachers Day

May 18, 2008

Dear Mr. Wang,

  Teacher's Day is around the corner. I write this letter to express my congratulation to you. I left Hebei University five years ago and I am an engineer now. But your amiable smile and wonderful lectures are so deeply embedded in my mind that they remain as fresh as in Hebei University years. You are a teacher of upright character, full of devotion to the work. You showed great concern for us students, not only importing us knowledge but also helping us train moral character. You often took pains to find and practice good teaching methods, and so we enjoyed attending your lecture as they were vivid and intelligible.

  I owe my progress to your teaching and instruction. I am determined to never give up the pursuit of learning, which is the best reward I can give you in return.

  Best wishes!

Yours respectfully,
Li Ming

B. Social Letter (社交书信)

(1) A Letter of Congratulation

June 20, 2006

Dear Wang Ping,

  I, with the greatest pleasure, offer you my sincerest congratulations on your having gained admittance as a graduate student. I'm so happy to learn about your achievements in study that I lose no time in writing to you.

  Your scholarly achievements are based on your diligent work during your four years in college. You have good reason to be proud of yourself. As a close friend of yours, I feel very happy to share your honor and pride.

  I believe you will make further efforts in your higher learning. With devotion to science, you will surely make yourself useful to society.

  I wish you great success in all that you undertake.

Yours,
Lin Yan

(2) A Letter of Thanks

May 25, 2008

Dear Susan,

  Now that I have become well enough to write, I want to express my sincere thanks not only to you, but also to your parents, for the kind treatment I received during my illness at your house.

  I am afraid that my being ill must have given you a great deal of trouble, but I know your parents and you will forgive me for being a burden to you against my will. I hope it will be in my power some day to repay this great kindness, and I shall always remember it with feelings of the greatest gratitude.

  Please give my best regards to your mamma and papa, and accept the same yourself from me.

Your affectionate friend,
Frieda

(3) A Letter of Acceptance

July 21, 2008

Dear Wu Dan and Xiao Lin,

  We are counting the days to our weekend with you in Emei. We are delighted that you have asked us, and we certainly won't let anything prevent us from going.

  We plan to take the four o'clock train on Friday afternoon, July 24th, as you suggest. And we'll take the early express back to Chengdu on Monday morning.

  Thanks so much for inviting us. We're looking forward to spending two wonderful days with you and the Smiths. We're also especially looking forward to the tennis you talk about. We haven't had a chance to play tennis for quite a long time.

With love,
Bob and Jane

(4) A Letter of Regret

July 21, 2008

Dear Wu Dan and Xiao Lin,

  We would love to go to Emei on Friday, July 24th, but that's the day when Jane's brother is arriving from England, and he is expecting us to meet him at the airport.

  If it were anything else, we would just change our plans and come. But we are sure you'll understand that we can't disappoint him when we know he'll be expecting to see us as he steps off the plane. He is scheduled to arrive at five-thirty this Friday. So we are very sorry to say that we will not be able to join you in Emei on the weekend you propose.

  But thanks so much for asking us, anyway. We know we're

missing a marvelous time! Please remember us to the Smiths, and tell them how sorry we are not to be able to join them for the weekend.

Affectionately yours,
Bob and Jane

C. Other Letters (其他书信)

(1) A Letter of Application for Financial Aid

June 1, 2009

Dear Sir,

    I am pleased to learn of my admission to your two-year program of studies leading to degree of M. S. in chemistry. Indeed, I have dreamed of this opportunity since completing my undergraduate study.

    In order to reduce the financial responsibility of my parents, I earnestly hope to obtain some kind of financial aid in the form of a teaching or research assistantship.

    Would you kindly consider this request and advise me as to the possibilities? Should further information be required, please let me know at your earliest convenience. I look forward to hearing good news from you.

Sincerely yours,
Wang Li

(2) A Letter of Application for a Place at the Graduate School of Physics

May 18, 2009

Dear Professor Smith,

I would like to apply for a place at the Graduate School of Physics of the University of Illinois for studies leading to the degree of Doctor of Science.

I was born in 1975, and graduated in Physics from Beijing Polytechnic University in July 1993. I have recently passed the English Proficiency Test (EPT) sponsored by the National Education Committee of China. This means that a government scholarship will be granted to me for my postgraduate studies in the United States. All my expenses will be covered by the Chinese government.

Enclosed please find a transcript of records of all the subjects which I completed at the university. Attached you will also find three letters of recommendation by three of my professors.

I hope a letter of admission will soon be issued to me for my visa, so that I shall be able to arrive in Chicago in time for the fall term.

I am looking forward to an early reply.

Yours sincerely,
Wang Kang

(3) A Letter of Introduction

July 30, 2009

Dear John,

My former roommate at college, Mark Chen, will be in Paris next month to study comparative literature under a scholarship. As you know, I've often wanted you two to meet, and this seems like an excellent opportunity.

Although Mark is a very serious student, he is one of the wittiest men I know—a good conversationalist in both French and English.

I've asked him to give you a call since he has no definite

address as yet. I know how busy you are with your work, so please do not regard this as an obligation. But if you have any free time, do show Mark around a bit. I would never have taken this liberty had I not been sure you would enjoy the meeting.

  I'll really appreciate any kindness you can show him, and I know Mark himself will, too.

Sincerely,
Charles

(4) A Letter of Recommendation

January 10, 2008

Dear Sir,

  I have the pleasure of recommending to you Mr. Zhu Hong as a postgraduate for further education in your college. He completed his undergraduate studies and obtained his B. A. degree in 1993 at Jilin University. Now he works as a teaching assistant in Shanghai Fisheries College. As his former English teacher, I deem it a pleasure to say what I know about him.

  Zhu Hong was one of the top students in my class. I know him to have been a promising student of intelligence and ability. In class he was an attentive and hard-working person, quick in apprehension and response to questions; out of class he had a very efficient method for studying and a keen sense of practical-ity. He always read a wide range of reference materials and was completely ready to be questioned in class. He was particularly good at speaking and writing. His independent and analytical ability was highly appreciated by teachers. Besides, his nice personality and great motivation also enable me to recommend him without any reservation to pursue further education at your college.

  It would be greatly appreciated if you would give him your kind consideration. If I can be of any further help, please let me know.

Sincerely yours,
Xu Li

(5) An Application for a Scholarship

Dr. Henry Ford
Chairman, Department of Chemistry
University of Colorado at Denver
Denver, Colorado 80208

April 10, 2008

Dear Dr. Ford,

I have read the announcement of the scholarship in chemistry that the University of Colorado is offering, and I would like to submit my application.

The enclosed application form for admission to the graduate school of your university will give my educational history. However, I would like to point out that I have just received an M.S. degree in chemistry with highest honors. For one semester, working with Professor Saramma, I acted as teaching assistant in chemistry. My thesis involves polymer chemistry, which I understand is a specialty at the University of Colorado. I would like to concentrate in that field for my advanced studies.

I would welcome the opportunity to have a personal interview.

Sincerely yours,
Wang Han

(6) A Letter for Applying a Post

May 25, 2006

Dear Sir or Madam,

I'm writing you to apply for a post in Beijing Olympic Organizing Committee. I will graduate from Hebei University with the MA Degree in English Literature this summer. I have a good academic record that ranks within top three in my class. In addition to my high proficiency in English language, I have rich experiences in organizing public activities and working with people. As the director of our English Drama Society, I've hosted several drama shows with my team, which have evoked the drama heat on campus. I'm honest, reliable, and ready to devote my knowledge and energy to my job! I do appreciate your time in reading this letter and I'm looking forward to hearing from you!

With best regards!

Sincerely yours,
Li Ming

(7) A Letter to a Reader

June 1, 2009

Dear Sir,

You have expressed your frustration and irritation with the city library over the past six months. There are usually lines waiting for assistance and for use of the computer card catalogs. You know that we have all kinds of readers coming to our library every day. They are keen on studying different subjects for different purposes. So, all the reading rooms are always full of people. We suppose that the situation may remain unchanged in the near future.

To avoid crowded conditions, we suggest you use the library during off-peak hours. You should have no trouble getting help and using the card catalog during the following periods: 11:30 am to 2:30 pm; 5:30 pm to 7:30 pm. The rest are our busiest time.

We always appreciate hearing your comments on the library.

Let us know what you think about the above suggestions.

Faithfully yours,
Li Ming

(8) A Letter to a House Agency

July 15, 2008

Dear Sir or Madam,

  I'm writing about the apartment on sale you advertised in the Classified Ad Section of *The Daily News*. I'm interested in the location of the apartment, and would like to buy it if everything turns out satisfactory. Is it possible for you to give more details concerning the following aspects?

  First, your advertisement said that the apartment was closed to downtown. Could you please tell me where it is located exactly? Are there many bus routes coming across this area?

  I'd also like to know when the apartment building was built, and the reason why the previous owner would like to put it on sale.

  I look forward to hearing from you soon.

Sincerely yours,
Li Ming

(9) Application Letter

May 20, 2007

Dear Sir,

  I was pleased to see your ad in the *Yangtze Evening Paper* on May 14, 2002 for a sales engineer. In July I will receive my Bachelor's degree in Electronic Engineering from Fudan

University, and I would like to be considered for the post.

I believe I could do satisfactory work for your company because both my education and work experience have been in line with the duties you outlined in your ad. As indicated in my attached resume, my main degree course is concerned with basic electronic topics. But I also have taken such courses as Marketing, Consumer Behavior Strategies and Psychology, and all available opportunities to increase my knowledge in both fields. The fact that I'm qualified for your job is *substantiated*[①] not only by my academic achievement but also by the moderate amount of experience I gained in participation in an electronic project last summer. As for my English ability, I have already passed the national CET(Band 6) with excellent results and I have even worked two summers as an English interpreter at Shanghai Travel Agency.

I would welcome an opportunity to join your staffs because your work is the kind I have been preparing to do and because the conditions under which it is carried out would help to demonstrate my abilities. If you also feel that I might fit your requirements I would be available for an interview any time at your convenience. I would greatly appreciate any word you might send me regarding my application.

Yours, Sincerely
Wu Yichen

(10) A Letter of Apology

June 6, 2006

Dear Bob,

    I am writing this letter to express my apologies for I have

---

① 证实,证明(陈述、主张等)有根据

mistakenly brought back the CD I borrowed from you during my stay in your house.

  The CD you lent me helped me a lot to pass the exam that was so important to me. I didn't realize that I still had the CD with me until I opened my luggage when I returned home. Now I am thinking about sending it back to you, so please tell me whether I should send it to your home address or to your work unit.

  I am very sorry for the inconvenience I may have caused you. I hope someday you will come to China and I will have the opportunity to repay your kindness and hospitality.

  Wish you all the best!

Yours sincerely,
Li Ming

(11) A Letter of Application

May 28, 2007

Dear Sir or Madam,

  I am writing in the hope that I may obtain an opportunity to further my study in Applied Physics toward master degree in your university.

  My name is Li Jin, an undergraduate student of the Department of Applied Physics, Tsinghua University, China. Next year in the summer, I will graduate and get my B. S. degree. I plan to continue my study and research in this field under the instructions of first class professors and in a dynamic academic atmosphere. I chose Boston University because there are a *congenial*[①] team of researchers, an array of databases and research projects in your School of Physics. I believe my interests

---

 ① 志趣相投的,志同道合的

are extremely congruent with[①] the strengths of the School. And my solid academic background will meet your general entrance requirements for graduate study.

  I will appreciate it very much if you could send me the Graduate Application Forms, the Application Form for Scholarship/Assistantship, a detailed introduction to the School of Physics, and other relevant information.

  I am looking forward to hearing from you soon.

Sincerely yours,
Li Jin

---

① 与……完全一致的

No.74 Practical Writings 应用文

A. Note (便条)

(1) Asking for Sick Leave(Ⅰ)

Apr. 10, 2009

Dear Mr. Fang,

　　Please excuse my absence from class today. I had a cold yesterday evening and could not fall asleep until late in the night. I'll go and consult the doctor today, and will resume my study if I feel better tomorrow.

Very truly yours,
Liu Wen

(2) Asking for Sick Leave(Ⅱ)

Nov. 27, 2009

Dear Mr. Wu,

　　I'm seriously ill today and can not come to class. I'm writing to ask for sick leave of two days.

Yours truly,
Li Jing

　　Encl[①]: doctor's certificate for sick leave

---

① Encl=enclosure 附件，内封物

(3) Asking for Business Leave (Ⅰ)

May 12, 2009

Dear sir,

  I beg to inform you that I shall be unable to attend classes today owing to important business in the family.

  I shall be very much obliged if you will grant me my application.

Yours truly,
Lin Hua

(4) Asking for Business Leave (Ⅱ)

Oct. 6, 2009

Dear Director Wu,

  A telegram has just come to hand, saying that my father is seriously ill and urging me to go home at once. Because of this, I should very much like to apply for one week's leave of absence from the 7th to the 13th *inst*.① I hope that my request will be given due consideration.

Yours sincerely,
Wang Lin

  Encl: a telegram from my mother.

---

① inst. = instant 本月的

B. Message (留言)

(1) Asking a Friend to Give a Ring

10:20 a.m. Mar. 28

Dear Li,

    I arrived here this morning by plane. I am staying at Room 1404, Peace Hotel. Please come over or ring me up as soon as you read this note. My telephone number:241316.

                                                               Chou

(2) Transmitting a Telephone Message

3 p.m. Tuesday

Dear Lin,

    Mr. Cheng of Hebei University has just rung you up saying that he will be expecting you in his office about ten tomorrow morning.

    Please give him a ring if the time does not suit you.

                                                            Xiao Wang

(3) Saying Good-bye

8 p.m. July 9

To Lao Zhang,

    I will leave by the train at 7:00 a.m. tomorrow morning. This is to say good-bye to you.

                                                            Ji Wen

(4) Requesting to Borrow Something

Mar. 10,1995

Dear Mr. Kent,

　　Will you please lend me your COD[①] for a few days? I hope you will let the bearer bring it to me.

　　Thank you very much.

Yours,

Zhu Yimin

(5) To Inform a Friend of Putting off a Meeting

Friday afternoon

Wu Qing,

　　Just a line to tell you that tomorrow's meeting has been put off because of the chairman's absence. Please notify the others concerned.

Liu Wen

C. Notice (启事)

(1) Lost

July 10,2009

　　Money lost. Whoever found it, please inform us about it. Tel. 5577577　Ext. 2202

Chemistry Department Office

[①] COD=Concise Oxford Dictionary

(2) A Wrist Watch Lost

Sept. 2, 2009

In the washroom, at noon, Sept. 2, a wrist watch was lost. Finder please return it to the owner, Wang Feng, Room 8, Dormitory 2.

(3) Found

Mar. 27, 2009

Lost money found. Whoever lost it may come to claim it.

The Office of Foreign
Languages Department

(4) A Briefcase Found

Dec. 6, 2009

A briefcase was found, inside of which are money and other things. Loser is expected to come to identify it. Please apply at the Lost Property Office, Room 107, the Office Building. Open from 8:00 to 11:00 a. m. and 2:00 to 5:00 p. m.

(5) For Sale

British-made bicycle
Excellent condition

Edward Lee
Tel: 21082318

(6) Needed

Portable typewriter
In good condition

Fan Yun
Room 208, Dorm. 5

(7) Book Wanted

Second-hand books on psychology for introductory course.

Ian Fleming
Tel: 441-8228

D. Poster (海报)

(1) Lecture

Under the Auspices of the Students Union
  A Lecture Will Be Given
      on Essential English Grammar
  by Prof. Li Pingfang
  in the Science Hall
at 7 p.m. on Wednesday, Oct. 19,1995
    All Are Welcome
Oct. 15,2009

(2) Talk

Speaker: Professor Frank Edward of the University of
    Southern California, U.S.A.

应用文 **Practical Writings** No.74

Subject: Contemporary American Literature
Time: 2:00. p. m. October 28, 2009
Place: Room 108, the Teaching Building.
  All Are Welcome
        The Foreign Affairs Office

(3) Basketball Match

    National Team *vs.* [1] Beijing Team
Time: 7:00 p. m. April 18, 2009
Place: School Gymnasium
 Please apply at the Students Union for tickets. Admission free.
       School Athletic Committee

(4) Women's Volleyball Match

    National Team vs U. S. Team
Time: 6:30 p. m. May 7, 2009
Place: Municipal Gymnasium
 Please contact the Students Union for tickets. Admission ten *yuan*. Tickets are limited to 50. Those who want to buy should be quick. The goers are expected to assemble at 5:50 p. m. at the school gate. The coach will leave at 6:00 p. m.

       The Physical Cultural Branch
       of the Students Union

---

 ① *vs.* = against,是拉丁文 *versus* 的简写

(5) This Week's Film

Name: Jane Eyre
Time: 6:30 p. m. 8:30 p. m. June 6
Place: Auditorium
Fare: 3 *Yuan*

Please apply at the Film Projection Group for tickets.

E. Notice (通知)

(1) Notice of the President's Office

Tomorrow being New Year's Day, there will be no class. All classes will be resumed as usual on the 2nd.

The President's Office

December 31, 2009

(2) Notice of the General Affairs Service

Notice is hereby given that the water supply is not available from 7:00 a. m. to 11:00 p. m. tomorrow, owing to the repairs of the water pipes.

The General Affairs Service

Feb. 2, 2009

(3) Notice of the Library Office

Readers are requested to note that from May 2, 1995, the library will be open during the following hours:

8:00 – 12:00 a. m.

1:30 – 5:00 p. m.

The Library Office

April 27, 2009

(4) Notice of the English Department

A short-term English conversation class will be given during the summer of 1995 (from July 15 to August 30). Only those who have passed CET-4 can participate. Applications should be filled in before June 30.

The English Department

June 21, 2009

(5) Notice of the Students Union

The Students Union has recently agreed to set up a Swimming Club. It aims to encourage swimming, to raise swimming standards and to form a college swimming team. During the summer there will be a number of lectures and demonstrations, and Mr. Wang, the swimming coach at the Wuhan Physical Culture Institute, has agreed to give us training.

Anyone in the school may join the club by filling in the application form and providing two passport-size photographs by the end of the month.

The inaugural meeting will be held in the school gym at 3 p. m. Thursday, June 30, 1995.

The Students Union

June 14, 2009

Appendix
附录

1. 英语章段写作常用词语

(1) 章段开头常用词语

As far as... is concerned	就……而论
As far as we know	据我们所知
As everybody knows	众所周知
As the proverb says	有句谚语说
As the saying goes	俗语说
As might have been expected	不出所料
At present	当前
At first	首先
At the start	开始
At this point	在这一点上
First of all	首先
Frankly speaking	坦白地说
Generally speaking	一般来说
I am of the opinion that...	我认为
I want to begin by saying...	首先我要说
In the beginning	首先
In the first place	第一
It can be easily proved that...	很容易证明
It can be said with certainty that...	可以肯定地说
It cannot be denied that...	无可否认
It goes without saying that...	不用说
It has been demonstrated that...	已经证明

It has been found that...	已经发现
It has been proved that...	业已证明
It has been shown that...	业已表明
It has to be noticed that...	必须注意
It is a common saying that...	俗语说
Adjacent to	紧接着
After a while	过了一会儿
All the same	虽然
Another special consideration in this case is that...	对此事的另一考虑是
As an illustration	作为例证
As a matter of fact	事实上
As has been already discussed	正如已经讨论过的
As has been explained before	正如已经解释过的
As has been noted	如上所述
As has been said before	正如已经说过的
As has been stated	如上所述
As is often the case	正如常常发生的那样
As it is seen from...that...	由……可以看出
As has been mentioned above	如上所述
As has been stated in the previous paragraph	如前段所述
As we can see from the above table	从表上可知
Aside from...	除了
At any rate	无论如何
At the same time	同时
At this point we agree that...	就此我们同意
Because of...	由于
Besides, we should remember that...	此外,我们应当记住
But for...	要不是
But it is a pity that...	但可惜的是
But the problem is not so simple. Therefore...	然而问题并非如此简单,所以
But rather	而宁可说
By comparison	比较起来
By contrast	对比起来

By now	至此
By reason of	由于
By the time	到……的时候
By the way	另外
By...we mean	所谓……我们指的是
Compared with...	与……相比
Considering...	考虑到
Contrary to...	与……相反
Contrary to all expectations	出乎意料
Despite the fact that...	尽管
Due to...	由于
Even if	即使
Even more	甚至
Even so	即使如此
Even though	即使
Except that...	除……之外
Far from...	非但
For a long period after...	……之后一个很长时期
For all that...	尽管
For all we know	据我们所知
For example	例如
For instance	例如
For no other reason that...	只是因为
For one thing...for another(thing)...	一则……二则……
For that matter	关于这点
For that same reason	同样道理
For this purpose	为此目的
For this reason	由于这个
From now on	今后
Further, we hold opinion that...	而且我们认为
Furthermore, I agree that...	此外,我同意
However, the difficulty lies in...	然而,问题在于
Whatever the case may be	不论怎样
If for no other reason than...	即使……也好
If so	倘若如此

If... then...	如果……那么……
In a broad sense	从广义上说
In a similar way	同样
In accordance with...	根据
It is one's belief that...	某人相信
It is one's opinion that...	某人认为
It is possible that...	有可能
It is probable that...	有可能
It is impossible that...	不可能
It is likely that...	有可能
It is calculated that...	据估计
It is evident from... that...	由……证明
It is estimated that...	据估计
It is generally agreed that...	人们通常认为
It is generally recognized that...	人们普遍认为
It is sometimes asked that...	人们有时问
It is asserted that...	有人主张
It is believed that...	有人(人们、大家)相信
It is considered that...	有人(人们、大家)以为
It is claimed that...	有人宣称
It is declared that...	有人宣布
It is expected that...	人们盼望
It is hoped that...	人们希望
It is predicated that...	据估计(预计)
It is proposed that...	有人建议
It is regarded that...	人们认为
It is reported that...	据报道(告)
It is supposed that...	据推测
It is thought that...	人们(有人、大家)以为
It is understood that...	不用说(谁都知道)
It is hardly too much to say that...	毫不夸大地说
It is no secret that...	不用讳言
It is well-known that...	众所周知
It is must be admitted that...	必须承认(毋庸讳言)
It must be emphasized that...	必须强调
It must be pointed out that...	必须指出

It should be made clear that...	应当讲明的是
It stands to reason that...	……是合乎情理的
No one can deny that...	谁也不可否认
Nothing is more important than the fact that...	最重要的事实是
Now that we know that...	既然我们知道
Of course	当然
On the subject of	关于
Once upon a time	从前
So far	迄今
So long as	只要
So the story goes	传说
Sometimes...sometimes...	时而……时而……
There is no denying the fact that...	无可否认
There is no doubt that...	毫无疑问
Therefore, we should realize that...	因此我们应当明白
To begin with	首先
To be sure	诚然
To start with	首先
To tell the truth	老实说
Until recently	直到前不久
We are all aware that...	我们都明白
We must recognize the fact that...	我们必须承认
We stand to it that...	我们坚决主张
What calls for special attention is that...	需引起特别注意的是
What is important is that...	重要的是
What we believe is that...	我们相信的是
What with...	由于……的原因
When it comes to...	就……而论
Whether one will or not	不管怎样
With a view to...	为……起见
With regard to...	至于
With respect to...	关于

(2) 衔接转折常用词语

A case in point is...	恰当的例子是

A more interesting thing is that...	更为有趣的是
A more important fact is that...	更重要的事实是
In addition	另外
In addition to...	除……之外
In analogy with...	与……相似
In answer to	为回答
In any case	无论如何
In fact	事实上
In the latter case	在后一种情况下
In line with...	根据
In much the same way as...	以和……大致相同的方式
In other words	换句话说
In spite of the fact that...	尽管
In that case	假使那样的话
In this case	在这种情况下
In this connection	就此而论
In view of the present situation	鉴于目前形势
It certainly would not be right to say that...	说……当然不行
It can be seen from this...	由此可见
It follows from this...	由此得出结论
It is true that... , but...	……是不错,但
Just as we have discussed earlier	正如我们早已讨论过的
Just as... , so...	正像……一样,……也……
Moreover, we should not forget that...	而且我们不该忘记
Next, we should all realize that...	其次,我们都应知道
The next important point is that...	下一个重要的论点是
No sooner... than...	刚……就……
Not because... but because...	不是因为……而是因为
Not only... but also...	不仅……而且
Not that... but that...	不是……而是
On account of	由于
On that account	为了那个缘故
On the advice of...	按……的劝告
On the assumption that...	假定

On the contrary	相反
On the left(right)	在左(右)边
On the other hand	另一方面
On the opposite side of...	在……对面
On this point we all agree that...	关于这点我们都同意
On second thoughts	经再三考虑
One thing which is equally important is that...	同样重要的是
Opposite to...	与……相反
Others may disagree, but I believe that...	其他人可能反对,但我相信
Owing to	由于
Perhaps you will question why...	也许你会问为什么
Seeing that...	既然
Similarly, we should pay attention to...	同样,我们应注意
Secondly, we must note that...	其次,我们必须注意
Thanks to the fact that...	多亏了
That is to say	也就是说
That is why...	这就是为什么
That is the reason why...	那就是……的原因
The reason is that...	理由是
This can be expressed as follows:	可以这样来表示
To take...for example	以……为例
The problem with regard to...is that...	与……有关的问题是
The question resolves itself into...	问题归结为
Therefore, we should realize that...	因此,我们应认识到
What is more	此外
With a view to...	为……起见
With regard to your proposal, I think that...	关于你的建议,我认为

(3) 章段结尾常用词语

Above all	最重要的是
After all	毕竟
All in all	总的来说

All things considered	总而言之
All this means that...	所有这一切都意味着
As a consequence	结果
As a result	结果
As the matter stands	事实上
At last	最后
At length	最后
At all events	无论如何
Consequently, most people believe that...	结果,大多数人相信
Finally, we hope that...	最后,我们希望
For short	简言之
From this point of view	就此而论
Hence, we conclude that...	因此,我们断言
I will conclude by saying...	最后,我要说
I want to make one final point...	我要说的最后一点是
In a word	总之
In brief	简言之
In conclusion	最后
In general	总之
In short	简言之
In summary	总之
In the end	最后
In the last analysis	归根结底
In the last place	最后
It may be confirmed that...	可以肯定
It may be safely said that...	可以有把握地说
Last but not least	最后但并不是最不重要的
Last of all	最后
On the whole	总的来看
That is all there is to it	仅此而已
The long and the short of it	总而言之
Therefore, we have the reason to believe that...	因此,我们有理由相信
Thus we are given to understand that...	所以我们懂得

To make a long story short	简言之；长话短说
To sum up	概括地说
With this end in view	为此

2. 英语写作常用过渡性词语及其实例

(1) 表示举例说明

a case in point, as a proof, as an illustration, for example, for instance, namely, such, specifically, that is, to illustrate

- a) That experiment, *for example*, was a total failure.
- b) *For instance*, a telegram often costs more than a telephone call.
- c) There are three colours in the British flag, *namely*, red, white and blue.
- d) *Such* an earthquake happened last year in China.
- e) An average student can be a top student with hard work. Cathy is *a case in point*.

(2) 表示增补意义

again, also, and, besides, equally important, furthermore, in addition, in other words, likewise, moreover, to put it another way, to repeat, then, too, what's more

- a) You need time, of course. *In addition*, you need diligence.
- b) *Furthermore*, the time for registration has been extended.
- c) They expected, *moreover*, to remove their house.
- d) The noise stopped for a moment, and *then* began again.
- e) He is an artist and, *what's more*, a good sportsman.

(3) 表示强调

above all, anyway, as a matter of fact, certainly, indeed, in fact, in particular, most important, obviously, surely, to be sure, truly, undoubtedly, without doubt

- a) *Certainly* the vacation was fun.
- b) *Indeed*, a dessert is always enjoyable.
- c) *Above all*, do not build an open fire in a forest.
- d) *Surely* you agree that she won the debate.
- e) *Most important*, the form has to be mailed by June 1.

(4) 表示对比或对照

by contrast, but, conversely, in contrast, instead, on the contrary, on the other hand, otherwise, unlike, whereas, while, yet

    a) *Unlike* his brother, he has a sense of humour.

    b) *In contrast*, the red fluid does not lose its colour.

    c) The husband wanted a boy, *whereas* the wife wanted a girl.

    d) Some students wanted to go on an excursion; others, *on the other hand*, wanted to go swimming.

    e) *Instead*, the new law caused many problems.

(5) 表示比较

by comparison, equally important, in the same way, in the same manner, like, likewise, similarly

    a) *Like* the owl, the fox hunts at night.

    b) *In the same way*, we look for a good doctor.

    c) *Similarly*, the Wilsons enjoy spicy foods.

    d) *Equally important*, the car drives thirty miles on a gallon of gas.

(6) 表示让步

after all, although, clearly, it is true(that), in spite of, nevertheless, still, yet

    a) *Although* she ran after the train, it left without her.

    b) I can't follow your advice. *Nevertheless*, thank you for giving it.

    c) *After all*, you have learned to cook Chinese food in this job.

    d) *Still*, a winter vacation can be pleasant.

(7) 表示结果

accordingly, as a result, consequently, for this reason, hence, in this way, so, therefore, thus

    a) I have never been to the museum and *therefore*, I do not know much about it.

    b) *As a result*, the hospital hired three nurses.

    c) *Consequently*, we opened an account at the bank.

    d) *Accordingly*, she telephoned three different companies.

    e) He wrote a very good composition, and *so* was much praised by our teacher.

    f) There has been no rain. *Thus* the crops are likely to suffer.

(8) 表示转折

but, however, although, though, yet, except for

a) *But* the clerk refused to answer.
b) The letter came two days too late, *however*.
c) *We* hoped, *though*, she would change her mind.
d) *Yet*, there was still a chance that he would win.
e) *Except for* one girl, all the hikers returned.

(9) 表示结论

as has been noted(mentioned, stated), at last, finally, in a word, all in all, in brief, in conclusion, in short, in sum, in summary, to conclude, to sum up, to summarize

a) *To sum up*, Christmas is the most important holiday.
b) *Finally*, the country agreed to issue more work permits.
c) *In conclusion*, a consulate offers more services.
d) *At last*, a treaty was signed.
e) *In summary*, recreation is a big business.

3. 英语作文常用格言和引语

On earth there is nothing great but man; in man there is nothing great but mind. ——A. Hamilton
（世上没有一件东西有人那么伟大；而人身上没有一件东西有心灵那么伟大。）

Man is the measure of things. ——Greek Proverb
（人是万物的度。）

My mind to me a kingdom is. ——Latin Proverb
（我的内心是我主宰的王国。）

What is a man but his mind? ——Clarke
（人无精神，何以为人？）

Other men live to eat, while I eat to live. ——Socrates
（别人为食而生存，我为生存而食。）

Life is like an onion: You peel it off one layer at a time, and sometimes you weep. ——Carl Sandburg
（人生像一个洋葱：你只有一层一层地把它剥开，有时还得流泪。）

The tragedy of life is not so much what men suffer, but what they miss.

——Thomas Carlyle
（人生的悲剧不在于人们受了多少苦,而在于人们没有得到什么。）
The principal thing in this world is to keep one's soul aloft.
　　——Gustave Flaubert
（人生在世的首要大事是保持灵魂的高尚。）
The supreme happiness of life is the conviction that we are loved.
　　——Victor Hugo
（人生最大的幸福是坚信有人爱我们。）
Nothing in life is to be feared. It is only to be understood.
　　——Marie Curie
（人生没有可怕的东西,只是需要理解。）
My philosophy of life is work.　　——Thomas Edison
（我的人生哲学就是工作。）
Nothing is impossible for those who have a strong will.
（天下无难事,只怕有心人。）
In life's earnest battle they only prevail, who daily march onward and never say fail.
（在严肃的人生斗争中,惟有日日前进,不屈不挠,才能获胜。）
When the fight begins within himself, a man is worth something.
　　——Robert Browning
（斗争在一个人心中产生时,其生存就有价值了。）
A man's life is limited, but there is no limit to serving the people. I will dedicate my limited life to the limitless job of serving the people.
　　——Lei Feng
（人的生命是有限的。可是,为人民服务是无限的,我要把有限的生命,投入到无限的为人民服务当中去。）
He who does not have a strong will can never achieve high intelligence.
（志不强者智不达。）
One crowded hour of glorious life is worth an age without a name.
　　——Scott
（光辉人生中一个小时,足可当得默默无闻的一生。）
Life is measured by thought and action, not by time.　　——Aubury
（衡量生命的价值,是思想言行,而非寿命之长短。）
Happiness, I have discovered, is nearly always a bound from hard work.
　　——David Grayson
（我发现,幸福几乎总是辛勤工作的回报。）

Ill-luck, you know, seldom comes alone.　——Cerventes
（祸不单行。）

Destiny: A tyrant's authority for crime, and a fool's excuse for failure.　——Ambrose Bierce
（命运：暴君犯罪的权利,傻瓜失败的借口。）

Chiefly the mold of a man's fortune is in his own hands.　——Petrarch
（一个人的命运主要是由他自己塑造的。）

To wait for luck is the same thing as waiting for death.　——Henry Ford
（等待走运无异于等待死亡。）

Be concerned about the affairs of state before others, and enjoy comfort after others.　——Fan Zhongyan
（先天下之忧而忧,后天下之乐而乐。）

Until death, I would spare no effort in the performance of my duty.
（鞠躬尽瘁,死而后已。）

Never may the will be relaxed, and never may time be wasted.
（志不可慢,时不可失。）

My interest is in the future because I am going to spend the rest of my life there.　——Charles F. Keltering
（我只对未来感兴趣,因为我将在那里度过余生。）

The childhood shows the man, as morning shows the day.　——Milton
（童年可预示成人,犹如早晨可预示白天。）

Youth is blunder; manhood a struggle; and old age a regret.　——Benjamin Disraeli
（青年是错误,成年是奋斗,老年是懊悔。）

At twenty years of age, the will reigns; at thirty, the wit; and at forty, the judgement.　——Benjamin Franklin
（在二十岁时是意志起支配作用,三十岁时是机智,四十岁时是判断。）

Youth is life's seed-time.　——Holmes
（青年时代是人生的播种期。）

The meaning of life is to strive. Without pursuit, what can one achieve?
（人生在勤,不索何获?）

Some thoughts always find us young, and keep us so. Such a thought is the love of the universal and eternal beauty.　——Ralph Waldo Emerson
（有些观念永远发现我们是年轻的,而且使我们保持年轻。这些观念就是对于普遍和永恒的美的爱。）

It is not by grey of the hair that one knows the age of the heart.

——Edward Lytton

（白发不能告诉你一个人心灵的年龄。）

If you do not plant knowledge when young, it will give us no shade when we are old.　——Chesterfield

（年轻时候不栽培知识，老了就没有乘凉的树阴。）

Lazy youth makes lousy age. (An idle youth, a needy age.)

（少年不努力，老大徒伤悲。）

To spend one's youth at leisure at the expense of reading will be too late for regrets in the evening of one's life.

（黑发不知勤学早，白首方悔读书迟。）

To get a broader view, climb to another floor of the tower.

（欲穷千里目，更上一层楼。）

Youth's stuff will not endure.　——Shakespeare

（青春易失，人生易老。）

One who keeps breast of times remains young.　——Stephen Phillips

（与时俱进的人，永远年轻。）

A man's not old, but mellow, like good wine.　——Stephen Phillips

（一个人不会衰老，而只会更成熟，正如醇酒一样。）

He who has never hoped can never despair.

（从不抱希望的人决不会失望。）

To travel hopefully is a better thing than to arrive.　——Bernard Shaw

（怀着希望去旅行，比到达目的地更有趣味。）

Hope springs eternal in the human breast.　——John Dryden

（人生永远满怀希望。）

Without hope, the heart would break.　——Camden

（没有希望，心灵就会衰竭。）

Hope is the thing with feather that perches in the soul.
　——Emily Dickinson

（希望是栖息于灵魂中的一种会飞翔的东西。）

Living without an aim is like sailing without a compass.　——J. Ruskin

（生活无目标，犹如航海无罗盘。）

He that seeks trouble never misses.　——George Herbert

（自寻烦恼者永不会寻不着烦恼。）

Anger is a wind which blows out the lamp of the mind.
　——Robert Ingersoll

（愤怒是吹灭心灵之灯的风。）

There is a crook in the lot of every one.
　（人生道路有坎坷。）
Calamity is a man's true touchstone.
　（灾难是人生的真正试金石。）
A gentleman never feels shameful to learn from and to consult with others.
　（君子不羞学，不羞问。）
Powerful is one who has knowledge.
　（人有知学，则有力矣。）
Joys are our wings, sorrows are our spurs.　——Richter
　（欢乐是人们的双翼，哀愁是人们的动力。）
Laugh, and the world laughs with you; weep, and you weep alone.
　——E. W. Wilcax
　（笑，世界与你同笑；哭，你独自去哭。）
He is not laughed at that laughs at himself first.　——Thomas Fuller
　（自己首先知道自己可笑之处的人，不会被他人耻笑。）
The pain of the mind is worse than the pain of the body.　——Syrus
　（心灵的痛苦比肉体的痛苦更难受。）
If winter comes, can spring be far behind?　——Shelly
　（冬天来了，春天还会远吗？）
A misty morning may have a fine day.　——Kelly
　（多雾的早晨之后，可能有一个晴朗的早晨。）
No prairie fire can burn the grass utterly: the spring wind blows it back to life again.
　（野火烧不尽，春风吹又生。）
A strong man will struggle with the storm of fate.　——Edison
　（坚强的人就是要同命运的风暴搏斗。）
Every noble crown is, and on earth will ever be, a crown of thorns.
　——Carlyle
　（世上高贵的王冠，都是用荆棘织成。）
Variety is the mother of enjoyment.　——Benjamin Disraeli
　（丰富多彩是快乐之母。）
Liberty is not license.
　（自由并非一张特许证。）
Give me liberty or give me death.　——Patrick Henry
　（不自由，毋宁死。）
Liberty means responsibility. That is why most people dread it.

——Bernard Shaw
（自由意味着责任，所以大多数人害怕自由。）

It matters not how a man dies, but how he lives. ——Samuel Johnson
（一个人怎样死去并不重要，重要的在于他怎样活着。）

A candle lights others and consumes itself.
（蜡烛燃烧自己，照亮别人。）

One may overcome a thousand men in battle, but he who conquers himself is the greatest victor. ——J. Nehru
（一个人能在战场上制胜千军，但只有战胜自己才是最伟大的胜利者。）

Victory won't come to me unless I go to it. ——M. Moore
（胜利是不会向我们走来的，我们必须自己走向胜利。）

Wherever true valour is found, true modesty will there abound.
——W. S. Gilbert
（真正的勇敢，都包含谦虚。）

Whatever you do, you need courage. ——Ralph Waldo Emerson
（无论你做什么事情，都需要勇气。）

Only a life lived for others is a life worthwhile. ——Albert Einstein
（只为别人而活的生命才是值得的。）

A good death does honor to a whole life. ——Petrarca
（死得光荣，一生荣誉。）

Truth sits upon the lips of dying men. ——Mattew Arnold
（人之将死，其言也真。）

The great tragedy of life is not that men perish, but that they cease to love.
——Somerset Maugham
（人生的大悲剧不是人们死亡，而是他们不再有爱。）

We would rather die on our feet than live on our knees.
——Franklin D. Roosevelt
（宁愿站着死，也不跪着生。）

Knowledge is power. ——F. Bacon
（知识就是力量。）

Long as the way is, I will keep on searching above and below.
——QuYuan
（路漫漫其修远兮，吾将上下而求索。）

A craftsman who wants to do good work must first sharpen his tools.
（工欲善其事，必先利其器。）

Love is ever the beginning of knowledge as fire is of light. ——Carlyle

（知识总是从爱好开始，犹如光总是从火起始一样。）

Knowledge is a treasure, but practice is the key to it. ——Fuller

（知识是一座宝库，而实践是开启这座宝库的钥匙。）

If a man empties his purse into his head, no one can take it from him.
　　——Franklin

（如果一个人倾其所有装入脑袋，则没有人能够拿走它。）

It is the peculiarity of knowledge that those who really thirst for it always get it.　——R. Jefferies

（凡真正渴求知识者，每能得之，这是知识的特性。）

He who has a good trade through all waters may wade.　——Howell

（有一技之长者处处可涉足。）

It is wise to announce one's comprehension and to admit one's confusion.
　　——Confucius

（知之为知之，不知为不知，是知也。）

He who reads tremendously owns a gifted pen.

（读书破万卷，下笔如有神。）

Learning without thinking leads one to perplexity, and thinking without learning puts one in calamity.　——Confucius

（学而不思则惘，思而不学则殆。）

Live to learn, not learn to live.　——Francis Bacon

（活着就要学习，学习不是为了活着。）

A little learning is a dangerous thing.　——Pope

（学问浅薄，如履薄冰。）

Fools learn nothing from wise men, but wise men learn much from fools.
　　——Johann Kaspar Lavater

（愚者不能从智者那里学到什么东西，但智者从愚者那里得益很多。）

Reading makes a full man, conference a ready man, and writing an exact man.
　　——Francis Bacon

（读书使人充实，谈话使人机智，而写作使人严谨。）

A good book is the best of friends, the same today and forever.
　　——M. Cillon

（好书是挚友，今日如此，永远如此。）

Choose an author as you choose a friend.　——W. Dillon

（择书如择友。）

In the highest civilization the book is still the highest delight.
　　——R. W. Emerson

(在最高层次的文明里,书仍是最高层次的乐趣。)

I have always come to life after coming to books. ——J. L. Borges
(一书在手,精神抖擞。)

Imagination is more important than knowledge. ——Albert Einstein
(想像力比知识更为重要。)

A good book is the purest essence of a human soul. ——T. Carlyle
(一本好书是人的灵魂最纯洁的本质。)

Truth lies at the bottom of a well. ——Greek Proverb
(真理深藏于井底。)

Paths are made by people treading on them. Where many people tread, there we have the paths. ——Lu Xun
(路是人走出来的。走的人多了,也就成了路。)

There is but one step from the sublime to the ridiculous. ——Paine
(真理到谬误,相去只一步。)

Judge nothing before the time. ——Bible
(不经时间,无可判断。)

Homer sometimes nods. ——Latin Proverb
(智者千虑,必有一失。)

He dares to be a fool, and that is the first step in the direction of wisdom.
——James G. Huneker
(敢于当傻瓜是走向聪明的第一步。)

Wisdom is to the mind what health is to the body. ——La Rochefoucauld
(智慧之于头脑,犹如健康之于躯体。)

A wise man never loses anything if he has himself.
——Friedrich W. Nietzsche
(聪明的人只要能认识自己,便什么也不会失去。)

Be wisely worldly, be not worldly-wise. ——Ed Howe
(要聪明地世故,不要世故地聪明。)

A wise man will make more opportunities than he finds.
——Francis Bacon
(聪明人创造的机会比他发现的要多。)

Genius is one percent inspiration and ninety-nine percent perspiration.
——Thomas Edison
(天才是百分之一的灵感加百分之九十九的汗水。)

Genius only means hard-working all one's life. ——Mendeleev
(天才只意味着终生不懈的努力。)

Towering genius disdains a beaten path. He seeks regions hitherto unexplored.
　　——Abraham Lincoln
　（卓越的天才不屑走旁人走过的路,他寻找迄今未开拓的地区。）
Genius is eternal patience.　——Michelangelo
　（天才是永恒的耐心。）
Virtue never grows old.　——Ray
　（美德永远不老。）
Virtue is to herself the best reward.　——Latin Proverb
　（善行本身即是对它自己的最好报酬。）
All men are equal; it is not birth but virtue alone that makes the difference.
　　——Voltaire
　（所有的人都是平等的;造成差别的不是门第,而只是美德。）
The wealth of the mind is the only true wealth.　——Hesiod
　（精神财富才是真正的财富。）
Character is the first and last word in the success circle.　——Marden
　（品德好是获得成功的先决条件。）
Personality is to man what perfume is to a flower.　——Schwab
　（人格之于人,犹如芳香之于花。）
The path of duty was the way to glory.　——Tennyson
　（本分尽职乃通向荣誉之大道。）
Life is measured by thought and action, not by time.　——Avebury
　（衡量生命的尺度是思想和行动,而不是时间的短长。）
Goodness is not tied to greatness, but greatness to goodness.
　　——Greek Proverb
　（善良不一定连着伟大,但是伟大必连着善良。）
True greatness is the greatness of the mind.　——Longfellow
　（真正的伟大是精神的伟大。）
The dome of thought, the palace of the soul.　——George Byron
　（思想的大厦是灵魂的宫殿。）
The best thinking has been done in solitude.　——Thomas Edison
　（最好的思想是在孤独中产生的。）
He that is master of himself will soon be master of others.　——Boho
　（能统治自己的人就很快能统治别人。）
Honesty is the best policy.　——Benjamin Franklin
　（坦诚是最明智的策略。）
Make yourself necessary to someone.　——Emerson

(要使你自己成为他人所需要的人。)

Praise the bridge he goes over.
　　(过河莫忘搭桥人。)

Genius is nothing but labor and diligence. ——Einstein
　　(天才无非是劳动加勤勉。)

The greatest of faults is to be conscious of none. ——Thomas Carlyle
　　(最大的缺点,莫过于意识不到自己的任何缺点。)

To err is human, to forgive divine. ——Alexander Pope
　　(失误人皆有之,宽恕乃超人之举。)

None but a fool is always right. ——Hare
　　(只有傻瓜才永远正确。)

He that knows others is learned, and he who knows himself is wise.
　　——Laotze
　　(知人者智,自知者明。)

A little pit is soon hot. ——John Tray
　　(器小易盈,量小易怒。)

Anger begins in folly, and ends in repentance. ——Decker
　　(愤怒起于愚鲁,终于悔恨。)

Patience is a virtue. ——Langland
　　(忍耐是美德。)

The hardest knife ill used loseth his edge. ——William Shakespeare
　　(使用不当,利刃也会变钝。)

Birds of a feather flock together. ——Cicero
　　(物以类聚。)

Like to like. ——Cicero
　　(物以类聚。)

Like kills like. ——Latin Proverb
　　(同类相克。)

Fire proves gold, adversity proves men. ——Seneca
　　(烈火炼真金,逆境识真人。)

Walls have ears. ——Shelley
　　(隔墙有耳。)

A life without a friend is a life without a sun. ——French Proverb
　　(人生没有朋友,犹如人生没有了太阳。)

A friend should bear his friend in informalities. ——William Shakespeare
　　(朋友要体谅朋友的弱点。)

All the splendour in the world is not worth a good friend. ——Voltaire
（人世间一切荣华富贵不如一个推心置腹的朋友。）
A friend in need is a friend indeed. ——John Ray
（患难朋友才是真朋友。）
Company in distress makes the sorrow less. ——Thomas Fuller
（患难中的同伴会减少你的痛苦。）
Tell me thy company and I will tell thee what thou are. —— Cerrantes
（告诉我你交什么样的朋友，我就可以说出你的为人。）
Be slow in choosing a friend, slower in changing. ——Franklin
（择友不须急，换友更宜慎。）
Friendship is the golden thread that ties the hearts of all the world.
——John Evelyn
（友谊是把全世界的心连在一起的一根金线。）
You must ask your neighbor if you shall live in peace. ——Clark
（邻睦则安。）
One good turn deserves another. ——Heywood
（好心值得好报。）
Do as you would be done by. ——Confucius
（己所不欲，勿施于人。）
He who is the most slow in making a promise is the most faithful in the
performance of it. ——Rousseau
（最难给你许诺的人，在履行的时候最真诚。）
Beauty is power; a smile is its sword. ——Charles Reade
（美丽是力量，微笑是其利剑。）
He who loves others is constantly loved by them; he who respects others is
constantly respected by them. ——Mencius
（爱人者人恒爱之，敬人者人恒敬之。）
Absence sharpens love, presence strengthens it. ——Bayly
（离别益增怅念，相逢加深爱慕。）
Both together do best of all. ——Latin Proverb
（二人同心，无往不胜。）
United we stand, divided we fall. ——Franklin
（团结则存，分裂则亡。）
You are much more likely to get rich from hard work than from a lucky win.
——Aesop
（靠艰苦的劳动比靠侥幸得来的收益更可能致富。）

It is no use doing what you like; you have got to like what you do.
　　——W. Churchill
　　(不能爱哪行才干哪行，要干哪行就爱哪行。)
Labour is often the father of pleasure.　——Voltaire
　　(劳动常常是快乐之父。)
Labour conquers all things.　——Virgil
　　(劳动战胜一切。)
Where there is a will, there is a way.　——Scott
　　(有志者事竟成。)
People do not lack strength; they lack will.　——Victor Hugo
　　(人们不缺少力量；他们缺少意志。)
Faith is the bird that feels the light when the dawn is still dark.
　　——Tagore
　　(信念是黎明前天尚黑时感到光明的鸟。)
Nothing is impossible to a willing heart.　——Heywood
　　(心头有志愿，无事不可能。)
Faith will move mountains.　——Bible
　　(信念能移动大山。)
Self-trust is the first secret of success.　——Emerson
　　(自信是成功的第一秘诀。)
A little of everything, and nothing at all.　——Montaigne
　　(事事浅尝辄止，结果一事无成。)
No rock is so hard but a little wave may beat admission in a thousand years.
　　——Tennyson
　　(石头再硬，浪击千年，也会被钻空进水。)
To strive, to seek, to find, and not to yield.　——Tennyson
　　(奋斗，探索，发现，而不要放弃。)
Great works are performed not by strength but by perseverance.
　　——Samuel Johnson
　　(成大事不在力量大小，而在持之以恒。)
Our greatest glory consists not in never falling, but in rising every time we fall.　——Goldsmith
　　(人生最大的光荣，不在于永不失败，而在于能屡赴屡起。)
Nothing venture, nothing have.　——Heywood
　　(不入虎穴，焉得虎子。)
I am a slow walker, but I never walk backwards.　——Abraham Lincoln

(我这个人走得很慢,但我从不后退。)

He who hesitates is lost. ——Joseph Addison

(犹豫不定,输得干净。)

Never in a steed pigsty-born; nor an evergreen pine potbound.

(猪圈难生千里马,花盆难养万年松。)

I have no secret of success but hard work. ——Turner

(除努力外,别无成功的秘诀。)

Try not to become a man of success but rather try to become a man of value.
——Albert Einstein

(不要为成功而努力,要为做一个有价值的人而努力。)

Time and tide wait for no man.

(时不待人。)

Today gold, tomorrow dust.

(今日值黄金,明日等尘土。)

Truth is the daughter of time.

(时间孕育着真理。)

One today is worth two tomorrows. ——Franklin

(一个今日等于两个明天。)

Time is money. ——Franklin

(时间就是金钱。)

A plant may produce new flowers; man is young but once.

(花有重开日,人无再少年。)

Take time while time is, for time will wear away. ——John Ray

(当有时间的时候要利用时间,因为时间即将消逝。)

To choose time is to save time. ——Francis Bacon

(选择时间就是节省时间。)

Time is a bird for ever on the wing. ——T. W. Robert

(时间是一只永远在飞翔的鸟。)

Strike while the iron is hot. ——Camden

(趁热打铁。)

Delays breed dangers. ——John Lyly

(拖延孕育危险。)

The proper function of man is to live, not to exist. ——Jack London

(人的正当作用是生活,而不是生存。)

Who saw life steadily and saw it whole. ——Matthew Arnold

(只有不断观察生活的人,才能全面了解生活。)

Travel, in the younger sort, is a part of educating; in the elder, a part of experience. ——Francis Bacon
(旅行对年轻人是一种教育,对老年人是一种体验。)

In our play we reveal what kind of people we are. ——Ovid
(游玩时,我们会泄露自己属于哪一类人。)

If we command our wealth, we shall be rich and free; if our wealth commands us, we are poor indeed. ——Edmund Burke
(如果我们能支配我们自己的财富,我们就会变得富裕而自由;如果我们的财富支配了我们,我们就会是真正的贫穷。)

Money can cure hunger. It cannot cure unhappiness. Food can satisfy the appetite, but not the soul. ——Bernard Shaw
(金钱可以疗饥,但不能治疗苦恼。食物可以满足食欲,但是不能满足灵魂的需求。)

Economy is of itself a great revenue. ——Cicero
(节约本身就是一大笔收入。)

Take care of the pence, and the pounds will take care of themselves. ——Chesterfield
(看管好了便士,英镑就自会看管自己了。)

Beware of little expenses; a small leak will sink a great ship. ——Benjamin Franklin
(留心微小开支;一条小裂缝会使一只大船沉没。)

The best sauce in the world is hunger. ——Cervantes
(世界上最好的调料是饥饿。)

Health is better than wealth. ——Ray
(健康胜于财富。)

The first wealth is health. ——Emerson
(健康是人生第一财富。)

Health and strength is above all gold. ——Francis Bacon
(健康和体力,黄金不可易。)

Happiness lies, first of all, in health. ——G. B. Curtis
(幸福所在处,首先是健康。)

Energy is eternal delight. ——W. Blake
(精力充沛是永恒的快乐。)

Health is not a condition of matter, but of mind. ——Merphy
(健康不是一种物质状态,而是一种精神状态。)

A merry heart lives long. ——Shakespeare

（豁达者长寿。）
Care killed the cat. ——Shakespeare
（忧能伤人。）
Gluttony kills more than the sword. ——Francisco Patrizz
（暴食致人死命甚于利剑。）
Prevention is better than cure. —— Charles Dickens
（预防胜于治疗。）
Nothing is really beautiful but truth. ——Nicolas Boileau
（惟真实的东西才是真正美丽的。）
A beautiful form is better than a beautiful face; a beautiful behaviour than a beautiful form. ——Ralph Waldo Emerson
（美丽的外形胜过美丽的脸蛋，美丽的行为胜过美丽的外形。）
First impressions are most lasting. ——Charles Dickens
（第一印象是最持久的。）
Never judge from appearance. ——Tindale
（不要以貌取人。）
Art is long, and time is fleeting. ——Longfellow
（生命短暂而艺术永恒。）
For art may err, but Nature cannot miss. ——Dryden
（艺术会失误，自然不失真。）
The pen is the tongue of mind. —— Cervantes
（笔乃思想之舌。）
The landscape belongs to the man who looks at it.
——Ralph Waldo Emerson
（风景属于欣赏风景的人。）
Brevity is the soul of wit. ——Shakespeare
（简洁为智慧的灵魂。）
Proper words in proper places, make the true definition of a style.
——Swift
（恰当的词用在恰当的地方，这就成为风格的真正定义。）
The scientist must not be a spider or an ant, but a bee. ——F. Bacon
（科学家不应是一只蜘蛛或蚂蚁，而应是一只蜜蜂。）
Give me where to stand, and I will move the world. ——Archimedes
（如能给我立足点，我将能撬动世界。）
What sculpture is to a block of marble, education is to the soul.
——Addison

(教育之于心灵,犹雕刻之于大理石。)

Education has for its object the formation of character. ——Spencer

(教育的目的在于品德的培养。)

Education is not the filling of a pail, but the lighting of a fire.
——W. B. Yeats

(教育不是注满一桶水,而是点燃一把火。)

The foundation of every state is the education of its youth. —— Diogenes

(每个国家的基础在于对其青年的教育。)

Example is always more efficacious than precept. ——Samuel Johnson

(身教胜于言教。)

Making peace is harder than making war. ——Stevenson

(促成和平比发动战争更困难。)

The best armor is to keep out of gunshot. ——Francis Bacon

(最好的盔甲是躲开枪炮。)

An eye for an eye, and a tooth for a tooth. ——Bible

(以眼还眼,以牙还牙。)

The law cannot make all men equal, but they are all equal before the law.
——Frederick Pollock

(法律不能使人人都平等,但是人人在法律面前是平等的。)

Law is order, and good law is good order. ——Aristotle

(法律就是秩序,有好的法律才有好的秩序。)

The good of the people is the highest law. ——Cicero

(人民的利益应是至高无上的法律。)

The best and wisest laws are mere words unless they are upheld.
——N. Hawthorne

(最好、最贤明的法律,如不加以维护,也只等于一纸空文。)

Change starts when someone sees the next step. ——William Drayton

(当有人看清下一步,变革就开始了。)

Discontent is the first step in progress of a man or a nation.
——Oscar Wilde

(不满足是一个人或一个民族进步的第一步。)

Prejudice is the child of ignorance. ——William Hazlitt

(偏见来自愚昧。)

It is easier to fight for principles than to live up to them.
——A. E. Stevenson

(为原则而斗争容易,按原则的要求活着难。)

If you have tasted bitterness of gall, you know better the sweetness of honey.
(吃过黄连苦,方知蜜糖甜。)

Rome wasn't built in a day.
(罗马非一日建成。)

He who laughs last, laughs best.
(谁笑到最后,谁笑得最好。)

Well begun is half done.
(良好的开端等于成功的一半。)

No road of flowers leads to glory.
(没有一条成功的道路是鲜花铺成的。)

Something attempted, something done.
(有所尝试,就有所作为。)

Fortune never helps the man whose courage fails.
(运气永远不会帮助没有勇气的人。)

Speech is silver, but silence is gold.
(雄辩是银,沉默是金。)

Never put off until tomorrow what can be done today.
(今日事今日毕。)

Early sow, early mow.
(早耕耘者早收获。)

When in Rome, do as the Romans do.
(入乡随俗。)